# Understanding Philosophy

# Understanding Philosophy

Edited by Brandon Taylor

CLANRYE
INTERNATIONAL
www.clanryeinternational.com

Clanrye International,
750 Third Avenue, 9th Floor,
New York, NY 10017, USA



ISBN: 978-1-64726-155-9

**Cataloging-in-Publication Data**

Understanding philosophy / edited by Brandon Taylor.
p. cm.
Includes bibliographical references and index.
ISBN 978-1-64726-155-9
1. Philosophy. 2. Philosophy--Study and teaching. 3. Philosophy, Modern. I. Taylor, Brandon.
B72 .U53 2021
190--dc23

For information on all Clanrye International publications visit our website at www.clanryeinternational.com

CLANRYE INTERNATIONAL

# Contents

# Preface

The main aim of this book is to educate learners and enhance their research focus by presenting diverse topics covering this vast field. This is an advanced book which compiles significant studies by distinguished experts in the area of analysis. This book addresses successive solutions to the challenges arising in the area of application, along with it; the book provides scope for future developments.

Philosophy deals with the study of fundamental and general questions regarding values, mind, existence, reason, knowledge and language. Some of the major categories of philosophy are epistemology, metaphysics, value theory, ethics, logic, mathematics and science. Epistemology refers to a branch of philosophy which is concerned with the nature of knowledge, justification and the rationality of belief. Various academic disciplines such as sociology, psychology, economics and linguistics emerged out of philosophy. There are a number of methods which are used in philosophy. These include rational argument, questioning, critical discussion and systematic presentation. This book discusses the fundamentals as well as modern approaches of philosophy. Some of the diverse topics covered in this book address the varied branches that fall under this category. The extensive content of this book provides the readers with a thorough understanding of the subject.

It was a great honour to edit this book, though there were challenges, as it involved a lot of communication and networking between me and the editorial team. However, the end result was this all-inclusive book covering diverse themes in the field.

Finally, it is important to acknowledge the efforts of the contributors for their excellent chapters, through which a wide variety of issues have been addressed. I would also like to thank my colleagues for their valuable feedback during the making of this book.

**Editor**

# 1

# On the Roots of Media Ecology: A Micro-History and Philosophical Clarification

**Corey Anton**

School of Communications, Grand Valley State University, 210 LSH, 1 Campus Drive, Allendale, MI 49401-9403, USA; antonc@gvsu.edu

Academic Editor: Robert K. Logan

**Abstract:** This paper provides a brief review of media ecology. It is partly a micro-history of the tradition, and partly a philosophical clarification of how and why "systems-theory orientations," literacy studies, and the rapid spread of new media were all essential to its germination, growth, and proliferation. Finally, the paper offers concluding remarks regarding social constructionist thought and how it relates to the media ecology tradition.

**Keywords:** media ecology; Marshall McLuhan; Jack Goody; systems-theory; literacy studies; new media; social construction

---

## 1. Introduction

To explore the ancestry line of media ecology, we first need to touch upon media ecology today, and then, after considering its current composition, we can identify its roots as well as the soil and overall atmosphere in which it sprouted and developed. This implies that we must differentiate between a history of media ecology as a field of study and a history of the ideas and thinkers that precipitated and nourished the emergence of the media ecology tradition in North America. The following, therefore, is partly a micro-history of the tradition and partly a philosophical clarification of how and why "systems-theory orientations", literacy studies, and the rapid spread of new media were all essential to its germination, growth, and proliferation. Finally, a concluding remark addresses how social constructionist ideas relate to the media ecology tradition.

The particular expression, "media ecology", grew out of a conversation in 1967 between Neil Postman, Marshall McLuhan and Eric McLuhan [1,2], and, within a year, Postman was using it in public talks. By 1971, New York University (NYU), Postman's home institution, had established a doctoral program by that name, and then, in 1998, NYU, The Toronto School of Media Studies, and St. Louis University joined resources to form the Media Ecology Association (MEA). Within four years of its establishment, the MEA launched an international journal, *Explorations in Media Ecology*, and, today, several books series are devoted to media ecology.

For many scholars, especially members of the MEA, media ecology refers to the study of media as environments and environments as media [1–3]. It focuses upon dominant communication technologies to account for both cross-cultural conflict as well as for the distinguishing characteristics of a given culture and/or historical period. Although media ecological thinking can be found back in the ancient world (e.g., admonishments against making "graven images", or in Plato's *Phaedrus*, where Socrates warns about the effects writing will have on memory and people's sense of wisdom), it was not until the 20th century that media ecological thought became more prevalent within popular sensibilities. Today, in the ultramodern 21st century, media ecological orientations are pervasive, mainly because communication technologies have altered countless patterns of interaction before people's very eyes: many people have witnessed cell phones change the nature of social interaction, video technologies alter notions of privacy, and robotic automation change the nature and meaning of employment. Hence, spanning and integrating ancient, modern and postmodern world-views, media ecology examines cultures and personhood as intricately intertwined with dominant communication technologies.

Three roots serve as the main nutrient sources to the media ecology tradition: Marshall McLuhan, Walter J. Ong, and Neil Postman [1–3]. These three—McLuhan arguably at the center—constitute a core, with a number of scholars branching out from that core. So, for example, thinkers such as Harold Innis, Lewis Mumford, Eric Havelock, Jack Goody, Susanne Langer, Edmund Carpenter, Elizabeth Eisenstein, Jacques Ellul occupy a major inner layer of branches, and then thinkers such as Ludwig Bertalanffy, Alfred Korzybski, Kenneth Boulding, Erving Goffman, Edward Hall, Dorothy Lee, Daniel Boorstin, Gregory Bateson, Paul Watzlawick, Tony Swartz, Susan Sontag, Denise Schmandt-Besserat, James Carey, David Olson, Leonard Shlain, Pierre Teilhard de Chardin, and Julian Jaynes occupy a further layer. There are also a number of contemporary scholars in the MEA who have produced books, manuscripts, and who remain active in the organization. This includes but is not limited to: Lance Strate, Thom Gencarelli, Janet Sternberg, Paul Levinson, Paul Soukup, Susan Barnes, Casey Lum, Paul Grosswiler, Sara van den Berg, Robert K. Logan, Brett Lunceford, Fernando Gutiérrez, Sheila Nayar, Ellen Rose, Brian Cogan, Phil Rose, Edward Tywoniak, Peter K. Fallon, Alex Kuskis, Steven Reagles, Valerie V. Peterson, Peter Zhang, Eric Jenkins, Robert MacDougall, and myself. And, finally, there are also many thinkers who contemporary media ecologists have enlisted as within the bounds of media ecology, scholars such as Elias Canetti, Georg Simmel, J.J. Gibson, René Girard, and Guy Debord among others.

## 2. The Larger Environment

Now that a few remarks have been made about media ecology today, we are ready to explore the soil and atmosphere in which the seedling took root. Media ecology, as may be evident from the scholars listed above, is not reducible to a single tradition or particular line of scholarship or even to a single discipline. Joshua Meyrowitz suggests that the specific, substantiating research lines of media ecology "have developed out of distinct disciplines (the classics, psychiatry, English, religion, anthropology, history, etc.)," and, accordingly, these works are not "generally conceived of as being parts of one body of literature" [4] (p. 22). Nevertheless, one complex multidisciplinary body of literature is exactly what media ecology has become.

As far back as the 1960's, Postman sought to express how multiple sources of thought were growing together, intertwining if only underground. He, along with Charles Weingartner, used the expression: "the Sapir-Whorf-Korzybski-Ames-Einstein-Heisenberg-Wittgenstein-McLuhan-et al. Hypothesis" [5] (p. 101). The motive behind this unwieldy agglutination—the expression that grew into "media ecology"—was to suggest that individuals across many different fields had come to some remarkably similar (or at least highly resonant) insights regarding humanity, perception, cultural evolution, and the constitution of social/psychological order. It also stressed the primacy of "relations" over "things" and pointed to mediation as a dynamic mode of connectivity. Postman and Weingartner promoted what Dewey and Bentley, in *Knowing and the Known*, called "trans-action" in distinction to mere "inter-action." More precisely differentiated, Dewey and Bentley write:

> *Inter-action*: where thing is balanced against thing in causal interconnection. *Trans-action*: where systems of description and naming are employed to deal with aspects and phases of action, without final attribution to "elements" or other presumptively detachable or independent "entities", "essences", or "realities", and without isolation of presumptively detachable "relations" from such detachable "elements." [6] (p. 108).

Increasing numbers of scholars were growing more and more suspicious of a detached observer, of assumptions regarding value-free language, of belief in a world complete unto itself to which persons and/or their material conditions could be added without any impact or effect. Postman and Weingartner sought accounts aligned with the idea that the "observer" cannot be separated from the "observed", especially where matters of technological mediation are concerned [5].

One of media ecology's main assumptions is that we can best understand technological mediation and the evolution (e.g., the socio-historical/material constitution) of human consciousness and culture through a systems-view. In 1974, Lee Thayer, a multidisciplinary systems theorist, established the journal titled *Communication*, with an astonishing editorial board that included not only Marshall McLuhan and Walter Ong, but such notable scholars as: Herbert Blumer, Daniel Boorstin, Kenneth Boulding, Kenneth Burke, George Gerbner, Harold Lasswell, Claude Levi-Strauss, Floyd Matson, F. S.C. Northrop, Ithiel de Sola Pool, Karl Pribram, Anatol Rapoport, David Riesman, Jurgen Ruesch, Wilber Schramm, Harley Shands, and Geoffery Vickers. As one of the intellectual predecessors to the MEA's current journal *Explorations in Media Ecology*, *Communication* brought together scholars from many different fields, areas such as psychology, sociology, physics, biology, engineering, mathematics, economics, etc. All were realizing how their fields of study and bodies of knowledge were caught within language practices and communication technologies more generally.

The 1960's and 70's witnessed a flood of scholarly reflection upon communication and symbolic processes not only because many fields were discovering how their objects of investigation were mediated, but also because of the rise of the telecommunication industries. Television, in particular, was central to burgeoning interest in media studies across North America. As TV sets entered people's homes, they poured out social unrest: concerns over gender and racial inequality, political strife, rapid shifts in values, and varieties of global conflict [4,7].

But other important elements in the soil need to be mentioned. In particular, the 20th century not only witnessed the first large scale attempt at universal mass education, it watched the project buckle under the weight of television and other electronic media. By the end of the century many people were concerned over growing illiteracy rates. Moreover, many scholars had become much more sophisticated in their inquires into the character and nature of alphabetic literacy. The year 1963 is marked by some scholars as a pivotal year for media ecological research [8]. Within a span of a little over twelve months, McLuhan's *The Gutenberg Galaxy* [9], Havelock's *Preface to Plato* [10], Goody and Watt's "Consequences of Literacy" [11], and Levi-Strauss's *The Savage Mind* [12] all were first published. These texts provocatively identify significant changes in the nature of the spoken word and in the nature of communicative practices with the advent of literacy; they pointed to the important role literacy had played in making the modern Western world.

Two other notable contributions were David Olson's *The World on Paper* [13] and Jack Goody's *The Interface between the Written and the Oral* [14]. Both masterfully address some of the more salient research lines on literacy at the roots of media ecology [13–18]. One line came out of psychology and concerned scholars such as Vygotsky, who claimed that certain mental abilities were dependent upon literacy, almost as if literacy single-handedly transforms basic intellectual operations. Along similar lines, Alexander Luria tested illiterate peasants to illustrate their apparent inability (or at least unwillingness) to think with abstract categories and/or to accept syllogistic reasoning [9]. Another line of contributions came from anthropology, especially turn of the century thinkers such as Sir James George Frazer, with his massive *The Golden Bough* [19] as well as Lucien Levi-Bruhl's highly influential *The Notebooks on Primitive Mentality* [20]. These two popular and widely read anthropologists significantly influenced subsequent thinking regarding the differences between "savages" and "civilized" human beings. Sylvia Scribner and Michael Cole, in their book *The Psychology of Literacy* camped all of the aforementioned thinkers together, basically accused them of something akin to technological determinism, and then set out to experimentally test the claim that literacy alters human consciousness and turns "savages" into "civilized human beings" [21]. Through a series of studies, they substantially refuted any claim to a great divide between oral and literate mind and sought to show, more modestly, the possibility of changes in skills but not general abilities. Along the way, however, they misunderstood and misrepresented the view that Goody, in particular, was espousing, and this returns us to the original point of departure about bringing systems-theory to the evolution (and socio-historical/material constitution) of human consciousness and culture.

An essential part of the task, as Goody identifies it, is to overcome the deeply entrenched kinds of "mentalism" in contemporary psychology [14]. That is, contemporary experimental psychology often traffics in the distinction between "abilities" and "skills" and therein reifies an "ahistorical", "acultural" mentalist sort of subject. This can be witnessed when Scribner and Cole try to test for something like abstract logical abilities as they could be produced by literacy. For Goody, in contrast, the main point is: what kinds of thought can people have—both in the short term and in the long term—because of pen and paper? In some ways, Goody was addressing what decades later would be called, "embodied cognition." The point is that the contemporary psychological distinction between "abilities" and "skills" is highly problematic. There's no such thing as "abilities" or "skills" in the abstract, that is, without the particular context and material conditions for the exercise of those abilities/skills. When we change our methods and means of communication we're actually changing the material conditions in which any skill or ability would develop or have influence. Goody employs the term "capacities" to undercut the ability/skill differentiation. I quote Goody at length:

> ... I myself could not, do not, remember the telephone number of my own office. That does not stop me from calling my colleagues because I look the number up in my telephone book, store it in my short-term memory, then dial. Now that I have a new type of telephone with its own memory I don't even need to look it up. My memory skills are not engaged. Yet I have a capacity to talk to vast numbers of people on this earth at short notice.
>
> To expect that this capacity would show up on a series of tests suffers from three theoretical difficulties. It assumes, first, that such capacities can be described, or better described, at a higher level of generality. Secondly, that this higher level of generality shows up in the "higher" mental processes. Thirdly, that these higher mental processes go on inside the mind alone. This last sentence sounds like a tautology. But if one defines skills and knowledge as "mental" in the sense that they are entirely contained within the mind, and have to be so tested, you quickly reach a point of no entry into the study of human interaction ... We are touching here upon the external-internal problem that has dogged so much thinking, in psychology, philosophy, and elsewhere ... Norbert Weiner asked his readers to imagine a mechanic with an artificial arm trying to repair an engine. Is the arm part of the machinery with which he is struggling, or part of the mechanic who is working on the engine? ... When a map or book intervene between the object and subject we are dealing with 'mind' out there as well as with mind inside ... writing presents us with an instrument capable of transforming our intellectual operations from the inside; it is not simply a question of a *skill* in the limiting sense but a change of *capacity*. The capacity depends upon interaction between individual and the objects mediated by writing, and so cannot in many cases be mocked-up in ways that would test general abilities (for example, of abstract reasoning and memory) ... [14] (pp. 253–256).

Scholars can continue to raise questions about what effects a technology has upon a person's general "abilities" or inner "mental" constructs, but they need not do so. On the contrary, they might chose to carefully document how individuals and/or whole cultures have been capacitated to function with technologies as extensions and as environments [13].

McLuhan's well-known response to General Sarnoff's claims regarding media effects cut directly to this point [7]. Sarnoff, talking about the relationship between technologies and their consequences, suggested, "The products of modern science are not in themselves good or bad; it is the way they are used that determines their value," to which McLuhan critically responded, "That is the voice of the current somnambulism ... It has never occurred to General Sarnoff that any technology could do anything but *add* itself on to what we already are" [7] (p. 23).

Media ecology grew, then, on one front, from a desire to show how print based literacy was blinding people to simultaneous interconnections and, on another front, from the nutrient soil provided by the electric age. Only as electric technologies began to be pervasive could the systematic complexity of social and psychological relations afforded by print be revealed. Atomistic, linear, and compartmentalized thought was the natural outcome of print, the symptom, as it were, of literate sensibilities. The abstract proclivity to separate "content" from "form" and the tendency to isolate items into a "one-thing-at-a-time" sequence of causal relations were products of literacy and obstacles to apprehending the dynamic nature of technological mediation.

Something should be said in this context about McLuhan's use of "formal cause". A key principle informing McLuhan's thought, one that only recently has come to adequate attention, was McLuhan's attunement to formal causality [22–24]. Aristotle distinguished four kinds of causality: material, efficient, formal, and final. For example, consider a spoon. It needs to be made of some material (steel, wood, plastic, etc.), and the materials must be fashioned in a particular sequence or process by the maker. In addition to these material and efficient causes, there are formal and final causes. The formal cause of the spoon is what the maker had in mind in setting out to produce the spoon. It is the idea guiding processes and expectations, thus enabling anyone to recognize the spoon "*as*" a spoon. Formal cause, therefore, enables the maker to know when the fashioning of the spoon is completed, when other people can clearly see "*what it is*". The final cause of the spoon is its "for-the-sake-of-which", the reason we wish to have the spoon, the end served by the spoon: a particular kind of eating. McLuhan appreciated how any environment or technology, as formal cause, grows an appetite, an orientating capacity, a set of sensibilities that seek satisfaction elsewhere. Formal cause is not only the source of "rear-view mirror" thinking (seeing the present through the past; e.g., "horseless carriage"), it is also what gives media forms the "Midas touch", the sense that anything touched by a media form gets made over in its image [7]. For example, print, as formal cause, had groomed people for uniformity, seriality, standardization, and lineal "one-thing-at-a-time" reasoning in countless areas of their lives, and, so too, the electric age was the formal cause of ground-awareness, attention to simultaneity, and interest in "relations" and "systems" rather than in "things" and their "properties".

Consider the NRA's slogan, "Guns don't kill people, people do" [2,7]. Such analytic compartmentalization typifies the need for a more robust systems-view of gun violence. Lance Strate, in his elucidation of the media ecology traditions, suggests, "If you disagree with this argument, and believe that there is greater potential for violence with firearms than without them, then you believe that the medium is the message" [2] (p. 130). Not only are there, annually, hundreds of accidental gun deaths in the US, but only the most *literal-minded* person could believe that anyone thinks "guns," in and of themselves, kill people. No one imagines that a gun somehow manufactures itself, fills itself with ammunition, hops off of a gun rack and starts shooting. The bogus separation of guns from people is already the literate dis-orientation, the non-systems view. Guns are *extensions* of people, and people who have extended themselves with guns kill more people than people who do not have such extensions. The systems-view informing the media ecological tradition would encourage people to understand how a technology does not merely get added to an environment; it changes everything. Paul Levinson nicely captures this issue where he writes that "The addition of a drop of blue dye to a glass of water results not in blue dye plus water, but in blue water: a new reality," as cited in [25] (p. 35).

## 3. Final Remarks

Before closing, one final observation should be made regarding the growth and proliferation of social constructionist thought, a neo-Marxist view that enlivened long-standing concern over the difference and/or relationship between "nature" and "nurture".

Social constructionist thought is mentioned only because it alludes to the rocky soil and arid conditions that motivated some scholars to seek the greener pastures of the media ecological tradition. Many who went to college in the 1980 and graduate school in the 1990s remember how popular social constructionist ideas were [26]. It was hard to go anywhere and not hear something (anything and everything) being described as "socially constructed". As a response, some scholars sought to more rigorously document the phenomenological constitution underlying social construction [27].

Phenomenological focus upon the body, especially the difference between the senses, offered a needed corrective to many social constructionist positions, but even a phenomenologically-informed social constructionist view seemed, all said, pretty lacking in historical depth and breadth [28–30].

Media ecology, more than any other tradition, provides a more robust manifestation of what so many social constructionist scholars had been seeking. We might call it, "socio-historical constructionism with teeth." Clearly, it is one thing to sweepingly proclaim that people socially construct "reality" or to vaguely suggest that "gender" or "race" or "self" or "intelligence" or "science" is socially constructed. It is quite a different matter to engage the socio-historical material technological conditions—the total human environment—which built the cultures and selves we now experience and take-for-granted. To explore the nature of alphabetic literacy, to learn how literate noetics alter and work with oral noetics, to examine features of social organization accomplished by printed material, to consider the effects of money on the experience of valuation and on practical commerce, to grapple with how calendars and clocks shape and organize our experience of time and social interaction, and to anticipate the likely side effects of new social media, these are main staples of today's media ecological research.

The overall human environment includes and incorporates technological extensions, and these are never merely add-ons. They alter our sensibilities and capacities, our notions of self and other, our notions of privacy and propriety, and our orientations in space and time. By bringing a systems-view to technological mediation, media ecology both undercuts the "one-thing-at-a-time" rationality fostered by print literacy and also provides a strategic vantage for understanding the kinds of changes currently afoot in the new media landscape.

**Conflicts of Interest:** The author declares no conflict of interest.

## References

1. Strate, L. *Echoes and Reflections: On Media Ecology as a Field of Study*; Hampton University Press: Cresskill, NJ, USA, 2006.
2. Strate, L. A Media Ecology Review. *Commun. Res. Trends* **2005**, *23*, 1–48.
3. Anton, C. History, Orientations, and Future Directions of Media Ecology. In *Communication Uncovered: General Semantics and Media Ecology*; Institute of General Semantics: Fort Worth, TX, USA, 2011; pp. 77–91.
4. Meyrowitz, J. *No Sense of Place: The Impact of Electronic Media on Social Behavior*; Oxford University Press: New York, NY, USA, 1985.
5. Postman, N.; Weingartner, C. *Teaching as a Subversive Activity*; Delta: New York, NY, USA, 1969.
6. Dewey, J.; Bentley, A.F. *Knowing and the Known*; Beacon Press: Boston, MA, USA, 1960.
7. McLuhan, M. *Understanding Media: Extensions of Man: Critical Edition*; Gingko Press: Corte Madera, CA, USA, 2003.
8. Havelock, E.A. *The Muse Learns to Write: Reflections on Orality and Literacy from Antiquity to the Present*; Yale University Press: New Haven, CN, USA, 1986.
9. McLuhan, M. *The Gutenberg Galaxy: The Making of Typographic Man*; University of Toronto Press: Toronto, ON, Canada, 1962.
10. Havelock, E.A. *Preface to Plato*; Harvard University Press: Cambridge, MA, USA, 1963.
11. Goody, J.; Watt, I. The Consequences of Literacy. *Compar. Studies in Society and History* **1963**, *5*, 304–345. [CrossRef]
12. Levi Strauss, C. *The Savage Mind*; University of Chicago Press: Chicago, IL, USA, 1966.
13. Olson, D. *The World on Paper: The Conceptual and Cognitive Implications of Writing and Reading*; Oxford University: Oxford, UK, 1994.
14. Goody, J. *The Interface between the Written and the Oral*; Cambridge University Press: Cambridge, MA, USA, 1987.
15. Goody, J. *The Domestication of the Savage Mind*; Cambridge University Press: Cambridge, MA, USA, 1977.
16. Illich, I.; Sanders, B. *The Alphabetization of the Popular Mind*; North Point Press: San Francisco, CA, USA, 1988.

17. Logan, R.K. *The Alphabet Effect: The Impact of the Phonetic Alphabet on the Development of Western Civilization*; William Morrow and Company, Inc.: New York, NY, USA, 1986.
18. Ong, W.J. *Orality and Literacy: The Technologizing of the Word*; Methuen: London, UK; New York, NY, USA, 1982.
19. Frazer, J.G. *The Golden Bough*; Macmillan Company: New York, NY, USA, 1909.
20. Lévy-Bruhl, L. *The Notebooks on Primitive Mentality*; Harper & Row Publishers: New York, NY, USA, 1975.
21. Scribner, S.; Cole, M. *The Psychology of Literacy*; Harvard University Press: Cambridge, MA, USA, 1981.
22. McLuhan, M.; McLuhan, E. *Media and Formal Cause*; NeoPoiesis Press: Houston, TX, USA, 2011.
23. Anton, C. McLuhan, Formal Cause, and the Future of Technological Mediation. *Rev. Commun.* **2012**, *12*, 276–289. [CrossRef]
24. Anton, C.; Logan, R.K.; Strate, L. *Taking up McLuhan's Cause: Perspectives on Media and Formal Causality*; Intellect Publishing: Bristol, UK, in press.
25. De Kerckhove, D. *The Skin of Culture*; Somerville House Publishing: Toronto, ON, Canada, 1995.
26. Berger, P.L.; Luckmann, T. *The Social Construction of Reality*; Doubleday: New York, NY, USA, 1966.
27. Anton, C. *Selfhood and Authenticity*; SUNY Press: Albany, NY, USA, 2001.
28. Anton, C. Beyond the Constitutive/Representational Dichotomy: The Phenomenological Notion of Intentionality. *Commun. Theory* **1999**, *9*, 26–57. [CrossRef]
29. Anton, C. Presence and Interiority: Walter Ong's contributions to a diachronic phenomenology of voice. In *Of Ong and Media Ecology: Essays in Communication, Composition, and Literary Studies*; Farrell, T.S., Soukup, P., Eds.; Hampton Press: Cresskill, NJ, USA, 2012; pp. 71–90.
30. Anton, C. Diachronic Phenomenology: A Methodological Thread within Media Ecology. *Explor. Media Ecol. J. Media Ecol. Assoc.* **2014**, *13*, 3–30. [CrossRef]

# 2

# Empathy and Vicarious Experience: Congruence or Identical Emotion?

**Patricia C. Brunsteins**

Escuela de Filosofía, Facultad de Filosofía y Humanidades, Universidad Nacional de Córdoba, Pabellón Francia, Ciudad Universitaria, Córdoba, C.P. 5000, Argentina; patriciabrunsteins@gmail.com

**Abstract:** Feeling empathy is something that happens, an experience we can remember once we have had it, or an experience we would like to have. I consider empathy, from an integral point of view (i.e., cognitive and emotive aspects are part of empathy), as the capacity of putting oneself in the place of others. Although, by this time, my general characterization of empathy will not be discussed, I will focus on one question about empathy for which there is still no agreement: whether the emotion of the person experiencing empathy must be identical or not to the emotion felt by the person being empathized with. The aim of this work is, firstly, to reduce the four possibilities about the relationship between the empathizer's emotion and the emotion felt by the person who is the target of empathy to two exhaustive and exclusive views: (1) the idea of identity of emotions between the empathizer and the target and (2) the point of view of the congruence of emotions between the empathizer and the target, both being cases of personal emotional experiences. Secondly, I suggest that these possibilities may make up an exclusive disjunctive argument, showing that problems with the first part of the argument or the premise would lead us to accept the second part: to feel empathy we do not need to feel exactly the same emotion that the object of empathy feels.

**Keywords:** empathy; emotion; cognition; emotional contagion; personal; subpersonal; perspective taking

## 1. Introduction

In recent years, the study of empathy as an intersubjective and non-reciprocal capacity has become increasingly relevant. In fact, during the last decades there has been an "explosion" of empirical and interdisciplinary work in evolutionary psychology, cognitive psychology, social neuroscience, psychology of development, philosophy of mind, and other disciplines that strongly modify the sense and the scope of empathy [1–4].

In this paper, and using a notion of empathy that I have been developing in other papers[1] as a starting point, I will focus on one particular characteristic of empathy to consider and to itemize that for which there is still no agreement: whether the emotion of the person experiencing empathy must be identical or not to the emotion felt by the person being empathized with. This problem, among others, is central to sustaining an ontological and epistemological plausible notion of empathy.

The aim of this work is, firstly, to reduce four possibilities about the relationship between the empathizer's emotion and the emotion felt by the person who is the target of empathy to two exhaustive and exclusive views: that the idea of identity of emotions between the empathizer and the target, and that the point of view of congruence [no identity] of emotions between the empathizer and the target. Both are cases of personal emotional experiences.

---

1 My view about empathy is developed in ref. [5–9].

Secondly, I suggest that these possibilities are parts of an exclusive disjunctive argument showing that problems with the first premise would lead us to accept the second one; the idea is that, for feeling empathy, we do not need to feel exactly the same emotion that the object of empathy feels.

## 2. The Central Core about Empathy

"Empathy" is usually defined in various ways and by different disciplines (psychoanalysis, philosophy, and social psychology, among others). Nowadays, taking into account studies in cognitive social neuroscience and philosophy of mind, it is possible to assume that there is a general agreement in considering empathy as a capacity of attaining the neuronal, affective, and cognitive levels to define it from a purely neuronal conception to an affective and/or a cognitive one. It is also conceived of as an integral view. This fact does not mean that consensus about ways of considering empathy has been reached, whether about its nature, scope, function, or criteria of differentiation, among other intersubjective capacities.

One of the unavoidable philosophical questions is to determine what kind of process the empathic experience is, particularly, what kind of emotional and cognitive experience it is. There are numerous theories to account for empathy, and there are many theories of emotion and cognition, too. However, there are very few conceptualizations about the type of theory of emotion adequate to account for empathy, as well as the type of cognition that is at stake in the empathic experience. This last fact leads us to have different ways of understanding empathy.

As previously mentioned, there are at least three different ways of conceiving the notion of empathy.

Empathy may be integrally conceived as Baron-Cohen, S. (2011) [2] or Decety, J. and Jackson, P. (2004) [3] conceptualize:

> "It is the ability to identify what someone is thinking or feeling and to respond to their thoughts and feelings with an appropriate emotion"
>
> (Baron-Cohen, S., 2011) [2]

> "It consists of affective sharing between oneself and the other; it is the cognitive ability to differentiate between self/other consciousness and the mental flexibility to adopt the subjective perspective of the other."
>
> (Decety, J. and Jackson, P., 2004) [3]

However, some philosophers hold that is the cognitive aspect of what specifies empathy:

> "Empathy is the cognitive consciousness of the internal state of another person [thoughts, feelings, intentions]"
>
> (Ickes, W., 1997) [10]

> "It is the cognitive consciousness of the thoughts, feelings, perceptions, and intentions of the other person"
>
> (Deigh, J., 2011) [11]

Finally, it is possible to sustain an emotive notion of empathy.

> "Empathy is the vicarious affective response to another person"
>
> (Mill, J., 1985) [12]

> "Empathy is the vicarious emotion that a person experiences when reflecting on the emotion of the other."
>
> (Prinz, J., 2011) [13]

The way empathy is defined is very important, since it is not a trivial differentiation or just a question of labeling or a way of talking. The way empathy is described depends on the abilities and processes involved in it, and this entirely modifies its social functions.

As a consequence of the different criteria about the complex notion of empathy, boundaries about other associated intersubjective phenomena like mindreading, perspective taking, personal distress, sympathy, emotional contagion, and empathy itself, among other phenomena, are ambiguous.

An interesting analysis that coheres all the different views about empathy described above is the Preston, S. and de Waal, F., (2001) [14] model of empathy that, by means of what they call the Action-Perception Model and its evolution processes, in different species, integrates diverse basic phenomena and higher cognitive processes as different levels of empathy.

## 3. My View on Empathy

Feeling empathy is something that happens, an experience we can remember once we had it, or an experience we would like to have. We may have empathy for our friend who has been stolen from or for our friend who got a Ph.D. To have empathy is "to know" or to feel what seems to be happening to the other person.

From my perspective, taking into account different ways of conceiving it as I described below, empathy could be understood as an imaginary extended line, the respective ends of which correspond to a notion of an entirely affective empathy on one side and an entirely cognitive notion on the other side. This line is integrated by different instances of empathy along it.

Each instance is merged with emotional and cognitive factors in different intensities depending on the type intensity of empathy. When emphasizing the integral nature of empathy, cases—defined as purely affective or purely cognitive—would not be, in fact, empathic cases[2].

I agree with the view that empathy is compatible with non-human animal empathy[3].

I claim that empathy is the ability to feel vicarious emotion congruent, but not identical, with the emotion that the other individual feels. To achieve empathy there are various factors at play: emotional, cognitive, contextual, and personal. While it requires several (but not all) cognitive abilities that are also used in mentalizing, it differs from mentalizing as another ability [16].

## 4. Empathy and Emotion

One of the important questions to be solved is what kind of emotion is involved in the empathic experience, since it seems that it is not what is called "a first-hand" emotion but, at the same time, the empathizer feels any kind of emotion.

A first-hand emotion is an emotion that happens to oneself and from oneself. However, there is another type of emotion, namely, the vicarious one. A vicarious emotion depends on another one. The vicarious emotional experience is whatever emotion a person manifests that is caused by the expression of another person's emotion. There is a vicarious emotional experience when our emotion does not arise from a first-hand experience [17].

The hypothesis developed in this paper aims to answer the following question: what is the relationship (if there is one) between the emotive aspect of the empathizer and the emotive aspect of the individual who is the object of empathy?

---

2 Cases of purely emotive aspects of empathy may be seen as emotional contagion, and cases of purely cognitive aspects would consider as mindreading or as theories of mind but not as empathy.

3 See ref. [6] "L'empatia animale: una caratterizzazione concetuale". In this article, (Brunsteins, 2017), within the framework of a position that rejects the anthropocentric thesis or the thesis of human exception from humanist ideas, gives a conceptual characterization of the notion of empathy applicable to both human and nonhuman animals. Along with and for this characterization, she proposes to consider emotions as processes ref. [15]. A notion of integral empathy would provide a tool that can be used to enhance knowledge of social cognition in different species, particularly differentiating empathy from other associated intersubjective phenomena such as compassion, cooperation, altruism, sympathy, emotional contagion, personal distress imitation, mindreading, and perspective taking, i.e., phenomena that are often confused.

This question allows at least two different and exclusive answers. The first one is proposed by [17]. They say that experiencing empathy is feeling the same as the person who is the object of empathy, posing an isomorphism between the emotional experiences.

In a different vein, ref. [3] and ref. [18] propose that, in order to have the experience of empathy, the emotion of the observer must be congruent with the emotion of the observed individual.

Each of these different answers supports two possibilities each: either identity between the emotional experiences is subpersonal, or either identity between the emotional experiences is at a personal level. The same occurs with the congruence between the emotional experiences; the congruence between the emotional experiences is and may be explained at a subpersonal level or at a personal one.

## 5. The Emotional Experience at a Subpersonal Level

As I expressed above, I will dedicate this part of the work to eradicate, as a possibility of empathic emotive experience, cases of identity or congruence of emotions between the empathizer and the person who is the object of empathy at a subpersonal level. In other words, I will disesteem the first and third possibilities, which posed that the identity between the emotional experiences is subpersonal or the congruence between the emotional experiences is subpersonal for empathy. In those cases, I suggest that the phenomenon referred to is not empathy but another intersubjective capacity, namely, emotional contagion.

Emotional contagion is a subpersonal process that happens when people tend to automatically imitate facial expressions or postures, and people feel a pale reflection of the emotions of others. The process of emotional contagion could be dissected in three stages: (1) mimicry, (2) feedback, and (3) contagion [19].

By means of mimicry, people tend to automatically imitate facial expressions, vocal, postures, and certain instrumental behaviors around them. They also have a tendency to feel a pale reflection of the emotions of others as a result of such feedback. The final result of the former is that people tend to capture the emotions of others.

Emotional contagion is closely related to empathy, although they are different phenomena.

The main difference between empathy and emotional contagion is that emotional contagion is an automatic and non-regulated capacity, while empathy may begin (in some cases, but not in all cases) with emotional contagion, particularly in cases in which empathy originated from direct perception. Thus, empathy may begin with emotional contagion, but other personal capacities are needed to have empathy, see ref. [1].

There are at least two main reasons to consider that empathy is more than emotional contagion and the emotion provoked in us. Firstly, there is empirical evidence that suggests that empathy can be modulated by other factors that are different from neuronal activation: the direct, automatic, and unconscious perception of another person's feelings. Empathy can be modulated through the intervention of external elements [20].Empathic modulation may be conceived of as voluntary through experience and practice (i.e., doctors, monks) using the control that each has on their emotions, or it may be modulated through implicit evaluative processes [20]. In the case of implicit evaluative processes, there are certain factors that modify the intensity of empathy and, in that sense, the very same empathy. The features of emotions (e.g., intensity, valence, and salience), the relationship between the empathizer and the person who is the object of empathy, characteristics of the empathizer (e.g., gender, age, past experiences), and contextual information modify the intensity and may even activate or obstruct empathy. For instance, there is empirical evidence that suggests that the intensity of empathy produced by others in pain decreases if the pain infringed is a means to cure, unlike pain infringed without justification [21]. The intensity of empathy of the observer also varies if the observer perceives the situation that the person in pain is involved in as fair or unfair. There is more intensity of empathy in cases of unfair situations [22]. In all these cases, it appears that, to empathize with someone, something more than affective correspondence is required, because, if that were the case, there should not be differences between cases of only affective correspondence between the empathizer and the target and those cases in which there was some additional information from the empathizer's side. In these cases, additional information has modified the very sense of empathy.

Secondly, from the conceptual point of view and taking into account the perspective of developmental psychology, it is important to highlight that conceiving of empathy as just mirroring at a subpersonal level would not fully explain differences due to maturation, nor would it explain the sophistication of complex forms of emotion and cognition during child development until maturity see ref. [23].

Thus, there are some cognitive abilities that I consider necessary in the empathic process, and they integrate the notion of empathy itself. If this is the case, emotional contagion would be the way of acquiring empathy but, to reach it, different capacities are also needed.

Perspective taking is related to a certain cognitive flexibility to be able to adopt the perspective of the other. This ability matures late, since it depends on the maturity of executive abilities that continue to develop until adolescence [24]. Together with perspective taking, the regulation of emotions is needed to be able to empathize. The latter states the similarity and differentiation between me and the other person. It consists of the ability to reply to the demands of the experience with a bearable emotional scope and to be flexible enough to allow or delay/inhibit spontaneous reactions. This ability allows empathizing without having personal distress, and it can lead to sympathy. According to Decety, J. and Lamm, C. [24], in addition to the cognitive abilities already mentioned with regards to empathizing with someone else, certain top-down process information is required; the executive functions implemented in certain areas of the cerebral cortex regulate cognition and emotion through selective attention and auto-regulation. They are capacities of focusing the context facilitating the intersubjective relationship and updating in terms of bottom-up information. It is a re-evaluation process. Finally, as the authors assume, bottom-up process information is required. In that process the "shared" emotion automatically activated in the observer through the direct perceptual inputs is accounted for. It refers to motor control and sensorial-affective domains.

Thus, given these four possibilities: (1) identity between the emotional experiences is subpersonal; (2) identity between the emotional experiences is personal; (3) congruence between the emotional experiences is subpersonal; and (4) congruence between the emotional experiences is personal, my suggestion leads us to eliminate cases 1 and 3 from the list of empathic experiences.

Emotional contagion is a punctually self-centered automatic capacity that may or may not be integrated into a more sophisticated notion, such as empathy. When experiencing empathy, reference to a capacity centered on the other occurs.

## 6. Identity between the Emotional Experiences is Personal

Having disesteemed the subpersonal emotive experiences as cases of empathy, let us consider the first part of the disjunctive premise of the principal argument.

Remember that the aim of this work is to reduce four possibilities about the relationship between the empathizer emotion and the emotion felt by the person who is the target of empathy to two exhaustive and exclusive views: the idea of identity of emotions between the empathizer and the target, and the point of view of congruence [no identity] of emotions between the empathizer and the target, both being cases of personal emotional experiences. Finally, I want to suggest these possibilities as parts of an exclusive disjunctive argument showing that problems with the first premise would lead us to accept the second one; the idea is that for feeling empathy, we do not need to feel exactly the same emotion that the person that is object of empathy feels.

The first part of the premise sustains that to have an empathic emotional experience is to feel the same emotion, in an identical way, that the person who is object of empathy is feeling. Wondra J.D. and Ellsworth, P.C. ref. [17] present the following example to develop this idea:

> "Imagine that your friend got sick following an international vacation that the two of you took together. You are waiting with your friend in the hospital to hear the results of a test for malaria. Both you and your friend think that a positive test result would be awful and that

your friend was extremely unlucky. Your friend feels fairly sure that the test will come back positive and feels sad. If you also feel confident that the test will be positive, then you will feel sad with your friend. We would call this empathy because you feel what your friend feels. If, however, you feel that you have no idea what the test result will be, then you will feel scared for your friend. We would call this a nonmatching vicarious emotion because it is not what your friend feels. The only difference is whether you have appraised the situation in the same way as your friend or not". [17] (p. 418)

**7. Why Should We Suspect about Identity?**

Firstly, I think that it would be problematic to accept the premise in hand, because it is difficult to determine whether, when Wondra, J.D. and Ellsworth, P.C. argue ref. [17] that empathy is the case, we actually have the same emotion as the person who is being empathized with; how can we know that an individual feels exactly (i.e., makes the same appraisals) what the other individual feels without entering into a subsequent intersubjective relationship to compare and adjust their own emotions or appraisals? If this is possible, what would be the justification criteria in this regard?

Secondly, it would be problematic to accept the premise at hand. Their proposal would place a great limitation on the empathic experience, since we could not have empathy with someone who experiences an emotion that we have not previously felt in the same sense as the individual feels it, unless we can achieve the same feeling through imagination and/or other cognitive functions. However, in that case, would it be effectively identical? Can we assume in that case that we have had the same appraisal? Thus, in order to admit the case of identity of emotions, it is necessary to give more reasons to overcome these problems.

It is also important to highlight that, in case of assuming congruence, it is impossible to explain why there is no identity between the empathizer's emotion and that of the target for the same reasons.

The very significant point is that there does not need to be some kind of identity for there to be empathy. Returning to Wondra, J.D. and Ellsworth, P.C.'s example, and reconsidering it through the light of my worries, there is empathy both feeling the same emotion of the friend or not. What really matters is to have put oneself into the other's situation, having an emotion that makes it possible to feel empathy. The emotion, no matter what that exactly emotion may be, is the vehicle for feeling empathy, with this emotion being congruent with the emotion the target feels.

Empathy is a flexible and malleable phenomenon due to a number of motivational and dispositional situations. Such situations, perspective taking, and the regulation of emotions modify the emotions we feel to go beyond emotional contagion, not suffering personal distress, and experiencing empathy.

Empathy may be generated by means of different mechanisms: through direct perception, through imagination, by perspective taking, or by means of top-down-type controls. Emotions can vary according to the rest of the intervening factors. These factors ensure that for there to be congruence between one's emotion and the other's emotion, the person takes what is relevant in the environment so that, with their own resources and through an emotional and cognitive experience, the person achieves the empathic experience. Since there are so many intervening factors when having the vicarious emotional experience, it would almost be begging the question to suppose that it will be the same type of emotional experience that is instantiated in both cases.

In addition, the way in which Wondra J.D., and Ellsworth, P.C. ref. [17] characterize emotions assumes, for example, that being afraid involves describing a series of emotional experiences that are traversed without clear boundaries because emotions are continuous. Thus, if this is the case, it is difficult to determine whether the case of vicarious emotion corresponds to the same type of emotional experience as the person who is the object of empathy, given that, for empathy, according to the authors, the subject should do the same type of evaluations that the individual who is the object of empathy has done.

A way to disentangle the problem is offered by Nanay, B. ref. [25], who makes an analogy between vicarious perception and vicarious emotion. The author assumes that it is possible, for instance, to feel vicarious fear without attributing any emotional state, because it is a relatively simple process that does not require any higher order thoughts. Nanay, B. ref. [25] uses the expression "vicarious emotional engagement" to refer to the form of emotional engagement with others in which we perceive entities around another person as emotionally relevant to that person. In this sense, when having empathy by means of some vicarious emotional engagement, it is not necessary to suppose identity of emotions between the empathizer[4] and the target, just a perceptual attribution of other centered-thick action properties to an object.

Moreover, it is important to take into account that, from the empirical point of view, evidence has been found suggesting a certain congruence but no identity of emotions. In fact, a study proposed by Morelli, S., Rameson, L., and Lieberman, M. ref. [26] reveals, from a quantitative and qualitative analysis, that empathy for positive and negative emotions selectively activates the regions associated with positive and negative affect, respectively. However, it is not possible to relate them to a specific emotion.

The problem is that if we define empathy in a narrow sense, we would exclude cases that I consider to reveal empathy contrary to Wondra, J.D and Ellsworth, P.C ref. [17].That difference is not a trivial question, since it refers to psychological processes. That is, there is an ontological commitment at stake. It also reveals different epistemological commitments.

Thus, reconsidering Wondra, J.D and Ellsworth, P.C.'s example, I think we may identify the case they refuse to consider: empathy as an actual and valid case of empathy. It is that way, because, by means of feeling scared, he or she feels empathy for his or her sad friend, being successfully placed in his or her shoes. In this case, being scared is congruent, but not identical, with his sadness. It provokes empathy as well. His or her fear of not knowing the outcome of the blood analysis is a result of his friend's sadness among other factors at play. He or she feels an emotion that is congruent, but not identical with, his or her friend, and it is sufficient to reach empathy. This result is in line with the empirical evidence just referred to. It may be possible to accept a broader sense of emotions matching, for instance, positive emotions with positive emotions or negative emotions with other negative emotions, enhancing, in that way, the notion of empathy.

## 8. Conclusions

Since there are space-time, body, perspective, and responsibility differences, it is necessary to explain in more detail the possibility that the emotion felt for the empathizer may be identical to that of the person who is the object of empathy.

Moreover, the rejection of the first part of the disjunctive premise leads us to a second one, that is, that the emotion of the observer must be congruent with the emotion of the observed individual.

**Acknowledgments:** Among the people I owe thanks is Liza Skidelsky and all organization committee members of the 2017 workshop on the Philosophy Cognitive Science in Buenos Aires, my research group, and those who participated in the workshop. Thanks also to reviewers for their advice and suggestions.

**Conflicts of Interest:** The author declares no conflict of interest.

## References

1. De Waal, F. *La Edad de la Empatía*; Tusquets Editores: Barcelona, Spain, 2013.
2. Baron-Cohen, S. *The Science of Evil: On Empathy and the Origins of Cruelty*; Basic Books: New York, NY, USA, 2011.
3. Decety, J.; Jackson, P.L. The functional architecture of human empathy. *Behav. Cogn. Neurosci. Rev.* **2004**, *3*, 71–100. [CrossRef] [PubMed]
4. Cuff, B.; Brown, S.J.; Taylor, L.; Howat, D. Empathy: A Review of the Concept. *Emot. Rev.* **2015**, *8*, 144–153. [CrossRef]

[4] See ref. [25] *Between Perception and Action*, cap.6. In this chapter the author develops his idea of vicarious perception.

5. Brunsteins, P. El carácter emotivo de la experiencia empática. In *La Segunda Persona y Las Emociones*; Pérez, D., Lawler, D., Eds.; SADAF: Buenos Aires, Argentina, 2017.
6. Brunsteins, P. L'empatia animale: Una caratterizzazione concettuale. *Anim. Stud.* **2017**, *1*, 72–77.
7. Brunsteins, P. La empatía y su contribución en el ámbito de los derechos humanos. In *La urdimbre de la Razón. Ensayos de Filosofía Teórica y Práctica Contemporáneos*; Lariguet, G., Ed.; Kazak Ediciones: Mar del Plata, Argentina, 2017.
8. Brunsteins, P. La delgada línea entre ser o no ser empático. In *Filosofía e Historia de la Ciencia en el Cono Sur Selección de trabajos del IX Encuentro y las XXV Jornadas de Epistemología e Historia de la Ciencia*; Editorial de la Universidad Nacional de Córdoba: Córdoba, Argentina, 2016; Volume 1, pp. 149–156.
9. Brunsteins, P. El rol de la empatía en la jurisprudencia desde la óptica de J. Deigh. Un análisis crítico a partir del caso Lilly Ledbetter. *Nuevas Fronteras en Filosofía Práctica* **2015**, *4*, 15–29.
10. Ickes, W. *Empathy Accuracy*; Guilford Press: New York, NY, USA, 1997.
11. Deigh, J. Empathy, Justice and Jurisprudence. *South. J. Philos.* **2011**, *49*. [CrossRef]
12. Mill, J.S. *Diario*; Alianza Editorial: Madrid, Spain, 1985.
13. Prinz, J. Against Empathy. *South. J. Philos.* **2011**, *49*, 214–233. [CrossRef]
14. Preston, S.; de Waal, F. Empathy: Its ultímate and proximate base. *Behav. Brain Sci.* **2002**, *25*, 1–20. [CrossRef] [PubMed]
15. Robinson, J. *Deeper than Reasons*; Oxford University Press: Oxford, UK, 2007.
16. Brunsteins, P. *La Psicología Folk: Teorías, Prácticas y Perspectivas*; Ediciones del Signo: Buenos Aires, Argentina, 2010.
17. Wondra, J.D.; Ellsworth, P.C. An Appraisal Theory of Empathy and Other Vicarious Emotional Experiences. *Psychol. Rev.* **2015**, *122*, 411–428. [CrossRef] [PubMed]
18. Decety, J. The Neural pathways, development and functions of empathy. *Curr. Opin. Behav. Sci.* **2015**, *3*, 1–6. [CrossRef]
19. Hatfield, E.; Rapson, R.L.; Le, Y.L. *The Oxford Companion to Emotion and the Affective Sciences*; Sander, D., Scherer, K.R., Eds.; Oxford University Press: New York, NY, USA, 2009; p. 99.
20. De Vignemont, F.; Singer, T. The empathic brain, how, when and why? *Trends Cogn. Sci.* **2006**, *10*, 435–441. [CrossRef] [PubMed]
21. Lamm, C.; Meltzoff, A.; Decety, J. How do we empathize with someone who is not like us? *J. Cogn. Neurosci.* **2009**, *22*, 362–376. [CrossRef] [PubMed]
22. Singer, T.; Seymour, B.; O'Doherty, J.; Stephan, K.; Doland, R. Empathic neural responses are modulated by the perceived fairness of others. *Nature* **2006**, *439*, 466–469. [CrossRef] [PubMed]
23. Hoffman, M. *Empathy and Moral Development*; Cambridge University Press: Cambridge, UK, 2003.
24. Decety, J.; Lamm, C. Human Empathy through the lens of Social Neuroscience. *Sci. World J.* **2006**, *6*, 1146–1163. [CrossRef] [PubMed]
25. Nanay, B. *Between Perception and Action*; Oxford University Press: Oxford, UK, 2013.
26. Morelli, S.; Rameson, L.; Lieberman, M. The Neural Components of Empathy: Predicting Daily Pro Social Behavior. *Soc. Cogn. Affect. Neurosci.* **2014**, *9*, 39–47. [CrossRef] [PubMed]

3

# The Modal—Amodal Distinction in the Debate on Conceptual Format

**Sabrina Haimovici**

Facultad de Filosofía y Letras, Instituto de Filosofía "Dr. Alejandro Korn", Consejo Nacional de Investigaciones Científicas y Técnicas (CONICET), Universidad de Buenos Aires, Buenos Aires, C.P. 1406, Argentina; shaimovici@filo.uba.ar

**Abstract:** In this paper, I review the main criteria offered for distinguishing the modal and amodal approaches to conceptual format: the type of input to which the representations respond, the relation they bear to perceptual states, and the specific neural systems to which they belong. I evaluate different interpretations of them and argue that they all face difficulties. I further show that they lead to cross-classifications of certain types of representations, using approximate number representations as an example.

**Keywords:** mental representations; concepts; grounded cognition; sensorimotor systems; symbols; approximate number representations

## 1. Introduction

Within the framework that takes concepts to be mental representations, one of the central and current debates concerns their format or vehicle. According to the traditional amodal approach, concepts are couched in a symbolic format that bears no structural similarity to perceptual states [1,2]. According to the modal or grounded approach, in contrast, concepts are couched in perceptual representations that become stored during perception and action, and can be later reenacted in absence of the stimuli that originally produced them [3,4].[1] Thus, a way of distinguishing amodal and modal vehicles relies on their relation to perceptual and motor systems, but besides this distinction, there is no general consensus on the specific characteristics of each type of format.

Some authors distinguish both types of representations in terms of the type of input to which they respond. For example, Dove states "[ … ] modal-specificity is defined with regard to input. Representations contained within a mechanism that has been shaped by natural selection to handle inputs from multiple modalities are amodal by definition" [5] (p. 424). Other authors appeal to the relation between a concept's structure and its content, and propose a distinction similar to that between icons and symbols. For example, Fodor identifies iconic representations with those that can be divided in any way obtaining a part that represents part of the content, whereas discursive symbolic representations are those that exhibit a canonical decomposition in which not every part represents part of the content [6]. In a similar vein, Martin opposes a "highly abstract, 'amodal,' language-like propositional format [ … ]" versus a "[ … ] depictive, iconic, picture-like format [ … ]" [7] (p. 983).[2] Other versions are based on evidence of neural organization, and claim that modal concepts consist of representations located on modality-specific pathways, while amodal

1 Within the grounded approach, perceptual representations are broadly understood, including the representations used by the systems that support perception, action, and internal states.

2 The debate on conceptual format continues in some aspects the debate between depictive and descriptive accounts of visual mental imagery. Proponents of depictive representations underlying imagery argued that they were picture-like [8], while

concepts reside in different independent systems [12]. Sometimes amodal representations are characterized in purely negative terms, as having a format that "differs from the format or formats of perceptual and motor representations" [13] (p. 1090), which has in turn elicited responses such that they constitute "black holes in conceptual space" [12] (p. 1127). It has also been suggested that the properties of concepts' vehicles are still unknown and in need of empirical research, yet the debate can advance without specifying those characteristics [13], and even that the question of format lacks "practical significance", given that we have no procedure for determining the format of the neural code [7].

I agree in that the debate is advancing, even though the characteristics of each type of representation remain underspecified. While the grounded or modal approach is still growing and is supported by an increasing amount of empirical evidence (for a review see [14], for discussion of the strength of the evidence see [15]), there is also evidence supporting amodal views (for reviews see [5,13]). Moreover, there are new hybrid and pluralist views that postulate both modal and amodal concepts [5,16–19]. The newer versions within each approach also search for biological plausibility and take into account recent neurological evidence. I think that it is therefore worth looking into the main criteria proposed for distinguishing modal and amodal representations. I will argue that all of them run into difficulties, either conceptual or of empirical application, and will also show that adopting different criteria leads to cross-classifications of representations taking as an example approximate number representations. This type of representations constitute an interesting example for several reasons. First, although they are sometimes held as direct evidence of amodal representations [5,20], their status as amodal is also discussed [21]. Second, there is a vast amount of evidence concerning the neural localization of these representations, and several functional models of how we encode this particular type of magnitude, which have considerable indirect support. Thus, these representations can be analyzed by all of the criteria that I will discuss.

In Section 2, I discuss the distinction in terms of the type of input to which the representations respond. I point out that this criterion offers an underspecified distinction, since it does not distinguish between multimodal and amodal representations. I also consider an alternative interpretation of this criterion that attributes a specific proprietary format to each modality, and places this criterion closer to one based on the neural systems of the representations that I analyze in Section 4. In Section 3, I analyze the isomorphism criterion. I consider two versions: an isomorphism between modal representations and their contents, and between modal representations and the perceptual states that produced them. I review several objections to the first interpretation, and argue that the second one resembles the neural one. Finally, in Section 4, I present the neural base criterion, and claim that it is the clearer and stronger of the three. However, I argue that this criterion also faces difficulties. In particular, it presupposes ways of individuating modalities and of determining which systems are constitutively involved in conceptual tasks and which ones are auxiliary, both of which encounter empirical difficulties.

## 2. Input Specificity

Some authors suggest that what distinguishes modal and amodal representations is the type of input to which they respond. According to this criterion, modal systems respond to a specific class of input, such as sound waves or molecule shapes, whereas amodal systems respond uniformly to inputs from different perceptual modalities [4,5]. It is usually assumed that a distinctive feature of perceptual systems is that they respond to specific physical magnitudes. It is less clear how modalities are individuated [21,22]. I will address this issue in Section 4. The main difficulty with this criterion is that,

---

proponents of descriptive representations argued for language-like, sentential representations [9,10]. Some of the criteria proposed for distinguishing modal and amodal representations partially overlap with those characterizing pictorial and sentential representations, in particular the appeal to isomorphic relations between the structure of the representations and their referential contents [11], that I will discuss in detail in Section 3. Although modal representations are sometimes identified with mental images, they differ since conceptual modal representations are not consciously experienced [3].

even assuming a clear individuation of modalities, it is underspecified. First, considering responding to perceptual inputs as a sufficient condition for modality would be too permissive. Given our physical constitution, every input route or modality of stimulation is perceptual. All of the information that we receive arrives to us through our senses, and as a consequence every representation is to a certain degree connected to perception. Thus, under this interpretation every representation would be trivially modal, and that does not seem to be the notion of modality endorsed by either side of the debate on conceptual format. As a consequence, proponents of this criterion emphasize a distinction between responding to a single class of input versus responding to several. However, this alternative does not allow to distinguish between amodal and multimodal representations, since both types represent several input classes [23].

In fact, amodal and multimodal representations are sometimes conflated. Barsalou reports an informal survey carried out by Martin, who asked researchers what they meant by the term "amodal" and found out they actually meant "multimodal" [12]. Sometimes the conflation is explicit. For example, Dehaene characterizes the horizontal intraparietal sulcus (hIPS), a brain area centrally involved in processing quantity, as amodal or plurimodal: "There are many indications that this region is indeed intimately involved with quantity, as opposed to other aspects of number. First of all, it responds to all the modalities of number presentation—whether the person is watching a set of dots, [ ... ] or looking at a symbol, like the Arabic numeral 3 or the written or the spoken word 'three.' This simple criterion, places the hIPS in what neuroscientists call 'plurimodal' or 'amodal' sectors of cortex—brain regions which, unlike the sensory areas, are not attached to a specific sensory modality, such as vision or touch, but lie at the meeting point of many input routes. If a brain region is to encode an abstract concept, one that is not tied to specific sensations, it is essential that it respond to all of the relevant modalities of stimulation in which the concept can be communicated" [24] (p. 239).

The problem with adopting this criterion is that every representation would be amodal. The ways in which concepts can be communicated will most likely include language, even for concepts that are "tied to sensations". Setting aside debates about phenomenal aspects of perceptual experience, and whether there are phenomenal concepts—e.g., concepts of specific shades of a given color—for a vast amount of sensations we not only have concepts, but also words to name those concepts. Thus, language constitutes one of the ways in which a concept can be communicated. As a consequence, every concept for which there is a term in natural language would be amodal, inasmuch as it responds to language plus the modality or modalities by which it can be communicated.

Considering the example of approximate number representations, the type of input to which they respond seems to be the main reason for considering them amodal. We have an ability to form approximate representations of the number of individuals in a set. This ability that is shared by human adults, human infants, and nonhuman animals (in particular pigeons, rats, and monkeys) has two distinctive characteristics, the distance and magnitude effects. First, the discriminability between two approximate representations is a function of their ratio, that is, the greater the numerical distance between two quantities, the easier it is to distinguish them. Second, for equal numerical distances, the smaller the magnitudes of the collections involved, the easier it is to distinguish them. These effects distinguish it from our ability to count and to represent exact quantities [24].

Studies have shown that performance is not affected by the modality of the stimulus [25]. Not only is performance in representing the approximate cardinality of visual and auditory stimuli similar, but there have also been studies of transfer from one modality to another [26]. It has been argued that these results reveal an underlying amodal system [5,13,20]. Dehaene explicitly refers to those representations as amodal [24,27,28]. As the quote above shows, he stresses that they not only respond to inputs from several modalities, but also to symbolic notations and words. Thus, he identifies them as amodal inasmuch as they respond to several input routes. However, he also refers to this ability as a "sense", talks of "number perception" (e.g., [24] p. 237) and even refers to these representations as evolutionary precursors from our symbolic number representations [28]. In order to be a precursor from a symbolic system, they must be different from symbols in a relevant sense. A candidate to make this difference is that they are analog, and in that sense different from amodal representations. This distinction involves an alternative criterion, based on the way the internal structure of the vehicles is related to what they represent, which I will discuss in the next section. Dehaene also stresses out evidence that the system's operation precedes symbolic education, suggesting that the format it employs is not symbolic. The fact that they respond equally to different modalities makes them amodal by the input specificity criterion. However, there are other considerations that lead to consider them modal. As I will argue, taking into consideration the internal features of the representations and the relation they bear to perceptual states, they would be modal. That is, according to alternative criteria these representations seem to be modal.

I have argued that this criterion underspecifies the distinction, given that it collapses multimodal and amodal representations and, as a result, there is a sense in which every representation would be amodal. Furthermore, casting the distinction in terms of the input to which the representations respond does not mention any characteristics of the vehicles, but only a relational property with their inputs. A related way of presenting this criterion that takes into account internal properties of the vehicles—i.e., the nature of the code—is as opposing a single amodal code or format to the multiple codes of perceptual modalities. It is usually assumed that the fact that the senses respond to different classes of inputs supports the thesis that they have proprietary formats [4,12]. As Barsalou explains, it is likely that the representations in modality-specific pathways exhibit evolutionary constrains that led them to specialize in specific types of computations over different kinds of inputs. As a result, it is likely that the representations and processes are proprietary for each modality. Furthermore, supported theories of perceptual processing postulate distinct representational primitives [4].

In order to classify approximate number representations by this last interpretation of the criterion, it is necessary to establish whether the way in which cardinality is encoded is shared by other magnitudes. If the codification is proprietary, i.e., specific for the codification of approximate numerosity and not shared by other systems, then these representations could belong to a distinct perceptual system. If, on the contrary, several magnitudes share the same type of code, then approximate numerosity would not have its own proprietary code. Still, these representations could be part of a broader perceptual system [21]. Finally, if all of our conceptual representations share this type of code, then they would be the result of a single amodal encoding scheme.

Evidence suggests that there is a specific system dedicated to approximate numerosity detection and codification. As Jones argues, there have been found neurons that selectively respond to specific numerosities in macaque homologous of the human hIPS, whose functioning resembles selective neurons in the visual system, such as edge- and face-detectors. In that sense, the system for approximate number representation is closer to a perceptual than to an amodal system [21]. Jones considers two possibilities: it could be itself a perceptual system dedicated to representing a specific numerical property in a proprietary code, or it could be a part of a broader perceptual system. I will address the particular way of encoding approximate numerosity in more detail in Section 4.

Considerations of the type of code and the systems to which the representations belong bring this criterion closer to the other criteria, i.e., isomorphism and neural base. I will analyze these two criteria in the following sections and then turn to the interrelations between the three.

### 3. Isomorphism

It is sometimes assumed that the main criterion for distinguishing both types of representations is the relation they exhibit between some properties of their vehicles and some properties of their contents. For example, in a recent introduction to the state of the debate between grounded and amodal approaches, Mahon and Hickok present the distinction between the formats they postulate as depending on whether "there is an isomorphism between the format of conceptual representation and conceptual content" [29] (p. 945). According to this criterion, whereas amodal representations are arbitrarily related to what they represent, modal representations, in contrast, are analog, i.e., they exhibit an isomorphism between their content and some properties of their vehicles [29,30]. In the context of this debate, isomorphism is not taken to be a strict one-to-one mapping between two sets or categories, but a "a structure-preserving function from elements in one domain onto elements in another, [ ... ] [that] may abstract away from detail in each domain" [31] (p. 177). This function also allows for "a certain degree of imprecision" [31].

There are two prevailing interpretations of this criterion. As Mahon and Hickok's introduction shows, it is commonly taken to be a correspondence between the format of conceptual representations and what they represent [4,11,30,31]. Although this criterion is usually attributed to Barsalou, this was not his original claim. As he states it: "The structure of a perceptual symbol corresponds, at least somewhat, to the perceptual state that produced it" [3] (p. 578). That is, there is a correspondence between the format of conceptual representations and the format of perceptual states. Barsalou clarifies that the intended correspondence is not between modal concepts and the world, because it might be the case that not every modal representation bears a structural resemblance to the physical world [3] (Note 1). Another way to state this criterion is as to whether the perceptual brain states that give rise to conceptual thoughts are constitutive of those thoughts or not [32]. The central tenet of the grounded approach claims that at least some of the perceptual states caused by encounters with category members become a constitutive part of the concept of such category. The modal representations that become stored for later reuse when thinking about, e.g., marshmallows, are a subset of the perceptual states that arise in interactions with marshmallows. That is, they are recorded patterns of activation in sensorimotor systems that can be reactivated to think about marshmallows off-line, i.e., in their absence. Thus, the format of modal representations exhibits a structural correspondence with the format of the brain states that produce them, not necessarily with what is represented in the world.

An objection to this interpretation of the criterion could be that a correspondence needs to be between two independent sets or entities. If conceptual thought constitutively involves reactivating the very same representations used during perception, in what sense are there two different things to bear the correspondence? The answer lies in the account of concept acquisition provided by the grounded approach. Not every perceptual representation becomes a part of a concept. There is a process of abstraction and selection (guided by attention and contextual factors such as specific goals). Thus, the two sets are not equivalent and therefore a structural correspondence can be established between them.

Still, some of Barsalou's claims against the amodal approach might suggest that he also has in mind certain correspondence between the format of concepts and what they represent. One of the objections against amodal approaches calls into question the plausibility of representations that are arbitrarily related to their contents: "I continue to doubt that the brain contains amodal conceptual representations that are arbitrarily related to modality-specific representations and to their corresponding referents in the world" [12] (p. 1127). This suggests that what distinguishes amodal from modal representations is not only their relation with sensorimotor states, but also with what they represent. This is problematic in at least two senses. First, the use of the term "arbitrary" in this context is confusing. It is generally accepted that, unlike analog representations, symbols are arbitrarily related to what they represent. This is the standard way for distinguishing them. For example, in characterizing amodal symbolic representations, Wilson and Foglia state: "Such representations are arbitrarily related to their referents because the way in which they are formed and deployed, along with their characteristics, bears no relationship to the physical and functional features of the referents" [30].

Nevertheless, in this context, the role of such arbitrariness is misleading. An empty symbol could be about anything, and there's nothing on its internal structure suggesting what content it will end up carrying. However, once it has acquired a content by whatever means are in place in the system, its relation to its content is not arbitrary anymore (it could be e.g., causal or nomological). That is, the semantic relation between a symbol and its referent is not necessarily arbitrary. Taking a paradigmatic example, words are arbitrarily related to their referents, in the sense of not bearing an internal correspondence or isomorphism to them, but are still systematically related to them [29]. Moreover, modal representations could bear the same type of semantic relation to their referents that amodal symbols (e.g., an informational relation). This reveals a problem in trying to distinguish types of vehicles by involving semantic considerations. The difference must be cast in terms of properties of the format, i.e., properties of the encoding scheme. These include the nature of the basic representational units and their principles or modes of combination [31].

A further problem of overlapping format and semantics is that it might suggest semantic consequences for the grounded approach that do not depend on the thesis concerning the format of representations, and thus, do not correspond to every version included under the approach. For example, Wilson and Foglia point out: "[ . . . ] not only do cognitive and perceptual mechanisms share representational states, but cognitive processing essentially re-activates sensorimotor areas to run perceptual simulations. A further implication is that perceptual symbols are not independent of the biological system that embodies them and the content conveyed would be likely to vary if intelligent systems varied physically" [30]. This consequence depends on the specific theory of content endorsed. Assuming a version of a dual factor theory of content that is compatible with embodied versions of format (e.g., [4]), the content carried by a certain representation not only depends on its internal structure, and thus in a way on its format, but also on its causal and nomological relations to the world.

Second, an appeal to isomorphism between the format of concepts and their contents is problematic in the more general sense that it does not specify the precise type of mapping between the properties of vehicles and their referents. Moreover, by considering that the mapping admits certain imprecision, it is not clear to what extent the structure of the referents is preserved.[3] Thus, the interpretation as isomorphism with the world is more problematic than that of isomorphism with perceptual states.[4] The adoption of the former interpretation might be related to the fact that it overlaps with the iconic–symbolic distinction (e.g., [6]). Fodor, one of the main advocates of amodal vehicles differentiates iconic from discursive representations in terms of the relation between the internal structure of their vehicles and what they represent. Whereas every part of an iconic representation represents a part of its content, not every part of a discursive representation does. Discursive representations have canonical constituents, and iconic ones have mere parts. In other words, icons represent in a continuous analog way, and any decomposition of them yields parts that represent parts of the content. Discursive representations, in contrast, represent in a discrete manner and have a canonical decomposition.

Adopting the iconic–symbolic distinction as a criterion seems to presuppose that all the representations used by sensorimotor systems are iconic. However, it has been argued that isomorphism between vehicles and what they represent is neither a necessary nor a sufficient condition for modality. First, Machery claims that it might not be a necessary condition, since it is an open empirical question whether every modal representation is isomorphic with its content [13]. The same cannot be argued with respect to the isomorphism to perceptual brain states. Until there is evidence of perceptual representations that do not exhibit a correspondence to the format of perceptual states, it seems that this offers a necessary condition for modality. Second, it has been argued that not every representation that is isomorphic with its content is modal. Machery mentions as an example the analog representations used by analog computers, that are isomorphic with their contents, but are not perceptual [13]. Prinz provides two further examples: Wittgenstein's suggestion that there is an isomorphism between true sentences and the world [33], and the possibility of a language of thought that is isolated from perception and exhibits a one-to-one correspondence with the world [4]. Analogously to the arguments against the necessity of isomorphism with the content, the arguments against its sufficiency have no weight against the interpretation as isomorphism with perceptual states. Understanding the isomorphism with perceptual brain states in the way I have presented it offers both a necessary and sufficient condition for modality. Yet, this interpretation has its own shortcomings.

3 I thank an anonymous reviewer for pointing this out.

4 I am not here defending that claiming that the format of all concepts bears a correspondence to the format of perceptual states will not be problematic for a theory of concepts, but only that it constitutes a clearer criterion for distinguishing modal and amodal representations.

Since this interpretation is similar to the neural base criterion, I will address its difficulties in the next section. In the remaining of this section, I will analyze how the isomorphism criterion classifies approximate number representations.

Going back to the numerosity example, the isomorphism criterion suggests that approximate number representations are modal. For example, as Carey describes it, approximate cardinality is represented by "a physical magnitude that is roughly proportional to the number of individuals in the set being enumerated" [34] (p. 118), that is, by a representation that is isomorphic to the quantity represented. Contemporary research in number representation supports this characterization. There are two main models of numerosity detection, both of which employ representations that are isomorphic to the brain states that produced them, as well as to what they represent.

The first one, the mode-control model by Meck and Church, proposes that numerosity is encoded sequentially in an iterative manner. The number of items in a set is encoded by an accumulator that receives an impulse pacemaker for each item in the set [35]. As a result, the amount of energy registered by the accumulator is a function of the number of items. The second one, the numerosity detector model by Dehaene and Changeux, detects cardinality in parallel [27]. It proposes an approximately constant number of active neurons for each item in a set, and summation units that pool activations from all the underlying units. Thus, the total neuronal activity estimates the number of items. The units that perform the summation operation become tuned to a selected range of values—i.e., a preferred numerosity—and in this way become numerosity detectors. Both models employ representations that add the number of items in the set in an analog way (either by an increased amount of energy in an accumulator or by an increased activation threshold in a neural cluster). Thus, approximate number representations seem to be analog and bear a correspondence both to what they represent, and to the perceptual states that produced them. Furthermore, their outputs seem to be couched in a proprietary code, specifically tuned to numerosity. They seem therefore modal.

Those who reject the isomorphism as a characterizing feature of modal representations, offer an alternative criterion based on the neural systems to which the representations belong. For example, Machery argues that, as the debate stands, the difference between both approaches is limited to the involvement of perceptual and motor systems in conceptual tasks. Thus, he proposes a purely negative characterization of amodal representations, as those recruited to solve conceptual tasks without involving perceptual and motor systems [13]. As a result, the problem of distinguishing modal and amodal representations is shifted to that of individuating perceptual and motor systems, and, moreover, their involvement on conceptual tasks. This is not without difficulties, as I will discuss in the next section.

## 4. Neural Base

Barsalou claims that the grounded approach does not actually focus on the format of representations, but instead on the neural reuse of the brain states that underlie perception [12]. That is, whatever the type of format that could be involved in perceptual streams, the central claim of the grounded approach is that conceptual thought consists (at least partially) on reactivating such streams. As a result the vehicles of conceptual representations will have the neural properties of the representations used in perception and action. In that sense, Barsalou seems to agree with Machery in that, whichever properties modal representations exhibit, what crucially distinguishes modal from amodal approaches is a commitment to the constitutive involvement of sensorimotor systems in conceptual tasks. This is not a new version of the grounded approach. As I pointed out in Section 3, the grounded account of concept acquisition has always implied that conceptual thought involves the reactivation of representations that were first activated in perception and action systems (e.g., [3,36]). "Simulation", "reenactment", or "reuse" all refer to the same processes by which the conceptual system reactivates perceptual brain states in the absence of the entities or events that would have produced those states.

What is new is an explicit emphasis in that the central grounded tenet is not about a specific type of format, but instead about the specific systems involved in cognition. Does this imply that format is actually not relevant to the debate? I will address this question at the end of this section, after better analyzing the reuse as a criterion for distinguishing types of representations. The proposal leaves the specific properties of conceptual vehicles underspecified and states instead that, as the empirical research stands, it can only go as far as to evaluate the involvement of perceptual systems in conceptual thought, and not to thoroughly describe the representations involved [12,13]. As a result, this criterion poses the involvement of perceptual systems or neural reuse of their representations in conceptual tasks as a necessary and sufficient condition for modal representations. In Sections 2 and 3, I have offered different interpretations for the type of input to which the representations respond and whether they are isomorphic, and at least under some of the interpretations, these two first criteria overlap with the neural base.

First, one of the ways of interpreting the type of input to which the representations respond, is opposing representations couched in a single domain general code, to representations couched in the multiple different codes of the perceptual modalities. This version is closely related to the notion of neural reuse, in that it opposes the reuse of the multiple codes used in perception and action to the transcription from those perceptual codes into a single amodal one. Thus, the difference between modal and amodal vehicles can be cast in terms of reuse or reenactment versus transcription. For example, as Vermeulen and colleagues describe: "The latter grounded or embodied cognition framework proposes that memory, language or judgments directly depend on simulations in sensory–motor systems that were active during the initial experience rather than on abstract symbols (i.e., amodal systems) that consist of transcriptions of neural states" [37] (p. 468). Second, the interpretation of the isomorphism criterion as a resemblance or correspondence between the structure of conceptual representations and the structure of perceptual brain states also overlaps with the reuse criterion. This is so because the isomorphism between modal representations and perceptual states is a direct consequence of the grounded account of concept nature and acquisition, which centrally involves the thesis of neural reuse, reenactment, or simulation. These interpretations offer a way around the problems I presented for the first two criteria. However, adopting the neural base as a criterion also runs into difficulties.

The first problem is that the evidence concerning the involvement of sensorimotor systems in conceptual tasks is not clear cut. The issue is how to determine when the use of certain systems in a given task is constitutive or merely auxiliary. It is not the aim of this paper to discuss in detail the evidence offered to defend either approach, but it is useful to briefly look into it in order to show the empirical problems of the neural base as a criterion. The modal approach has been defended by both behavioral and neuroimaging results that suggest the involvement of perceptual systems in conceptual tasks, such as evaluating whether certain features belong to a given category or whether a sentence is sensible (for a detailed review see [14]). This strategy has received several objections that point out to alternative interpretations of the evidence. For instance, in reply to this strategy and as part of his defense of the amodal approach, Machery advances the offloading hypothesis as an alternative interpretation of this evidence [13]. According to this hypothesis, in order to solve some tasks we manipulate perceptual and motor representations. Machery speculatively suggests that this might be so because the information relevant to solve such tasks is not encoded in the conceptual system, or because certain tasks are more efficiently solved in that way.

An unintended consequence of this strategy is that it conflicts with the very criteria for identifying concepts. If perceptual and motor representations can be used to solve conceptual tasks by themselves, or in Barsalou's terms in a "stand-alone" manner, then what prevents them from being conceptual? I'd like to propose a reason why they seem to be concepts. If the offloading occurs as a strategy to solve certain tasks more efficiently, and this becomes the default way to deal with such cases, this would qualify those representations as concepts or at least as parts of concepts by Machery's own criterion, since it identifies concepts with the "bodies of knowledge that are used by default in the processes underlying the higher cognitive competences" [38] (p. 11). It is not clear whether Machery is proposing that when offloading to the perceptual systems, the amodal systems are involved as well, or that the conceptual tasks are solved by resorting solely to perceptual and motor representations. In any case, both alternatives entail that modal representations used by default in certain tasks are at least parts of conceptual representations. If the evidence under discussion is of involvement of perceptual systems in conceptual tasks, then the offloading hypothesis is not sufficient for discarding modal conceptual representations.

At the same time, an analogous argument can be pressed against some alternative interpretations suggested by modal advocates to explain the evidence supporting amodal theories. There is a growing body of evidence for amodal systems. One type of evidence comes from patients suffering from semantic dementia. In these cases, damage to the anterior temporal lobe is followed by impaired conceptual abilities that seem to be general across modalities. Semantic dementia is associated with multimodal deficits and, as a consequence, is taken as evidence that amodal concepts are stored in the specific damaged areas [13,39,40]. However, there are alternative interpretations of this evidence. As Kiefer and Pulvermüller review, it has been argued that, instead of hosting amodal representations, the anterior temporal lobe acts as a facilitation area for conceptual processing, while the conceptual representations per se remain hosted in perceptual systems [41]. This brain region acts as a supramodal convergence zone that integrates information from different modalities and guides the reactivation of stored perceptual representations. In an analogous way to my objections to the offloading hypothesis, it is not clear what prevents this "supramodal" representations from being concepts. Both strategies exhibit the difficulties in discriminating the systems that constitutively host conceptual representations from those that are auxiliary in conceptual processing. As a consequence, they are not sufficient to discard either type of format.

A further problem in interpreting behavioral evidence is the "mimicry problem" [42]. As Anderson argued, given that it is not possible to perform tests of types of representations in isolation, but only of pairs of representations and processes, it is always possible to exploit tradeoffs between representations and processes in order to offer alternative accounts of the evidence. He offered a formal proof showing that: "Given any representation-process pair, it is possible to construct other pairs with different representations whose behavior is equivalent to it. These pairs make up for differences in representation by assuming compensating differences in the processes" [42] (p. 263). A usual response to this problem is the appeal to other notions for evaluating competing theories, such as their plausibility and complexity [43]. Still, the assessment of a theory's plausibility and complexity is not always straightforward, and the difficulties in interpreting behavioral evidence constitute a significant limitation for the empirical application of certain criteria.[5]

The difficulties in providing an empirical distinction between modal and amodal representations are closely related to the ones in providing characterizing features for being a concept. At a minimum, authors seem to be working with an operationalization notion of a concept as what is constitutively involved in solving certain types of tasks, such as categorizing or understanding language. This raises a problem: it is unlikely that any of those tasks is solved by resorting exclusively to concepts, and, as a consequence, they do not provide an ultimate empirical test for distinguishing the representations and systems that implement our conceptual repertoire from mere auxiliary or concomitant ones. Thus, although in principle the involvement of perceptual systems or neural reuse of their representations should be both a necessary and sufficient condition for modal representations and thus a criterion for distinguishing them from amodal ones, it is problematic to distinguish constitutive from auxiliary systems empirically.

---

[5] I thank Mark Keane and an anonymous reviewer for their observations on this issue.

The second problem is how to individuate perceptual systems. That is, even if there was a way for distinguishing constitutive from auxiliary systems, this criterion presupposes a way for identifying perceptual systems. As I pointed out in Section 1, there seems to be an underlying assumption that perceptual systems are the ones that respond to a specific physical magnitude. However, as Machery argues, "perceptual systems are not delineated in a principled and uncontroversial manner" [13] (p. 1091, see also [22]). Although there are clear cases of at least parts of perceptual systems (such as the primary visual cortex or area V1), the limits of such systems are not clear. Thus, identifying the representations that are constitutively involved in conceptual tasks will not be sufficient as a criterion if there is no way to determine whether those representations belong to sensorimotor systems or not.

Finally, some authors argue that localizing the neural bases of conceptual processes is not informative of their format [7,44]. Martin argues that the format question has no "practical significance", given that we have no procedure for determining the format of the neural code [7]. As a consequence, the neural base would not serve as a criterion for distinguishing types of format. Martin's point goes beyond the problem of determining whether a certain brain region belongs to a perceptual system or not. He calls into question whether knowing that certain representations belong to a perceptual system tells us something about their format. Knowing more about how different areas of the brain encode information and the processes by which it is retrieved and combined is not in principle impossible. In fact, there are steps towards "decoding" some neural populations. Going back to the example of approximate number representations, some studies suggest the way in which neurons in the intraparietal sulcus (IPS) might encode cardinality. For example, Roitman and colleagues recorded neurons in the lateral intraparietal area in macaques whose responses resembled the summation units from the two models of numerosity detection mentioned in the previous section [45]. Assuming Roitman and colleagues' results were replicated in humans, and further, the discharge patterns proposed by a model of numerosity detection were found in a specific neural population, this would inform the classification. If certain neurons in the IPS present a discharge rate that increases or decreases in proportion to the cardinality of the stimulus, this suggests that they bear a structural isomorphism both to what they represent and to the perceptual representations that originated them. Furthermore, it offers a starting point to compare how other magnitudes are encoded in order to determine whether approximate number representations have a proprietary format or not.[6] However, the knowledge of how information is encoded is not available for every concept.

Therefore, even though the overlap between the three criteria, considering the way in which the information is encoded, the systems to which the representations belong and whether there is reuse of the representations underlying perception and action, constitutes a strong interpretation that promises to allow a better assessment of the evidence, its empirical application still encounters limitations.

## 5. Conclusions

The debate between amodal and modal—or grounded—views is one of the central ones within the mental representations approach to concepts. Although much research focuses on determining the type of vehicles concepts are couched in, the distinction between the amodal and modal format is not a clear one. On the one hand, there is not a general consensus on the specific properties that distinguish modal and amodal representations, and different authors adopt different criteria, which leads to a cross classification of certain representations depending on the chosen criterion. On the other hand, as I argued, the main criteria that have been proposed have difficulties. The distinction in terms of the type of input to which the representations respond is underspecified, given that it collapses multimodal and amodal representations. An alternative version of this criterion, that opposes a single amodal code to multiple proprietary codes corresponding to each modality, avoids this consequence, and places

---

6 Studies of visual imagery offer further interesting examples of decoding. Several studies have recently provided evidence of decoding mental images from patterns of brain activity in area V1 (for a brief review see [46]).

this criterion closer to one based on the neural systems of the representations. The isomorphism criterion has two interpretations, both of which encounter difficulties. One of them, an isomorphism between modal representations and their contents, has been objected as neither sufficient nor necessary for modality, given that it is unlikely that every perceptual representation is isomorphic with its content, and there are cases of isomorphic representations that are not perceptual. The other one, an isomorphism between modal representations and the perceptual states that produced them is better suited for the distinction, given that it offers a necessary and sufficient condition for modality. Nevertheless, it resembles the neural base criterion, and shares its problems. There seems to be a convergence on the neural base criterion: a distinction between the reuse in conceptual tasks of the neural systems underlying perception and action, versus the transcription from the sensorimotor systems to a different code in a separate system (or systems). Although this criterion offers a clearer conceptual distinction, it has limitations in its empirical application. As I argued, it presupposes modes of individuating modalities and of determining which systems are constitutively involved in conceptual tasks and which ones are auxiliary. Although the distinction between modal and amodal representations is at the center of one of the main debates on concepts, the available criteria for the distinction are problematic. Without a criterion that offers an adequate conceptual and empirical distinction, a proper assessment of the evidence for each type of format is not possible.

**Acknowledgments:** I am grateful to Liza Skidelsky, Abel Wajnerman Paz, Nicolás Serrano, Sergio Barberis, Fernanda Velázquez, Mariela Destéfano, and Cristian Stábile for their helpful discussion of earlier versions of this paper. I would also like to thank the participants of the Workshop on the Philosophy of Cognitive Science (WPCS 2017) and two anonymous reviewers for their comments and suggestions.

**Conflicts of Interest:** The author declares no conflict of interest.

## References

1. Fodor, J.A. *The Language of Thought*; Crowell: New York, NY, USA, 1975; ISBN 0-690-00802-3.
2. Fodor, J.A. *Concepts: Where Cognitive Science Went Wrong*; Oxford University Press: Oxford, UK, 1998; ISBN 978-0-19-823637-5.
3. Barsalou, L.W. Perceptual symbol systems. *Behav. Brain Sci.* **1999**, *22*, 577–609. [CrossRef] [PubMed]
4. Prinz, J.J. *Furnishing the Mind: Concepts and Their Perceptual Basis*; MIT Press: Cambridge, MA, USA, 2002.
5. Dove, G. Beyond perceptual symbols: A call for representational pluralism. *Cognition* **2009**, *110*, 412–431. [CrossRef] [PubMed]
6. Fodor, J.A. *Lot 2: The Language of Thought Revisited*; Oxford University Press: Oxford, UK, 2008.
7. Martin, A. GRAPES—Grounding representations in action, perception, and emotion systems: How object properties and categories are represented in the human brain. *Psychon. Bull. Rev.* **2016**, *23*, 979–990. [CrossRef] [PubMed]
8. Kosslyn, S.M.; Pinker, S.; Smith, G.E.; Shwartz, S.P. On the demystification of mental imagery. *Behav. Brain Sci.* **1979**, *2*, 535–548. [CrossRef]
9. Pylyshyn, Z.W. What the Mind's Eye Tells the Mind's Brain: A Critique of Mental Imagery. *Psychol. Bull.* **1973**, *80*, 1–24. [CrossRef]
10. Pylyshyn, Z.W. The Imagery Debate: Analogue Media Vs. Tacit Knowledge. *Psychol. Rev.* **1981**, *88*, 16–45. [CrossRef]
11. Paivio, A. *Mental Representations: A Dual Coding Approach*; Oxford University Press: Oxford, UK, 1986.
12. Barsalou, L.W. On Staying Grounded and Avoiding Quixotic Dead Ends. *Psychon. Bull. Rev.* **2016**, *23*, 1122–1142. [CrossRef] [PubMed]
13. Machery, E. The amodal brain and the offloading hypothesis. *Psychon. Bull. Rev.* **2016**, *23*, 1090–1095. [CrossRef] [PubMed]
14. Pecher, D. The perceptual representation of mental categories. In *The Oxford Handbook of Cognitive Psychology*; Reisberg, D., Ed.; Oxford University Press: Oxford, UK, 2013; pp. 358–373.
15. Machery, E. Concept empiricism: A methodological critique. *Cognition* **2007**, *104*, 19–46. [CrossRef] [PubMed]

16. Lambon, R.M.A.; Sage, K.; Jones, R.W.; Mayberry, E.J. Coherent concepts are computed in the anterior temporal lobes. *Proc. Natl. Acad. Sci. USA* **2010**, *107*, 2717–2722. [CrossRef] [PubMed]
17. Reilly, J.; Peelle, J.E.; Garcia, A.; Crutch, S.J. Linking somatic and symbolic representation in semantic memory: The dynamic multilevel reactivation framework. *Psychon. Bull. Rev.* **2016**, *23*, 1002–1014. [CrossRef] [PubMed]
18. Shallice, T.; Cooper, R.P. Is there a semantic system for abstract words? *Front. Hum. Neurosci.* **2013**, *7*. [CrossRef] [PubMed]
19. Zwaan, R.A. Embodiment and language comprehension: Reframing the discussion. *Trends Cogn. Sci.* **2014**, *18*, 229–234. [CrossRef] [PubMed]
20. Machery, E. Two Dogmas of Neo-Empiricism. *Philos. Compass* **2006**, *1*, 398–412. [CrossRef]
21. Jones, M. Number concepts for the concept empiricist. *Philos. Psychol.* **2016**, *29*, 334–348. [CrossRef]
22. Macpherson, F. Individuating the Senses. In *The Senses: Classic and Contemporary Philosophical Perspectives*; Macpherson, F., Ed.; Oxford University Press: New York, NY, USA, 2011; pp. 3–43.
23. Wajnerman Paz, A. Using neural response properties to draw the distinction between modal and amodal representations. *Philos. Psychol.* **2018**. under review.
24. Dehaene, S. *The Number Sense: How the Mind Creates Mathematics, Revised and Updated Edition*; Oxford University Press: New York, NY, USA, 2011; ISBN 978-0-19-991039-7.
25. Dehaene, S.; Dehaene-Lambertz, G.; Cohen, L. Abstract representations of numbers in the animal and human brain. *Trends Neurosci.* **1998**, *21*, 355–361. [CrossRef]
26. Izard, V.; Sann, C.; Spelke, E.S.; Streri, A. Newborn infants perceive abstract numbers. *Proc. Natl. Acad. Sci. USA* **2009**, *106*, 10382–10385. [CrossRef] [PubMed]
27. Dehaene, S.; Changeux, J.-P. Development of Elementary Numerical Abilities: A Neuronal Model. *J. Cogn. Neurosci.* **1993**, *5*, 390–407. [CrossRef] [PubMed]
28. Nieder, A.; Dehaene, S. Representation of number in the brain. *Annu. Rev. Neurosci.* **2009**, *32*, 185–208. [CrossRef] [PubMed]
29. Mahon, B.Z.; Hickok, G. Arguments about the nature of concepts: Symbols, embodiment, and beyond. *Psychon. Bull. Rev.* **2016**, *23*, 941–958. [CrossRef] [PubMed]
30. Wilson, R.; Foglia, L. Embodied Cognition. Stanf. Encycl. Philos. 2017. Available online: https://plato.stanford.edu/archives/spr2017/entries/embodied-cognition (accessed on 22 March 2018).
31. Camp, E. Thinking with Maps. *Philos. Perspect.* **2007**, *21*, 145–182. [CrossRef]
32. Evans, V. What's in a concept? Analog versus parametric concepts in LCCM Theory. In *The Conceptual Mind: New Directions in the Study of Concepts*; Margolis, E., Laurence, S., Eds.; MIT Press: Cambridge, MA, USA, 2015; pp. 25–29. ISBN 978-0-262-02863-9.
33. Wittgenstein, L. *Tractatus Logico-Philosophicus*; Routledge: London, UK, 1919.
34. Carey, S. *The Origin of Concepts*; Oxford University Press: New York, NY, USA, 2009; ISBN 978-0-19-988791-0.
35. Meck, W.H.; Church, R.M. A mode control model of counting and timing processes. *J. Exp. Psychol. Anim. Behav. Process.* **1983**, *9*, 320–334. [CrossRef] [PubMed]
36. Barsalou, L.W.; Kyle Simmons, W.; Barbey, A.K.; Wilson, C.D. Grounding conceptual knowledge in modality-specific systems. *Trends Cogn. Sci.* **2003**, *7*, 84–91. [CrossRef]
37. Vermeulen, N.; Mermillod, M.; Godefroid, J.; Corneille, O. Unintended embodiment of concepts into percepts: Sensory activation boosts attention for same-modality concepts in the attentional blink paradigm. *Cognition* **2009**, *112*, 467–472. [CrossRef] [PubMed]
38. Machery, E. *Doing Without Concepts*; Oxford University Press: New York, NY, USA, 2009; ISBN 978-0-19-530688-0.
39. McCaffrey, J. Reconceiving conceptual vehicles: Lessons from semantic dementia. *Philos. Psychol.* **2015**, *28*, 337–354. [CrossRef]
40. McCaffrey, J.; Machery, E. Philosophical issues about concepts. *Wiley Interdiscip. Rev. Cogn. Sci.* **2012**, *3*, 265–279. [CrossRef] [PubMed]
41. Kiefer, M.; Pulvermüller, F. Conceptual representations in mind and brain: Theoretical developments, current evidence and future directions. *Cortex J. Devoted Study Nerv. Syst. Behav.* **2012**, *48*, 805–825. [CrossRef] [PubMed]

42. Anderson, J.R. Arguments Concerning Representations for Mental Imagery. *Psychol. Rev.* **1978**, *85*, 249–277. [CrossRef]
43. Thomas, N.J.T. Mental Imagery. Stanf. Encycl. Philos. 2018. Available online: https://plato.stanford.edu/archives/spr2018/entries/mental-imagery (accessed on 22 March 2018).
44. Leshinskaya, A.; Caramazza, A. For a cognitive neuroscience of concepts: Moving beyond the grounding issue. *Psychon. Bull. Rev.* **2016**, *23*, 991–1001. [CrossRef] [PubMed]
45. Roitman, J.D.; Brannon, E.M.; Platt, M.L. Monotonic Coding of Numerosity in Macaque Lateral Intraparietal Area. *PLoS Biol.* **2007**, *5*, e208. [CrossRef] [PubMed]
46. Pearson, J.; Kosslyn, S.M. The heterogeneity of mental representation: Ending the imagery debate. *Proc. Natl. Acad. Sci. USA* **2015**, *112*, 10089–10092. [CrossRef] [PubMed]

# 4

# Undetachable Concepts in Non-Human Animals

**Laura Danón**

Centro de Investigaciones de la Facultad de Filosofía y Humanidades, Facultad de Filosofía y Humanidades , Universidad Nacional de Córdoba (National University of Córdoba), Pabellón Agustín Tosco 1° Piso, Ciudad Universitaria, Córdoba 5000, Argentina; ldanon@unc.edu.ar

**Abstract:** In this paper, I would like to explore the idea that some non-human animals may be incapable of detaching or separating some of their concepts both from other concepts and from the larger thought contents that they are part of. This, in turn, will make it impossible for them to recombine these undetachable concepts with others in every admissible way. I will begin by distinguishing three different ways in which one concept may be undetachable from others, and I will show how each of them leads to specific restrictions in the kinds of conceptual re-combinations that they admit. Finally, I will try to provide some theoretical reasons, as well as some empirical evidence, to give at least initial support to the hypothesis that some non-human animals actually suffer from the limitations previously identified.

**Keywords:** concepts; animal cognition; the Generality Constraint; conceptual recombination; conceptual detachability

## 1. Introduction

It is widely accepted in Philosophy that paradigmatic examples of propositional contents involve representing some particular entities as being thus and so or, putting it differently, as having certain properties or characteristics.[1] Thus, having a thought with a propositional content such as *John is tall* involves thinking about John, about the property of being tall, and attributing the latter to the former [2–6]. Once this is accepted, it can also be argued that, when we have thoughts about particular objects, two kinds of concepts, with their own distinctive semantic functions, compose the contents of our thoughts: "concepts of particulars", or "object concepts", and "concepts of properties" [2–4,7].[2] Now, property concepts are usually thought to be *general,* in the sense that they can be attributed to many different particulars. In turn, those who defend the existence of concepts of particulars frequently claim that they involve the capacity to think about individual entities as the *same ones* in our different encounters with them, despite the fact that their properties may change or differ from one encounter to another [2,3,8,9]. If all this is correct, then it seems that the concepts that compose propositional contents should be redeployable in different contexts.

Some philosophers have taken this idea one step further and argued that, besides being capable of generalizing their predicative concepts to different particulars and thinking about particulars as

---

1 It seems plausible to think that the most basic cases of propositional contents will refer to physical particular objects. Nevertheless, one may also find propositional contents that refer to other kinds of particular entities, such as abstract objects, instances of properties, or instances of relations. Additionally, there are also propositional contents that do not refer to any propositional entity at all, as happens in the case of a content like "some cabins are red" [1].

2 Following Evans [4] and Camp [3], I will understand concepts as amounting to some specific cognitive abilities and I will use the terms "concepts" and "conceptual abilities" interchangeably.

having different properties, genuine thinking creatures must satisfy a strict version of what Evans calls the Generality Constraint (GC)[3].

According to Evans' original statement:

> "... if a subject can be credited with the thought that *a is F*, then he must have the conceptual resources for entertaining the thought that *a is G*, for every property of being G of which he has a conception" [4] (p. 104).

As stated here, GC is a demanding constraint according to which thinking creatures must be capable of recombining each of their concepts of particulars with every property concept in their possession.[4] In addition, even if he does not state it explicitly in this quote, Evans also requires that they must be capable, inversely, of recombining every property concept with every particular concept in their conceptual baggage. In brief, according to Evans, genuine thinkers must be capable of combining their concepts of properties and particulars in any admissible way.[5]

Some philosophers have suggested that, if we understand GC in this demanding sense, we will have to refrain from ascribing concepts to non-human animals, since empirical evidence indicates that there are limits to the ways in which they can recombine their representations to form new thoughts [3,13,14]. What is more, Camp [3] and Carruthers [14] have pointed out that, if we claim that creatures who are incapable of some conceptual combinations do not possess concepts at all, we may end up having to exclude adult human animals from the realm of concept users.[6] These philosophers suggest, instead, that we should adopt a more inclusive and gradualist view of concept possession and defend that at least some species of non-human animals have some basic conceptual abilities.

Now, if we accept that there may exist non-human concept users that do not satisfy the full-blown version of GC, we still have much to explore regarding the kinds of limitations that these creatures could suffer when it comes to recombining their concepts in order to form new thought contents. In this paper, I would like to advance in the exploration and charting of this scarcely-known terrain by focusing on how, sometimes, the capacity of different animals to recombine some of their concepts might be affected by another closely related capacity: detaching, or separating, those concepts from the larger thought contents in which they are embedded.

Consider the case of a mental content such as *a is F*, in which a property concept *F* is combined with the concept of a particular *a*. If, in order to think such a thought, animals had to satisfy GC in its full-blown version, they would have to be capable of combining each of these two concepts with every other concept in their repertoires in every admissible way. However, if we admit, following philosophers such as Camp and Carruthers, that animals may entertain such a thought, and possess the concepts *F* and *a*, while only satisfying GC up to a certain grade, then an interesting possibility opens up: they may be capable of combining those concepts with others in *some* ways, but not in *every* way. Thus, a creature C may, for example, be capable of combining *a* with G and *H*, but not with *J*, and she may be capable of combining *F* with *b* and *c*, but not with *d*.

---

3 Lievers [5] and Dickie [10] reconstruct the main reasons given by Evans [4] and Peacocke [11] in favour of such a distinction.

4 Strictly speaking, Evans uses a different terminology: he speaks of "concepts", to refer to property concepts, and of "Ideas", to refer to what I am calling here "concepts of particulars". My terminological choice follows contemporary presentations of the Generality Constraint, which usually refer to all the components of thoughts as concepts (see [3,12–16]).

5 The requirement that it should be possible to recombine concepts of particulars and concepts of properties in every admissible way can be interpreted in two different senses. Philosophers like Evans [4], Peacocke [11], and Strawson [17] seem to think that some conceptual combinations are too heterogeneous to form a complete and intelligible thought. According to them, concepts have "categories of appropriate application" and only those thoughts that combine concepts within these categories are intelligible. In other words: there are restrictions on the kinds of categories that can be recombined in an intelligible way. Consequently, GC should only require from concept possessors that they can make categorically appropriate combinations of their concepts. Camp [12] has argued, on the contrary, that we should not impose any categorial restrictions on conceptual significance or on conceptual competence. Consequently, she thinks that GC, in its full-blown sense, should require from concept possessors that they can recombine their concepts in every syntactically admissible way.

6 Evans himself seems to endorse a similar idea. See [4] (p. 105).

With these possibilities in mind, what I would like to do here is to explore the following hypothesis: in some occasions, the limitations in a creature's capacity to recombine her concepts will be the result of a different inability: that of *detaching* or *separating* some of her concepts both from other concepts and from the larger thought contents that they are part of.[7]

In the following sections, I will try to elaborate this idea by undertaking two different tasks. I will begin by distinguishing, without pretending to be exhaustive, three different ways in which some creatures' abilities to recombine their concepts could be restricted by distinct kinds of limitations in their capacities to separate some of their concepts from others. The main purpose, here, will be to show that these limitations constitute a coherent conceptual possibility. What is more, as we will see, these different kinds of undetachable concepts will be constituent parts of different sorts of *sui generis*, semi-structured contents, that have not been considered in the literature and deserve further exploration.

My second aim in this paper will be to show, even if in a rough and tentative way, that these conjectures may turn out to be explanatory fruitful. In order to do so, I will try to provide some theoretical reasons, as well as some empirical evidence, to give initial support to the hypothesis that there are non-human animals that do suffer from the limitations previously identified.

Before turning to these two tasks, I think it is worthwhile to spend some time clarifying a bit further three notions—i.e., those of *detachability*, *recombinability* and *redeployment*—that will play a central role in the rest of the paper. This preliminary task will be undertaken in the next section.

## 2. Detachability, Recombinability, and Redeployment of Concepts

Suppose that a creature C thinks that *a is F*. It seems almost a truism that in order to be able to recombine the concepts *a* and *F* with other concepts in her possession, C needs to be previously capable of separating or detaching them from such content. Let us consider now what would happen in the opposite situation: imagine that C is capable of having some thoughts with contents composed by some specific concepts, but that she is incapable of separating *some* of these concepts from those contents. In such a case, she will be able to deploy the latter, but only as long as they are embedded in the former. She will not, instead, be capable of recombining these undetachable concepts with other concepts, nor will she be capable of redeploying them in further thoughts.

Even if we accept this picture of the way in which detachability and re-combinability of concepts are related, one may still wonder: what does it mean to say that some concepts can be detached (or not) from others? If we want to avoid circularity, we cannot merely claim that detachable concepts are those that can be freely recombined with others in further contents and, inversely, that undetachable concepts are those that cannot be so recombined. We need to characterize detachability in a way that is different from, and helps to explain, the capacity of some creatures to freely redeploy and recombine their concepts.

What I would like to suggest is that we may gain a better understanding of what is for a concept to be detachable (or not), by thinking about the conditions in which a creature may, or may not, be able to deploy and understand that concept. I will be assuming here that deploying concepts in thoughts is not a blind and brute activity, but an intelligent one. Consequently, deploying a concept involves having some understanding (even if minimal or tenuous) of its meaning. If this is so, we may understand the detachability and undetachability of concepts following terms: C has a concept that is undetachable from another one if in order to deploy the former, C needs to combine it with the latter. This is so, basically, because it is only when the undetachable concept is thus combined that it can

---

7 The combinatorial limitations of non-human animals may have other sources. Thus, Beck [13] has claimed that some animals are incapable of combining some representations with others as a result of their analogical format. Carruthers [14], in turn, has argued that some insects, like bees, may suffer from combinatorial limitations due to the fact that they use different representational systems and lack a way of integrating the representations from one of those systems with the representations from the other. Clearly, these cases seem to be independent and have different origins than undetachability.

actually mean something to the thinking creature. Thus, if C's concept *F* is undetachable form concept *a*, C simply cannot grasp the meaning of *F* when it is not combined with *a*. A thought such as *b is F* is just unintelligible for her.

On the contrary, a concept is detachable for creature C when her capacity to use it, having some understanding of its meaning, does not depend on C's simultaneously combining it with any other specific concept. C may manifest this capacity to detach her concepts in two different ways. In its full-blown sense, C has a detachable concept, such as *F*, if she can think about *F*, grasping the meaning of such a concept, regardless of whether *F* is combined with any other concept.[8] However, C may also have a detachable concept *F*, in a weaker sense, if, even when she must always deploy *F* combining it with other concepts to form propositional contents, she can still understand or grasp the meaning of *F* regardless of which specific concepts in C's repertoire it is combined with. In any of these two cases, I think it can be claimed that C's concept satisfies what I would like to call the Detachability Condition (DC).

Let us suppose that C possesses a variety of concepts of properties and of particulars, but she cannot deploy some of these concepts with complete independence from some others. Thus, to take just one extreme example, imagine that C can only deploy concept *F* when she attributes *F* to one specific particular that C conceptualizes as *a*. For her, *F* does not mean anything when it is not combined with *a*. In such a case–as in others that I will examine below—the Detachability Condition is clearly violated, and it can be stated that *F* is undetachable from *a*. What is more, undetachability of concept *F* from certain concepts of particulars clearly implies that there will be limits to the ways in which it will be possible to recombine *F* with other concepts, and to redeploy it in further thoughts. If, returning to our previous example, concept *F* can only acquire its stable meaning when combined with the concept of particular *a*, it will not be possible to combine it with other concepts of particulars in intelligible ways. Moreover, something similar applies to other kinds of undetachability, as will be argued later on. Thus, detachability, as I have characterized it here, seems to be a necessary pre-condition for full-blown *redeployability and recombinability*.

Leaning on these general ideas, in the next section I will distinguish–without aiming to be exhaustive—three different kinds of incapacities that some creatures may suffer to separate or detach some concepts in their possession from others and, consequently, to satisfy the Detachability Condition. In turn, I will also try to show that each of these specific failures to satisfy DC leads to specific limitations in the creatures' capacities to recombine and redeploy their concepts in further thoughts. Once that preliminary task is completed, I will present reasons in favor of the idea that having concepts with these limitations might end up being of adaptive value for some non-human animals, and I will examine several empirical examples of animal behavioral patterns, in order to show how they can be explained by one or other of the limitations to detach and recombine concepts that were previously identified.

Before moving on, however, some preliminary caveats are in order. First, I am not claiming here that the detachability limitations to be presented below constitute a general feature of *all* the concepts and contents of non-human animals. In other words, I am neither claiming that these varieties of conceptual undetachability constitute a general feature of animal cognition, nor that they are a general feature of some species' cognition. I am only defending the much more modest

---

8 It seems to me that having concepts of properties that are detachable in a full-blown sense involves different cognitive capacities than having analogously detachable concepts of particulars. To be capable of detaching property concept *F* in a full-blown sense involves understanding what *being an F* would consist in for any arbitrary particular. Arguably, this is the kind of capacity that allows a creature to entertain contents with existential quantifiers like: *There is an x such that x is F.* To be capable of detaching the concept of particular *a*, instead, involves being capable of thinking about *a* without entertaining any propositional content in which some property is explicitly predicated of *a*. But this does not necessarily mean that one must think about *a de re*. Another alternative is to defend that there are object-directed mental states—like, for example, *imagining my grandmother*—that are about particular objects, and represent these objects under specific aspects, but are non-propositional [18].

claim that there might be some animals who find it impossible to detach some particular concepts in their possession from others. This will, in turn, preclude them from making specific conceptual combinations. However, the whole problem might be quite local, and only restricted to a few concepts in the creatures' repertoire.

Secondly, many doubts will probably arise when it comes to classifying the kind of undetachable representations that I will be discussing below as *concepts*. The main reason for those doubts is that it is usually assumed, even by those who are willing to defend deflationary notions of concepts and concept-possession, that if a creature C has genuine concepts of properties (e.g., *F*) and of particulars (e.g., *a*), she must be at least capable of combining *a* with a second property concept, different from *F*, and *F* with another concept of particular different from *a*. Otherwise, it might be argued that all C has is a non-decomposable holistic representation of *a-as-being-F* and, moreover, that C lacks a separate understanding of what each of these components means on its own [14,19].

Even though I feel the force of these arguments, on what follows I will try to show that the kind of undetachable representations that I will be presenting in Section 3 are not holistic representations, and that the contents constituted by them are not entirely devoid of structure either. On the contrary, these representations compose contents that have some kind of structure, admit some (partial) decomposition and, arguably, still fulfill different (and differentiable) semantic functions. All of these are central features that these undetachable representations share with the fully-detachable concepts of properties and of particulars. This is, basically, the reason I will opt to call them "concepts" as well. Nevertheless, if someone prefers to reserve the notion of "concept" strictly for those representational units that can be detached and recombined at least in some ways with others, I have no problem with this more traditional use of the term. All I want to defend here is the possibility, and the heuristic value, of positing contents composed by more basic representational units that suffer from specific kinds of detachability and recombinability limitations. A change in the way in which we name these representations is not so relevant–we may, for example, call them "proto-concepts" instead of concepts—as long as we are clear on which their main features are.

Let me briefly introduce one final worry. It seems that, in order to provide empirical evidence in favor of the existence of undetachable concepts, we should carefully select which kind of animal behavior to focus on. Why? Mainly because if we focus on animals that are so cognitively primitive that the attribution of concepts (or even of proto-concepts) to them seems to be out of the question, or highly unlikely, we would be completely unjustified in arguing, from their behavior, that they have *undetachable concepts* (or proto-concepts). This issue is closely related to a second problem: which are the conditions that a creature should satisfy in order to be credited with the possession of concepts? These are both highly controversial topics whose proper treatment would require a thorough discussion on which the requirements that should be imposed on concept possession are and whether the empirical evidence to be presented below satisfies them. Clearly, I cannot undertake such a task here. However, I would like to point out, nevertheless, that I have tried to provide empirical examples of animal behavior that reveal rather complex forms of cognition. In fact, all the behaviors to be examined below involve (relatively) flexible responses to objects in the animals' environments and not merely to specific proximal stimuli. Furthermore, in many of them, the animals are capable of learning new things about those objects that they are interacting with, of extrapolating what has been learnt to new contexts, etc. Arguably, these animals are also capable of improving their ways of discriminating and responding to some objects and its varying properties, etc. Now, the capacity to learn, acquire and integrate new information, the flexibility and versatility of the responses, the possibility of taking some distance (or gaining some independence) from the impinging stimuli, etc., are among the requirements that, according to several philosophers, must be satisfied by non-linguistic animals if we are to credit them with some (basic) conceptual abilities ([3,20,21]). Thus, even though the topic would deserve a more extensive and careful treatment, there are some reasons to conjecture that these could be conceptual (or at least proto-conceptual) creatures and to further explore what kind of concepts and contents are required in order to explain their behavior.

## 3. Varieties of Undetachability

### *3.1. The Undetachability of Some Concepts of Particulars from One Specific Property Concept*

The first case that I would like to consider is the following one: imagine that there is a creature C who is incapable of thinking about some kind of particulars without thinking of them *as being F*. Provided that **a**, **b** and **c** are the members of the class of particulars in question, each time C deploys her concept of one or another of these particulars, she will not be able to avoid representing them as possessing the property *F*. Thus, each time C deploys a concept such as a, *b* or *c*, she will inexorably embed it in a content like: *a is F*, *b is F* or *c is F*. Clearly, such a constraint in C's representational capacities will put a substantive limitation on her abilities to recombine and redeploy concepts. Basically, she will not be capable of thinking about any content which involves representing **a**, **b** or **c**, as having properties different from **F** (like, for example, *a is G*, *b is H*, etc.) at least as long as she does not represent them *as being F* at the same time.[9] Interestingly, this does not preclude C from detaching her concept *F* from the contents *a is F*, *b is F and c is F* and redeploying it in new contexts, attributing it to any other particular entities and forming new thought contents such as *d is F* or *e is F*.

It is important to notice that, despite the fact that C cannot detach concept *a* from concept *F*, when C thinks *a is F*, she is not entertaining an entirely unstructured thought which admits no decomposition into smaller representational units, each with its distinctive and stable representational function. Rather, she seems to be entertaining a thought that has some kind of structure. That is, a thought with a content composed by (at least some) smaller, re-deployable units, with stable representational functions. Basically, this is so for two reasons. Firstly, because it is possible to identify at least one constituent conceptual unit–property concept *F*—that can be detached from this whole content and redeployed in other contents, making always the same stable semantic contribution.[10] However, it is also true that C will not be capable of thinking about **a** without ascribing property **F** to it. In this sense, this is not either a wholly structured content, entirely composed by conceptual units that can be freely detached and fully-recombined.

If these ideas are correct, it seems that what we have here are contents that occupy some sort of previously unexplored middle-ground between holistic unstructured contents and fully-structured ones. These are, if we want to give them a name, "semi-structured" contents, composed by some smaller parts that can be freely decomposed and re-deployed, and other parts that remain irrevocably embedded in the larger contents that they constitute. As it will become clear later on, the same is true, *mutatis mutandis*, for contents constituted by the other kinds of undetachable concepts to be examined below.

Now, what kind of behavior should be expected from a creature when she is deploying these sorts of undetachable concepts of particulars? In addition, do we have any evidence suggesting that there are, indeed, creatures that entertain contents composed by such undetachable concepts?

---

9 This point is tricky. Strictly speaking, in the kind of cases I am thinking about, nothing precludes C from representing **a** as having other properties different from **F**, but only if, at the same time, she also thinks that *a* is *F*. What she cannot do is to think about **a** as having a different property from **F**, while not thinking about it as also *being F*. This is important since, as some empirical examples below will illustrate, even if some animals seem to be incapable of representing some particulars without simultaneously attributing certain properties to them, they can still represent them as having other properties as well. Thus, assuming that gazelles always represent lions as dangerous, they also seem to be capable, at the same time, of detecting and integrating other relevant properties of lions (as their sizes, how far away they are from them, etc.). My main point here, then, is only that if gazelles are indeed incapable of detaching their representations of lions from their representations of danger, they will be also incapable of entertaining some contents: those in which lions are represented as having other properties while they are not simultaneously represented as being dangerous.

10 Interestingly, this will allow us, at least in principle, to single out the semantic contribution of concept *a*, even despite *a*'s undetachability from *F*. Why? Because *a* will be making the specific semantic contribution that is absent from all those other contents in which *F* appears combined with other concepts. At least in the case of a simple thought like *a is F*, all we need to do is somehow isolate the semantic information that this content bears, which is both different from the semantic contribution of *F* and absent in all other contents in which *F* is redeployed in combination with other concepts of particulars.

Regarding the first question, one thing that should be expected from creatures that, when thinking about particulars **a**, **b** or **c**, can only think of them as *being F*, is a very specific kind of *cognitive* or *representational rigidity*. Since these creatures cannot help thinking, for example, of **a** *as F*, one may expect that they will not be capable of changing their way of characterizing **a**, attributing to it different properties from *F*–while at the same time refraining from thinking about it *as an F*—even if they should rationally do so, in light of their other beliefs or available evidence. In other words: these kinds of contents should be irresponsive to disconfirming evidence. Furthermore, since these creatures cannot entertain contents in which *a* is combined with *G*, or *H* (but not *F*), one may expect them to be also incapable of having any other kind of psychological states with such contents. They will not only be incapable of believing that *a is G*. They will be neither capable of imagining, conjecturing, doubting that *a is G*, etc., (and, of course, the same applies to *b* and *c*).

This *cognitive rigidity* will likely have, as one of its consequences, a specific kind of *behavioral rigidity*. Let us assume that believing that *a is F* typically guides C's behaviors in some specific ways, and that, if C deploys concept *a* at all, then she is compelled to combine it with property concept *F*. In such a case, we may expect that, each time C conceptualizes particular **a** as *a*, the same content–i.e., *a is F*—will be making the same contribution to influence her behavior. Of course, this does not mean that C will necessarily act in the exact same way each time she thinks the content *a is F*. Her behavior may still change as a result of her other mental states, of her moods, situation, etc. Nevertheless, her responses to the particular entity **a** will still be much more rigid than those of another creature C*, capable of representing **a** in other ways, different from *being F*. An example may help to clarify this point: imagine that whenever C represents **a**, she must inexorably represent it as *a menace*. Clearly, her behavior towards **a** may still suffer many variations, depending on her other beliefs, desires, fears, etc. Thus, if she believes that *a is a menace* but she also believes that *one should try to avoid menaces as long as possible*, she will presumably behave very differently than how she would act if she believed that one *should face menaces as soon as possible*. Nevertheless, her behavioral dispositions will still be less flexible and varied than those of a creature C* that is capable of representing **a** as being *harmless*, *useful*, *desirable* (and not representing **a** as *a menace* at the same time).

It seems quite clear that this kind of cognitive and behavioral rigidity will have its costs. For example, creatures suffering from it will retain irrational beliefs about some particulars having certain properties, even when evidence should lead them to think otherwise. Besides, they will find it difficult (or even impossible) to adapt to those situations in which the particulars in question have lost the property that they rigidly attribute to them, since they will be incapable of representing such a fact. In addition, they may not be capable of responding adequately in certain situations, as a result of their incapacity to conjecture counterfactual scenarios in which any of these particulars loses the aforementioned property, etc.

Nevertheless, it may still be of adaptive value, for some species, to have a rigid disposition to always represent certain particulars as having some specific property, especially when they live in environments in which it is frequent for these particulars to have the property in question, and when registering such a fact is relevant for their survival. Thus, some animals might, for example, tend to rigidly represent different individual predators as dangerous, no matter which contexts they find them in, or they may always perceive food as desirable, etc. This would allow them to respond in a fast and usually adequate way to the presence of those entities, without wasting valuable time and cognitive resources on representing them as having other properties that may be less relevant, highly unlikely, absurd, etc. Additionally, it may free them from the complex task of having to determine on which properties of a particular to focus on in a given context, which properties this particular actually has in the present moment, etc.

However, are there animals that actually suffer from this incapacity to detach some concepts of particulars from certain property concepts? It seems to me that, in order to answer this question, it is useful to distinguish between two kinds of evidence that might be offered in favor of this hypothesis.

Firstly, one could have evidence that, for all one knows, there are non-human animals that always represent some particular entities as having some specific property. This would be the case, for example, if all the evidence that we had about a species S were consistent with members of S always treating some particular entities as having property **F**, and nothing indicated that, on the contrary, in some contexts or situations, members of S do not represent these particulars as *being F*, but as having other properties. What I would like to suggest is that this would give us some initial, although admittedly rather weak, reasons to conjecture that members of S have the kind of detachability and combinatorial limitations that I have described so far. In fact, such a hypothesis would provide an explanation of the fact that they always represent these particular entities *as being F*: because it is impossible for them to do something different. If we endorse this line of thinking, we can turn to the behaviors of many non-human species that uniformly respond to certain particulars in the same way in different contexts and treat them as initial evidence suggesting that these animals suffer from the specific kind of conceptual undetachability that I am describing here.

Let us consider just one example of this kind of evidence: California ground squirrels' abilities to recognize snakes as predators. According to researchers, these squirrels do not require experience with snakes during development in order to recognize their danger. Pups born and reared in the lab without previous contact with snakes distinguish them from novel animate objects. Moreover, they behave in the complex ways adults do towards snakes, that is, flagging their tails, approaching cautiously, investigating in elongated postures, and jumping back [22]. In brief: their behavior shows that very early on, and without previous learning, they consistently behave towards snakes by treating them as dangerous predators.

This does not mean, of course, that the behavior of squirrels towards snakes cannot change with experience and context. As researchers remark, experience is indeed important in the development of subtler aspects of anti-snake cognition. Squirrels learn to distinguish, for example, changes in the body temperature of a snake as a sign of the amount of their dangerousness (as the body of the snakes heat up, the biochemical processes that support their behavior speed up, and they deliver strikes with greater velocity, less hesitation and greater accuracy) [22]. They also respond differently to snakes depending on where they discover them. If, for example, the rattlesnake is found near their burrow, squirrels are more confrontational than when they detect it near someone else's burrow [23].

Nevertheless, the fact that ground squirrels always react towards snakes, even from their first encounter, in a cautious, inquisitive, and evasive/aggressive way, suggests that they always represent them as predators, or as some kind of menace, rather than, for example, as friends, preys, tools, etc. One could further hypothesize that this is due to the fact that they cannot detach the representation of the particular snakes that they interact with from the predicate "predator" (or some other similar concept) that always comes associated with it. If such were the case, this could be a plausible empirical example of the kind of content that I have just described.[11]

However, from the fact that some animals always think about some particulars as having certain properties it does not necessarily follow that, whenever they think about these particular, they *cannot help* representing them in such a way. Yet, the latter was, precisely, the hypothesis to be tested. Then, it still seems that in order to obtain a stronger support for the claim that some animals, such as California ground squirrels, suffer from the kind of conceptual undetachability sketched here, we would need to acquire evidence that these animals are incapable of changing their way of representing snakes, even when confronted with relevant evidence against it. If, for example, we could arrange an experimental scenario in which squirrels were confronted with harmless snakes, they were shown other creatures playing with them, etc., but they still reacted in a fearful way towards these

---

[11] It should be noted, though, that since squirrels learn new things about snakes, and react differently to them in different contexts, they must also be capable of having thoughts in which snakes are represented as having other properties besides that of being a predator (like being hot, or cold). As seen above, nothing in my proposal precludes that alternative, as long as these more complex contents always include the "threat" or "predator" predicate as well.

predators, this would give us additional reasons to think that they are incapable of detaching their representation of each particular snake that they encounter from a property concept such as *threatening* or *dangerous*.

As far as I know, we lack relevant studies on the capacity or incapacity ground squirrels to stop representing snakes as dangerous in light of relevant evidence. Consequently, we do not have yet strong evidence that whenever these animals face a particular snake they are incapable of detaching their representations of that particular from some specific property concept like: *dangerous*! Still, I would like to suggest that this is the evidence that we should be looking for if we are interested in basing the conjecture that they are incapable of detaching some of their concepts of particulars from specific property concepts on stronger ground.

There is, still, an additional point to consider. Let us suppose that an animal is, at present, incapable of detaching her concept *a* from her concept *F*. Must it be also impossible for her to overcome this limit in order for us to conclude that she suffers from the kind of undetachability that is being discussed here? It seems to me that we do not need to demand so much. Let me roughly explain why.

There are reasons to think that, at least on some occasions, an animal's rigid disposition to think about some particulars as having a specific property might have been acquired, for example, after a process of associative learning.[12] In such a case, one could go on arguing that the rigid link between the creatures' concepts may break after another conditioning process. Arguably, this is what happens even in cases of extremely rigid associations, such as phobias, after behaviorist desensitization therapy. Now, let us focus, to take just one toy example, on a hypothetical subject S suffering from a phobia to spiders at a period of time $T_1$. It seems reasonable to claim, in such a case, that in $T_1$, S has a rigid tendency to represent spiders as being, say, *extremely dangerous*. Furthermore, her disposition may be so strong that she is simply incapable of thinking about spiders without thinking about them as *extremely dangerous*, she cannot spontaneously negate that thought, she does not respond to evidence against it, etc. Let us also suppose that, later on, S's situation changes through a conditioning process that puts an end to her phobia. It still seems to me that if during a given period of time $T_1$, S was incapable of detaching her representations of spiders from the predicate *extremely dangerous* in the way previously described, one may legitimately claim that, despite later changes, during $T_1$, she suffered from the kind of undetachability and combinatorial limitations described here. Thus, what this case suggests is that the incapacity of a creature to detach some of her concepts from others, and the limits to recombine the concepts following from it, may be only temporary, but still genuine. *Mutatis mutandis*, this idea can be extended to the other kinds of undetachability described in Section 3.2. and Section 3.3.

Let us now turn to one final objection that I would like to consider. Someone might wonder why I am interpreting these empirical evidence as showing that squirrels' defensive responses to snakes are actually guided by a mental state with a content composed by two different concepts: a concept of the particular snake in question and a concept of a property like: *dangerous* or *threatening*. Why shouldn't one think, instead, that our squirrels are merely forming a simpler holistic representation of a specific kind of danger instead?

Roughly, there are two reasons in favor of thinking that ground squirrels are forming complex mental contents composed by two different kinds of concepts instead of an unstructured representation of a specific kind of danger. On the one hand, squirrels seem capable of treating other animals—like hawks, dogs, golden eagles, etc., —as dangerous. Since, presumably, their behavior is flexibly guided, in all these situations, by some representation of these different animals' dangerousness, it does seem plausible (and economic) to conjecture that, in fact, they are attributing the same property concept to

12 Some may doubt that the semi-structured contents described so far could be acquired by a process of associative learning. This kind of skepticism probably stems from an inclination to think that associative learning must necessarily produce associative structures–merely composed by a sequence of concatenated representations and involving no attribution of properties to particulars. However, as Mandelbaum [24] has argued, logically speaking, there are no reasons to bar the possibility that any kind of representational structure may arise from a process of associative learning.

these different particulars (instead of having a separate specific representation of the danger generated by snakes). On the other hand, as mentioned above, they are capable of learning new things about snakes and integrating this new information when dealing with them. In a sense, then, they do not seem, either, to be merely detecting the property of a specific kind of danger out there. Rather, they are detecting and tracking a particular entity: an entity that they always represent as dangerous, but which is also something more than a mere kind of danger to them.

### *3.2. The Undetachability of a Specific Property Concept from Some Concepts of Particulars*

What I will examine now is the inverse incapacity from the one presented in Section 3.1. What happens in this second situation is that a creature C is incapable of putting to use a property concept *F* without representing *F* as a property of a specific particular such as **a**. In this case, each time our creature deploys property concept *F*, she must necessarily do it by combining *F* with concept *a*. Thus, C will not be capable of detaching *F* from *a* at all and, consequently, she will not be capable of entertaining concepts such as *b is F* or *c is F*. However, of course, she will still be able to combine her concept *a* with other property concepts in all kinds of ways.

Once again, it seems that these are semi-structured contents in which it is possible to identify two basic components–*a* and *F*—with different semantic functions. Basically, this is so because one (and only one) of these constitutive elements (concept *a*) can be freely detached and recombined, while the other (concept *F*) remains embedded in the original larger content *a is F.* In addition, one may also expect to find here a representational and behavioral rigidity similar to the one described in Section 3.1. In this case, creature C will not be capable of attributing property *F* to any particular different from **a**, even when she should do so, given the available evidence. In turn, since each time she deploys concept *F* she will do it by entertaining a content such as *a is F*, her behavior will always be influenced by such a content, and never by contents such as *b is F*, *c is F*, etc. Presumably, this should have a restrictive impact on the kind of behaviors that she may manifest.

What about the explanatory credentials of positing this second kind of detachability limitations? It seems to me that, in general, this rigid disposition to combine a given property concept with a specific concept of a particular could be useful when the following conditions are met. Firstly, when there is a reliable correlation between the presence of property **F** and the presence of particular **a** as the bearer of **F**. Secondly, when in order to deal with their environments, it is particularly relevant, for some animals, not only to register the presence of property **F**, but also to be prepared to deal with the situations in which a specific particular, such as **a**, is **F**.

Thus, for example, a certain noise **N** may indicate many disparate things, in different counterfactual scenarios. Now, it may also be true that, in the environment of creature C, this noise is usually produced by a particular animal **e**, an enemy of C. In addition, it might be especially relevant for C to get prepared, whenever she detects **N**, for the possible presence of that specific enemy. In such a situation, having a rigid disposition, when detecting **N**, to think that *e is producing N*, might result a valuable tool for C.

This kind of undetachability may help us to explain some empirical evidence on the way in which some animals keep track of specific individuals in their environments. It might be useful, for example, to explain extant evidence of signature vocalizations that allow animals from different species to communicate information about their individual identities to other members of their group. Among these individually distinctive signals, one may include the squeaks of adult timber wolves [25], the calls of sub-Antarctic fur seal pups [26], the calls of bank and cliff swallow chicks [27], etc.

According to researchers, signature vocalizations fulfill a variety of functions. In some animals, they allow the mutual recognition of parents and offspring. To focus on just one example, after giving birth, sea fur seal mothers must go to the sea to feed and to build nutrient reserves for lactation. Once they return to land, they need to reunite with their pups. However, in order to be able to do this, both the mother and the pup must be capable of recognizing each other among their conspecifics. That seems to be the evolutionary reason they both develop their own signature vocalizations [26,28].

What I would like to suggest, in addition, is that one way to explain how these signature vocalizations accomplish their function is by claiming that the receptors of such signals have a rigid and automatic tendency to link them to one and only one individual. Consequently, when hearing, for example, the signature vocalization of her mother, the pup cannot avoid entertaining a content such as *mum is calling*$_1$.[13] This rigid link between the representation of a specific signature vocalization and a particular individual would explain the effective way in which the former fulfills its singularizing function.[14]

Of course, a skeptic may legitimately ask, at this point, why should one attribute to these animals a complex content such as *mum is calling*$_1$, composed by a concept of a particular and a property concept, instead of attributing to them a simpler unstructured representation such as "mum"? In a nutshell, the answer is that we may presume that the pups will also be capable of tracking and recognizing their mothers as the same individuals even when they are not calling them but, instead, behaving in other ways. If this is indeed the case, such a capacity will be manifested in two features of their response to these different situations. On the one hand, they must show (in the familiarity of their behavior towards their mothers, in the way in which they integrate different information acquired in the past about them, etc.), that they recognize or re-identify their mothers in their different encounters with them. On the other hand, they must also show, in the versatility and variances of their responses to these same individuals in these different situations, that they are sensitive to the fact that they have different properties, act in different ways, etc. Now, if pups do have this capacity, it seems that what we need, in order to explain the variances and invariances of their responses to their mothers in all these situations, is to attribute to them different contents in which the same mother is represented as having different properties (like *mum is calling, mum is asleep, mum is eating*, etc.).

Now, strictly speaking, what this evidence suggests is that, when animals such as seals hear certain sounds, they always associate them with a particular individual, even when they have no perceptual access to that individual at the time. However, once again, this only gives us weak evidence in favor of the existence of a specific conceptual undetachability of certain properties from certain concepts of particulars. One can interpret the empirical evidence as indicating that these animals have a strong tendency to link some representations of properties with specific representations of particulars. However, as happened in Section 3.1., it can be argued that what we need to have is a different kind of evidence: evidence not only that, for all we know, certain animals always think about some properties as the properties of the same particulars, but also evidence that they are not capable of combining these property concepts with concepts of other individuals, even when they have good reasons–like, for example, being faced with relevant evidence—to form these new combinations. Until we have this further evidence, our conjecture is a very tentative one. Nevertheless, for the reasons given above, it deserves further exploration.

### *3.3. The Undetachabilty of some Concepts of Particulars from the Determinate Property Concepts Belonging to a Determinable Class*

The last kind of undetachability that I am going to present is, clearly, the weaker one. Consequently, it is also the one that imposes less restrictions to the ways in which a creature may combine her concepts. What happens in this more lenient case is that each time a creature C deploys a concept of a particular from a specific group (e.g., *a*, *b* and *c*), she is inexorably compelled to combine it with one or another of the property concepts belonging to a determinate range ($F_1$.... $F_n$).

[13] I am using "calling$_1$" to refer to that specific signature call that the mother of the pup (and only her) can elicit.

[14] Bottlenose dolphins also produce individuating signature whistles. Now, dolphins can copy the signature whistles of others, and use such mimicking to label and address their social companions (even though they do this very rarely). Moreover, dolphins occasionally respond to hearing their own whistles (elicited by others) by calling back with the same whistle type [29]. Such flexible use of signature whistles suggests that dolphins who hear a signature whistle need not attach it inexorably to the same individual caller.

It may be of help, in order to clarify what this last kind of undetachability consists in, to introduce a well-known logical distinction between two kinds of property concepts: *determinate* and *determinable* ones. Roughly, determinable property concepts are higher-level concepts that have other concepts–determinate ones—as their sub-species. To mention a paradigmatic case, *color* is a determinable concept, while *blue, red, yellow*, etc., are the determinate concepts falling under it [30]. Pure determinate concepts, in turn, are such that no other determinate concept is subsumable under them [31].

With the determinable/determinate distinction in hand, it is possible to characterize the kind of cases that are being examined as having the following general structure: a creature C has some concepts of particulars (like *a, b, c*) and, whenever she thinks about any of them, she rigidly tends to combine it with one or another of the different determinate concepts which are subsumed under a certain determinable property concept *D*. Alternatively, it could be claimed that the determinable concept *D* fixes the range of determinate concepts that C can combine her concepts of particulars *a, b* and *c* with.

Clearly, in this kind of case, C will be capable of representing a particular, such as **a**, as having one or another of the corresponding determinate concepts that fall under determinable concept *D*. In this sense, her concept *a* will be detachable from any specific determinate concept that one may choose. However, it will be not possible for C to detach *a* from every determinable concept that fall under determinable concept *D*. Hence, she will not be capable of thinking about *a* as having any other properties different from the ones that can be subsumed under *D* (at least without also attributing to *a* one or another of the determinate concepts falling under *D*).

Following a similar argumentative line to the one employed in Section 3.1., it could be argued that it may be of adaptive value, for some species, to count with a rigid disposition to represent some particulars as having one or another of the determinate concepts that fall under a specific determinable one. This may be what happens, for example, in the case of an animal that cannot avoid thinking about particular items of food as *fresh or rotten*, about particular preys as *strong* or *weak*, etc. Such an innate tendency to attribute to certain particulars one or another property concept belonging to a specific determinable range may be of use to ensure that, in normal conditions, they register and focus on the aspects of those particulars that are the most important to enhance their possibilities of reproduction and survival. In other words, such a rigid link between the representation of some particulars and the attribution of one or another property from a limited class to them, will guarantee that these animals provide an answer, in their thoughts, to questions that might be relevant for their survival, like: Is this edible? Is this dangerous? In addition, animals with such tendencies will avoid wasting both time and cognitive resources selecting, among a much wider range of possibilities, which important properties to focus on when dealing with specific particulars, etc.

Let us now turn to the question of whether there are animals who actually suffer from these limitations to detach and recombine their concepts. In a recent paper on baboon's ways of conceptualizing other individual members of their group, Cheney and Seyfarth [32] remind us that Old World monkeys live in societies where their possibilities of survival and reproduction depend, to a large extent, on their social abilities. What they suggest is that these kinds of contexts "have favored individuals who can recognize other animals' social attributes *and treat these properties as inextricable parts of an individual's identity*" (italics are mine) [32] (p. 57). To illustrate this general idea, they focus on how female baboons recognize two kinds of social properties in other members of their group: their social rank and their kinship. According to them, rank and kinship are "social concepts" or "representational primitives" that these female baboons possess. Knowing the rank and kinship of the individual members of their group is of vital importance for baboons, since it is the best way to predict their behaviors and it is essential to forming the kind of stable and enduring bonds that lead to high reproductive success [32] (p. 60). Now, what different experiments show is that when a baboon hears another one vocalize, the listener encodes information about the caller's identity (i.e., about *who* is emitting the call), but also about her dominance rank and family membership. Interestingly, they add that this encoding is both immediate and automatic. In fact, according to them:

> " . . . just as we cannot hear a word without thinking about its meaning, a baboon cannot hear a vocalization without thinking about the animal who is calling, what she looks like and her rank and family membership" [30] (p. 61).

Now, other evidence suggests that this automatic categorization of individuals according to rank and kinship takes place not only when a baboon hears the calls of other baboons, but also when they interact with them in all kinds of ways. In this line, Cheney and Seyfarth make the following general claim:

> "Individual recognition, then, is more than just recognition of an individual. It includes the recognition of that individual's place in society" [32] (p. 61).

I find Cheney and Seyfarth's claims about how baboons represent other individual members of their group to be congenial with the idea that these animals have the kinds of semi-structured contents that compel them, whenever they represent other individual members of the group, to think of them as having a determinate position in the social hierarchy and as belonging to a certain family. If this is right, baboons' thoughts about other baboons will always have to include the attribution of one of several concepts of determinate properties: those related to different positions in the social hierarchy, or to different family memberships.

Baboons' societies are dynamic, and ranks may change over time (especially in the case of male baboons). Moreover, baboons are, for all we know, experts at tracking those changes. Thus, at least when they are representing the social rank of other individuals, they may need to attribute to them different ranks at different moments in time. Nevertheless, they may well be incapable, as Cheney and Seyfarth claim, of representing these individuals and of identifying them without attributing to them some rank or another. If this were the case, the notion of content sketched here might be just what we need to account for the specific ways in which they track and represent other group members and (some of) their social properties.

## 4. Conclusions

Tradition in Philosophy has tended to distinguish neatly between propositional and non-propositional contents. Now, there are many different alternative ways of understanding these notions. According to the most deflationary use of the term, a content is propositional if it represents things as being in a certain way and can be evaluated as true or false or, more leniently, as correct or incorrect. A more robust notion requires, additionally, that propositional contents have sentential structures and that they are composed by stable conceptual units that can be freely detached and recombined in every admissible way, satisfying a full-blown version of Evan's Generality Constraint.

Now, imagine that someone adopted the robust notion of propositional contents recently mentioned, and came to think, in addition, that the only other kind of content that we need to posit are unstructured, non-propositional contents, lacking all the characteristic features of full-blown propositional ones: such contents should be non-conceptual, they must have no truth conditions and they should admit no decomposition into more basic constituent units. My first and central aim in this paper has been to defend, against such a view, that there is conceptual space for (at least) another kind of contents, occupying a middle-ground space between these two extreme alternatives. These are semi-structured contents, composed by constituent representational units—concepts of particulars and properties—that do not satisfy the more demanding versions of GC for a very specific reason: it would not be possible for the creature entertaining such contents to freely detach some of their constituent concepts from others. Like robust or full-blown propositional contents, these semi-structured contents represent things as being in certain ways, and they have correctness conditions. Moreover, it seems possible to identify different representational or conceptual units composing these contents and making a distinctive contribution to them. Nevertheless, unlike full-blown propositional contents, they have, among their constituents, one conceptual unit that cannot be freely detached from all others.[15]

Once I had accomplished the initial conceptual task of providing a general characterization of these semi-structured contents and its constituent concepts, I went on distinguishing some ways in which one concept may be undetachable from others, failing to satisfy what I had called the Detachability Constraint. Additionally, I argued that each of them leads to specific restrictions in the kinds of conceptual re-combinations that they admit. Finally, I took some tentative steps in order to show the empirical plausibility and heuristic value of the idea that there are animals that possess some concepts which do not satisfy the Detachability Constraint, and some semi-structured contents partially composed by them. Firstly, argued that there are reasons why it would be adaptive for some animals to have these kinds of concepts. Secondly, I suggested which sort of empirical evidence we should be looking for in order to strengthen the conjecture that some species do, indeed, suffer from the detachability and combinatorial limitations distinguished in this paper. Admittedly, these are only initial and tentative steps, but I think they can help us see both undetachable concepts and semi-structured contents as theoretical tools that deserve further exploration.

**Funding:** This research was funded by SECYT UNC (05F829, 2016-2017), FONCYT 2015-2572 and PIP 2014-2016, CONICET.

**Acknowledgments:** I would like to thank Daniel Kalpokas, Federico Castellano and the participants of the *Workshop on the Philosophy on Cognitive Science* (WPCS 2017) for their helpful comments on an earlier version of this paper.

**Conflicts of Interest:** The author declares no conflict of interest.

## References

1. Burge, T. *Origins of Objectivity*; Oxford University Press: New York, NY, USA, 2010; pp. 1–624, ISBN 978-0-19-958140-5.
2. Camp, E. Logical Concepts and Associative Characterizations. In *The Conceptual Mind: New Directions in the Study of Concepts*; Margolis, E., Laurence, S., Eds.; The MIT Press: Cambridge, MA, USA, 2015; pp. 591–621, ISBN 978-0-262-02863-9.
3. Camp, E. Putting Thoughts to Work: Concepts, Sistematicity and Stimulus-Independence. *Philos. Phenomenol. Res.* **2009**, *78*, 275–311. [CrossRef]
4. Evans, G. *The Varietes of Reference*; Oxford University Press: New York, NY, USA, 1982; pp. 1–416, ISBN 0-19-824686-2.
5. Lievers, M. The Structure of Thoughts. In *The Compositionality of Meaning and Content*; Verning, M., Machery, E., Schurz, G., Eds.; Ontos Verlag: Frankfurt, Germany, 2005; Volume 1, pp. 169–188, ISBN 3-937202-52-8.
6. Proust, J. *The Philosophy of Metacognition: Mental Agency and Self-Awareness*; Oxford University Press: Oxford, UK, 2013; pp. 1–366, ISBN 978-0-19-960216-2.
7. Dickie, I. *Fixing Reference*; Oxford University Press: Oxford, UK, 2015; pp. 1–333, ISBN 978-0-19-875561-6.
8. Millikan, R. *On clear and Confused Ideas*; Cambridge University Press: New York, NY, USA, 2000; pp. 1–258, ISBN 0-521-62553-X.
9. Strawson, P.F. Particular and General. *Proc. Aristot. Soc.* **1953**, *54*, 233–260. [CrossRef]
10. Dickie, I. The Generality of Particular Thought. *Philos. Q.* **2010**, *60*, 508–531. [CrossRef]
11. Peacocke, C. *A Study of Concepts*; The MIT Press: Cambridge MA, USA, 1992; pp. 1–266, ISBN 0-262-16133-8.
12. Camp, E. The Generality Constraint and Categorial Restrictions. *Philos. Q.* **2004**, *54*, 209–231. [CrossRef]

---

[15] But, one may still insist: should these semi-structured contents be classified as propositional or as non-propositional? I think the answer to this question will depend, once again, on how the notion of "propositional" is understood. If we take it in a minimal sense, according to which a propositional content is merely a content that has truth conditions and represents things as being in certain ways, semi-structured contents would clearly count as propositional. But if we adopt the full-blown notion, they would not qualify as such. Moreover, it is an open question if there are other relevant features–besides the limits to detach and recombine some of their constituent concepts that we have examined—which differentiate semi-structured concepts from full-blown propositional ones.

13. Beck, J. The Generality Constraint and the Structure of Thought. *Mind* **2012**, *121*, 563–600. [CrossRef]
14. Carruthers, P. Invertebrate Concepts Confront the Generality Constraint (and Win). In *The Philosophy of Animal Minds*; Lurz, R., Ed.; Cambridge University Press: New York, NY, USA, 2009; pp. 89–107, ISBN 978-0-521-88502-7.
15. Prinz, J. *Furnishing the Mind*; The MIT Press: Cambridge, MA, USA, 2002; pp. 1–358, ISBN 0-262-26207-5.
16. Heck, R. Nonconceptual Content and the Space of Reasons. *Philos. Rev.* **2000**, *109*, 483–523. [CrossRef]
17. Strawson, P.F. *Individuals*; Routledge: London, UK, 1959; pp. 1–255, ISBN 0-415-05185-1.
18. Crane, T. *The Objects of Thought*; Oxford University Press: Oxford, UK, 2013; pp. 1–179, ISBN 978-0-19-968274-4.
19. Newen, A.; Bartels, A. Animal Minds and the Possession of Concepts. *Philos. Psychol.* **2007**, *20*, 283–308. [CrossRef]
20. Allen, C. Animal Concepts Revisited: The Use of Self-Monitoring as an Empirical Approach. *Erkenntnis* **1999**, *51*, 33–40. [CrossRef]
21. Allen, C.; Hauser, M.D. Concept Attribution in Non-Human Animals: Theoretical and Methodological Problems in Ascribing Complex Mental Processes. *Philos. Sci.* **1991**, 221–240. [CrossRef]
22. Owings, D.H. The Cognitive Defender. In *The Cognitive Animal: Empirical and Theoretical Perspectives on Animal Cognition*; Bekoff, M., Allen, C., Gordon, M., Eds.; The MIT Press: Cambridge, MA, USA, 2002; pp. 19–26, ISBN 0-262-02514-0.
23. Swaissgood, R.R.; Owing, D.H.; Rowe, M.P. Conflict and Assessment in a Predator-Prey System: Ground Squirrels vs. Rattlesnakes. *Anim. Behav.* **1999**, *57*, 1033–1044. [CrossRef] [PubMed]
24. Mandelbaum, E. Associationist Theories of Thought. In *The Stanford Encyclopedia of Philosophy*, (Summer 2017 ed.); Zalta, E., Ed.; The Metaphysics Research Lab: Stanford, CA, USA, 2017; Available online: https://plato.stanford.edu/archives/sum2017/entries/associationist-thought/ (accessed on 4 April 2018).
25. Goldman, J.A.; Phillips, D.P.; Fentress, J.C. An Acoustic Basis for Maternal Recognition in Timber Wolves (*Canis lupus*)? *J. Acoust. Soc. Am.* **1995**, *97*, 1970–1973. [CrossRef] [PubMed]
26. Charrier, I.; Mathevon, N.; Jouventin, P. How Does a Fur Seal Mother Recognize the Voice of Her Pup? An Experimental Study of *Arctocephalus Tropicalis*. *J. Exp. Biol.* **2002**, *205*, 603–612. [CrossRef] [PubMed]
27. Stoddard, P.K.; Beecher, M.D. Parental Recognition of Offspring in the Cliff Swallow. *Auk* **1983**, *100*, 795–799.
28. Charrier, I.; Mathevon, N.; Jouventin, P. Vocal Signature Recognition of Mothers by Seal Pups. *Animal Behav* **2003**, *65*, 543–550. [CrossRef]
29. King, L.S.; Janik, V.M. Bottlenose Dolphins Can Use Learned Vocal Labels to Address Each Other. *Proc. Natl. Acad. Sci. USA* **2013**, *11*, 13216–13221. [CrossRef] [PubMed]
30. Hannah, R. *Kant, Science and Human Nature*; Oxford University Press: New York, NY, USA, 2006; pp. 1–483, ISBN 0-19-928554-3978-0-19-928554-9.
31. Johnson, W.E. *Logic (Part 1)*; Cambridge University Press: Cambridge, UK, 1921; pp. 1–255.
32. Cheney, D.; Seyfarth, R. The Evolution of Concepts About Agents: Or, What Do Animals Recognize When They Recognize an Individual? In *The Conceptual Mind: New Directions in the Study of Concepts*; Margolis, E., Laurence, S., Eds.; The MIT Press: Cambridge, MA, USA, 2015; pp. 57–75, ISBN 978-0-262-02863-9.

# 5

# Human Cognition, Patterning and Deacon's Absentials: The Value of Absent-Mindedness in the Sense of Minding What is Absent

**Marlie Tandoc [1] and Robert K. Logan [2,*]**

1 Book and Media Studies, University of St. Michael's College, University of Toronto, 60 St. George, Toronto, ON M5S 1A7, Canada; marlie.tandoc@mail.utoronto.ca
2 Department of Physics, University of Toronto, 60 St. George, Toronto, ON M5S 1A7, Canada
* Correspondence: logan@physics.utoronto.ca

**Abstract:** Important aspects of human cognition are considered in terms of patterning, which we claim represents a shift from focusing on what is present to what is absent. We make use of Deacon's notion of absentials and apply it to the patterning that underscores human cognition. Several important aspects of human cognition are considered that represent a shift from focusing on what is present to what is absent, namely, language as representing the transition from percept to concept-based thinking, mathematical grouping and patterning of items into sets that gave rise to verbal language, as well as imaginative thinking which is so critical for the development of the arts, mathematics and science. The connection between information and absence is also examined, in which we claim that information is an absential, paralleling an idea of Deacon's.

**Keywords:** absentials; abiotic matter; patterning; constraints; cognition; imagination

---

*There is more here than stuff. There is how this stuff is organized and related to other stuff*

—Terrence Deacon

*The spoken word was the first technology by which man was able to let go of his environment in order to grasp it in a new way*

—Marshall McLuhan

## 1. Introduction

Important aspects of human cognition are considered in terms of patterning, a key factor in the development of human cognition and culture, which also represents a shift from focusing on what is present to what is absent. We make use of Deacon's notion of absentials by which he understands the emergence of life and sentience from abiotic matter in his book *Incomplete Nature*. Logan and Tandoc asserted in "Thinking in Patterns & Patterns of Human Thought as Opposed to AI Data Processing" that the patterning that underscores human cognition is re-examined in terms of Deacon's absentials. Several important aspects of human cognition are considered that represent a shift from focusing on what is present to what is absent, namely, language as representing the transition from percept to concept-based thinking, as described in *The Extended Mind*, mathematical grouping and patterning of items into sets that gave rise to verbal language, as well as imaginative thinking which is so critical for the development of the arts, mathematics and science. The connection between information and absence is also examined, in which we claim that information is an absential, paralleling an idea of Deacon's.

In ref. [1] (available through open access at http://www.mdpi.com/2078-2489/9/4/83) we posited that a key factor in the development of human cognition and culture was the unique ability of humans to both recognize and create patterns, which we will henceforth refer to as *patterning*. Patterning led to the emergence of verbal language, the ability to deal with information overload, conceptualization, imagination, invention, mathematics, and the sciences, both natural and social. Patterning is also an essential part of the visual arts, music, and narratives which are oral, literate and cinematic in nature.

In that study [1] we proposed that the ability of humans to identify and create patterns led to the unique aspects of human cognition and culture as a complex emergent dynamic system consisting of the following human traits that co-emerged: patterning, social organization, rudimentary set theory or categorization, spoken language, and the ability to deal with information overload. We argued that these traits are interrelated, as they all involve the ability to flexibly manipulate information from our environments via pattern restructuring. We argued that the human mind is the emergent product of a shift from external percept-based processing to a concept and language-based form of cognition [1] based on patterning. We described the evolution of human cognition and culture, arguing that they emerged from the ability of humans to think in terms of patterns. One example of the way patterning contributed to human cognition is the role it played in the emergence of language, which involved the ability of humans to create **patterns** by distinguishing a set of objects or activities that are similar, differentiating them from other objects or activities, and giving a name to that set, namely, a word.

## 2. Deacon's Incomplete Nature

In this essay, we will show that while patterning involves relationships among the elements that make up the pattern or the set, the most essential feature that makes the pattern possible is actually absent. What is absent is the definition of what constitutes the pattern or set, which is an absential, as defined by Deacon [2] (p. 2) in his groundbreaking study *Incomplete Nature*. According to Deacon, life and sentience emerged from abiotic matter in terms of absentials defined as "there is something not-there there." The something that is "not-there there" is the way the abiotic matter is organized, or as Deacon proposed explaining how life and sentience emerges from abiotic matter or "stuff": "There is more here than stuff. "There" is how this stuff is organized and related to other stuff [2] (p. 544)." This according to Deacon is how life and sentience emerges from abiotic matter in terms of absentials or "something not-there". Those who are unfamiliar with Deacon's work might have a look at a review and precís of his book [3].

The thesis that we develop in this article is dependent on the ideas that Deacon developed in his book *Incomplete Nature*. Deacon developed the paradoxical notion that it is something absent, an absential, that allows him to understand the origin of life and sentience. Deacon [2] (p. 2) contends that one cannot relate the phenomena of "a function, reference, purpose, or value", so essential for understanding life and cognition to physical matter, and that each of these phenomena "is in some way incomplete." Deacon suggests that organization be thought of in terms of constraints that create absences, or what is not there. Constraints prevent things from happening, and hence, create absenses.

> But although the specific absences that constitute a constraint do not suffer the epiphenomenality of descriptive notions of organization, they are nevertheless explicitly not anything that is present. This requires that we show how what is absent is responsible for the causal power of organization and the asymmetric dynamics of physical or living process [2] (p. 195)

Deacon associates information with constraints, making reference to Kauffman, Logan, et al. [4], where the notion that information and constraints are intimately connected was developed.

## 3. Patterning, the Basis of Human Cognition Involves Something That Is Absent

We suggest that, in addition to understanding the nature of life and sentience in terms of absentials or something that is not there a la Deacon, the patterns in the arts and sciences created by human sentience or cognition can also be understood in terms of something that is not there. This is consistent with the fact that living organisms and sentience are themselves essentially patterns. Furthermore, human cognition not only recognizes and identifies patterns, but it also creates patterns in the form of language, mathematics, science, music, the visual arts, and narratives to mention only a few. Indeed, we agree with Deacon that there is immense *value* in thinking in terms of absences not only for the natural sciences, but also for human cognition and culture in general. For example, Deacon concurs that there are some "serious inadequacies" with our current scientific theories, as well our notions of life in general, that thinking in terms of absences could remedy:

> A counterintuitive figure/background reversal, focusing on what is absent rather than present, offers a means to repair some of the serious inadequacies of our conceptions of matter, order, life, work, information, representation and even consciousness and conceptions of value [2] (p. 44)

We believe that the human mind already excels at this figure-ground reversal, but in an intuitive, everyday sense, which allows us to "repair" our *personal* understandings of our world. Focusing via patterning on what is absent rather than present is the property of the human mind that allows us to extract information and make *meaning* of our world. This paper aims to focus on some of the ways in which human cognition has already evolved to think in terms of absences, via recognizing and minding the *organizational* properties of our world. We will examine several of these patterning processes of the human cognition including language, mathematics, science, and imaginary thinking, as well as the cultural concepts or artifacts that such thinking creates. The issue of formalizing this type of thinking in the natural sciences, as noted by Deacon, will also be discussed.

We will first review how ref. [1] came to the conclusion that patterning is an essential and unique feature of human cognition and culture. We will then describe Deacon's notion of absentials and show how patterning also involves absentials, or how patterns involve something that is not there in the elements making up the pattern itself. To paraphrase Deacon, there is more to the pattern than the elements making up the pattern, there is the way in which these elements are organized, and how they relate to each other.

## 4. Thinking in Patterns and the Patterns of Human Thought

As humans gained complete control of fire and began to live around their campfires in clans instead of nuclear families, information overload developed. Logan [5] argued that verbal language emerged to deal with this information overload. Verbal language, which replaced the mimetic communication of pre-verbal vocalization, gestures, hand signals, and body language, allowed for conceptualization, and hence, planning and the co-ordination of group activity. The first words acted as concepts that represented all of the percepts that were associated with that concept. The use of the word "water", for example, instantly triggers all of one's direct experiences and perceptions of water, such as the water we drink, the water we cook with, the water we wash with, rain water, and the water that is found in rivers, ponds, lakes, and oceans. The word or concept of water is not there; only the actual material water made up of $H_2O$ molecules is there.

Before humans had verbal language, the brain was basically a percept processor; however, with language, the brain became a mind that was capable of conceptualization, with the ability to plan and co-ordinate its activities. The mind is the brain plus language (mind = brain + language). Language is not just a medium to communicate thoughts; it is also the medium in which thoughts are formulated. Indeed, the shift from percept-based to concept-based thinking that emerges with language parallels Deacon's emphasis on a shift from solely what is present to what is absent as well. The words of a language that are absent in the physical world describe the objects of the world that are present in the world in the physical sense. This parallels McLuhan's idea that language was the first tool we used to "let go of [our] environment in order to grasp it in a new way," i.e., to let go of our environment **perceptually** and grasp it **conceptually**. Percepts are present in the material world, in the sense they are sensations detected by the subject; in contrast, concepts do not have a material presence, as they are thoughts in the mind of the subject. We are quite comfortable with the idea that a picture may be worth a thousand words. However, in our view, a word also brings to mind thousands of individual images (percepts). It is in this *absence* of any present perceptual experience that the power of language and conceptual thinking resides.

Language gave us the tool to formulate "absences" in terms of concepts or words, and move from a percept-based form of thinking to a concept-based form of cognition which is capable of dealing with things not present in the here and now. For example, Alison Gopnik [6] argued in her book *Philosophical Baby* that a major part of childhood cognition is *imagination*, or the ability to consider "what could have been" and "what could be." Concepts are imagined, not perceived or sensed. It takes imagination to conceive. For example, it takes imagination to see that the various forms of water that we encounter perceptually are related. One must imagine what is not there, namely, the categories that language allows us to create.

Forming or positing a pattern is a form of hypothesizing. A hypothesis is something that is not there; there is only the data that is sensed or perceived from which the hypothesis is formulated or imagined. A paradox: Hypothesizing is a form of minding what is absent, which is the opposite of being absent-minded. Similarly, creative impasses are also highly reflective of Deacon's argument that we have stubbornly fixated too long on the "stuff" in the world. Creative insight may be defined as the ability to *reorganize knowledge* (i.e., patterning) to overcome a particular problem. This is why, when faced with a problem, it is often recommended that we "sleep on it" or "take a break and come back to it". When we return to the problem, the "stuff", of course, is exactly the same as it was before; nothing has changed in the physical material world. But perhaps we may recognize a new *organizational property* in-between the "stuff". Creative thought and creating hypotheses is the perfect example of thinking in terms of absences. Thinking in absences frees us from the material world, and gives us a mental sandbox of possibilities and hypotheses to play with. Indeed, just like manipulating various parameters or constraints in a mathematical model or computer simulation to produce different outcomes, imagination is also like playing around with constraints in our mental sandbox to create novel scenarios, of what could have been, what could be, or what will be. Thus, viewing imagination as the importance of "absence" in Deacon's notion of constraints and absentials demonstrates that a lot of human cognition parallels the figure-ground reversal, as first formulated by Marshall McLuhan, and later incorporated in Deacon's shift from what is present to what is absent.

> The term *constraint* thus denotes the property of being restricted or being less variable than possible, all other things being equal, and irrespective of why it is restricted [2] (p. 193)

## 5. Patterning and the Origin of Language

A key cognitive ability that led to language was to see the pattern in all of one's experiences or percepts with water, and to use the word "water" accordingly, acting as a concept to describe the set of all of one's experiences or percepts of water. We argue that the human mind is the emergent product of a shift from external percept-based processing to a concept and language-based form of cognition based on patterning. Logan and Pruska-Oldenhof [7], in a book entitled *A Topology of Mind—Spiral Thought Patterns, the Hyperlinking of Text, Ideas and More*, developed the thesis that "the human mind is intrinsically verbal and mathematical, and that language and mathematical thinking in the form of set theory co emerged at the dawn of the emergence of Homo sapiens." A word is created as a concept representing the set of percepts that relate to that concept.

The unique human ability of patterning, i.e., the ability to identify and create patterns, led to the flowering of human cognition and culture based on conceptualization. We claim therefore that humans basically think in terms of patterns. We will show that patterning and patterns themselves, which are so essential for the emergence of verbal language and all that followed in its wake, are based on something that is missing, or an absential, as defined by Deacon [2]. We therefore turn to a description of absentials and the role they play in the emergence of life and sentience from abiotic matter.

### 6. Deacon's Incomplete Nature and the Role of Absentials in the Emergence of Life and Sentience

Deacon [2] in *Incomplete Nature: How Mind Emerged from Matter* attempts to understand how life, sentience, and the human mind emerged from abiotic matter. He posits that these phenomena are not the result of the properties of the matter that give rise to them, but rather, the way that the abiotic physical matter is organized. The *pattern* of the organization of this abiotic matter that gives rise to life and sentience is what he defines as an absential. The matter is there physically, but the pattern is an absential that is not explicitly there physically.

Deacon contends that one cannot explain the phenomena of "function, reference, purpose, or value" in terms of the properties of physical matter, and that each of these phenomena that are essential to life and sentience "is in some way incomplete [2] (p. 2)". Each of these phenomena cannot be explained in physical terms or linked to physical processes, which is why Deacon suggests that there is something missing which he labels as an "absential" or an "absential feature [2] (p. 3)", his neologism for what is missing from our understanding of the physical dimension of these phenomena. Absential features are the "defining property of life and mind [2] (p. 3)."

Deacon's formulation of absentials represents what McLuhan would call a figure/ground reversal, in which, instead of focusing on matter, one focuses on their interactions, or as Deacon puts it:

> A counterintuitive figure/background reversal, focusing on what is absent rather than present, offers a means to repair some of the serious inadequacies of our conceptions of matter, order, life, work, information, representation and even consciousness and conceptions of value .... It requires reframing the way we think about the physical world in thoroughly dynamical, that is to say, process terms, and recasting our notion of causality in terms of something like the geometry of this dynamics, instead of thinking in terms of material objects in motion affected by contact and fields of force. [2] (p. 44)

Deacon suggests that organization be thought of in terms of constraints, or what is not there, i.e., absences. It is the constraints that give rise to the pattern.

> Constraint is a property of a collection or ensemble of some sort, but a negative property. It is a way of referring to what is not exhibited, but could have been, at least under some circumstances ... But although the specific absences that constitute a constraint do not suffer the epiphenomenality of descriptive notions of organization, they are nevertheless explicitly not anything that is present. This requires that we show how what is absent is responsible for the causal power of organization and the asymmetric dynamics of physical or living process [2] (pp. 193, 195)

### 7. Absentials and Patterning

We suggest that patterning or the creation and identification of patterns, which is so essential to the origin of verbal language and conceptual thought in human cognition that verbal language made possible, also depend on absentials. The absential of a pattern of elements is the something that it is missing. It is the constraint that allows the elements making up the pattern to be recognized as a pattern, but it, itself, is not part of the pattern. A set is, in a certain sense, also a pattern. The set of all fruits that are apples is composed only of apples, yet the constraint or definition of what is considered to be an apple is not part of the set; it is absent. The set of all even numbers does not contain the constraint that for a number to be a member of the set of even numbers, its division by two must be a whole number. This defining constraint for the set of even numbers is not a member of the set itself. The constraint or information that defines a set is not part of the set, and hence, is absent, i.e., it is an absential. In other words, the qualia, or the whatness that defines a set, a category, or a pattern is an absential.

We will claim that basically, the absential, which Deacon defines as a constraint, is information based on ideas developed in [4]. In *Incomplete Nature*, Deacon begins Chapter 13, entitled *Significance*, with the following super heading:

> The first surprise is that it takes constraints on the release of energy to perform work, but it takes work to create constraints. The second surprise is that constraints are information and information is constraint—Stuart Kauffman, Personal Communication.

This Personal Communication references the article "Propagating Organization: An Enquiry [4]". In this referenced article, the following claim is made:

> Constraints are information and information is constraints. The first part of this twosome, constraints are information is, we believe, secure. The second part, information is constraints, may be more problematic [4].

The idea that constraints are the information, instructional, or biotic information, was first formulated in a conversation when Stuart Kauffman asked Robert Logan how cells were able to do the work to build constraints that allowed them to convert external energy from their environment into work if the constraints did not exist in the first place (a chicken and egg problem). Logan told Kauffman he could not answer his question but that **the constraints are the information**, which he came up with by channeling Marshall McLuhan and his notion that "the medium is the message".

If the absential that defines a pattern is a constraint, and a constraint is information as is claimed in [6], then we feel justified in claiming that information is an absential. In fact, Deacon makes the same claim that, "Information is the archetypical absential concept [2] (p. 374)." The information about or the organization of a system, whether it is organic or abiotic, is an absential. The natural sciences are forms of information that are absentials, in that they are not part of the phenoemona they are describing. The phenomena that natural science describes is present in the material sense, but the description is not present materially, and hence, is absent.

Another argument that information is absential is as follows: Constraints which are information create absences. How? Consider a glass of water. The glass is a constraint preventing the water from leaving the glass, and hence, creates an absence of the water outside of the glass. Names and words are also absentials—words are concepts, and therefore absentials. Absent are all the percepts not related to the word or the concept the word represents.

If constraints are absentials and also information, then perhaps it follows that information is also an absential. Information is grammatically a noun, but it describes a process of informing and informing is a verb. As such, information appears even further removed or absent in the material sense. Information is not a currency, a material thing, an object, or as [2] (p. 333) puts it, it is not "a physical commodity; a kind of stuff that one can acquire, store, sell, move, lose, share, and so on"; instead, information is a process. It is a word that describes a process, i.e., how parts interconnect, relate, and work together in a system.

Let's consider whether the information that a stop sign conveys is an absential? The stop sign is only the red octangle with the letters s, t, o, and p on it, and therefore, the information is not there in the material sense; it is absent. The red octangle and the letters: s, t, o, and p are not the information. The information is in the process of the interpretation of the stop sign by the motorist. It is the effect on the motorist.

If information is a process, then measuring it should be, in terms of its effects, not the number of its bits, as Shannon [8] defined it. If information, on the other hand, is a noun, a material thing, then yes, the number of bits is a measure of it. But information is not a static thing, but rather, a dynamic process, and therefore, not a material thing that can be measured in terms of the number of bits of which it is composed. Although "information" is a noun, it certainly behaves like a verb. Linguistically and grammatically, the word "information" is a noun, but in actuality it is a process, and hence, is verb-like. The word is derived from Latin through French by combining the word "inform", meaning giving a form to the mind, with the ending "ation", denoting a noun of action. This earliest definition refers to an item of training or molding of the mind. Shannon's form of information is a noun or a thing. Both MacKay's [9] "information is a distinction that makes a difference" and Bateson's [10] (p. 428) "information is a difference that makes a difference" are definitions that assume information is a verb or a process. These are two different ways in which the same term, information, is used; one is noun-like, in the case of Shannon, while the other is verb-like, in the case of MacKay and Bateson. Basically, what we are suggesting is that Shannon's theory is not so much a theory of information, but a theory about the transmission of signals, since it does not deal with the interpretation of the signal by the receiver, which is an essential element of information.

The connection of information with the idea of giving form to the mind is the key to the notion that information is not a thing, but rather, a process by which the mind is formed or informed, and hence, it is intimately tied to the meaning and the effect on the recipient of the information. What we normally call information as a thing in our everyday use of the term is actually information as signs, which only inform when they have meaning for their recipient or receiver, the interpreter of the signs.

## 8. Culture as an Absential: The Product of the Patterns of Human Thought

As the human mind has often been described as an information-processor, it makes sense that our cognitive abilities and cultural concepts have evolved to best process information, a Deacon *absential*. Culture can be viewed as the product of the transmission of *information*, with the human mind acting as the medium for that information. Hence, a la McLuhan [7,11], "the medium is [indeed] the message".

Because humans think and process concepts in terms of absentials, our cultural concepts are also absential as well. For example, in a recent article in the journal of Theology, Moritz [12] argued that the notion of God (perhaps one of the most ubiquitous aspects of human culture) is an example of Deacon's absential concept. As the notion of God is prevalent across human cultures all over the world, it does seem that there is a property of the human mind, a "*way* in which we think, that allowed this idea to emerge across space and time. We believe this "way" to be thinking in terms of *absences* and *patterns*. Indeed, owing to the fact that there are universal concepts such as God, religion, honor, music, art, science, mathematics, marriage, etc. across diverse cultures, as Brown [13] has suggested, it follows that certain properties of human cognition, such as thinking in absences and patterns, over time, converged on these abstract absential concepts. In a similar way, Deacon's notion of teleodynamics, of self-reproducing self-correcting systems, has also led to the universal *human phenomena* of culture, language, organization, science, economics, and technology [3]. As teleodynamics requires that "presence and absence must be mutually inter-defined" Ref. [14], it can also be argued that these human cultural concepts are also largely defined by their absential qualities. Cultural artifacts are formulated in terms of absentials produced by the human mind, which is capable of thinking in terms of language and concepts, both of which are, in turn, absentials.

**Author Contributions:** Both authors contributed to this article equally.

**Funding:** There is no external funding.

**Conflicts of Interest:** The authors declare no conflict of interest.

## References

1. Logan, R.K.; Marlie, T. Thinking in Patterns & Patterns of Human Thought as Opposed to AI Data Processing. *Information* **2018**, *9*, 83. [CrossRef]
2. Deacon, T.W. *Incomplete Nature*; WW Norton & Company: New York, NY, USA, 2011.
3. Logan, R.K. Review and Précis of Deacon's Incomplete Nature: How Mind Emerged from Matter. *Information* **2012**, *6*, 290–306. [CrossRef]

4. Kauffman, S.; Logan, R.K.; Este, R.; Goebel, R.; Hobill, D.; Smulevich, I. Propagating Organization: An Inquiry. *Biol. Phil.* **2007**, *23*, 27–45. [CrossRef]
5. Logan, R.K. *The Extended Mind: The Emergence of Language, the Human Mind and Culture*; University of Toronto Press: Toronto, ON, Canada, 2007.
6. Gopnik, A. *The Philosophical Baby*; Picador: London, UK, 2010.
7. Logan, R.K.; Pruska-Oldenhof, I. *A Topology of Mind—Spiral Thought Patterns, the Hyperlinking of Text, Ideas and More*; Springer: Cham, Switzerland, 2018.
8. Shannon, C.E. A Mathematical Theory of Communication. *Bell Syst. Tech. J.* **1948**, *27*, 379–423, 623–656. [CrossRef]
9. MacKay, D. *Information, Mechanism and Meaning*; MIT Press: Cambridge, MA, USA, 1969.
10. Bateson, G. *Steps to an Ecology of Mind*; Paladin, Frogmore: St. Albans, UK, 1973.
11. McLuhan, M. *Understanding Media: Extensions of Man*; Mac Graw Hill: New York, NY, USA, 1964.
12. Moritz, J.M. How Absence Makes Things Grow: Absential Metaphysics and the Teleodynamics of God as Love. *Theol. Sci.* **2016**, *14*, 449–455. [CrossRef]
13. Brown, D.E. *Human Universals*; Mac Graw Hill: New York, NY, USA, 1991.
14. Deacon, T.W.; Cashman, T. Steps to a Metaphysics of Incompleteness. *Theol. Sci.* **2016**, *14*, 401–429. [CrossRef]

6

# Post-Modernism, Agency and Democracy

**Matthew McManus**

Department of Political Science and International Relations, Tec de Monterrey, C.P 52926 Atizapan, Mexico; garion9@yorku.ca

**Abstract:** This essay presents a general summary of post-modern philosophy's conception of agency. It argues that while post-modern philosophers offer formidable intellectual tools for criticizing contemporary restrictions on agency, their conception falters for a variety of philosophical and political reasons. This implies we should develop a more robust conception of agency to provide a foundation for progressive politics. The essay concludes by analyzing several recent steps to develop such a conception.

**Keywords:** post-modern culture; Wittgenstein; Heidegger; agency

---

## 1. Introduction

Post-modernism is currently one of the most highly contentious areas in academia. From the right, critics such as Jordan Peterson and Stephen Hicks have criticized post-modernism for abandoning the Enlightenment and embracing irrationalism.[1] From the left, Slavoj Zizek and Alain Badiou have criticized post-modern "democratic materialists" for their sophistry and alleged support for PC culture [2] (p. 2). It has even attracted considerable attention in the media as part of the ongoing culture wars, with pundits and journalists taking sides in the ongoing academic furor. All this makes it ever more important to have a reasonably thorough grasp of the virtues and limits of post-modern discourse. This essay is designed as a contribution to the ongoing discussion. In particular, I discuss the post-modern account of agency, as presented in the work of several seminal authors. I also discuss how this account of agency relates to the arguments of many post-modern philosophers and theorists for a greater embrace of democracy. While I largely agree with the democratic ambitions of the post-modern philosophers, I argue that the account of agency they present remains too thin and riddled with theoretical problems to serve as a sufficient intellectual basis for greater democratization. In particular, I argue that post-modern accounts of agency remain bound to what I follow Heidegger in calling a "technical mindset" which limits their capacity to develop a robust description of what unconstrained agency might look like. After discussing this technical mindset and its application to post-modern theories of agency, I then briefly conclude this paper by sketching some preliminary arguments about what a more robust philosophical account of agency might look like.

Before I begin, I should also offer a single important qualification. This essay operates at a high level of generalization and draws numerous links between different authors who justify the post-modern account of agency for different reasons. While their individual arguments are exceptionally important, and often highly interesting, I have not been able to discuss them all in any depth in this piece. In a later work, I hope to address some of the more exemplary accounts of agency more directly, both for exegetical and practical purposes. However, I will not do so here. This is because my ambitions are narrower. I hope to showcase the limitations of post-modern approaches

---

1 Perhaps the most famous, if highly problematic, account is in Hicks' book. See [1].

to agency, not to imply that we should do away with post-modernism generally, but to preserve the valuable insights of the tradition against superficial and mean-spirited attacks. This requires looking at the weaknesses of post-modernisms' approach to agency, so that its worthwhile claims can be extracted and incorporated into a more robust progressive project in the future. In the last parts of this paper, I will very briefly discuss several authors who have already engaged in such a project. These figures should give us hope for the future, as they are models for how to engage the most important theoretical enterprise in progressive political today.

## 2. A (Very) Brief History of Post-Modernism

The forerunners of post-modern theory emerged in the 1940s, during an unusual time in the history of European thought. Many Europeans had been deeply horrified by the atrocities perpetuated during the Second World War. More cynically, European intellectuals also reacted staunchly to the growing awareness that both the ideological and concrete influence of the Continent was on the wane. It seemed to many that the promise of modernism, and Western Civilization more generally, had proven a bust. Some, such as Martin Heidegger [3], looked upon this shift with cautious pessimism. Others, such as Herbert Marcuse, Theodor Adorno, and Max Horkheimer, took it upon themselves to explain how Western reason, and the Enlightenment promises associated with it, could be turned to such violent and seemingly nihilistic ends [4,5]. In so doing, they undertook a novel effort to fuse the Marxist critique of society with psychoanalysis, the newly discovered science of individual psyche [6,7].

While the work of the Frankfurt school was important in initiating the shift away from modernism and its optimistic rationality, the post-modern conception of agency truly blossomed in France during the 1960s.[2] It was initiated by a group of young scholars against the then dominant schools of thought in French intellectual circles. These include: semiotics, Hegelian dialectics (particularly as understood by Alexandre Kojev and Jean Hippolyte), Sartrean existentialism, and (especially for many) Marxism. Each of these became associated with some vestige of the rationalized established discourses, whether it was the historical tyranny of dialectics or the transcendental narcissism of Sartre. Thinkers such as Michel Foucault, Gilles Deleuze, Felix Guattari, Jean Francois Lyotard, Jean Baudrillard, and Jacques Derrida have since become synonymous with the intellectual attempt to undermine not just these discourses, but the very idea that one can ever get beyond discourse and reach and objective philosophical standpoint from which to see the world as it truly is.[3] Many came up with insightful accounts for why this realization should help liberate us, particularly by revealing the contingency behind powerful and often institutionally backed discourses. Others produced influential social theories which purported to explain how the discourses of modernity emerged and were propagated across society. Most critically, while these thinkers differed on many important, many of them stressed that their criticisms were neither objective observations, nor did they rest on some alternative normative theory that should be propagated in place of the discourses they criticized.[4] This leads to the question of what type of philosophical approach was being offered, and what its consequences might be for different concrete instantiations of their arguments.

While the post-modern theorists differed on a great many of central points, they shared two crucial beliefs in common. The first was that there could be no Archimedean standpoint from which a subject could assess the world. To invoke Richard Rorty [9] (p. 155), we must become anti-foundationalists. In addition, the second related belief was that previous theories of morality and agency, themselves

---

2 The relationship of French post-modern theory and the critical theories of the German Frankfurt school is the subject of ongoing debate. It seems clear that both have had a formative impact on North American critical theory.

3 The case of Deleuze is somewhat more complex. While his logic of transcendental empiricism does stress the need to continuously create new concepts in line with "deterritorializing" one's subjectivity, his earlier work on univocity and difference occasionally suggests there are such things as ontological truths. See [8].

4 On the Deleuze point see [8].

based on those objectivizing discourses, were both unsustainable and undesirable. These were explosive claims, though the ramifications of each were of course unpacked differently depending on the thinker in question.

Each of the major post-modern theorists arrived at their belief that there was no objective standpoint from which to assess the world differently. Lyotard [10], who coined the designation "post-modern", based his belief on empirical observation that individuals had lost faith in "meta-narratives" which bridge disciplines and social practices. As he puts it in his classic work *The Postmodern Condition*:

> *In contemporary society and culture—post-industrial society, postmodern culture—the question of the legitimation of knowledge is formulated in different terms. The grand narrative has lost its credibility, regardless of what mode of unification it uses, regardless of whether it is a speculative narrative or a narrative of emancipation.* [10] (p. 37)

Lyotard was largely a historically minded thinker, who approached the subject of post-modernism in epochal terms. In the works for which he was most famous, he largely eschewed the more analytical and philosophically technical arguments made by thinkers such as Foucault and Rorty. Instead he discussed the way in which grand narratives had ceased to be attractive to many in post-modern society. Jean Baudrillard was even more historically minded and developed often brilliant arguments concerning why post-modern societies became ones where any conception of truth was increasingly ambiguous. Baudrillard claimed that modern societies had gradually gone beyond even Marx in surrounding themselves with symbolic simulacrums of real simulacra out there in the material world. On this Marxist vision, there was a real world of material objects and relations which ideology prevented us from apprehending.[5] One of the tasks of critical theory was to help rid us of these illusions. Baudrillard thought this Marxist optimism was fundamentally outdated. We no longer lived in an environment where the real world was accessible to us. Instead, we exist in an increasingly hyper-real environment in which simulacrum do not stand in for anything; what is being presented to the subject is not standing in as a representation of something, a "parodic rehabilitation of all lost referentials" [12] (p. 39). In this symbol saturated world, it became ever more difficult to distinguish what is being referred to from the hyper-real symbols that are intended to stand in for it.

Lyotard and Baudrillard both approached the topic of post-modernism from a socio-historical perspective. To invoke Fredric Jameson [13], they were interested in the "condition of post-modernity" which was in some sense understood as "cultural logic". They understood it as an epoch in human history where narratives and symbols associated with truth came under pressure by post-modern conditions. Other thinkers were post-modern in quite a different sense. They were also keen to provide arguments about the "condition of post-modernity" as a "cultural logic". However, they also offered deeper epistemological and linguistic arguments as to why achieving some kind of correspondence theory of truth-to develop a mirror of nature in Rorty's [14] famous metaphor-was unlikely to ever happen. I will provide a few accounts of this deeper set of arguments below.

Perhaps the most famous post-modern theorist is Jacques Derrida, who made his name criticizing and to some extent building the then ascendant school of Saussurean structuralism. Structuralism, simplifying a great deal, held that the determinate meaning of a sign was dependent on its holistic association with other signs [15]. This meant that language did not really represent the world in terms of a one-to-one correspondence between word and object but was rather system that needed to be understood as a totality. Derrida built upon these insights, while also pointing out their limitations. Derrida argued that logocentric societies privileged that idea of representation in language because they believed that signs could make present what was absent. This in turn flowed from a phonocentric understanding of subjects as making statements which have specific meaning which in turn must

[5] The most famous example of this is Marx's account of the fetishism of the commodities [11] (p. 163).

be interpreted by other subjects. What was not acknowledged in this was that language could not make something present that was absent, and that the belief that it could do so involved pathologically attempting to suppress the other possible meanings latent within both an individual proposition and language as a whole [16]. In this respect, even the ambitions of the structuralists to demonstrate the systematicity fell short of the vastness of what language did, both on the surface of a text and beneath it. Part of the goal of deconstruction, as it came to be called, was to indicate that these meanings could not be so suppressed. Deconstructionist interpreters were encouraged to follow the "trace" back to indicate what an author or speaker was attempting to keep buried.[6] This did not mean, as some have crudely put it, that Derrida was a relativist per se. However, it did mean that there could be no final interpretation of a text, since both the surface and potential substratum of meanings could beget a limitless number of different, playful, interpretations.

Finally, Foucault also reacted violently against the dominant intellectual traditions of hiss time; whether it be the structuralism of Saussure or the Marxism of figures such as Sartre or Althusser. Foucault developed a discursive approach to language and knowledge which followed Nietzsche's [18] (pp. 437–599) *Genealogy of Morals* in privileging history as an ur-discourse that casts insight into the continuous transformation of all other discourses. One of the virtues of such a historical analysis is revealing that what might appear an objective discourse on truth is often a very specific episteme which emerges in a given place and time for complex socio-historical reasons [19,20]. Often, Foucault believes these reasons have far more to do with the power simultaneously providing support for and being supported by a given episteme than its intrinsic truth. The power of these discourses can often blind us to their disturbingly pervasive effect, particularly when they become associated with disciplinary institutions such as prisons and schools [21]. This is where he made his famous connection to the productive, but occasionally insidious relationship between knowledge/and power. For Foucault, echoing Bacon, every system of knowledge presupposes a system of power.[7] An institutional system of law, for instance, establishes a given episteme for legal practitioners and subjects to operate within, while enforcing the consistency and constancy of the episteme with carceral power. This meant that a knowledge could never be understood independently of power; a discursive episteme always needed to be situated in networks of power and enforcement, even when these happened to be practically useful. This also meant that Foucault's account of knowledge and power went well beyond the standard Marxist critique of ideology, as for instance was popularized by well-known French thinkers such as Althusser [23]. While the Marxist critique of ideology at least held out the hope of overcoming the false consciousness imposed by super-structures and the culture industry, for Foucault we would never have any knowledge or truth that could be meaningfully disconnected from a system of power.

This brief summary is meant to demonstrate how an array of otherwise distinct thinkers reached similar conclusions about the possibility of subjects making objective assessments about the world. Whether they reached this conclusion through the empirical observation of contemporary society as was the case for Lyotard, a historical assessment of post-modernity relative to other historical epochs in the case of Baudrillard, o by illustrating the inability of language to adequately represent the world as it is in Derrida and Foucault, the philosophical and concrete outcomes were the same. We should abandon the long held belief that one can arrive at anything resembling truth, or at least truth as defined by the correspondence theory designating that truth means a coincidence between our mental and linguistic representations of the world, and the world as it actually is.

Once this step towards epistemological skepticism was taken, it is not hard to see why post-modern theorists would quickly reach related conclusions about the status of theories concerning agency and morality. This relates to the second point of agreement between the major post-modern theorists: as with epistemic theories of knowledge, most moral theories, especially those associated

---

6 For an indicative text applying Derrida's approach to the "ethnocentrism of knowledge" see [17] (p. 289).

7 For a helpful account see [22].

with the political and economic status quo, rest on an insecure foundation. Indeed, almost all the post-modern theorists agree that one of the tasks theory should take upon itself is to liberate us from moralizing demagogues by unmasking the spuriousness of their moral claims. This can often be very difficult, since many demagogues operate from entrenched positions of power and socio-economic influence which are institutionally perpetuated over time. This was most artfully put by Michel Foucault, who in an almost Kantian vein went as far as to frame freedom as the ontological condition for all ethics:

> *Freedom is the ontological condition of ethics; but ethics is the deliberate form assumed by freedom.* [24]

While I largely agree with Foucault's sentiment here, it is important to note that many of the post-modern accounts which share his belief rest on a moral assumption that increasing the agency of individuals is desirable. I say "moral assumption" because why and whether freedom/agency is good in and of itself is rarely discussed. This can be a substantial problem if one adopts a different moral or meta-ethical position which does not give freedom such pride of place, as would be the case for many utilitarianism and virtue ethicists. However, given I agree with this post-modern emphasis on agency, I will not take substantive issue with the assumption in this paper. Instead, this section will conclude by discussing what the post-modern theorists understand to be constraints imposed on the exercise of human agency, and what they offer as an alternative model.

Each of the major post-modern theorists offers a distinctive and unique account of what constraints are imposed on the exercise of human agency. Many of these accounts of the constraints imposed on human agency, such as those of Lyotard, Baudrillard,[8] and Deleuze and Guattari[9] offered frequently brilliant analyses of Western modernity and the many complex forces which enforced and even fostered support for anti-democratic and even fascistic impulses. Foucault went even further with penetrating genealogies of knowledge/power formations; particularly medical associations, the penal system, sexual norms, before finally announcing that we had entered a new age of bio-politics wherein the state would become responsible for the biological functioning of its populations ([27,28], pp. 139–140). Strangely, Derrida wrote very little about political and ethical concerns until very late in his oeuvre ([29,30], pp. 54–81). However, all his writings imply the need to dissociate one's self from propounded certainties, whether through breaking them down wholesale or approaching them ironically.

> *If I had invented my writing, I would have done so as a perpetual revolution. For it is necessary in each situation to create an appropriate mode of exposition, to invent the law of the singular event, to take into account the presumed or desired addressee, and at the same time, to make as if this writing will determine the reader, who will learn to read (to 'live') something he or she was not accustomed to receiving from anywhere else. One hopes that he or she will be reborn differently, determined otherwise, as a result...* [31] (pp. 30–31)

While each of these distinct analyses has features to recommend them, and I shall not evaluate any specific one here. Instead, I will attempt to generalize their common features to discuss what unites these various philosopher's arguments about agency and its limitations. In addition, this is where the problems begin. Unfortunately, as I will elaborate below, both the post-modern theorists and their many admirers have been notably wary of providing a model of what unconstrained agency would look like, or what positive measures can be taken to realize it.[10] Indeed, beyond appeals to the virtue of greater democratization, non-fascist living, and the ecstasy of a liberated aesthetics of the self, it is hard to tell what emancipated agency might look like. As I shall discuss later, this silence is not incidental. Indeed, I believe it flows from the structure of post-modern accounts of the relationship between subjectivity and agency. Despite their many innovations, I believe that post-modern theories

---

8 For an indicative example see [25] (p. 25).
9 For the Deleuze and Guattari reference see [26] (pp. 296–322).
10 Deleuze and Guattari [32] are the notable exception.

of agency remain dependent on many of the same presuppositions they sought to disprove. This meant that their accounts are bound by the same restrictions, necessitating we move beyond post-modern accounts of agency where possible.

### 3. The Limitations of the Post-Modern Approach to Agency

In this section, I will claim that the unwillingness of many post-modern theorists to develop a more robust approach to agency is unsurprising for two interrelated reasons. In later sections, I will elaborate how this also problematizes the post-modern support for greater democratization.

Firstly, if post-modern theorists pushed their various philosophical arguments about the influence of language and social structures to their logical conclusion, they would once again be forced to place the contingent individual, in all his/her particularity, at the center of their theory.[11] This would abnegate much of the political motivation behind adopting post-modernism as a philosophical support due to its critiques of liberal individualism. Indeed, it comes perilously close to the Lockean position that individuals begin as a blank slate whose subjectivity is gradually constituted through engagement with the determinants of the empirical world.[12] Moreover, given that the individual is regarded exclusively as the product of various socio-historical effects, a post-modern theorist is handicapped when developing a robust theory of freedom. This is because the post-modern approach remains beholden to what I claim is a deterministic "technical mindset" common to scientism and its offshoots throughout Western thought. Secondly, I believe the claim that agency is determined entirely by socio-historical circumstances is unattractive not just because of its ramifications, but because it is, at base, fallacious.

My first claim can be illustrated by an appeal to the late Ludwig Wittgenstein, and his argument that a private language cannot be conceived. This is because he defines language by focusing on its communicative function in a given semantic community. Wittgenstein [33] denied that one could conclusively discover a determinate master rule from which all potential "language games" branch. If there were such a determinate rule, it might be possible to develop a rationalistic model of human consciousness that could then account for the universal objectivity of empirical phenomena. This is because the universal rule which determines all semantic "forms of life" would have been understood. From there, one could try to move from the particularities of language use to its universal pre-conditions. Since Wittgenstein was convinced that there was no such rule, we are left with accepting that language, and thence all linguistically mediated approaches to "truth," can only leave things exactly as they were. Much as in his earlier work, one who truly understands this realizes that there are better things to engage in. As Wittgenstein artfully put it in the *Tractatus*:

> *My propositions serve as elucidations in the following way: anyone who understands me eventually recognizes them as nonsensical, when he has used them as steps to climb up beyond them. (He must, so to speak, throw away the ladder after he has climbed up it.) He must transcend these propositions, and then he will see the world aright.* [34] (p. 89)

Languages emerged because of the "games" that we played in various "forms of life" and made up a "vast system" of interconnected semantic meanings. None of these could be arranged in some philosophical hierarchy. As he composed the *Philosophical Investigations* in the 1940s and early 50s, Wittgenstein seems to have become convinced that the very attempt to draw a one-to-one correspondence between classes of linguistic statements and forms of knowledge did a disservice to the variety of language games existing in the world. He came to feel that one could not determine *a priori* whether some language games were more valuable than others. The only way to determine whether a given language game might serve a valuable purpose within a historical community of speakers was

---

11 I refer to the internal logic of the argument rather than the criteria of another logical system.

12 I say perilously with a bit of sarcasm. Given Locke's peerless bourgeois credentials, I cannot imagine any post-modern theorist would accept such an association.

to internally understand the "forms of life" common to that community [33] (para 241). These forms of life can be meaningfully compared to several post-modern conceptions of language and meaning, including Foucault's discourses, Derrida's texts, Lyotard's narratives and so on. While there are important technical differences between them, each other believes that discourses, texts, and narratives operate largely independently of the wills and subjectivities of those who interact with them. Instead these subjects are largely determined by these discourses, texts, and narratives. In Wittgensteinian terms, the private subject was less important than the "forms of life" which determined the language games that we play.

By extension, Wittgenstein felt it made little sense to speak about a private human consciousness whose inner content can be analyzed independently of the social and linguistic world around it.[13] To do so would be to presume that one could semantically think the "I" without some language inherited from a given set of socio-historical contexts. On this Wittgensteinian account consciousness is now seen, at best, as the ability to assimilate and engage in linguistic behavior.[14] Many post-modern theorists have attempted to build on this insight. Post-modern theorists hope to demonstrate how diffuse forms of discursive formations, logocentric interpretations, grand narratives, and the micro-power of modern politico-legal institutions inhibit the agency[15] of individuals.[16] However, they have been very reluctant to suggest what this agency itself is, even in such an uninhibited form. Pushed to their extreme, I think post-modernist arguments would wind up back in the very liberal modernism they seek to eschew.

If one accepts that all things are determined through being interpolated within diverse socio-historical contexts, then one is pushed to accepting a political variant of liberal universalism. This is because, the post-modernist must believe that all experiences can be made explicit through a shared language, in effect becoming universalized. Otherwise the post-modern theorist would be pushed to believing that there was some private self that transcended and stood outside the determinations of the socio-historical contexts. From this, some post-modern theorists have argued that the no subjective position can be epistemically privileged over any other. In other words, the post-modernist is pushed towards valuing all epistemic positions equally. This is because one can no longer claim that there are private experiences that operate at a radical level beyond the socio-historical contexts through which subjects interact and define themselves.[17] Or, to put it in Derridean language, it becomes unclear that we can meaningfully talk about even our subjective interpretations of events since there is "no outside text." If it is true that all subjectivities are determined by the socio-historical contexts, there are no such private experiences.

This has obvious normative consequences. If there is no private subjectivity that transcends the determinations of the socio-historical contexts, and we cannot privilege any epistemic position over another, it seems plausible that each individual's opinions should be accorded equal weight on normative issues. This is because there is no transcendent position from which one might speak "truth" to the power dynamics which determine the makeup of our society and our subjectivity.[18] Ironically, as Jeremy Waldron claimed, this would compel post-modernists to also accept the strong claims of liberal universalists who argue for the metaphysical, rather than just political, tenability of their argument.[19] Or, as put by Brian Barry, claiming that there is no universal core from which one can derive values

---

13 This was central to his argument in [35].

14 Rorty employs the term "mind" rather than "consciousness". For the sake of consistency I have chosen to stick with the terminology I have worked with throughout this piece.

15 In many respects this runs counter to Wittgenstein's belief that even a critical analysis of language can only leave things as they are; philosophy cannot impede on what he called "forms of life".

16 I rely primarily on Foucauldian terminology here both because I think it is the clearest and most consistent.

17 The classical example is of course the Marxist emphasis on the class consciousness of the proletariat. Marx cannot be accused of being a liberal in disguise however, either at a political or philosophical level.

18 For the references to "forms of life" see [33] (para 241).

19 See, amongst other works, his paper "Particular Values and Critical Morality" in [36].

must lead one to the uncritical acceptance of all systems of value, including the systems of those who believe there is such a universal core [37] (p. 252).

If, on the other hand, there is something incommunicable in the experiences of persons that must be understood in and of itself, and not truncated by semantic translation into communicable discourses, post-modern theorists are forced into a different position. They would have to argue that there are some features of knowledge and human agency that cannot be accounted for through a critical analyses of the socio-historical contexts. This would include the experiences of legally marginalized individuals whose voices have been silenced. There must exist some core of self-hood and agency which exists beyond that determined by the socio-historical contexts we share with others. In other words, the perfect post-modern theorist becomes some kind of a Kantian in the end, much like Foucault himself did by re-engaging with the critical project.[20]

Indeed, Foucault's analyses are perhaps most representative here. As indicated, in *The Order of Things*, Foucault initially seems to have agreed with the quasi-Nietzschian argument that history was something of an ur-science which enabled us to understand all others [19] (pp. 400–407). Later, as he moved into the *Archaeology of Knowledge* and *Discipline and Punish*, this early optimism gave way to a cynical belief that knowledge/power was an often oppressive force. It took the form of discourses engendered by various institutional authorities, such as the nexus between law and prisons, which were in turn supported by immense apparatus of oppression. These determined even the subjectivities of those who were incorporated into them. Or to paraphrase his striking aphorism in *Discipline and Punish*, our subjective soul becomes a prison for the potentialities of our body [21]. What is odd when analyzing this is the unusual degree of determinism latent within the analysis, which is reflective of what I will later describe as the technical mindset. Foucault understands agency as primary being about material potentialities which are in turn constrained by external socio-historical contexts which determine our inner subjectivity. Only late in his life did he seem to recognize the inherent limitations in such an analysis, turning as mentioned to Kant as a potential source of insight.[21] However, Foucault, as with most of his post-modern kin, was unable ever to articulate a comprehensive response to these problems fully. The same is true in the work of other post-modern theorists such as Baudrillard and Lyotard, who regarded human subjectivity as largely defined by our new hyper-reality of the post-modern condition, and Derrida who as I shall discuss below never fully managed to explain how agency could be possible in a linguistic environment where texts operated independently of the will of subjects who interpreted them.

Some, post-modern philosophers such as Derrida and Deleuze, made tentative movements in the direction of developing more robust conception of agency I am calling for. For instance, Derrida consistently stressed the ethical openness that deconstruction was meant to engender. This can certainly be understood as an argument for a kind of interpretive agency; albeit one I would argue that I still strongly constrained by its emphasis on the text being determinative. In addition, Derrida did extend such arguments to innovative claims about a democracy to come. This would be defined by a politics of friendship and allowing the Other to exist in their undecidability, rather than interpolating them into the rigid categories characteristic of logocentrism [39]. In other words, Derrida's politics is about allowing the Other to remain what it is fundamentally, in all its alterity. Many of his most important arguments in the political and ethical realm center around this normative commitment. Derrida will often observe how standard approaches to politics and ethics will often try to incorporate the other into a standard horizon of understanding.[22] Drawing on his work, commentators such as Spivak [17] will observe that this is as true of liberalism as any other ethics and politics. While superficially tolerant, liberalism is often unwilling or even unable to allow the subaltern to "speak" because its

---

[20] See Michel Foucault "What is Enlightenment?" in [38] (pp. 32–50).

[21] See Michel Foucault "What is Enlightenment?" in [38] (pp. 32–50).

[22] The reference to "horizon of understanding" is not Derridean, but rather by own terminology meant to summarize an approximation of his position.

voice would reflect the fundamental limitations of the liberal outlook. So, in historical practice, even apparently tolerant political ideologies such as liberalism have ultimately engaged in imperial and repressive projects. For Derrida and followers such as Spivak, this totalizing impulse is antithetical to any progressive politics that is truly concerned with difference.

Many of these arguments are inspiring, and their critical dimension is well taken. However, they are also left frustratingly empty of determinative content. When not engaging in critical discussions, Derrida and Spivak discuss constructive politics and agency at such a level of generality that it is difficult to determine what they actually want in concrete terms. Defenders might respond by saying this is a deliberate gesture to refrain from setting guidelines intended to determine future actions by free agents. However, it is one thing to discuss a future that is to be left open to acts of human agency. It is another to provide little theoretical guidance on how to ensure this future is available to as many people as possible. Moreover, they generally do not systematically relate to the broader problems post by post-modern theorists about the determinacy of discourse, text, narrative and the socio-historical contexts and institutions which support them.

Aside from some of the examples discussed above, post-modern theorists have generally tried to avoid these theoretical problems by not actually engaging with them at a philosophical level. Rather than engage substantially with developing a robust account of agency, they have focused theoretical attention on the practical activity of those who engage in socio-political struggles in an attempt to avoid theorizing about foundationalist accounts of knowledge and agency. All other attempts to mute these limitations philosophically, for instance by establishing an account of "strategic essentialism", can only evade the limitations by appealing to the sensibilities of those already converted to the worth of a particular cause.[23] Indeed, these limitations, perhaps more than any others, explain the current emphasis placed on the German idealists and their accounts of freedom; whether one is talking about Kant for Foucault, or Hegel and Schelling for Zizek [40] (pp. 137–138).

Moreover, my argument stresses that the political consequences of wholesale embracing a post-modernist approach to agency are not at all desirable; indeed, they would directly contradict the political sentiments of those theorists who advocate for post-modern approaches to breaking down the socio-historical contexts. This is because many post-modern theories are predicated on accepting the ultimate determinacy of socio-historical contexts. As such, a post-modern theorist unable to consistently develop any robust theory of agency which deviates significantly from those common to the Western tradition is unsurprising. This is because post-modern theory is beholden to what I call the "technical mindset."

The claim that human agency is primarily or entirely determined by socio-historical contexts is predicated on accepting determinism. More particularly, post-modern theorists take socio-historical contexts to be the true determinants constituting the various forms of human subjectivity. If the determinants of human subjectivity are the socio-historical contexts within which we come into existence, then the particularities of a subject's experiences must occupy a privileged explanatory position when determining who we are, and how we relate to social phenomena such as legality. Since these particularities are unique to each subject, there can be no fixed, or "Archimedean" point, from which to begin constructing a universal theory of human subjectivity beyond saying that difference is the only universal.[24] To invoke Foucault, our intersectional subjectivity is molded into a soul which becomes a prison for the body through interactions within distinct socio-historical contexts.

The embrace of such a historicized account of human subjectivity is often seen as highly emancipatory. The claim is that universalistic discourses on the "proper" essence of human nature were employed as a weapon intended to marginalize the experiences, and thus the subjectivity, of various "others". It would not be going too far to claim that, for some scholars, this polarity between accounts

---

[23] Political engagement in "strategic essentialism" was pioneered by Spivak [17] (pp. 282–284) in a number of works.
[24] The idea of an Archimedean point is critiqued by Rorty [41].

of "universal" consciousness, always understood as being consistent with Western metaphysics and values, and the production of its deficient "Other" is what most defines our intellectual history. This polarity between the legitimate universalism of Western liberal "agency" and its pre-determined and deficient "Others" is seen as contributing to the emergence of sexism, racism, and a host of other historically significant prejudices. The counter claim is that by embracing the post-modern account of subjectivity one can avoid making essentialist claims either about human beings or the phenomena they experience.[25] Post-modern theorists often take this as laying the critical groundwork for a more emancipatory politics to follow; one that will do away with the prejudicial polarities which define the intellectual history of the Western world. As I shall indicate below, I do not believe this genealogy is inaccurate.[26]

### 4. Post-Modernism, the Technical Mindset, and Human Agency

Heidegger claimed that at the base of Western thought is not simply an emphasis on crude polarities, but the ontological claim that reality consists of what Heidegger calls "beings in Being". He held that this ontological presumption, far from simply being the purview of a few philosophers, influenced the way most individuals understood both themselves and the world around them. The ontological claim maintains that the world is ultimately divisible into different fragmented things, each of which exists in a complex set of relations with other similarly fragmented things.[27] This is what I call the technical mindset; the belief that the world is ultimately a collection of "things"; with individuals being a specific class of things.

As Heidegger put it in *What is Called Thinking*:

> *Accordingly—what is called thinking, insofar as it follows this call. Thinking means: letting-lie-before-us and so taking-to-heart also: beings in being. Thinking so structured pervades the foundation of metaphysics, the duality of beings and Being. Such thinking develops its various successive positions on this foundation, and determines the fundamental position of metaphysics.* [43] (p. 224)

The account of subjectivity offered by post-modernism is beholden to this same ontological presumption that reality consists of "beings in Being" specifically that individuals are determined by the various socio-historical contexts within which they exist. The entire subjectivity of an individual, on this account, can be understood by looking at the bundle of determinants that constitute them. In this respect, post-modern theory does not break from the parameters of modern Western thought, which is largely oriented by the technical mindset.

If post-modern theorists understand human subjectivity to be exclusively determined by socio-historical contexts, they understand human beings in a manner that is analogous to that of "things". Once one has developed a properly mechanical understanding of the impact of particular but intersecting socio-historical contexts on the plastic *tabula rasa* of our un-determined subjectivity, the post-modern theorist can then understand how a given type of subject emerges. Of course, developing a post-modern analysis powerful enough to make entirely accurate claims about all the determinants of subjectivity may be practically impossible. However, by definition, the possibility of developing such a technique cannot be ruled out *a priori*. This variant of the technical mindset exemplified by post-modernism also has serious political consequences. The claim that human subjectivity is entirely determined by socio-historical contexts has not just been embraced by those focused on theorizing how individuals might deploy their agency to be rid of prejudice and structural forms of injustice. It is also, as Arendt brilliantly assessed in *The Origins of Totalitarianism*, the working

---

25 Chomsky [42] (p. 90) has often touched on the political association frequently drawn between empiricism and the emancipation of marginalized subjectivities.

26 The reference to "one dimensionality" is drawn from Marcuse [5] (p. 12), though adapted here.

27 Heidegger's most sustained commentary on the metaphysics of "beings in Being" appears in [43].

assumption of authoritarian and totalitarian regimes bent on molding the perfect human beings to ensure the functioning of the regime [44] (Part III).

This is no coincidence. Post-modernism emerges with the development of the technical idea that human subjectivity is indefinitely plastic because there is no core set of features which define us. The idea the human subjectivity is plastic is a precondition for arguing that those subjects who grew up in socio-historical contexts not amenable to the technical requirements of our modern and now post-modern world should be treated unequally.[28]

Of course, few if any post-modern theorists have argued for authoritarianism; quite the contrary. For many, various post-modern arguments are adopted to show sensitivity to the plurality of human experiences in given socio-historical contexts and reflects a rejection of authoritarianism. However, it is hard to see how post-modernism can generate what Chomsky referred to as a "soft theoretical" boundary against the idea that the subjectivity of human beings is indefinitely malleable, and therefore open to manipulation by authoritarian institutions [42] (pp. 90–91). This is because post-modernism cannot develop an account of human agency beyond a negative one. Post-modern arguments can only critique the socio-historical contexts which constrain individuals. However, it is not enough to examine which particular socio-historical contexts impede human agency if one does not have an account of what agency is.

The post-modern approach to agency cannot explain how, despite the emergence of an immense plurality of human subjectivities, there none the less remain tremendous commonalities in the way we think, interact, and develop even within very different socio-historical contexts. Superficially, the idea that there are tremendous commonalities between people might appear to be simply false. How could it be true given the immense plurality of differences one can encounter for instance in moral, political, and religious systems? However, what post-modern theorists do not sufficiently appreciate is that no such particularities would be possible unless the capacity to transcend such particular contexts was also possible. The most evident example of this is language. It is entirely possible to imagine a private individual, or a collection of entirely private individuals, who are incapable or perhaps even unwilling to speak to one another or even with themselves. In such circumstances, the range of variation one would see in human subjectivities would be entirely minimal.

However, this is not the case for human beings. As Chomsky [46] indicates, our common capacity to develop novel syntactic structures is what accounts for the linguistic diversity we see in the world. Chomsky attributes this shared capacity to a linguistic organ which develops a language in accord with the rules of universal grammar. This capacity is what enables the development of a wide variety of syntactic structures which then assume different semantic meanings in given socio-historical communities.[29] The members of such communities can then plausibly speak of themselves as having a unique group history. Without this common capacity, no diversity could emerge. In other words, what is common to us all is what enables us to be different.

This indicates the limitations of post-modern theory. Post-modern theories characterize human beings as determined by the socio-historical contexts within which we exist. This indicates how post-modernism remains beholden to the technical mindset; the approach regards human beings as ultimately the product of their environment. For these reasons, post-modern theorists are unable to develop a more robust approach to human agency without going beyond the theoretical limitations of the mindset. They become limited to developing critiques of the socio-historical contexts without accounting for what an emancipated agency would resemble either in theory or in practice.

This is not to suggest we should abandon the insights of post-modern theories. In many respects, I think their political and historical critiques of the socio-historical contexts to agency provide a great deal of insight on why and how we must overcome their false necessity. What is required is linking the

---

[28] The basis of this critique goes as far back as Rousseau [45] (p. 171).

[29] Noam Chomsky refers to his hypothesis that there exists a "language organ" several times.

critical approach post-modern theory takes towards contemporary society to a more robust normative conception of what emancipated human agency should be.

This is especially true regarding the emphasis both place on democracy. One of the great virtues of the post-modern theory has been exposing the still deeply undemocratic propensities that exist in our society. This is true along many dimensions which have been exposed by a variety of post-modern theorists. Whether it is through disciplinary institutions, an emphasis on the positivity of law, or favoring a simulated democratic public sphere over an authentic one, there are many sites in our society which call for greater democratization and public involvement.

### 5. Post-Modern Democratic Theories

Despite the inability or unwillingness of many post-modern theorists to develop a robust model of agency, this has not prevented many from engaging in positive normative theorizing on the great political issues of the day.[30] Perhaps unsurprisingly, most are self-declared democrats who make consistent and impassioned calls to emancipate the demos from the limitations of the liberty oriented conception of agency in theory, and of liberal-capitalism in practice. Indeed, the propensity of post-modernists to become democrats is so common that some radicals, most notably Alain Badiou and Slavoj Zizek, have taken to caricaturing it as the guiding ideology of modern "critical theory."[31] Democracy is invoked by post-modern theorists as a way of shifting a population away from the "conservative" autocratic narratives of tradition oriented philosophies which privilege the totalizing views of experts over the considered opinions people faced with practical tasks [9] (pp. 29–30). Other post-modern theorists place tremendous stress on developing the authentic "democratic intuitions" of individuals [48] which can be directed against the false-idols of representational parliaments where the rituals of democracy are falsely "staged" [17] (p. 257). In some cases, the possibility of a democratic multitude coming to inherit the earth is all but transformed into a true political theology, as in this indicative statement by *Empire* authors Michael Hardt and Antonio Negri:

> *Certainly, there must be a moment when reappropriation and self-organization reach a threshold and configure a real event. This is when the political is really affirmed-when the genesis is complete and self-valorization, the cooperative convergence of subjects, and the proletarian management of production become a constituent power. This is the point when the modern republic ceases to exist and the postmodern posse arises. This is the founding moment of an earthy city that is strong and distinct from any divine..* [49]

Or as they put it more directly in a later work:

> *Freedom and equality also imply an affirmation of democracy in opposition to the political representation that forms the basis of hegemony...The logic of representation and hegemony in both these instances dictates that a people exists only with respect to its leadership and vice versa, and thus this arrangement determines an aristocratic, not a democratic, form of government, even if the people elect that aristocracy.* [50] (pp. 304–305)

On the one hand, it might appear odd that so many post-modern theorists would argue so consistently and uniformly for greater democracy given their rejection of foundationalism. However, many post-modern theorists seem to regard their skeptical arguments towards the epistemological and ontological status of knowledge as a corollary to a normative disposition which is highly emancipatory. By breaking down a belief in meta-narratives, post-modern theorists hope to create greater space at the philosophical level for new epistemes to emerge which might serve to challenge hegemonic ideologies;

---

30 It is worth noting that all of the theorists I subsequently mention share an often under-theorized belief that increasing agency is valuable because they presume that the free development of the self is "what matters". Unfortunately this meta-ethical argument, and its consequent limitations, are rarely scrutinized directly.

31 See Badiou's dismissive references to democratic materialism which opens Alain Badiou [2] (pp. 1–9) and Slavoj Zizek [47].

for instance, the widespread belief in the universality of the liberty oriented conception of agency. This is also related to the critiques of the socio-historical contexts engaged in by many post-modern theorists [49]. Once belief in these meta-narratives is shaken, many post-modern theorists believe the institutional arrangements they support will be similarly undermined as their false necessity is recognized and rejected [51].

It is important to note that while many post-modernists might acknowledge that the rejection of meta-narratives means that there can be no necessary connection between their philosophical and normative positions, the latter are characterized as immanently implied by the former.[32] Critical theory should become reflected in a critical approach to hegemonic practices inhibiting the "multitude" from organizing and emancipating itself from the powers that bind it.

However, I think that this radicalizes the immanent political dimensions of post-modern theory too much. There seems little inherent reason one must become politically radicalized at the normative level, even if one accepts the democratizing potential of the various post-modern philosophical arguments. To paraphrase Barry again, the rejection of foundationalism need not lead to the view that all normative positions are or should be considered equal [37] (p. 252). It is just as possible that one might accept Rorty's generally liberal vision of a pragmatic approach to politics. One could also draw conclusions about the need for a strong, even authoritarian state required to arbitrate between moral disagreements given the existence of moral relativism.[33] It is even possible that, by rejecting foundationalism, one might draw more conservative conclusions about what is morally proper. Indeed, Edmund Burke [54] directly linked his skepticism towards philosophical foundationalism and rationalism with a distinctively British conservatism.

That post-modernism has often led theorists in a democratic direction is, to my mind, partly explained as an accident of culture. As I explained, given that it initially arose in France as a reaction against modernist meta-narratives associated with the political status quo, or the Marxist alternative seen as dominated by the Soviet Union. However, to my mind, the deeper reason is that many post-modern critiques are predicated on normative judgments which are meant to be universalized. Most important is their belief that the agency authentically development of the self is morally desirable. One must presume that even anti-essentialist post-modern theorists such as Gayatri Spivak [55] express concern with whether the "subaltern" can speak because they believe that expression is of some intrinsic value to those who have been marginalized.

This inability to evade the burden of moral judgment reflects Ronald Dworkin's [56] very Kantian point about the impossibility of evading moral judgment. However, it is worth noting that I do not believe that the democratic arguments of many post-modern theorists are therefore invalid. I simply believe that they should be made explicit. If it is true that individuals should have the agency to define themselves, as many post-modern theorists implicitly seem to believe, then this can be directly linked to a moral argument for both democracy and the amplification of an individual's overall capacity for agency. By linking this to a more robust model of agency, post-modern theorists can also avoid the limitations of the technical mindset I accounted for in the section above. I believe that progressively minded thinkers should focus their energies more on developing such an account of agency, and less on the various critical attractions offered by post-modern philosophy. This is especially important in the contemporary political climate, when so many regard progressive thinkers as exclusively involved in identity politics and trashing the other side. We should be attempting not just to criticize, but to inspire. To do so we will need more formidable philosophical resources than post-modernism can truly offer. In addition, indeed, some philosophers emerging from the post-modern tradition-most notably Judith Butler [57], once considered the critic par excellence-have attempted to accomplish just this. In doing so, they have often been forced to move gradually away from the limits of post-modernism's approach

---

32 For the reference to "immanence" see [52] (p. 584).

33 This is how Richard Tuck [53] (pp. 62–65). interprets Thomas Hobbes.

to agency, as Butler [58] did in *The Psychic Life of Power* where she incorporated psychoanalytical themes into a Foucauldian analysis of power. This was a necessary step towards giving a more robust twist to agency necessary to provide a normative underpinning to a democratic theory. I believe this is a positive development which bodes well for the future of progressive philosophy.

## 6. Conclusions

In this paper, I unpacked what I take to be the basic features of the post-modern approach to agency. I began by briefly summarizing the history of the approach and outlined the arguments of some of the major theorists. This included quickly analyzing the work of seminal figures such as Baudrillard, Derrida, and Foucault. In particular, we looked at their approach to truth and agency. In the next two sections, I argued that post-modern theories were unable to get beyond certain limitations. Firstly, if the logic of the post-modern arguments was unpacked thoroughly it would wind up re-embracing the liberal individualism it sought to eschew. Secondly, I argued that this was not coincidental. This is because post-modern theorists are unable to develop a more robust approach to agency because they remain bound up in the limitations of what I called the technical mindset. Ultimately, post-modern theorists must regard human beings as determined by the socio-historical contexts within which we exist. This problematizes the arguments many post-modern theorists make for greater democracy. In many respects it leads to conclusions that were not intended or desired. I therefore argued that, especially given the intellectual and political climate surrounding post-modernism today, we should be more ambitious in developing truly robust accounts of democracy that can inspire people to genuine social change. Such an account is truly needed in today's world, when many increasingly associate progressive thinking with offering only critical visions of the world, without any substantial alternatives being on offer.

**Funding:** This research received no external funding.

**Acknowledgments:** Thank to you Marion Trejo for her support in writing this paper.

**Conflicts of Interest:** The author declares no conflict of interest.

## References

1. Hicks, S.R. *Explaining Postmodernism: Skepticism and Socialism from Rousseau to Foucault*, Expanded Edition; Ockam's Razor Publishing: Beijing, China, 2014.
2. Badiou, A. *Logics of Worlds: Being and Event II*; Alberto, T., Ed.; Continuum: London, UK, 2006.
3. Heidegger, M. *The Question Concerning Technology and Other Essays*; William, L., Ed.; Harper Perennial: New York, NY, USA, 1977.
4. Adorno, T.; Horkheimer, M. *Dialectic of Enlightenment: Philosophical Fragments*; Edund, J., Ed.; Stanford University Press: Palo Alto, CA, USA, 2002.
5. Marcuse, H. *One Dimensional Man*; Beacon Press: Boston, MA, USA, 1964.
6. Marcuse, H. *Eros and Civilization: A Philosophical Inquiry into Freud*; Beacon Press: Boston, MA, USA, 1974.
7. Fromm, E. *Escape from Freedom*; Henry Holt and Company: New York, NY, USA, 1994.
8. Deleuze, G. *Difference and Repetition*; Paul, P., Ed.; Columbia University Press: New York, NY, USA, 1994.
9. Rorty, R. *Philosophy and Social Hope*; Penguin Books: New York, NY, USA, 1999.
10. Lyotard, J.-F. *The Postmodern Condition: A Report on Knowledge*; Geoff, B., Brian, M., Eds.; University of Minnesota Press: Minneapolis, MN, USA, 1984.
11. Marx, K. *Capital: Volume I*; Ben, F., Ed.; Penguin Press: London, UK, 1990.
12. Baudrillard, J. *Simulacra and Simulation*; Sheila, F.G., Ed.; University of Michigan Press: Michigan, MI, USA, 1994.
13. Jameson, F. *Postmodernism, or, the Cultural Logic of Late Capitalism*; Duke University Press: Durham, NC, USA, 1991.
14. Rorty, R. *Philosophy and the Mirror of Nature: Thirtieth Anniversary Edition*; Princeton University Press: Princeton, NJ, USA, 2009.

15. De Saussure, F. *Course in General Linguistics*; Wade, B., Ed.; McGraw-Hill Book Company: New York, NY, USA, 1966.
16. Derrida, J. *Of Grammatology*; Gayatri, S., Ed.; The John Hopkins University Press: Baltimore, MD, USA; London, UK, 1976.
17. Spivak, G. *A Critique of Post-Colonial Reason: Toward a History of the Vanishing Present*; Harvard University Press: Cambridge, MA, USA, 1999.
18. Nietzsche, F. *Basic Writings of Nietzsche*; Walter, K., Ed.; The Modern Library: New York, NY, USA, 2000.
19. Foucault, M. *The Order of Things: An Archaeology of the Human Sciences*; Routledge: New York, NY, USA, 2002.
20. Foucault, M. *The Archaeology of Knowledge*; Routledge: New York, NY, USA, 2002.
21. Foucault, M. *Discipline and Punish: The Birth of the Prison*; Alan, S., Ed.; Vintage Books: New York, NY, USA, 1977.
22. Turkel, G. Michel Foucault: Law, Power, and Knowledge. *J. Law Soc.* **1991**, *12*, 170–193. [CrossRef]
23. Althusser, L. *On Ideology: Second Edition*; Ben, B., Ed.; Verso Books: London, UK, 2008.
24. Foucault, M. The Ethic of Care for the Self as a Practice of Freedom: Interview Conducted by Raul Fornet-Betancourt, Helmut Becker, and Alfredo Gomez-Muller on January 20, 1984. *Philos. Soc. Crit.* **1987**, *12*, 112–131.
25. Baudrillard, J. *The Spirit of Terrorism*; Chris, T., Ed.; Verso Press: London, UK; New York, NY, USA, 2012.
26. Deleuze, G.; Guattari, F. *Anti-Oedipus: Capitalism and Schizophrenia*; Robert, H., Mark, S., Helen, B.L., Eds.; Penguin Books: New York, NY, USA, 1977.
27. Foucault, M. *The History of Sexuality Volume One: An Introduction*; Robert, H., Ed.; Vintage Books: New York, NY, USA, 1980.
28. Foucault, M. *The Birth of Biopolitics: Lectures at the College De France 1978–1979*; Graham, B., Ed.; Picador: New York, NY, USA, 2008.
29. Derrida, J. *The Gift of Death and Literature in Secret*; David, W., Ed.; University of Chicago Press: Chicago, IL, USA, 2008.
30. Derrida, J. *On Cosmopolitanism and Forgiveness*; Routledge: London, UK, 2001.
31. Derrida, J. *Learning to Live Finally: The Last Interview*; Pascale-Anne, B., Michael, N., Eds.; Melville House Publishing: Brooklyn, NY, USA, 2007.
32. Deleuze, G.; Guattari, F. *A Thousand Plateaus: Capitalism and Schizophrenia*; Brian, M., Ed.; University of Minnesota Press: Minneapolis, MN, USA, 1987.
33. Wittgenstein, L. *Philosophical Investigations*; Anscombe, G.E.M., Hacker, P.M.S., Joachim, S., Eds.; Blackwell Publishing: Oxford, UK, 2001.
34. Wittgenstein, L. *Tractatus Logico Philosophicus*; David, p., Brian, M., Eds.; Routeledge Classics: London, UK, 2003.
35. Wittgenstein, L. *On Certainty*; Dennis, p., Anscombe, G.E.M., Eds.; Harper Torchbooks: New York, NY, USA, 1969.
36. Waldron, J. *Liberal Rights: Collected Papers 1981–1991*; Cambridge University Press: Cambridge, UK, 1993.
37. Barry, B. *Culture and Equality: An Egalitarian Critique of Multiculturalism*; Polity: Cambridge, UK, 2000.
38. Foucault, M. *The Foucault Reader*; Paul, R., Ed.; Pantheon Books: New York, NY, USA, 1984.
39. Derrida, J. *The Politics of Friendship*; Verso Books: London, UK, 1997.
40. Zizek, S. *Less than Nothing: Hegel and the Shadow of Dialectical Materialism*; Verso Books: London, UK, 2012.
41. Rorty, R. Solidarity and Objectivity. In *Relativism: Interpretation and Confrontation*; Michael, K., Ed.; University of Notre-Dame Press: Notre Dame, IN, USA, 1989.
42. Chomsky, N. *On Language: Chomsky's Classic Works Language and Responsibility and Reflections on Language*; The New York Press: New York, NY, USA, 2007.
43. Heidegger, M. *What is Called Thinking*; Gray, J.G., Ed.; Harper Torchbooks: New York, NY, USA, 2004.
44. Arendt, H. *The Origins of Totalitarianism*; Harcout: New York, NY, USA, 1955.
45. Rousseau, J.J. *The First and Second Discourses*; Roger, D., Judith, R.M., Eds.; Bedford/St Martins: London, UK, 1969.
46. Chomsky, N. *Language and Politics*; AK Press: Chico, CA, USA, 2004.
47. Zizek, S. Democracy is the Enemy. Available online: http://www.lrb.co.uk/blog/2011/10/28/slavoj-zizek/democracy-is-the-enemy/ (accessed on 28 October 2001).

48. Gairola, R. Interview with Gayatri Spivak. Occupy Education: An Interview with Gayatri Chakravorty. Available online: https://politicsandculture.org/2012/09/25/occupy-education-an-interview-with-gayatri-chakravorty-spivak/ (accessed on 25 September 2012).
49. Hardt, M.; Negri, A. *Empire*; Harvard University Press: Boston, MA, USA, 2000.
50. Hardt, M.; Negri, A. *Commonwealth*; The Belknap Press of Harvard University Press: Boston, MA, USA, 2008.
51. Unger, R. *Politics Volume One: False Necessity*; Verso Press: London, UK, 2004.
52. Tushnet, M. Postmodernism and Democracy. *Am. Lit. Hist.* **1995**, *7*, 582–590. [CrossRef]
53. Tuck, R. *Hobbes: A Very Short Introduction*; Oxford University Press: Oxford, UK, 2002.
54. Burke, E. *Reflections on the Revolution in France*; Oxford University Press: Oxford, UK, 2009.
55. Spivak, G. Can the Subaltern Speak? In *Marxism and the Interpretation of Culture*; Cary, N., Lawrence, G., Eds.; University of Illinois Press: Champaign, IL, USA, 1987.
56. Dworkin, R. Objectivity and Truth: You'd better Believe It. *Philos. Public Aff.* **1996**, *25*, 87–139. [CrossRef]
57. Butler, J. *Notes Towards a Performative Theory of Assembly*; Harvard University Press: Cambridge, MA, USA, 2015.
58. Butler, J. *The Psychic Life of Power: Theories in Subjection*; Stanford University Press: Stanford, CA, USA, 1997.

# 7

# The Natural Philosophy of Experiencing

**Robert Prentner** [1,2]

[1] Department of Cognitive Sciences, University of California, Irvine, CA 92627-5100, USA; robert.prentner@uci.edu

[2] Department of Humanities, Social and Political Science, ETH Zürich, 8091 Zürich, Switzerland

**Abstract:** A new philosophy of nature is urgently needed. The received ontological view, physicalism, is unable to account for experiential phenomena and in particular for consciousness in all its varieties. We shall outline the concept of experiencing which should figure as a new conceptual primitive in natural philosophy. Experiencing refers to a process which comprises the interaction of an agent with its world through action based on phenomenal experience. This process can be viewed under two different aspects. One regards the subjective aspect of experiencing, the other one regards it in terms of physical objects. The first case illustrates the "what-it-is-likeness" of experiencing, the second illustrates how experiencing gets "objectified" in nature. We furthermore wish to delineate our concept of experiencing from the concept of (meta-cognitive) awareness. Scientific theories that explain how awareness comes about in sufficiently organized brains should respect the distinction between experiencing and awareness. We also sketch how experiencing could be related to theoretical biology in terms of information processing by organisms. Experiencing is non-exclusive; it refers to a primitive and a-personal natural process and not to a property possessed only by humans or other persons.

**Keywords:** natural philosophy; subjective experience; process; dual aspects; consciousness; information-theory; theoretical biology; 1st-person and 3rd-person perspectives

## 1. Introduction

Natural philosophy (*philosophia naturalis*) fell into oblivion in the course of the 20th century, because it appeared that the natural sciences—an outgrowth of natural philosophy which originated in the 17th and 18th century—could in principle account for any natural phenomenon. In academic philosophy, the scientific success story led to the broad endorsement of a position known as "physicalism", which could roughly be stated as the ontological claim that all being is or "supervenes on" the physical [1]. To put this definition into the perspective of natural philosophy, we hasten to add that physicalism, as we understand it in this article, implies the thesis that being is describable comprehensively[1] in terms of our best physical theories, and only in their terms.

Physicalism is still the dominating metaphysical view in contemporary analytic philosophy (a little less so on the continent). Yet, a big shortcoming of physicalism is its seeming inability to account for subjective experience as part of the natural world, most notably for consciousness in all its forms. Even though the cognitive and neural sciences made substantial progress in understanding the relation of brain and world, it is still unclear (to some it is even "inconceivable" [3]) how a science of the brain could ever explain the inherently subjective and qualitative nature of consciousness. This is

[1] Up to some phenomena which seem not relevant for subjective experience: This is expressed most clearly in Sean Carroll's idea of a "core theory" [2] that accounts for the vast majority of natural phenomena, including meaning and consciousness, but not quantum gravity or grand unification.

clearly an area where a rejuvenated philosophy of nature that provides conceptual space for subjective experience is urgently needed. One possibility is to embrace "emergentism", understood roughly as the idea that complex arrangements of matter give rise to novel properties in nature [4]. But emergentism, while *prima facie* plausible and conceptually close to physicalism in its "non-reductive" variety [5], has its inherent problems: So far, no universal theory of emergence has been accepted within the scientific or philosophical community. Even less intelligible are accounts of emergence in the field of consciousness studies: Suppose that "emergence" in fact turns out to be a useful concept for science, it will probably not be useful enough to account for a supposed emergence of thought [6,7].

An alternative view regards subjective experience as fundamental, which would mark—in contrast to emergentism—a true rival to physicalism in its conception of nature. But how best to conceive of such a new philosophical world view? In contrast to mainstream physicalists, we propose that nature is only intelligible in terms of processes which comprise subjective experience (qualia) but also decisions and actions. We refer to such processes as *experiencing*, objectified by *any* natural phenomenon. Our concept of experiencing is based on the interaction of an agent with its world. A comprehensive understanding of experiencing necessitates a description of it in terms of dual aspects [8]: one in terms of phenomenality, another one in terms of object-structures. Importantly, we do not equate "agents" and "persons". The notion of "person" is taken to refer to an evolved biological structure. Agents are primitives; persons are historical and biological entities.

To start the analysis, we shall first look at the most difficult problem for physicalists: explaining consciousness. One could make the case that there is *not even conceptual space* to allow for consciousness within physicalism. In Section 2 "Working definitions of consciousness", we briefly outline and discuss two often-heard proposals which try to give a (short but concise) "working definition" of consciousness. Closer inspection reveals that both definitions are each limited to a particular perspective. On the one hand, it is the perspective of a naturalist who looks at biological systems "from the outside"; on the other hand, it is the perspective of an introspectionist who only looks at the system "from the inside". Both are faced with difficulties when urged to account for consciousness as natural property. Any notion of consciousness which is (i) adequate to its phenomenology and (ii) conceives of it as referring to a natural phenomenon should be able to consistently relate a subjective 1st-person and an objective 3rd-person perspective without reducing one to the other. We call this the "consistency requirement" for studying consciousness, and we propose that the resolution of the distinction "subjective-objective" shall be found on a higher, ontological level.

In Section 3 "Experiencing", we thus introduce a conceptual stance which regards the process of experiencing as primitive[2]. It derives from the simple idea that an agent (a primitive, a-personal entity) perceives its environment, autonomously makes decisions and acts. An agent's environment could be regarded as entity that carries the disposition to cause (qualitative) experiences in the agent, whereas the agent could be regarded as entity that is responding appropriately. The subjective perspective of the agent is assumed to be the dual of a theorist's description of the whole process. "Awareness", referring to a (meta-cognitive) biological phenomenon, could then be understood as complexification of the process of experiencing. A description of this complexification should explain the transition from a-personal embodied agents to evolved persons, and it should satisfy the consistency requirement. Once we have accepted the conceptual innovations proposed in this section, there exists a chance to make substantial progress on the problem of consciousness. If we stick with physicalism, this will likely not be the case.

As a concrete example, we introduce and discuss the prospects of the notion "meaningful information" (in the *phenomenal* sense of meaning) in biological systems and its relation to experience and awareness in Section 4 "The biology of meaning". We shall first review some empirical work

---

2 We are not the first to propose this. Similar ideas could be found, for example, in the works of Charles S. Peirce [9], William James [10] or Alfred North Whitehead [11].

that might justify the belief in the ubiquity of experiencing in biology, which is closely related to an understanding of "information", not as purely syntactic but as inherently meaningful (semantic) concept. This will eventually lead to a tentative discussion of awareness, understood as biological phenomenon based on experiencing. Our model bears some formal similarities to established approaches in theoretical biology; however, the concepts that underlie it are quite different.

## 2. Working Definitions of Consciousness

### 2.1. *Consciousness = Whatever-Is-Lost in Dreamless Sleep*

"Everybody knows what consciousness is: it is what vanishes every night when we fall into a dreamless sleep and reappears when we wake up or when we dream" [12] (p. 216). Does this mean that consciousness is an object that could be lost just as one could lose his car keys? Could we perhaps locate it somewhere in the brain? Does it "consist of [other things, such as] inner, qualitative, subjective states and processes of sentience or awareness" as John Searle [13] (p. 559; our italics) believes? Is it of a certain size or at least a concrete "going-on" that is located in space and time [14] (p. 3)?

These and similar descriptions ground most research that is done in consciousness studies today. Phenomenologically, this seems to miss an important point. This can be illustrated using a metaphor that likens consciousness to the process of waking up in the morning. After a deep and peaceful slumber, our metaphor's protagonist awakes in the morning when the first rays of sunlight are tickling his eyes. While he senses the smell of coffee from the kitchen, the thought of his overdue tax filing is forming in his mind and enters his consciousness together with a stream of perceptual experiences: the visual scenery of his bedroom, the sounds that are coming from the streets through the window, and a strong itching in his left foot. Is it reasonable to assume that something emerged here? Clearly, the answer is "yes": Certain objects formed in the protagonist's conscious mind when he woke up, but it is not consciousness that (re-)emerges, nor is it "phenomenal experience" or its "what-it-is-likeness".

This could further be illustrated by taking a phenomenologist's perspective: We never experience a world without being consciousness, all there is for us is the world as it is "given to consciousness". It would be even more adequate to say that as soon as we fall asleep the (experienced) world is what "vanishes overnight and reappears when we wake up or when we dream"—not consciousness. The guiding intuition behind this is that we should not think of consciousness as a property of some (natural) object, but (perceived or intentional) objects as emerging within consciousness. Phenomenologists have argued for this on philosophical grounds at least since Edmund Husserl has criticized the "natural attitude" [15]. (Cf. [16,17] for a similar point in a contemporary setting). We need to let go of the intuition that consciousness corresponds to a property of physical objects: Being conscious is unlike having mass and position. Consciousness is what lets us see objects in space and what lets us feel their masses.

But why is it so natural to suppose that consciousness is just like any other (physical or biological) property of an organism, something which might be lost or regained? "Consciousness = whatever-is-lost in dreamless asleep" is a useful circumscription, when we read it the following way: Given an outside perspective on a particular organism, part of its (overt and neuronal) behavior is such that it vanishes when the organism falls into a dreamless sleep and reappears again when it wakes up or when it dreams. But this does not directly inform us about phenomenality—how it feels like for the organism to have an experience. It is a description of how the organism would appear to an external observer. However, we must not confuse this external perspective with the subjective experience of the organism itself.

### 2.2. *Consciousness = Having Qualia*

Another competitor for a working definition of consciousness stems from the fact that being conscious implies that "it-is-something-like" [18] to have a particular experience. It is sometimes heard that consciousness is tantamount to having certain things, namely qualia[3], where, more precisely, qualia are understood as intrinsic, non-representational and unstructured properties of experience; or for short: "consciousness = having qualia".

It therefore comes as no surprise that with respect to a 1st-person perspective this definition is more adequate. Yet, it seems that this definition does not help much when trying to relate consciousness to the (neuronal or manifest) behavior of an organism just because the definition is only about the intrinsic perspective of a subject. Whereas the first definition, "consciousness = whatever-is-lost in dreamless sleep", misrepresents the subjective perspective of an organism, the definition "consciousness = having qualia" seems to imply that consciousness is an inaccessible, ineffable and purely internal thing. It precludes any chance of relating it consistently with a scientific account of the world (even if consciousness figures as primitive concept in our account of it).

This finds expression in the skeptical claim that, as involved as it might get, no explanation could ever make it plausible why physical dynamics should be accompanied by phenomenology at all, instead of "going-on in the dark". It seems to imply a form of dualism, which is mirrored in conceiving of a purely internal 1st-person perspective and a purely external 3rd-person perspective. Some thinkers have hoped this would give rise to two corresponding sets of "data" [22]. Accordingly, one would be able to arrive at a science of consciousness by demanding consistency between these two kinds of data and derive "bridge laws" between them. So far, this dualist proposal has not been fruitful, though, and it is doubtful whether the notion of "1st-person data" is at all coherent. Data, by definition, belong to the domain of recordings. They result from reports or measurements, they are inherently "post-subjective", or, as one might wish to say: "they only exist in the world of objects". 1st-person data are thus more like the chimera than like pointer readings of measuring devices for subjectivity.

### 2.3. *Consistency between Perspectives*

Neither "consciousness = whatever-is-lost in dreamless sleep" nor "consciousness = having qualia" is able to express an adequate concept for the phenomenon of consciousness as natural property. The former because it misses a crucial property of experience: To any conscious being, consciousness means its world; to any outside observer, consciousness is invisible and all she could see are correlated brain states or the conscious being's behavior; the latter if it is taken to imply an ineffable, purely internal notion of experience.

This indicates a fundamental conceptual asymmetry. Given one perspective, consciousness is all there is, and the experienced world with all its objects emerges within consciousness. Given the other perspective, all there is are atoms in the void; no consciousness to be seen anywhere, neither in our heads nor behind curtains, but only neurons firing and ions moving. An important constraint for a theory of consciousness then is that the first story—call it "the phenomenal story"—is consistent with the second—"the physical story". We call this the consistency requirement which states that two descriptions of the very same process need to be consistent with each other.

To respect the consistency requirement, it is logically not necessary that consciousness is identical to a certain physical structure (e.g., the brain) or is caused by it. In other words, it is not the case that only forms of physicalism could guarantee such a consistency. The challenge for many contemporary approaches in consciousness studies is therefore not (only) to overcome skepticist arguments regarding

---

[3] For example, Hameroff & Penrose [19] (p. 40) in a review of their Orch-OR theory of consciousness state that "phenomenal conscious awareness, experience, or subjective feelings [are] composed of what philosophers call 'qualia'". To be fair, the authors arguably do not explicitly state that consciousness is a thing-like substance, composed of elementary qualia. However, they could easily be seen to imply exactly this. In another example, Leopold Stubenberg wrote a book centering around the notion of "consciousness as the having of qualia". [20] Importantly, he notes that both the notions "having" and "qualia" need to be qualified due the problematic relation between qualia and their bearers. Stubenberg finally arrives at a "bundle theory" of experience that is very dissimilar from the (ordinary-language) concept of "thing-ness". Similarly, Galen Strawson argues for "selves", the subjects of experiences, to be "things" but later qualifies this to be understood in a "thin" way [21], actually more in line with Buddhist teachings of the no-self and primarily referring to an a-personal phenomenon.

the bridging of an "explanatory gap" [23] but also to state the mind-matter relation in a way which satisfies the consistency requirement. But there are possibilities other than stating subject-object identity to ensure consistency. Recall, for example, the assumption of "functional coherence" proposed by David Chalmers [3]. This assumption restricts the possible structure of theories of consciousness to those theories where "awareness" (taken as an access-related psychological property, cf. [24] is systemically linked to phenomenology without being identical to it. In contrast to the notion of functional coherence, however, we propose that consistency should be understood as perspectival and dynamical. If our concepts only referred exclusively to the "intrinsic" or "extrinsic" properties that things have, then it would be hard to see how statements about experiences could be related to statements about physical structures without making a Cartesianist assumption (that is, without assuming that consciousness resembles a "thing-like" substance that "is contained" in a body). A different strategy would think of consciousness as pertaining to the interaction between an organism and its environment (hence consistency is dynamical), and that a comprehensive description would correlate different aspects of these interaction (hence consistency is perspectival), without reducing one to the other. In many cases it is futile to approach a resolution of a conceptual distinction (such as "subject-object" or "mind-body") at the same descriptive level. Rather, one could only resolve it on a more fundamental descriptive level. Such is what we wish to propose in Section 3 "Experiencing", where we introduce the concept of experiencing, which eventually plays the role of establishing consistency on a fundamental level.

## 3. Experiencing

### *3.1. Experiencing as Fundamental and A-Personal Process*

It is sometimes heard (e.g., by Eric Kandel [25]) that the mind will be to the sciences of the 21st century what the gene was to the sciences of the 20th. We believe this to be an accurate prediction, however, one that will only turn out to be true, once the philosophical image of nature is revised such that it includes the concept of *experiencing as primitive.*

We would also like to distinguish two senses in which the notion of "consciousness" is used in the literature: On the one hand it refers to the notion of "subjective experience", which we take to be an irreducible part of experiencing; on the other hand, it refers to a particular biological phenomenon which we henceforth denote as "awareness" to distinguish it from pure experiencing (we simply use the term "awareness", which is sometimes also referred to as meta-cognitive form of consciousness). In addition, we postulate that *experiencing is a-personal,* whereas awareness is intimately related to the concept of a "person". Awareness should be explained on the basis of the more fundamental notion of experiencing.

Experiencing has a subjective aspect and is assumed to manifest itself in any natural phenomenon, which we could study in the physical, chemical and biological sciences. Experiencing gets "objectified in nature", in the terminology of Arthur Schopenhauer [26], or it is "embodied" in a slightly more contemporary façon de parler. While awareness denotes a species-specific (and hence evolutionary constrained), 1st-personal phenomenon, experiencing denotes a fundamental process in nature and thus a primitive concept for a renewed philosophy of nature, similar as "mass" or "extension" were primitive concepts in the mechanistic philosophy of René Descartes [27]. We could circumscribe the concept of experiencing as follows:

> *Experiencing refers to a* structured process of interaction *of an agent with its world. Experiencing can be studied under different* aspects. *One of these pertains to the* subjective *perspective of the agent, which is irreducibly* phenomenal *for that (and only for that) particular agent; the phenomenality of experiencing couldn't thus be accessed by an external observer. However,* experiencing is also structured. *This makes it possible to precisely describe this structure and trace experiencing empirically. This leads to a second perspective which corresponds to the* physical aspect *of experiencing.*

The onto-epistemic thesis says that experiencing manifests itself in any natural phenomenon. Given this, experiencing could be scientifically studied. The thesis does not say that subjectivity or consciousness reside "within" matter or that physical objects "ground", "produce" or "give rise" to experience. For the onto-epistemic thesis to be substantial, though, it should be the case that whenever we look closely enough at nature, we find bits and pieces that hint at experiencing.

### 3.2. A Post-Kantian Model

It seems helpful to illustrate the concept of experiencing using a model inspired by Immanuel Kant's transcendental philosophy put forward in his *Critique of Pure Reason* [28]. (But we shall also point out some necessary adjustments that need to be made to this framework in our opinion). There, mind is "affected" by a "thing-in-itself", and the raw sensory material is structured according to space-time and categories such as causation[4]. Using a schematic representation this could be depicted as:

$$W \overset{p}{\rightarrow} X, \tag{1}$$

where a "world" $W$ stands for Kant's (hypothetical) thing-in-itself that affects a receptive mind in the act of "perception" $p$ which, in turn, sculpts experience $X$. It is crucial to note that the only things one could attend to are the contents of $X$. Neither the "world" as such nor the mind's conceptual faculty that "sees through" the sensory apparatus is consciously given to it. That is why the world must first and foremost be regarded as a hypothetical entity that triggers perception. This should not be confused with the "world" in a physicalist's sense, i.e., with the totality of material systems, but could simply be taken as everything that has the disposition to cause changes in $X$.

While the Kantian analogy serves an illustrative purpose, there are many differences between Kant's transcendental philosophy and our proposed natural philosophy. First, we explicitly reject any notion of a world-mind dualism on our account. Our model comprises a "world" of dispositions to cause (changes in) the experiential content of a receptive "mind". "World" and "mind" do not, however, refer to two distinct entities of our ontology but merely to different conceptual abstractions (cf. the notion of a "conceivable world" by Ivan Havel [30]). Second, there are cognitive connotations when discussing "conceptual schemes" or "categories", eventually turning into a kind of neuro-Kantianism, which we reject. Experiencing is taken to refer to any natural process, rather than to processes ascribable to only humans or other persons. Third and perhaps most importantly, the mind-world relationship is sometimes conceived of as merely passive "stimulus-matching" relationship. We approach it instead in terms of active participation or interaction. In other words, instead of a (passive) mind-world model, we need to consider the *agent-environment interaction*,

$$W \underset{p}{\overset{a}{\leftrightarrows}} X, \tag{2}$$

which is reminiscent of the sensory-motor (perception-action) cycle known to biologists [31,32] and philosophers (e.g., John Dewey [33]). In particular, from an empirical point of view, the feedback component of such a model is crucial because it permits us to experimentally engage with the agent: Without having the possibility of getting responses from the agent there would in principle be no way to test any claims pertaining to the structure of experiencing, and researchers would need to exclusively rely on philosophically motivated *a priori* arguments. Even though the phenomenality of an agent's

---

4 To be a little more precise, Kant explicitly distinguishes between "forms of intuition" (=space and time) and genuine "mental" categories such as causation, substance or unity. For the sake of this article, however, we shall not ponder deeply on this distinction. In the course of 19th and 20th century philosophy, the Kantian a-priori has been subject to various interpretations and modifications, see for example the symbolic constructivism of Ernst Cassirer [29]. We do not wish to engage in the debate how to best conceive of the a-priori in this article.

perceptions is in principle inaccessible from an external perspective, a stimulus-response architecture of the kind expressed in Equation (2) in principle allows us to derive and test predictions relative to the dynamics of the agent-environment system, unlike a "negative theology of experience". This also marks a methodological advance compared to physicalist approaches toward the mind, where the mental is often defined solely in terms of the "negative" (the so-called *"via negativa"* approach to physicalism; cf. [34,35]). While our model seems primarily related to perceptual processes, any general account also needs to say something about "internal" mental phenomena, such as abstract thoughts, emotions or moods. The following is preliminary (self-consistency and empirical adequacy need still to be worked out further), but it shows how the model seems in principle able to accommodate such phenomena as well. In general, there exist two possible approaches toward internal mental phenomena. The first reduces them to (implicit or explicit) representations of the workings of the physical body. Such a strategy is the default approach in physicalism, and largely faces the same problems as physicalist accounts of perception. Another strategy would acknowledge the possibility of endogenous "self-interactions" of agents. A description of this process is projected onto an "external world" relative to the agent. (Recall that "world" should not be understood in terms of a *physical* environment, but rather in the sense of a totality of dispositions to cause experience.) The consistency requirement furthermore demands this projection to be consistent with a description in terms of the agent's subjective experience.

To make the model more powerful, we consider in addition some "internal processing" or "decision-mechanism" that connects the agent's experiences to the agent's actions. This can be motivated on empirical grounds too. Decision mechanisms are now found to be ubiquitous in biological systems (see also Section 4 "The biology of meaning"). Such a model has been proposed recently in terms of a very general mathematical structure by [36],

$$W \underset{p}{\overset{a}{\leftrightarrows}} \begin{pmatrix} G \\ \uparrow d \\ X \end{pmatrix}, \tag{3}$$

which consists of perception-, decision-, and action-Kernels p, d and a that loop through the world $W$, the experiential content of an agent $X$, and the group of possible actions $G$ available to that agent[5]. Such an account aims at understanding what experiencing *does*, not what it is; it is a model of experiencing and not a theory about its essence.

In the next section we discuss how the new philosophy of nature could be related to recent empirical studies. We argue that (i) the biological dynamics should be re-conceived in terms of *information* theory. This is largely an epistemic point, based on well-established scientific work[6]. It could be interpreted along the lines that it merely "appears as if" a system were processing information meaningfully, but one might alternatively conclude that (ii) it refers to an embodied process of experiencing. One could justify this second interpretation by appealing to the necessity to account for jointly irreducible perspectives in order to exhaustively describe biological phenomena. In other words, the physical dynamics of biological systems could be thought to *objectify* experiencing in the physical world. One could relate this (iii) to the study of *awareness* as biological phenomenon which arises from a complexification of experiencing. While this would explain, why it is "something-like"

5 Expressed mathematically, $\boldsymbol{W}, \boldsymbol{X}$, and $\boldsymbol{G}$ each represent measurable spaces, i.e., a set $\boldsymbol{Y}$ equipped with a sigma algebra $\boldsymbol{Y}$; and the "pda-loop" represents the succession of Markovian Kernels $\boldsymbol{p}$, $\boldsymbol{d}$, and $\boldsymbol{a}$ which mediate between these spaces such that $z$: $\boldsymbol{Y_j} \times \boldsymbol{Y_k} \rightarrow [0, 1]$. Intuitively, this means that the Markovian Kernel $\boldsymbol{z}$ assigns to any combination of an "element" $\boldsymbol{j} \in \boldsymbol{Y_j}$ and an "event" $\boldsymbol{k} \in \boldsymbol{Y_k}$ some probability between 0 and 1. Finally, there exists an integer n that counts the number of pda-loops executed by the agent.

6 There is a well-known difficulty in exhaustively defining the concept of "information" when used other than in the syntactical (Shannon) sense. Any appeal to "information" is therefore provisional. However, we note that "information" does not refer to an ontological primitive in our philosophy. It thus resembles notions such as "cause", "probability" or "purpose" which all need further conceptual clarification in a renewed philosophy of nature (cf. also the discussion in Section 4.2).

to be conscious (because experiencing has an irreducibly phenomenal aspect), two important and non-trivial constraints are that any description of this complexification should make it intelligible why it results in a 1st-person perspective and that it satisfies the *consistency requirement* for the study of consciousness introduced in Section 2.3. In contrast to the "hard problem", this line of inquiry seems promising and is rooted in a philosophy of nature that takes experiencing as primitive.

## 4. The Biology of Meaning

### 4.1. "Meaning" and Information

The principles governing biological systems are increasingly studied from the angle of information theory [37–39], and it is often claimed that the study of energy transfer through these systems should be re-conceived in the language of information theory in order to arrive at a more comprehensive understanding of biological processes. Consistent with this, one could regard biological systems as units that process information acquired via sensory organs to adjust their behavior.

We also know from genetic, cellular and systems-level analyses that the behavior of biological systems is not only dependent on the incoming (sensory) information but, as least as much, on the organization and the internal processing (sometimes also referred to as "internal decision mechanisms") embodied in the organism, for example, in gene regulatory networks or predictive neuronal mechanisms [40–43].

This is not premised on any ontological account of "information," but it only requires acceptance of the claim that certain systems are best described in terms of information-processing units and could be regarded as quasi-intentional or quasi-perceptual. In biology, this has been recently argued for a large class of systems (e.g., [44,45]); in philosophy, similar claims were put forward as "mind-life continuity thesis" based on sensory-motor coupling (for example [46]). This perspective necessitates understanding of how biological systems manage information flows and integrate exteroceptive signals with bodily sensations (interoception), anticipations about the future (predictions) and past experiences (memories). The information processed by a biological system could then be regarded as "meaningful" in the sense that it underlies behavior which limits entropic tendencies or leads to various adaptive changes. Accordingly, organisms embedded in an environment could be conceived of in terms of systems that use information that "stands for" and thus "refers to" external entities or internal processes in order to guide adaptive behavior.

One particular approach that has been postulated to analyze information processing in (neuro-) biological systems is "integrated information theory" (IIT: [12,47]), originally conceived as "measure of consciousness" but recently applied to information processing in biological systems more generally [48]. The main idea behind using IIT to analyze information flows in biological systems is to quantify how much an element or a set of elements within the system constrain the system's past and future states. The exact mathematical form of how this should best be measured has changed over the course of publications, but it crucially involves calculating differences between state repertoires, e.g., KL-divergences or the "earth mover's distance" (for details we refer the reader to [47]). This distance measure is evaluated for the total system and a "minimum information partition", and thus quantifies the amount of information in the system "as whole" as compared to the sum of its parts. Importantly, while one might be skeptical regarding the claim that IIT resembles a modern-day version of panpsychism [49,50] or whether its "central identity" claim does not in fact propose a reductionist account of consciousness "through the backdoor", its concepts might still be useful to study the properties of information-processing networks, in particular, how "meaningfulness" could be encoded by the way how an organism's current state constrains its (past and future) evolution, mirroring Bateson's dictum that "information is a difference that makes a difference" (cf. [51]). In other words, IIT could be thought of as pertaining to the physical aspect of a meaningful process objectified in biological networks.

*4.2. Meaning and Perspective*

The previous subsection argued that sufficiently complex biological systems could be understood in terms of entities that process information "meaningfully". But are we justified to conclude that such processing really is meaningful (from the system's perspective), rather than merely "appearing as if" it were meaningful (from a theorist's perspective)? "Meaning", as it was used in the last paragraph, refers primarily to our 3rd-person perspective as theorists or observers, and it is unclear how this is related to any notion of subjectivity at all.

Let us repeat the discussion so far. By interacting appropriately with the world, we recorded some physical dynamics which looks as if they were meaningful. We could interpret this along the lines that we have interacted with a complex mechanism that "causes our perceptions" and "informed our minds" accordingly. Another, perhaps more natural, interpretation would be that we have interacted with something that in fact is (phenomenally) meaningful and the physical dynamics we have recorded reflected this. The benefit of this position—in addition to being metaphysically more parsimonious, that is, without postulating a "jump" from the physical to the subjective at some place—is that it explains why it can only look "as if" (because the physical dynamics merely provides an extrinsic perspective on the process) and that it explains the seeming increase of "mental-looking properties" emerging within the hierarchy of natural phenomena (because of the complexification that characterizes the transition from the physical to the biological). This is different from saying that there is meaning "inside" the organism, a claim which strikes us as dualist.

One way of justifying (ii) is rooted in the rejection of the claim that a mechanistic model could comprehensively account for biological phenomena, a claim which unfortunately seems to be the mainstream opinion of current physicalism. An argument against a mechanistic philosophy of nature was famously laid out in Kant's *Critique of the Power of Judgement* [52]; for a modern appreciation of the Kantian Critique in developmental and molecular biology see, e.g., [53]. The argument is usually based on the inability of theoretical frameworks to explain prototypical examples of biological mechanisms such as the seemingly intentional behavior during pattern formation or embryogenesis. We do not wish to enter the specific debates here. Instead, we wish to present some more principled reasons to doubt the claim that mechanistic descriptions are sufficient to exhaustively describe biological phenomena. This is, on purpose, *not* an empirical claim but relates to some concepts any philosophy of nature needs to be clear about:

1. Scientific concepts usually have a long history, and to a philosopher it seems puzzling that their genesis is sometimes overlooked in their conceptual analysis. Take the concept of entropy that is now very well known in the physical sciences (though often confusedly employed). Whereas many believe that entropy refers to an objective property of thermodynamic systems (but see for example E.T. Jaynes [54] who argued that entropy is an "anthropomorphic concept"), the inventor of the term "entropy", Rudolf Clausius, purposely conceived it to refer to a natural process that derives from our everyday experiences in and outside the laboratory. ("Entropy" derives from the Greek word εν-τϱοπη meaning "content of transformation". [55]) It could even be argued that all scientific concepts such as "energy", "force" or "field" have their genesis in a multitude of subjective experiences that led to an inter-subjectively true description of the world (cf. [56]). This suggests that, in fact, apparently objective descriptions are not necessarily about the "true states of the world out there" but result from a generalization of concrete experiences.
2. One of these concepts, the concept of *probability*, is still in need of clarification. Objectivists conceive of probability as (ignorance about) a property of the system under study and compete with subjectivists that tie probability to the degree of belief of an observer (see, e.g., the overviews in [57,58]). Objectivists would need to show that their concept of probabilities is really free from any reference to (subjective) belief; subjectivists would need to demonstrate the explanatory benefit of their position. Settling this dispute is beyond the present state of play in logic. Until it

is settled, however, we need to be careful when interpreting theoretical frameworks that explain a system's behavior primarily in terms of probability.

3. Biological systems (such as, but not limited to, the brain) are often described as probabilistic systems under thermodynamic constraints. Generalizations about the workings of such systems are subject to the caveats that pertain to thermodynamics and probabilities. In particular, this pertains to any explanation in biology cast in terms of information-theory. If it is the case that the concept of probability *logically necessitates* a subjectivist approach, both observational *and* theoretical statements must not be regarded as being about some "objective truth out there". It then follows that generalized biological theories too must not lightheartedly be regarded as being "objective" (in the same sense), and a description purely in terms of physical concepts would not exhaustively describe a system's behavior.

The above indicates that some of the concepts we employ in scientific theorizing might indicate an irreducibly subjective (and as a corollary: phenomenal) ontological counterpart, in particular the concept of probability as applied to systems dealing with uncertainty. This also pertains to other "more biological" concepts such as "function" or "purpose", which hinge on the status of more primitive concepts such as causation, probability or chance. This therefore defines another area where conceptual work in philosophy is relevant for the scientific enterprise. A new philosophy of nature would probably lead to very different conceptions than those of physicalism.

We can summarize this subsection by saying that a minimal account of "phenomenal meaning" seems to be necessary for understanding biological phenomena expressed in the language of information-theory. We henceforth shall say that "information is meaningful" to a particular organism, noting that we thereby do not claim that organisms resemble "little persons". The notion "information is meaningful" arises naturally from regarding experiencing as primitive concept in our ontology, together with the onto-epistemic thesis that experiencing gets objectified in nature. We could also justify this by pointing to a deficiency of the "received view" of physicalism, according to which purely mechanical (literally meaningless) descriptions supposedly afford exhaustive explanations of biological phenomena—a claim which should be rejected eventually.

### 4.3. *Meaning and Awareness*

How could this lead to a model of awareness? When discussing a potential "referential nucleus" for consciousness studies, [59] noted that, while the presence of perception-action cycles might indicate the presence of experience, the ascription of awareness to such systems might nevertheless be precluded by an apparent lack of reportable 1st-personal content. Thus, any empirically accessible conception of awareness should involve such contents. This seems consistent with ideas coming under the heading of "global workspace" theory [24] where awareness supposedly derives from accessibility of neuronally encoded information, which ultimately leads to subjective reports. This framework has recently been developed into a neuro-computational direction [60]. Some might doubt, however, that the notion of computation is more than a convenient fiction by which one represents the system's dynamics (from a scientist's 3rd-person perspective), rather than referring to the idea that certain complex biological systems actually do take a 1st-person perspective on their environment. In other words, it does not become intelligible how the consistency requirement as sketched in Section 2.3 would hold for such an explanation.

The things that organisms perceive are not detached Cartesian ideas but the inferred objects and structures that constitute the organism's *experienced world*. A good example that lets one see the difference between descriptions of mere behavior and awareness is provided by a discussion of "time consciousness". Many organisms are able to vary their action according to temporal cues they get from their environment. Yet, this does not imply that they represent time from a 1st personal perspective; rather their action is simply coded to an external periodic pattern (expressed, e.g., in circadian rhythms [61]). While the latter is sometimes understood in terms of an intricate mechanism pertaining to biological homeostasis, this is different from the "time consciousness" of a personal subject, which (phenomenally) experiences an enduring "now". The canonical phenomenological discussion of this is due to Edmund Husserl [62]: Awareness is structured according to temporal patterns (according to Husserl these are the "temporal moments" of "retention", "primal impression" and "protention"), which lets the organism see distinguishable objects that appear in consciousness. Similarly, this might hold for the representation of space in terms of spatial patterns.

How could a merely computational mechanism account for this difference? Our concept of experiencing comes to help. While we do acknowledge the role of computational mechanisms in generating reportable (or otherwise accessible) content, we add that the information thereby processed is already meaningful. Making it available to the system could make intelligible how biological systems become aware by computing over "meaningful information" and thus create the rich phenomenal structure such as the one coming under the header of "time consciousness".

The important meta-theoretical constraints are (i) that such reportable content could be identified, in some non-trivial sense, with 1st-personal descriptions and (ii) these descriptions are consistent with the overall biological dynamics. (We have suggested earlier that the consistency requirement should be taken as referring to the interaction of an organism with its environment and not merely to the functional organization of its nervous system.) At this point, it is good to remind ourselves that we have defined experiencing itself to be subject to two different and dual descriptions – a phenomenal one and a physical one. We have thus good reason to assume that the problem of awareness might be resolvable when accepting the conceptual innovations proposed in this article.

## 5. Discussion

A novel philosophy of nature should overcome the impasse of our current naturalist world view. In physicalism, this is the inability to account for subjective experience, in particular consciousness in all its forms, as natural property of the world. We therefore put our focus on this question and pointed at novel concepts that should be incorporated into natural philosophy. Unsatisfied with "emergentist" solutions to the problem of consciousness, we proposed that experience should figure as primitive concept in the theory.

The conceptual inadequacy to account for consciousness in physicalist terms can readily be seen when looking at two widespread "working definitions" of consciousness that are frequently found throughout the literature. After briefly stating them in Section 2 "Working definitions of consciousness", we noted that both seem to reduce the phenomenon of consciousness to either its physical or its subjective aspect. In contrast to this, we have put forward a "consistency requirement" which demands that any account of consciousness as natural property should treat it as perspectival entity that defies mutual reduction. Such consistency will likely be given by appealing to a more fundamental ontological primitive.

We then elaborated on a philosophical alternative to physicalism in Section 3 "Experiencing", according to which "experiencing" refers to the structured process of interaction of an agent with its world. Experiencing refers to an a-personal process in nature and can be studied under different aspects. One of these aspects pertains to the subjective perspective of the agent, which is irreducibly phenomenal for that (and only for that) particular agent. A second perspective on this process corresponds to the physical (or "objective") aspect of experiencing. Furthermore, experiencing is assumed to be an a-personal phenomenon, marking a clear distinction between experiencing and any notion of awareness. The latter should then be understood to "arise" from a hierarchy of objectivations of experiencing in sufficiently complex organisms, making intelligible how a 1st-personal perspective arises from experiencing. The consistency requirement serves as constraint on such theories.

This is the broad outline. Yet, there are many issues which still need to be addressed in more detail, for example, how the mechanism of complexification of experiencing works or how experiencing is related to biology more generally. We have discussed a model in Section 4 "The biology of meaning", which illustrates how the process of experiencing could be regarded as being objectified in a biological setting. Information processing in biological systems was argued to be meaningful.

However, the biological system does not correspond to a "person" in any substantial sense of the word. The model is formally consistent with recent trends in theoretical biology, for example, Friston's cognitive-biological approach [63], which could aptly be named "the physics of belief", since the mathematical description of the dynamical system appears to be a functional on "beliefs" (a "Lagrangian" according to [64], that is, a functional on probabilities derivable from the internal states of a network). This type of "belief" is a-personal. Furthermore, our approach is not about specific "causal powers" [13] of the brain but about natural tendencies of self-organizing biological systems *tout court* and lends itself to a very different interpretation, more in line with naturalized phenomenology and models of dynamical agent-environment couplings. Of course, the brain has an important role to play in the process of generating awareness, but it is not the role of "magically" creating phenomenology. Rather, the brain seems to afford a particularly efficient way of systematically correlating and processing a vast amount of (sensory and endogenous) inputs that result in suitable (behavioral) output. The brain, on our view, should be thought of as processing information that is literally meaningful to the organism by regulating an organism's self-sustaining and adaptive behavior.

The transition from simple information-processing to complex representation furthermore indicates how personalist human psychology might be related to an a-personal precursor phenomenon embodied in biological systems. Personalist psychology could be regarded as a scaled-up and evolutionarily constrained result of natural biological processes. Our approach has much in common with the cell-theory of life: The minds of complex (psychological) agents arise from the minds of simpler (biological) agents. However, the mind is not emergent, it is fundamental and objectifies itself in nature.

The model promises to be productive for the scientific project. We have illustrated this along the (seemingly hopeless) problem of consciousness. If true, is this enough reason to abandon physicalism? One could be skeptical. Nothing could directly verify (or falsify) physicalism, as long as physicalism has the last say on what does or does not count as substantial anomaly to the framework. The best one could do is show how certain assumptions eventually lead to self-contradicting consequences. The reason to reject physicalism (or any other philosophical view) is usually not to be found in an *experimentum crucis* but derives from its inability or inadequacy to account for the experiences we make inside and outside of our laboratories. It is thus the task of natural philosophy to make experience intelligible again.

**Funding:** This research was funded by the Swiss National Science Foundation, grant P2EZP1_175109.

**Acknowledgments:** The author thanks present and past colleagues for discussions related to this article, two anonymous referees for insightful comments, and UC Irvine and ETH Zürich for institutional support.

**Conflicts of Interest:** The author declares no conflict of interest. The funding sponsor had no role in the design of the study, the writing of the manuscript, or the decision to publish the results.

## References

1. Stoljar, D. *Physicalism*; Routledge: New York, NY, USA, 2010.
2. Carroll, S. *The Big Picture. On the Origins of Life, Meaning, and the Universe Itself*; Dutton: New York, NY, USA, 2016.
3. Chalmers, D.J. The Conscious Mind. In *Search of a Fundamental Theory*; Oxford University Press: Oxford, UK, 1996.
4. Stephan, A. Emergentism, irreducibility, and downward causation. *Grazer Philos. Stud.* **2002**, *65*, 77–93.
5. Crane, T. The significance of emergence. In *Physicalism and Its Discontents*; Loewer, B., Gillett, G., Eds.; Cambridge University Press: Cambridge, UK, 2007; pp. 207–224.
6. Seager, W. *Natural Fabrications: Science, Emergence and Consciousness*; Springer: New York, NY, USA, 2012.
7. Prentner, R. Chemistry, context and the objects of thought. *Found. Chem.* **2017**, *19*, 29–41. [CrossRef]
8. Atmanspacher, H. 20th Century Varieties of Dual-Aspect Thinking. *Mind Matter* **2014**, *12*, 245–288.
9. Peirce, C.S. *Collected Papers of Charles Sanders Peirce*; Hartshorne, C., Weiss, P., Eds.; Harvard University Press: Cambridge, MA, USA, 1931–1935; Volumes 1–6.

10. James, W. *The Works of William James: Essays in Radical Empiricism*; Harvard University Press: Cambridge, MA, USA, 1976.
11. Whitehead, A.N. *Process and Reality*; Corrected Edition; Griffin, D.R., Sherburne, D.W., Eds.; Free Press: New York, NY, USA, 1978.
12. Tononi, G. Consciousness as Integrated Information: A Provisional Manifesto. *Biol. Bull.* **2008**, *215*, 216–242. [CrossRef] [PubMed]
13. Searle, J.R. Consciousness. *Annu. Rev. Neurosci.* **2000**, *23*, 557–578. [CrossRef] [PubMed]
14. Strawson, G. Realistic monism: Why physicalism entails panpsychism. *J. Conscious. Stud.* **2006**, *13*, 3–31.
15. Husserl, E. *Logical Investigations*; Routledge: London, UK, 2001.
16. Varela, F. A science of consciousness as if experience mattered. In *Toward a Science of Consciousness II: The Second Tucson Debates*; Hameroff, S., Kaszniak, A.W., Scott, A., Eds.; MIT Press: Cambridge, MA, USA, 1998; pp. 31–44.
17. Bitbol, M. Science as if situation mattered. *Phenomenol. Cogn. Sci.* **2002**, *1*, 181–224. [CrossRef]
18. Nagel, T. What is it like to be a bat? *Philos. Rev.* **1974**, *83*, 435–450. [CrossRef]
19. Hameroff, S.; Penrose, R. Consciousness in the universe: A review of the "Orch OR" theory. *Phys. Life Rev.* **2014**, *11*, 39–78. [CrossRef] [PubMed]
20. Stubenberg, L. *Consciousness and Qualia*; John Benjamins Publishing Company: Amsterdam, The Netherlands; Philadelphia, PA, USA, 1998.
21. Strawson, G. *Selves. An Essay in Revisionary Metaphysics*; Oxford University Press: Oxford, UK, 2009.
22. Chalmers, D.J. How can we construct a science of consciousness. In *The Cognitive Neurosciences III*; Gazzaniga, M., Ed.; MIT Press: Cambridge, MA, USA, 2004; pp. 1111–1120.
23. Levine, J. Materialism and Qualia: The Explanatory Gap. *Pac. Philos. Q.* **1983**, *64*, 354–361. [CrossRef]
24. Baars, B. Global workspace theory of consciousness: Toward a cognitive neuroscience of human experience. *Prog. Brain Res.* **2005**, *150*, 45–53. [PubMed]
25. Kandel, E. Biology and the Future of Psychoanalysis: A New Intellectual Framework for Psychiatry Revisited. *Am. J. Psychiatry* **1999**, *156*, 505–524. [CrossRef] [PubMed]
26. Schopenhauer, A. *The World as Will and Representation*; Dover Publications: New York, NY, USA, 1958.
27. Descartes, R. *Principles of Philosophy*; Springer: Dordrecht, The Netherlands, 1982.
28. Kant, I. *Critique of Pure Reason*; The Cambridge Edition of the Works of Immanuel Kant; Cambridge University Press: Cambridge, UK, 1998.
29. Cassirer, E. *The Philosophy of Symbolic Forms*; Yale University Press: New Haven, CT, USA, 1953–1957.
30. Havel, I.M. Living in Conceivable Worlds. *Found. Sci.* **1998**, *3*, 375–394. [CrossRef]
31. Von Uexküll, J. *Theoretical Biology*; Harcourt, Brace & Co.: New York, NY, USA, 1926.
32. Sperry, R.W. Neurology and the mind-brain problem. *Am. Sci.* **1952**, *40*, 291–312.
33. Dewey, J. *Experience and Nature*; Open Court: La Salle, IL, USA, 1925.
34. Montero, B.; Papineau, D. A defense of the via negativa argument for physicalism. *Analysis* **2005**, *65*, 233–237. [CrossRef]
35. Bishop, R. The Via Negativa: Not the Way to Physicalism. *Mind Matter* **2010**, *8*, 203–214.
36. Hoffman, D.D.; Prakash, C. Objects of consciousness. *Front. Psychol.* **2014**, *5*, 577. [CrossRef] [PubMed]
37. Kussel, E.; Leibler, S. Phenotypic Diversity, Population Growth, and Information in Fluctuating Environments. *Science* **2005**, *309*, 20. [CrossRef] [PubMed]
38. Nurse, P. Life, logic, and information. *Science* **2008**, *454*, 424–426. [CrossRef] [PubMed]
39. Davies, P.C.W.; Walker, S.I. The hidden simplicity of biology. *Rep. Prog. Phys.* **2016**, *79*, 102601. [CrossRef] [PubMed]
40. Kauffman, S. *The Origins of Order: Self Organization and Selection in Evolution*; Oxford University Press: Oxford, UK, 1993.
41. Perkins, T.J.; Swain, P.S. Strategies for cellular decision-making. *Mol. Syst. Biol.* **2009**, *5*, 1–15. [CrossRef] [PubMed]
42. Friston, K.J. The free-energy principle: A unified brain theory? *Nat. Rev. Neurosci.* **2010**, *11*, 127–138. [CrossRef] [PubMed]
43. Lan, G.; Tu, Y. Information processing in bacteria: Memory, computation, and statistical physics: A key issues review. *Rep. Prog. Phys.* **2016**, *79*, 052601. [CrossRef] [PubMed]

44. Pattee, H.H. Cell phenomenology: The first phenomenon. *Prog. Biophys. Mol. Biol.* **2015**, *119*, 461–468. [CrossRef] [PubMed]
45. Mitchell, A.; Lim, W. Cellular perception and misperception: Internal models for decision-making shaped by evolutionary experience. *BioEssays* **2016**, *38*, 845–849. [CrossRef] [PubMed]
46. Kirchhoff, M.D.; Froese, T. Where There is Life There is Mind: In Support of a Strong Life-Mind Continuity Thesis. *Entropy* **2017**, *19*, 169. [CrossRef]
47. Oizumi, M.; Albantakis, L.; Tononi, G. From the Phenomenology to the Mechanisms of Consciousness: Integrated Information Theory 3.0. *PLoS Comput. Biol.* **2014**, *10*, e1003588. [CrossRef] [PubMed]
48. Marshall, W.; Kim, H.; Walker, S.I.; Tononi, G.; Albantakis, L. How causal analysis can reveal autonomy in models of biological systems. *Philos. Trans. R. Soc. A* **2017**, *375*. [CrossRef] [PubMed]
49. Koch, C. *Consciousness. Confessions of a Romantic Reductionist*; MIT Press: Cambridge, MA, USA, 2012.
50. Tononi, G.; Koch, C. Consciousness: Here, there and everywhere? *Philos. Trans. R. Soc. B Biol. Sci.* **2015**, *370*, 20140167. [CrossRef] [PubMed]
51. Schroeder, M. The Difference that Makes a Difference for the Conceptualization of Information. *Proceedings* **2017**, *1*, 221. [CrossRef]
52. Kant, I. *Critique of the Power of Judgment*; The Cambridge Edition of the Works of Immanuel Kant; Cambridge University Press: Cambridge, UK, 2000.
53. Roth, S. Mathematics and biology: A Kantian view on the history of pattern formation theory. *Dev. Genes Evol.* **2011**, *221*, 255–279. [CrossRef] [PubMed]
54. Jaynes, E.T. Gibbs vs. Boltzmann entropies. *Am. J. Phys.* **1965**, *33*, 391–398. [CrossRef]
55. Clausius, R. *The Mechanical Theory of Heat—With Its Applications to the Steam Engine and to Physical Properties of Bodies*; John van Voorst: London, UK, 1867.
56. Peschard, I.; Bitbol, M. Heat, Temperature and Phenomenal Concepts. In *The Case for Qualia*; Wright, E., Ed.; MIT Press: Cambridge, MA, USA, 2008; pp. 1–38.
57. Primas, H. Basic elements and problems of probability theory. *J. Sci. Explor.* **1999**, *13*, 579–613.
58. Beisbart, C.; Hartmann, S. *Probabilities in Physics*; Oxford University Press: Oxford, UK, 2011.
59. Pereira, J.; Ricke, H. What is consciousness? Towards a preliminary definition. *J. Conscious. Stud.* **2009**, *16*, 28–45.
60. Dehaene, S.; Lau, H.; Kouider, S. What is consciousness, and could machines have it? *Science* **2017**, *358*, 486–492. [CrossRef] [PubMed]
61. Rosbash, M. Nobel Lecture: The Circadian Clock, Transcriptional Feedback and the Regulation of Gene Expression. 2017. Available online: http://www.nobelprize.org/nobel_prizes/medicine/laureates/2017/rosbash-lecture.html (accessed on 5 October 2018).
62. Husserl, E. *On the Phenomenology of the Consciousness of Internal Time (1893–1917)*; Brough, J.B., Trans.; Kluwer Academic: Dordrecht, The Netherlands, 1991.
63. Friston, K.J. Life as we know it. *J. R. Soc. Interface* **2013**, *10*, 20130475. [CrossRef] [PubMed]
64. Sengupta, B.; Tozzi, A.; Cooray, G.K.; Douglas, P.K.; Friston, K.J. Towards a Neuronal Gauge Theory. *PLoS Biol.* **2016**, *14*, e1002400. [CrossRef] [PubMed]

# 8

# Quantum Discontents, or What is Wrong with our Science Practice

**Gennady Shkliarevsky**

Historical Studies Program, Bard College, Annandale-on-Hudson, NY 12504, USA; shkliare@bard.edu

**Abstract:** For more than eighty years, quantum theory (QT) has dominated physical science. This domination remains unchallenged to this day. Some physicists celebrate this remarkable stability. Others lament this fact and argue that QT inhibits our understanding of physical reality. They feel that numerous problems that have accumulated in physical science require stepping beyond the horizon outlined by QT. The article offers a critical examination of the foundational assumptions of QT that shape its practice. It uses two interpretations of QT as case studies—Copenhagen interpretation and the theoretical perspective advanced by American physicist David Bohm—to explain one major problem that continues to plague our study of physics. The article sketches a path to a possible solution and outlines a new science practice that this solution will require.

**Keywords:** quantum theory; Copenhagen interpretation; Bohmian mechanics; quantum uncertainty; determinism; subject-object relations; systems theory

---

## 1. Introduction

For more than eighty years, quantum theory (QT) has dominated the science of physics. It has been a rich source of ideas and perspectives that have shaped many spheres of our knowledge, from physics to chemistry, computer science, information, chemistry, biology, psychology, philosophy, and even social sciences. One cannot think of our civilization without thinking about quantum theory.

In the course of its history, QT has experienced many changes. Indeed, QT as we know it today is in many ways very different from and much richer than its original formulation in the early 20th century. Yet its fundamental features remain unchanged. Today, many basic premises and conclusions of QT are still the same as they were at the time of its inception; its controversies and paradoxes still provoke hot debates. The most important and controversial problems of QT are still awaiting their solutions.

Many researchers feel that this remarkable staying power proves that QT is fundamentally correct. There are, however, others—and their number is growing—who are very resentful of the fact that physics has not been able to step much beyond the horizon circumscribed by QT. They see its continued domination as the principal cause of what they see as stagnation in our physical science. In their view, QT has become an obstacle to the evolution of our knowledge about physical reality and a hindrance to its progress. They feel that numerous problems that have accumulated in physical science require stepping beyond the horizon outlined by QT.

The article offers a critical examination of the foundational assumptions of QT that shape its practice. It uses two interpretations of QT—the Copenhagen interpretation and the theoretical perspective advanced by American physicist David Bohm—as case studies to explain one major problem that continues to plague our study of physics. The article sketches a path to a possible solution and outlines a new science practice that this solution will require.

## 2. The Copenhagen Interpretation and Its Critique

The Copenhagen interpretation (CI) is the original interpretation of QT that to this day remains one of the more widely used. The rise of CI has marked a significant progress in our understanding of physical reality. It has also, however, produced a great deal of confusion. For one thing, the formulation of CI has created a profound rift in our knowledge of physical reality. As a result of its rise, our knowledge has become divided into two very different parts—classical and nonclassical physics; so different, in fact, that one often gets the impression that we are dealing with two different, if not totally incommensurable, realities. Perhaps nothing illustrates this difference better than visualizability. Classical physics frequently uses images of objects—balls, bricks, planets, galaxies, etc.—that we envision moving and interacting with each other. Nonclassical physics is all about mathematical formulas and equations that describe processes and effects that are impossible to visualize. In Erwin Schrödinger's apt description, CI is "a formal theory of frightening, indeed repulsive, abstractness and lack of visualizability" [1] (p. 681).

The lack of visualizability, to which Schrödinger points, is not a whim of the framers of CI; it is due to the main innovation that CI has made. One of the principal novelties in CI is the recognition of the agency of the observer. According to CI, we cannot observe physical reality in isolation. When we conduct observations, we act upon reality and our actions produce effect. As Bohr has stressed: "when searching for harmony in life one must never forget that in the drama of existence we are ourselves both actors and spectators" [2] (p. 236). Quantum reality manifests itself by responding to actions by the observer. Strictly speaking, CI does not deal with individual particles. It assigns individuality to interactions. According to Bohr,

> The individuality of the typical quantum effects finds its proper expression in the circumstance that any attempt of subdividing the phenomena will demand a change in the experimental arrangement introducing new possibilities of interactions between objects and measuring instruments that in principle cannot be controlled [2] (p. 210).

And elsewhere:

> In quantum mechanics, we are not dealing with an arbitrary renunciation of a more detailed analysis of atomic phenomena, but with a recognition that such an analysis is in principle excluded [2] (p. 235).

In other words, CI tells us that we observe the interaction, made possible by mediation, between reality, on one hand, and the observer and the instruments that the observer chooses to use, on the other. This approach basically recognizes that mediation is necessary for the production of knowledge. Such mediation involves both the instruments chosen and the interpretation of results by the observer. Incidentally, this recognition applies to reality in general, not just to quantum reality.

This approach has had a profound impact on research methodology. CI guides researchers to deal strictly with the experimental results that they observe, rather than reflect on reality that they, according to CI, cannot in principle observe. In light of CI, such reflections are but idle speculations. When quantum experiments produce what from the common sense view appears as paradoxes, we should accept these paradoxes as given, no further questions asked.

Paradoxes create conflicting images that defy our imagination and are impossible to visualize. Indeed, how do you picture such well-known quantum phenomena as entanglement, superposition, or wave function? Moreover, the framers of CI have specifically forewarned us against making any attempts to envision quantum processes. Richard Feynman, a renowned physicist and a recipient of a Nobel Prize for his achievements in quantum physics, cautioned:

> Do not keep saying to yourself, if you can possible avoid it, "But how can it be like that?" because you will get 'down the drain', into a blind alley from which nobody has yet escaped. Nobody knows how it can be like that [3] (p. 129).

Since CI does not allow any probing beyond the phenomena accessible to observation, those who subscribe to CI must accept paradoxes and reject visualizability. CI guides researchers to practice instrumental approach and rely on formidable mathematical formalism that allows them to calculate and predict the results of quantum experiments. Summarizing his understanding of the achievement of CI, Werner Heisenberg, one of the principal framers of this perspective, wrote:

> The conception of the objective reality of the elementary particles has thus evaporated not into the cloud of some obscure new reality concept, but into the transparent clarity of mathematics that represents no longer the behavior of the particles but rather our knowledge of this behavior [4] (p. 2).

Mathematical formalism expunged visualizability from quantum mechanics. "Shut up and calculate" has become the most widely applied rule among practitioners.

As has already been indicated, the rejection of visualizability has become one of the markers of the dominant interpretation of QT. As has already been mentioned, this fact has left the system of our knowledge of physical reality deeply divided into two parts: Classical and nonclassical physics. The continued popularity of CI perpetuates this division. The perpetuation of the division hinders the equilibration of two parts (classical and nonclassical) of the system of our knowledge of physical reality. The equilibration of differences is the process that creates new and more powerful levels of organization, which is essential for the evolution of systems, including systems of knowledge. The failure to equilibrate our knowledge of physical reality explains the repeated attempts to create alternative interpretations that challenge CI.

There is another reason why CI spurs the creation of new interpretations. As has been indicated earlier, CI recognizes the agency of the observer. According to this interpretation, we cannot in principle observe reality by itself, but only the way it manifests itself in interactions with the instruments selected by the observer. In other words, what the observer observes is not reality by itself, but only the phenomenal level of interactions. Thus, CI formalism describes interactions between reality and the observer, not reality itself, since it is only this level that is accessible to the observer in experiments. The bizarre quantum phenomena that mathematical formalism describes appear on the phenomenal level of interactions—the only level accessible to observation. Therefore, strictly speaking, the conclusions that CI draws from observations of the phenomenal level cannot be extended to reality as it is; such extension is unwarranted by the interpretation itself.

When CI observes uncertainty on the phenomenal level of interactions, it cannot really extrapolate from these observations that reality is uncertain. According to its own premises, the only correct conclusion that it can make is that we do not know how reality is, since uncertainty is observed only on the phenomenal level. We cannot assume that observing the manifestation of reality is the same as observing reality itself. Therefore, CI does not warrant the conclusion about uncertainty of reality that is accepted by the proponents of CI unquestionably and without any qualifications.

Since, strictly speaking, quantum experiments do not warrant any conclusions about the nature of reality, the key proposition that CI makes about the inherent uncertainty of physical reality can only be accepted as an axiom. However, in order to be accepted as a foundational proposition, it must be justified. Otherwise, we can only see such a proposition as subjective and arbitrary. CI does not provide such justification. Moreover, such justification is in principle impossible. As Ernest Nagel and James R. Newman explain in their widely-accepted exposition of the celebrated achievement of Kurt Gödel, the famous Austrian logician and mathematician, Gödel's proof shows "that it is impossible to establish the internal logical consistency of a very large class of deductive systems unless one adopts principles of reasoning so complex that their internal consistency is as open to doubt as that of the systems themselves [5] (p. 5)". Nagel and Newman further explain:

> The import of Gödel's conclusions is far-reaching, though it has not yet been fully fathomed. These conclusions show that the prospects of finding for every deductive system an absolute proof of consistency that satisfies the finitistic requirements of Hilbert's proposal is most

> unlikely. They show also that there are an endless number of true statements which cannot be formally deduced from any given set of axioms by a closed set of rules of inference [5] (p. 109).

According to Nagel and Newman, Gödel did not think of his results as due "to some odd defect in the specific system PM (Principia Mathematica)," but "are applicable to *any* system" [5] (p. 95) (italics in the original).

Many computer scientists have argued in the same way that true uncertainty may exist, but its existence cannot be demonstrated logically since the metaprocedures required for such a demonstration will necessarily reveal inconsistencies that contradict the original axiom. Hans Primas, for example, shows that if an axiomatic principle, such as determinism, cannot be satisfied, "it can be enforced by choosing a larger state space [6] (p. 10)." Such enforcement, according to Primas, is perfectly compatible with mathematical probability theory because:

> Every mathematically formulated dynamics of statistically reproducible events can be extended to a description in terms of a one-parameter group of automorphisms on an enlarged mathematical structure which describes a fictitious hidden determinism. Consequently, randomness in the sense of mathematical probability theory is only a weak generalization of determinism [6] (p. 1).

Jean Bricmont also sees ontic determinism lurking behind the appearance of quantum randomness [6–8].

There is only one conclusion one can draw from the above discussion. CI does not and cannot provide either empirical evidence or logical justification for its foundational proposition about reality. It is impossible to prove that reality is uncertain. Thus, CI may be true, but it is impossible to prove that it is true. In the absence of such proof—either empirical or logical—we have no choice but to view CI as subjective and arbitrary. In other words, CI cannot and does not produce a definitive interpretation of quantum mechanics. This fact and also the need to solve the problem of the division in the system of our knowledge of physical reality (so that the system could further evolve) justifies and legitimizes efforts to construct interpretations based on different foundational propositions that rival CI.

**3. Bohmian Mechanics**

There are many interpretations that challenge the dominant position of CI. They include Bohmian mechanics, the pilot-wave theory, the hidden variable interpretation, the many-worlds interpretation, the many-minds interpretation, the consistent histories approach, and some others [9–12]. However, despite the growing variety of new versions, CI still retains its commanding presence. Some critics explain these failures by the power of scientific establishment that backs CI and controls the resources necessary for developing these alternative interpretations. Indeed, the power of scientific establishment is considerable. It controls much of research funding, access to publications, the power of appointments and tenure decisions, etc.; and it certainly uses this power to support the theoretical perspective it has chosen to back up. In his famous book *The Structure of Scientific Revolution*, Thomas Kuhn points out a high degree of inertia in our scientific community. Many other researchers have expressed similar concerns [13–19]. However, force alone cannot explain the enduring dominance of CI. In order to explain the failure of alternative versions to open new vistas in studying physical reality, one should take a closer look at the challengers. Examining these failures is certainly important for making progress.

It is beyond the scope of this article to provide a detailed analysis of all theoretical perspectives that offer alternatives to CI. Such an analysis requires a separate study. This paper will focus only on one interpretation that has attracted more attention than others. It is what has been dubbed as Bohmian mechanics, named after its creator, American physicist David Bohm.

Bohm first formulated his theory back in the early 1950s [20]. Initially, the theory was quite successful and was able to gain some support in the physics community. However, as time passed, its influence waned and it has only recently experienced some revival [12,20].

Bohm certainly accepts the most important contribution of CI—its mathematical formalism. In contrast to CI, however, in Bohmian mechanics, this formalism is more than just a convenient way to calculate and predict outcomes of quantum experiments. The phenomena that quantum equations formalize are, for Bohm, the actual aspects of reality. Bohmian mechanics explains even the weirdest quantum phenomena—such as nonlocality, superposition, and backward causality—in terms of causes and effects. In Bohm's theoretical perspective, for example, nonlocality—a quantum phenomenon that involves speeds faster than the speed of light—is not merely a mathematical representation of some results of quantum experiments. It is, for Bohm, a fundamental property of reality. The famous wave function is not just a convenient formula for calculating outcomes of quantum experiments; in the Bohmian world, it actually guides particles and determines their state.

Quantum formalism is essentially mathematical equations of motion that, like all other mathematical equations, obey the logic of mathematics. Viewing this mathematical formalism as more than just the way of calculating and predicting the outcomes of the phenomena it describes, but as representing the actual aspects of quantum reality, entails one inevitable consequence. In order to conserve the logical necessity of mathematical equations, Bohm has to recognize determinism as the fundamental property of reality. Thus, in contrast to CI that sees uncertainty as a fundamental property of reality, Bohmian mechanics recognizes that quantum reality is fully determinate. Indeed, Bohm acknowledges the existence of uncertainty, but this uncertainty is strictly epistemological, that is, it is due to our lack of knowledge about reality, rather than the way this reality is [12,20].

One can see from the above that Bohm completely and radically reverses CI. The strategy of reversal results in several consequences that do not work in favor of the Bohmian alternative. As a mere inversion of CI, Bohmian mechanics has the same explanatory power as CI. Like CI, Bohm also essentially interprets, or rather reinterprets, the phenomena that can be observed on the level of interactions. When he accepts these phenomena as fundamental properties of physical reality, he commits the same logical mistake by attributing to reality what essentially belongs to the phenomenal level, which is unwarranted. We certainly cannot view the manifestations of reality on the level of phenomena as the actual and real properties of reality by itself. Since Bohm's fundamental proposition about the determinate nature of reality is derived from mathematical formalism, we must view it as an axiomatic proposition that Bohm uses to organize his theoretical perspective. However, he also does not provide a logical justification for this claim. Moreover, there can be no proof for ontic determinism. Just like the existence of uncertainty and randomness is impossible to prove, their existence is also impossible to disprove, which undermines any claim of ontic determinism: If there is a possibility that reality can be uncertain, then the claim that reality is determinate must be in doubt.

Jean Bricmont simply dismisses the entire issue of the intrinsic nature of determinism as ultimately irrelevant. Bricmont examines two current definitions of determinism. He finds that one definition in which determinism is conflated with predictability renders determinism trivially false. Considering the other definition that avoids the conflation, Bricmont asks a pertinent question: Is there a function—in a Platonic sense (that is, independent of our ignorance)—that determines a finite sequence of sets of numbers that never repeats itself in a unique way? His answer is that the existence of such a function is simply impossible to disprove because one can always find a function or even many functions that map "each set into the next one" [7] (p. 2). Bricmont's conclusion dismisses the whole issue of determinism as utterly irrelevant to science. In his view, "there is no notion of determinism that would make the question [of determinism] scientifically relevant ontically it [determinism] is true but uninteresting [that is, impossible to disprove]" [7] (p. 2). "I don't know," he adds, "how to formulate the issue of determinism so that the question becomes interesting" [7] (p. 1). The point is that either determinism or uncertainty may actually exist in the ontic sense, but this existence is impossible to prove; and if the claim that reality is either uncertain or determinate cannot be justified, any theory based on either of these claims cannot be accepted as definitive.

In a practical sense, Bohmian determinate mechanics also offers no advantages in comparison with CI. While its determinism suggests that since all particles in the universe have a determinate position, we can calculate their positions at any moment if we know their initial position and the wave function of the universe, in practice, the acquisition of such knowledge encounters an insurmountable problem. In order to perform such calculations, one should know the initial position of particles, including particles in the brain of the observer and their wave function. Observing particles in one's own brain requires constructing a position from which such observation can be conducted. However, the problem is that such a position should also be accessible to observing, which will inevitably lead to the problem that Niklas Luhman defined as infinite regress that inevitably results from observing the observing. Bohmian mechanics does not resolve this problem. In principle, we can know the position of every particle in the universe; in practice, however, such knowledge is impossible [12] [21] (p. 479) [22] (p. 329).

In contrast to CI, Bohmian mechanics is visualizable. But that is probably the only significant difference between the two interpretations. Just like CI, Bohm's perspective also rests on the shaky foundation of a subjective and arbitrary axiomatic proposition. It offers few, if any, practical advantages in comparison with CI. As a result, one cannot accept Bohmian mechanics as a definitive interpretation of quantum theory. Just like CI, it offers nothing that can help to integrate classical and nonclassical physics and, consequently, does not contribute to the further evolution of the system of our knowledge of physical reality. Due to these reasons, Bohmian mechanics fails to present a real and constructive alternative to CI.

## 4. The Solution

As has been indicated earlier, the division in the system of our knowledge of physical reality creates a problem. It prevents this system from evolving and transcending the boundaries of the existing knowledge. The achievement of this goal requires the creation of a new perspective that would be broad enough to include both classical and nonclassical physics as its two specific cases—that is, cases that are true under special circumstances or assumptions. How can we solve this problem of division and create such broader perspective? Ironically, CI suggests a solution, but it fails to follow through on its own suggestion.

CI claims that the observer has access only to interactions between quantum reality and the instruments that the observer chooses to conduct observations. So, what is this interaction and what is its nature?

According to CI, observations affect the objects that we observe. In other words, they change these objects in some way. Therefore, the act of observing is a creative act that changes reality.

However, there is more to this interaction. The objects of observation are not passive. They also respond to the action by the observer and affect the outcome of interactions. Therefore, the response of objects to observing changes the outcome and, consequently, also represents a creative act.

The conclusion that follows from the above considerations is that the process of interaction that takes place between the object and the observer (subject) is a creative act. CI is absolutely correct: The only reality available to us is the process of creation. This process creates our knowledge.

We are part of the universe. Like any other object in our universe, we interact with other objects. Hence, we are fully justified in generalizing our interactions with objects we observe to all other interactions. Therefore, interactions with objects we observe are a subset of a more general type of interactions that take place among all objects in our universe. It is a universal process of interactions and this process is creative. It creates objects in our universe and our universe as a whole.

The main property of our universe is its uniqueness: It is all there is. There is nothing outside it; in fact, there is no outside. As there is nothing outside our universe, nothing can come into it and nothing can disappear from it because there is nowhere to disappear. Consequently, everything must be conserved. Conservation is fundamental to our universe; it originates in the uniqueness of our universe and it gives rise to the process of creation.

Our universe contains an enormous variety of different forms. All these forms are finite; and the resources for sustaining finite forms are also finite. In order to conserve finite forms, their range of possibilities, or degrees of freedom, must expand, which will allow them access to new resources. Gaining new possibilities requires new properties, that is, properties that have had no prior existence; in other words, it requires an act of creation. New properties can arise only as a result of the integration of differences that leads to the emergence of the new and more powerful levels of organization. Conservation is impossible without the process of creating such new and more powerful levels of organization. If a system does not evolve and does not create new levels of organization, it begins to disintegrate.

We humans are also creations of this process. As its creations, we are also part of this process. We have inherited from this process our capacity to create. Over the course of our history, we have demonstrated this capacity in works of art, in science and technology, in organizing our society and its institutions. Our civilization itself is remarkable evidence of our creativity. It is the source of our power and prosperity.

Given the importance of the process of creation in our life, one would expect that we would use it as the main organizing principle of our practice. Yet, odd as it may seem, this process is not central to our civilization. Our civilization is decidedly anthropocentric. Since at least the Enlightenment, if not earlier, we have made the human subject the main organizing principle of our civilization, its practice, and institutions.

This article has shown that the adoption of subjectivity as the main organizing principle of our mental universe is essentially a subjective and arbitrary act—it is not supported either by justification or by experimental verification. For this reason, it cannot and does not provide us with a definitive way of interpreting reality. It generates confusion, inconsistencies, and paradoxes that hinder the progress of our civilization and create many current problems that we as a civilization face today, including the stagnation of our physical science that remains split between two separate and rather incommensurable, despite some similarities, conceptions of reality.

As this article suggests, the solution of the problem that plagues the system of our knowledge of physical reality is in creating the frame for a new theoretical perspective that would be able to integrate both classical and nonclassical physics as its particular cases; that is, cases that are true under special circumstances or axioms. Such a frame will require a foundation that is capable of including axiomatic propositions upon which both classical and nonclassical physics rest.

The process of creation can serve as the basis for such integration. The foundational proposition for classical physics is the centrality of the object. By contrast, nonclassical physics is organized around the recognition of the centrality of the subject and subjectivity. This article agrees with CI that we cannot observe quantum reality as it is; we can only access the interaction between this reality and the observational instruments chosen by the subject. This article has shown that the process of creation is the essence of this interaction, and this process is ultimately the source of everything that exists in our universe. Therefore, this process can serve as a foundational proposition that integrates subjectivity and the object. A theoretical perspective constructed on this foundation can integrate classical and nonclassical physics. Therefore, we should adopt the process of creation as the main focus of our science practice.

The process of creation appears in different guises (the process of emergence or the construction process) in a variety of theoretical perspectives: Systems theory, theory of emergence, complexity theory, theory of self-organization, creativity studies, and others.

Different researchers define this process in different ways. The definition that in the view of this author fits best is the following: The process of creation is an operation that generates new levels and forms of organization of reality. The distinct feature of such created forms of organization is their irreducibility. We cannot reduce them. That is to say, we cannot establish linear causal relations between the new form that has emerged and the level of organization of reality from which it has emerged. We cannot reduce life, for example, to chemical elements. We cannot reduce consciousness to biological processes that, according to the theory of evolution, gave rise to it. We cannot explain the behavior of insects that have clear signs of intelligence present. We cannot reduce order to the chaos that has preceded it (for more on the process of creation see [23–26]).

One important advantage of using the process of creation as the organizing principle of our science practice is the fact that, unlike determinism or uncertainty, it can be both justified and empirically validated. One can imagine reality without uncertainty or determinism, as the Copenhageners and Bohm do. However, one cannot imagine reality without the process of creation. If there were no creation, there would be nothing. Leibniz, among other philosophers, had a clear understanding of this fact when he asked his famous question that he considered the fundamental question of metaphysics: "Why is there something rather than nothing?" Moreover, all humans have a capacity to creation. There are numerous creations that prove the existence of this capacity. Our universe has numerous examples of creation—from particles and atoms, to stars and galaxies, and everything else. These are powerful empirical confirmations of the existence of the process that created them all.

What will such new science practice organized around the process of creation involve? It is beyond the scope of this article to provide a detailed answer to this question; such an answer has been provided elsewhere [27]. However, an outline of the main points may be in order.

First of all, we must recognize that the main motive of our intellectual activity is not knowledge. Knowledge is merely a byproduct of this activity. Its true motivation is the construction of new and increasingly more powerful levels of our mental organization as a way of conserving our mental constructions. These new and more powerful levels of organization will allow us to establish new one-to-one correspondences between our mental constructs and reality, thus generating new knowledge.

Since the construction of new and more powerful levels of organization involves integrating differences, the most important form of validation of new knowledge is its inclusiveness and comprehensiveness. This does not mean that experimental support is not necessary. Our mental activity emerges from practical activity. Therefore, this process should also allow the inversion from theoretical constructs to practice. However, mental constructs are the most powerful forms of organization of reality and they can always create one-to-one correspondences with physical reality, and such correspondences alone cannot validate knowledge.

This approach follows from the understanding that the process of creation is the source of our knowledge and, in fact, the source of everything that exists in our universe. By understanding this process and applying this knowledge to our practice, we will place our practice on the solid foundation of our reason and rationality and will no longer rely on domination and force in determining what constitutes knowledge and what does not.

## 5. Conclusions

Over fifty years ago, Thomas Kuhn in his now famous book *The Structure of Scientific Revolutions* addressed the issue of stagnation in the evolution of our knowledge [13]. It is in many ways a pessimistic book. It recognizes that our science community has a tendency to succumb to inertia that leads to long periods of stagnation. Moreover, the author suggests that such stagnation is inevitable and there is nothing that we can do to ameliorate this condition. He does not believe that human reason and rationality are capable of overcoming this inertia and prevent it from hindering the progress of our knowledge. In a way, he suggests a very anti-Enlightenment conclusion that human reason cannot be the arbiter in our practice, including our science practice. According to Kuhn, only death and destruction can ultimately settle the conflict between stasis and change, between old ways and innovation. The old generation should die out so that the new one could pave the way for new ideas and theories. But even death and destruction may not necessarily be a guarantee against inertia and stagnation, and assure the ascension of new ideas. The modern tools of indoctrination and thought control may be powerful enough to prevent the rise of a new generation and the spread of new ideas. Inertia and stagnation may very well become an inescapable condition of our civilization.

In a way, Kuhn tells us that we are the source of our progress. For this reason, the only guarantee we can have against stagnation is our full commitment to a science practice that is based on reason and rationality—not domination and force, no matter how benevolent the motivation behind them may be. We need to understand the process that plays a critical role in knowledge production—the process that is fundamental to the existence of our universe and that we have inherited in the course of a long and arduous evolution. We need to place our hope in the capacity of our reason to understand even this fundamental process that transcends our own existence; and we must work hard to realize this hope.

To conclude, this article has argued that quantum physics is based on assumptions about reality. In the cases examined in this piece, they are assumptions that reality is uncertain (the Copenhagen interpretation) or, on the contrary, that it is deterministic (Bohm). Both assumptions are unjustified. The absence of justification means that there was no rational control over the construction of the theory, that the theory may very well be based on a wrong assumption, that reality is neither uncertain nor deterministic, that these are false choices, and that we should start asking once again some fundamental questions as to how reality actually is. It means that it may be time to leave our safe communities of common faith and start sailing toward new shores.

**Funding:** This research received no external funding

**Conflicts of Interest:** The author declares no conflict of interest.

## References

1. Cramer, J.G. The Transactional Interpretation of Quantum Mechanics. *Rev. Mod. Phys.* **1986**, *58*, 647–687. [CrossRef]
2. Bohr, N. Discussion with Einstein on Epistemological Problems of Atomic Physics. In *Albert Einstein: Philosopher-Scientists*; Schilpp, P.A., Ed.; Open Court: La Salle, IL, USA, 1969.
3. Feynman, R. *The Character of Physical Law*; The M.I.T. Press: Cambridge, UK, 1985.
4. Stapp, H.P. Quantum Theory and the Role of Mind in Nature. ArXiv:Quant-Ph/0103043. 9 March 2001. Available online: http://arxiv.org/abs/quant-ph/0103043 (accessed on 28 June 2012).
5. Nagel, E.; James, R.; Newman, J.R. *Gödel's Proof*; University Press: New York, NY, USA, 1953.
6. Primas, H. Hidden Determinism, Probability, and Time's Arrow. In *Between Chance and Choice: Interdisciplinary Perspectives on Determinism*; Atmanspacher, H., Bishop, R., Eds.; Imprint Academic: Thorverton, UK, 2002.
7. Bricmont, J. Determinism, Chaos, and Quantum Mechanics. Available online: http://www.freeinfosociety.com/pdfs/mathematics/determinism.pdf. (accessed on 22 June 2010).
8. Bricmont, J. *Making Sense of Quantum Mechanics*, 1st ed.; Springer: New York, NY, USA, 2016.
9. Ballentine, L.E. *Quantum Mechanics: A Modern Development*; World Scientific: River Edge, NJ, USA, 2014.
10. Putnam, H. A Philosopher Looks at Quantum Mechanics (Again). *Br. J. Philos. Sci.* **2005**, *56*, 615–634. [CrossRef]
11. Belavkin, V.P. Quantum Probabilities and Paradoxes of the Quantum Century. 2005. Available online: http://arxiv.org/abs/math.PR/0512415 (accessed on 23 April 2011).
12. Albert, D.Z. Bohm's Alternative to Quantum Mechanics. *Sci. Am.* **1994**, *270*, 56–67. [CrossRef]
13. Kuhn, T.S. *The Structure of Scientific Revolutions*; University of Chicago Press: Chicago, IL, USA, 2012.
14. Weiler, H.N. Whose Knowledge Matters? Development and the Politics of Knowledge. In *Entwicklung Als Beruf*; Theodor Hanf, T., Weiler, H.N., Dickow, H., Eds.; Nomos: Baden-Baden, Germany, 2009.
15. Araya, D. Cultural Democracy: Universities in the Creative Economy. *Policy Futures Educ.* **2010**, *8*, 217–232. [CrossRef]
16. Latour, B. *Politics of Nature: How to Bring the Sciences into Democracy*; Harvard University Press: Cambridge, MA, USA, 2004.
17. Lopez-Corredoira, M. Sociology of Modern Cosmology. 2008. Available online: http://arxiv.org/abs/0812.0537 (accessed on 17 July 2013).

18. Brown, R.H. Modern Science and Its Critics: Toward a Post-Positivist Legitimization of Science. *New Lit. Hist.* **1998**, *29*, 521–550. [CrossRef]
19. Charlton, B.G. Why Are Modern Scientists so Dull? How Science Selects for Perseverance and Sociability at the Expense of Intelligence and Creativity. *Med. Hypotheses* **2009**, *72*, 237–243. [CrossRef] [PubMed]
20. Bohm, D. A Suggested Interpretation of the Quantum Theory in Terms of 'Hidden' Variables. I. *Phys. Rev.* **1952**, *85*, 166–179. [CrossRef]
21. Luhmann, N. *Social Systems*; Stanford University Press: Stanford, CA, USA, 1995.
22. Shkliarevsky, G. The Paradox of Observing, Autopoiesis, and the Future of Social Sciences. *Syst. Res. Behav. Sci.* **2007**, *24*, 323–332. [CrossRef]
23. Shkliarevsky, G. Understanding the Process of Creation: A New Approach. *Manag. J. Sustain. Bus. Manag. Solut. Emerg. Econ.* **2017**, *22*, 1–13. [CrossRef]
24. Kauffman, S. A God of Creativity. *New Sci.* **2008**, *198*, 52–53. [CrossRef]
25. Kauffman, S. *Humanity in a Creative Universe*; Oxford University Press: Oxford, UK, 2016.
26. Prigogine, I.; Stengers, I. *Order out of Chaos: Man's New Dialogue with Nature*; Bantam Books: Toronto, ON, Canada; New York, NY, USA, 1984.
27. Shkliarevsky, G. *The Civilization at a Crossroads: Constructing the Paradigm Shift*; Glasstree Publishing: Raleigh, NC, USA, 2017.

# 9

# The Naturalization of Natural Philosophy

**Joseph E. Brenner**

International Center for the Philosophy of Information, Xi'an Jiaotong University, Xi'An 710049, China; joe.brenner@bluewin.ch

**Abstract:** A new demarcation is proposed between Natural Philosophy and non-Natural Philosophy—philosophy *tout court*—based on whether or not they follow a non-standard logic of real processes. This non-propositional logic, Logic in Reality (LIR), is based on the original work of the Franco-Romanian thinker Stéphane Lupasco (Bucharest, 1900–Paris, 1988). Many Natural Philosophies remain bounded by dependence on binary linguistic concepts of logic. I claim that LIR can naturalize—bring into science—part of such philosophies. Against the potential objection that my approach blurs the distinction between science and philosophy, I reply that there is no problem in differentiating experimental physical science and philosophy; any complete distinction between philosophy, including the philosophy of science(s) and the other sciences is invidious. It was historically unnecessary and is unnecessary today. The convergence of science and philosophy, proposed by Wu Kun based on implications of the philosophy of information, supports this position. LIR provides a rigorous basis for giving equivalent ontological value to diversity and identity, what is contradictory, inconsistent, absent, missing or past, unconscious, incomplete, and fuzzy as to their positive counterparts. The naturalized Natural Philosophy resulting from the application of these principles is a candidate for the 'new synthesis' called for by the editors.

**Keywords:** common good; contradiction; ethics; information; logic; naturalization; realism; science; synthesis

---

## 1. Introduction

In 1949, it was still possible for Alfred Ayer [1] to write: "... the function of the philosopher is not to devise speculative theories which require to be validated in experience, but to elicit the consequences of our linguistic usages. That is to say, the questions with which philosophy is concerned are purely logical questions; and though people do in fact dispute about logical questions, such disputes are always unwarranted. For they either involve the denial of a proposition which is necessarily true or the assertion of a proposition which is necessarily false."

Fortunately, this binary, apodictic position has been largely deconstructed by more recent philosophical work, especially by transdisciplinary, realist approaches to consciousness and mind. Examples are the concept of the embodied mind of Lakoff and Johnson [2], an extension of basic phenomenological positions introduced by Merleau-Ponty, and the philosophy of neuroscience of Bennett and Hacker [3]. This period has also seen the development of the philosophy of process, extensions of the work of Whitehead [4], Rescher [5], and Seibt [6]. Another current field of research is that of the philosophy of information, pioneered by Wu Kun in China [7] and Luciano Floridi in Italy [8].

Unlike Ayer, I expect of philosophy that, like science in a different way, it tells us something about nature, man's unique position in nature and his interaction with it. It is nevertheless a body of knowledge, a theory of reality that can fail in two major ways. It can overemphasize the difference with science, as in the anti-scientific aspects of phenomenology and idealism in general, and it can relegate all non-tangible phenomena, not demonstrable by physical experiment, to the realm of epiphenomenalism. The concept of a Natural Philosophy, which has evolved into science, raises the further complication of what *it* is and how it differs from philosophy *tout court*. The domain of philosophy is further in fact divided by its relation to science. Analytical philosophy recognizes the central role of science, but applies to it an inadequate conception of the logical operation of complex processes and living systems. Continental philosophers and anti-realists such as Bas van Fraasen ('Constructive Empiricism') are fundamentally anti-scientific and thus lack a necessary link to reality. Both kinds of theories thus fail for similar reasons.

### 1.1. Outline of Paper

In this paper, three lines of discussion will be pursued: (1) the demarcation of Natural Philosophy by a non-standard, non-propositional philosophical logic which I have called Logic in Reality [9] (LIR); (2) the application of LIR to stubborn problems within the philosophies of process and science, as well as in Natural Philosophy itself as previously delimited; and (3) the role of recently developed philosophies of information, consistent with LIR, in bringing a new ontological dimension to philosophy. I begin by a first exposition in Section 2 of the differences I see between Natural Philosophy and Philosophy in general, philosophy *tout court*. Section 3 is a brief outline of LIR. LIR is grounded in physics, but its elements are the evolving states of natural processes, biological, cognitive and social. Section 4 presents some of the conceptual precursors to LIR in relation to Natural Philosophy, including the ontological philosophies of physics and process [10] for comparison with speculative linguistic–epistemological philosophies. Section 5 centers on phenomenology and its relation to Natural Philosophy, and addresses the issue of naturalization as a hermeneutic strategy. The next Section 6 analyzes the developing philosophies of information of Floridi and Wu. I argue that the latter anticipates the convergence of science and philosophy foreseen for Natural Philosophy.

### 1.2. A New Synthesis

In their Introduction to this special issue for *Philosophies*, its editors, Gordana Dodig-Crnkovic and Marcin Schroeder, refer to the disjunction above in their call for a new synthesis of scientific and philosophical knowledge. Whatever else may be true about it, such a synthesis, re-integration or rejunction of knowledge with its origins must provide for a grounding of human value systems in that knowledge. This is a minimum necessity for its use in support of the common good.

A new synthesis should, among other things, go beyond the familiar analytic/synthetic distinction. One can envisage the appearance of a new Synthetic Philosophy that will be a better natural partner, in both senses, of Analytical Philosophy than is the diffuse and not very useful concept of Continental Philosophy. I propose this paper as a contribution to such a new synthesis.

## 2. Philosophy and Natural Philosophy

### 2.1. What Is Philosophy?

It seems essential to first outline my position as to what philosophy and Natural Philosophy are and how they differ. Before addressing the status of contemporary Natural Philosophy, let us therefore try to answer the question posed in 1991 by Deleuze and Guattari: "What is philosophy?", "*Qu'est-ce que la philosophie?*" [11]. In their view, philosophy is neither contemplation, reflection nor communication. It is the cognitive activity of creating concepts in a domain of pure immanence, in contrast to science and logic which involve functions and observers, and to art which operates with percepts and affects. Most importantly, philosophy does not operate with propositions: the relations that compose the concept are not those of comprehension or extension but of ordered variation, processual and modular, pure events, real without being actual, ideal without being abstract. I can agree with these authors that standard logic has an 'infantile' conception of philosophy.

Concepts, hence philosophy, should not be confused with the energetic cognitive states-of-affairs in which they are found. "There is no energy; only intensities" in philosophy, whereas energy involves intensity in an extensive context. Taking this line of reasoning one step, the level of immanence itself is pre-philosophic, becomes philosophic under the influence of the concept and then evolves is a philosophic relation with non-philosophy. Finally, while the two domains—of immanence and event—are inseparable, philosophic concepts do not 'intervene' in scientific functions or functionalities and vice versa. I will introduce a similar demarcation, to use a term familiar to philosophers of science, to distinguish between philosophy and Natural Philosophy.

The philosophy of Deleuze illustrates the results of applying the concepts of immanence and transcendence without defining and including any dynamic dialectical relation between them. It constitutes a domain, governed by a binary logic of undetermined, idealized entities, Humean in its lack of effective interactions. In the domain of reality to which LIR applies, the existence of all beings depends and is defined by that of others. Infinities and infinitesimals do not exist, but are replaced by transfinite values, and immanent and transcendent aspects of phenomena are mutually and alternately actualized and potentialized. Thus, LIR can discuss philosophical issues in physical, dynamical terms that do not require recourse to any imaginary, abstract structures which to separate aspects of reality. The aspects that are considered 'virtual' or 'possible' in Deleuze are so 'in philosophy' but 'in reality' are instantiated as potentialities.

The answer to the question posed in 2.2 below by the contemporary philosopher of information and information ethics Rafael Capurro [12] is the following: philosophy deals with the question about reality as a whole stated by beings (ourselves) that finds ourselves in reality without having the possibility of a holistic view of being ourselves in reality and not beyond it. The fact that we are able to ask this question means that we have some kind of pre-knowledge about reality as a whole while at the same time this pre-knowledge is problematic, otherwise we would not ask the question and would not be able to become philosophers.

### *2.2. What Is Natural Philosophy? The Ontological Turn*

I continue with Capurro's response in the same format as above: Natural Philosophy deals with the question about nature as a whole stated by beings (ourselves) that finds themselves in nature without having the possibility of a holistic view of being ourselves in nature and not beyond it. The fact that we are able to ask this question means that we some kind of pre-knowledge about nature as a whole while at the same time this pre-knowledge is problematic, otherwise we would not ask the question and would not be able to become natural philosophers.

The question then changes to the difference between nature and reality as a whole, including fictions, non-verifiable beliefs and intangible objects of thought. Since the idea that classical Natural Philosophy evolved into science seems correct, we are left, for the domain of Natural Philosophy, a speculative interpretation of nature viewed in its entirety. This interpretation is, *ipso facto*, at a lower ontological level than the science which has largely replaced it. Much of the 20th Century linguistic turn, expressed in both analytical and phenomenological and residual transcendental traditions, is still visible in contemporary philosophy.

The reaction to this unsatisfactory state of affairs has been the reinstatement of realisms and materialisms of various kinds, associated today with the names of Derrida, Badiou, Zizek, and others. The 'ontological turn' in philosophy is a term of art that designates dissatisfaction with descriptions of reality based on analytical, semantic criteria of truth. Starting with Heidegger's critique of hermeneutics and the basing of philosophy on human life, the ontological turn is a challenge to neo-Kantian epistemologies, and looks to what the structure of the world might be like to enable scientific, that is, non-absolute knowledge. Unfortunately, ontological theories have been hobbled by the retention of static terms whose characteristics are determined by bivalent logic.

In 2002 [13], Priest suggested that an ontological turn in philosophy was taking place, away from language in the direction of a contradictory nature of reality. However, Priest proposed paraconsistent logic as appropriate to this turn. Lupasco anticipated this ontological turn by some 60 years, but his logical system lacks the epistemological limitations of paraconsistency.

We may thus say that contemporary philosophy is largely natural and realist: I note the landmark date of July 2012 and the Summer School in German Philosophy at the University of Bonn: "The Contemporary Turn in German Philosophy". I have no difficulty in associating this group of thinkers with the term 'natural philosophers', but I do not believe that the issue of what is natural has been exhausted by them.

The most important point for me is that Natural Philosophy tells us something real about the world that is consistent with our best science, physical, biological and cognitive. Speculative philosophy can always re-illuminate 'eternal' questions such as what it means to be a thinking being in a non-thinking environment, but it cannot in itself be other than part of philosophy *tout court*. This non-Natural Philosophy, to repeat, exists for 'natural' reasons: it is a natural necessity for human beings to create it, by a natural process, but it is not part of nature *qua* content.

### *2.3. Nature and Non-Nature: Belief*

Capurro suggests that we humans are the *tertium datur*, the included third (see below), living the paradox of a being who is able to ask questions about the whole of reality (of nature, the soul, god) from a perspective that is the negation of such an 'absolute' perspective. The kind of 'relative' transcendence (going 'beyond' but remaining 'inside') that is characteristic of philosophy (as different from theology and myth) is that this philosophical perspective on the whole of reality (or nature, the soul, god) is the one of indeterminateness or 'nothingness'. This paradox, our own way of existence, might 'explain' while we, humans, asking some kind of true and permanent knowledge about what is at stake concerning what is, was, will/can be, have looked and still look for answers in myths and religions.

The result is not an answer but a dead end. It is a fact that people who believe in a transcendental deity, outside and/or including nature believe that it is the true reality and all else is illusion. Realists such as the writer think that the believing of such believers is real but its objects are illusions. Neither side can accept that the other is even partly correct without invalidating their respective theses. Since such absolute polarization is not a part of nature, it cannot be part of any Natural Philosophy. The demarcation problem is simpler than that between science and non-science.

### *2.4. A New Role for a New Logic*

This sub-Section outlines my core thesis: I take the Logic in Reality mentioned above and see how it might provide a criterion for distinguishing between Natural Philosophy and philosophy in general. Obviously, if one takes 'nature' to be all of 'reality', there is no difference between them. I think it is more useful to define the following three domains and their respective theories and logics:

- Philosophy
    - The non-natural domain: fictions[1], beliefs, especially, transcendental beliefs, computational programs
    - Epistemology
    - Classical bivalent/multivalent propositional logic, present or 'projected' (Sherlock Holmes behaves logically)
    - Being (abstract: the being of Being)
- Natural Philosophy

[1] A discussion of fictionalism is outside the scope of this paper.

- The natural domain of physical and mental reality
- Ontology
- Dynamic logic of processes (Logic in Reality—LIR)
- Becoming (real; the link to 'Being')

There is no sharp cut between these domains: in some one perceives that epistemology is dominant, but there is also a longing for ontology, while propositional/predicate logic is largely retained.

I will refer below to aspects of Natural Philosophy in the work of some contemporary thinkers coming from biological and social scientific fields, such as Terrence Deacon [14] and Wolfgang Hofkirchner [15], who almost by definition work at the interface of Natural Philosophy and philosophy. It is not by accident that these people, as well as myself, are involved in the development of the science and philosophy of information and their naturalization.

It is now time to present the basic principles and formalisms of Logic in Reality, as described in detail in my 2008 book, *Logic in Reality* (Dordrecht, Springer) [9]. We will see among other things that the boundaries between the indicated domains should not be considered absolute, and why the word 'pure' should be banished from discussion.

## 3. Logic and Logic in Reality (LIR)

### 3.1. *The Logical Line. Change*

Part of the difficulty for the Lupasco concepts and LIR to gain acceptance is that it requires changes in perspective not only in the content of logic and logical analyses and the process of using it, but in our common-sense views of parts and wholes, sets, categories, truth, determinism, causality and time and space, all based on a more complex view of the principles underlying thought [16]. What is gained is a better perception of the dynamics of first-person experience, consciousness and other complex psychological and socio-economical processes, creativity and art.

The discussion of Logic in Reality, as it has emerged from the pioneering work of Lupasco, is formulated in this paper in language I have used previously, as it remains the best I have found to make this unfamiliar approach understandable. I am encouraged to note that at least two of the contributions to this Special Issue include references to LIR.

### 3.2. *The Principle of Dynamic Opposition: The T-State*

The antagonistic dualities of our world can be formalized as a structural, logical, and metaphysical principle of opposition or contradiction instantiated in complex higher-level phenomena (Principle of Dynamic Opposition—PDO). The fundamental postulate of LIR is that for all energetic phenomena (all phenomena) alternate between degrees of actualization and of potentialization of themselves and their opposites or 'contradictions' but without either going to the absolute limits of 0% or 100%. The point at which a logical element and its opposite are equally, 50% actualized and potentialized is one of maximum interaction from which new entities can emerge. It is designated by Lupasco and Basarab Nicolescu, the physicist colleague and major continuator of Lupasco [17], as a 'T'-state, T for included middle or third (*Tiers-inclus*). I use the concept of T-states to evaluate both philosophical and scientific theories, including patterns of human individual and social behavior. A dynamic systems view can be used to focus on the feedback in all natural processes.

### 3.3. *Philosophy and the Philosophy of Mind*

Regarding philosophy as such and the vast subject of the philosophy of mind, I will restate my criticism [18] of philosophical arguments. They often depend on some form of absolute separability of opposing or dichotomous terms, which use, in one way or another, the principles of binary logic which exclude the functionality of complex interaction.

For a philosophy of mind, the central problem is to show how physical tokens, the neuro-physiological processes occurring in the brain, can give rise to mental tokens that retain the properties of intentionality, 'aboutness', individuality and some level of causal powers or functionality. I have discussed the Lupasco conception of the operation of the human mind on which these capacities may be based in an article forthcoming in an *APA Newsletter* [19].

### 3.4. Insights from Chemistry

For clarity, I should explain that my ideas of process and change have been influenced by my training as a chemist. In chemical reactions one has, at the same time, reactants; an environment, for example a solvent in a reaction vessel; energy being added as heat or light; and some of the reactant atoms or molecules absorbing that energy to move toward a transition state from which, given favorable thermodynamic criteria, most of them will become products. However, also at the same time, some products are absorbing sufficient energy to move in the opposite direction and re-become reactants. I claim that not only is this a picture of what happens in other physical and biological sciences, but also in real cognitive and social situations. No description of processes, not relations as such but changes in relations or ideas, theories, etc. can be less complex, in a thermodynamic world, than this one from chemistry.

In more logical-philosophical terms—those of Lupasco—the movement described is from potentiality to actuality, from the point of view, say, of reactants to products, but this movement, to repeat, is not total and is always accompanied, even to a minor degree, by the opposite movement from actuality to potentiality, the 'regeneration' of reactants. We can always change our mind—twice. We do it from a point, a T-state in Lupasco or a transition state in chemistry—where the driving forces for change in direction are approximately equal.

I claim that the LIR approach can redefine the domains of philosophy: theories of reality which follow a bivalent or multivalent logic of propositions are satisfactory for philosophy, idealist or reductionist-materialist. The domain of Natural Philosophy can only be described by a logic of real processes that shows the origin and evolution of change.

### 3.5. Scientific Structural Realism (SSR)

I have positioned LIR as a theory of reality by comparing it to formulations of other realist theories. The conception of structures in LIR as real processes permits an alternate to Scientific Realism which I defined in [9] as a kind of scientific structural realism (SSR). The ontological structure of reality of LIR supports a non-naïve and above all non-absolute scientific realism, so that a theory of scientific structural realism is possible that includes the best of both worlds.

Details of this approach, including the relation to Ontic Structural Realism (OSR) are provided in my book. Basically, the answer to the question asked by Lupasco—"What is a structure?" [20]—is that structures also must be looked at as processes-in-change, dynamic entities (cf. [21,22]).

The metaphysics of LIR provides for a fundamental vagueness in nature. Any semantic conception, such as that of Kuhn, according to which the most basic laws in a theory or paradigm are true in some absolute sense is excluded as anti-realist.

### 3.6. A New Synthetic Philosophy

LIR statements look like what are termed synthetic statements, that is, ones whose truth depends on matters—in particular, contingent facts about the world—to which I have ascribed a certain dialectic structure. Such statements are to be distinguished from analytic statements that are true by virtue of the meaning of their constituent terms alone.

LIR thus provides support to a naturalistic, causal-role theory of mental content and a naturalistic means of drawing the analytic/synthetic distinction. This can be part of Natural Philosophy, even if a 'pure' analytic theory cannot be. LIR always defines a real relation between the intensional notions or aspects of a phenomenon and the extensional ones. Analytic claims can provide insight into external reality, but only if coupled with a non-semantic theory that provides some basis for explanation of the coincidence between our concepts and the properties or real phenomena of the world. By starting from the side of the phenomena, LIR permits progress toward a new 'synthetic' philosophy that if not entirely is more within the domain of Natural Philosophy[2].

## 4. Conceptual Precursors of LIR in Relation to Natural Philosophy

To support my new approach to and content of Natural Philosophy, reference needs to be made to its precursors to see where the LIR Principle of Dynamic Opposition might apply. Precursors include both non-contemporary and contemporary thinkers, and both philosophers and scientists. I will not attempt to review the entire history of knowledge from 'Heraclitus to Hegel to Heidegger', recognizing that significant elements of Logic in Reality are to be found in all of them. To repeat my thesis, to the extent that a component in these theories is present explicitly or implicitly equivalent to Logic in Reality, the relevant doctrine is *ipso facto* in the domain of a Natural Philosophy.

### *4.1. An Historical Line: Gare on Fichte, Schelling, and Engels*

The contribution of Arran Gare to this special issue [24] suggests a dialectic line of development of Natural Philosophy from Hegel through Fichte, Schelling, and Engels to Whitehead. He has set himself the objective of specifying the difference between natural philosophy and science in order to give the former a more functional role for making progress in knowledge. My approach in this paper can be summarized as specifying the difference between philosophy and natural philosophy in order to give the latter a more functional role for making progress in knowledge. In my approach, what is emphasized is the similarity or overlap between natural philosophy and the non-experimental sciences.

I refer the reader to Gare's article, but I will cite here some highly suggestive passages in the work of these authors that foreshadow the basic principles of Logic in Reality. Despite the 'bad press' which contradiction usually receives, Fichte said quite clearly [25] that the "thing-in-itself ... is a contradiction though as the object of a necessary idea it must be set at the foundation of all of our philosophizing, and has always lain at the root of all philosophy and all acts of the finite mind, save only that no one has been clearly aware of it, or of the contradiction contained therein. This relation of the thing-in-itself to the self forms the basis for the entire mechanism of the human and all other finite minds. Any attempt to change this would entail the elimination of all consciousness, and with it of all existence." It is this positioning of the concept of active, ontological contradiction, in Fichte and Lupasco that defines its place in Natural Philosophy.

As Gare points out, it was dialectics as developed by Schelling that "provided the forms of thinking required to develop natural philosophy". Schelling developed Fichte's notions of the appreciation of subjects as activities (JEB: processes) rather than objects and of cognition as the process by which nature has come to comprehend itself. The notion of synthesis rather than analysis is central, and so, as in Lupasco, is opposition. "Thought is inherently synthetic, Schelling argued, and begins with a genuine opposition between thought and something opposing it, or between other factors within thought." As in Lupasco, the dynamic basis is provided for emergence from a state of contradiction of a "new synthetic moment that can be treated as a product or factor in the next level of development". I only suggest, based on the principles of LIR, "product and factor". Emergent entities, as 'products', enter into oppositional relations as 'factors'. Lupasco specifically refers to his method as a 'dialectomethodology' which he saw as requiring the identification of the dialectically opposing forces operating in a process, their reciprocal degree of actualization and potentialization and the direction of the trend toward predominantly one or the other, as noted in Section 3 above.

It is equally relevant for this study to note the central place Gare gives to the unfinished 1883 work of Friedrich Engels, *Dialektik der Natur*. It can be described both as a philosophy of the natural

---

2 Let us not forget, at this point, from Schroeder's charter for *Philosophies*: "Synthesis through Diversity" [23].

sciences and a Natural Philosophy, demonstrating not the identity but the overlap of these concepts. As summarized by a Soviet writer, Boniface Kedrov (in a curious work found in an East German bookstore in the 1980s [26]), Engels gives ample justification for considering dialectics as a fundamental natural as well as epistemological process: "What is called objective dialectics is found throughout nature, and subjective dialectics, dialectical thought, only reflects the dominance, again throughout nature, of movement by opposition of contraries." This statement could be considered a philosophical foundation for the Natural Computation of Dodig-Crnkovic [27] (see below). Engels said that a dialectical method was the only one that could enable an understanding of reality. Engels made dialectics the basis of his and Lenin's materialism, but we do not need to follow him here. It is ironic that Lupasco adopted and developed the logic of this dialectics coming from a bourgeois background of *petite noblesse*. His rehabilitation of dialectics, however, was routinely attacked and denigrated (as well as plagiarized) by some of the armchair Marxists of the French *intelligentsia* such as Yves Barel. As for Lupasco, the point of departure for knowledge for Engels was the "qualitative aspect of things and phenomena and not their quantitative side".

In his further citations from the *Dialektik der Natur*, Gare suggests a relation to Lupasco with which I agree: "Dialectics is the science of universal interconnection, of which the main laws are the transformation of quality and quantity—mutual penetration of polar opposites and transformation into each other when carried to extremes—developments through contradiction or negation of negation—spiral form of development." Logic in Reality is a way of avoiding the dogmatism of Engels' thesis when it is stated this rapidly: the transformation of the polar opposites operating in complex systems is never complete; extremes of 0 and 1 are never reached except in trivial cases. Contradiction inheres in physical processes, and negation of negation remains at the level of linguistic logic. The concept of spiral form of development is an absolutely essential one which I have described in detail as a consequence of Deacon's concepts of "incomplete nature" [28]. I will discuss the work of both Whitehead and Deacon below.

### 4.2. A Scientific Line: Gödel, the Philosophy of Physics and LIR

Contemporary Natural Philosophy cannot be discussed without reference to the most important developments in 20th Century physical science: quantum physics, including the Pauli Exclusion Principle; the uncertainty principle of Heisenberg; and the Gödel principle of the reciprocity of completeness and consistency in mathematics. I call attention in particular to the work of Sklar on the Philosophy of Physics [29]. Let me state the relation between quantum mechanics and Logic in Reality apodictically: the superposition of quantum states is isomorphic to the T-state in LIR at macroscopic levels of reality. Together with uncertainty, a physical basis is provided for the Lupasco physical-logical Principle of Dynamic Opposition. As I have shown in [9], LIR can be usefully compared with quantum logics, but further conceptual changes are necessary to make quantum-type logics applicable to macroscopic change. It should be clear that an explanation of the experimentally demonstrable quantum features of the world will (still) require a radical rethinking of our metaphysical picture of it. At the latter level, the one of greatest generality, the definition of some principle that is missing or has been ignored would have major consequences for the future of 'reason' in the broadest possible sense. As indicated above, there may exist aspects of physics, expressed in the PDO, that are already accessible and could fit this description. In a recent paper [30], Bishop and I have discussed how Heisenberg's conception of potentiality, his *res potentiae*, should apply at a macroscopic level.

In has ontological approach to modern physics with regard to the development of field theories, Cao [21] sees the synergy—'mutual penetration'—between physics and metaphysics, considering that physics has also provided us with a direct access to metaphysical reality. Cao describes a debate, over the nature of energy suggest: "What if energy is taken as substance *with the new feature of being always active, always changing its form while keeping its quantity constant* (emphasis mine)? Then energeticism would seem to be a precursor of James's functionalism and Whitehead's ontology of process." This doctrine is close to LIR and perhaps should be how a philosopher could appreciate the first law of thermodynamics.

My interim conclusion is that a philosophy of physics embodying these principles lies comfortably within Natural Philosophy. The links to nature are extensively described in a crucial 2012 compendium by Kuhlmann and Pietsch: "What Is and Why Do We Need Philosophy of Physics?" [31]. Very much in the spirit of my analysis is the authors' thesis (ii): the boundary between physics and philosophy of physics is blurry, particularly with regard to foundational questions (e.g., the physical 'ground' of existence).

Nature's Metaphysics?

As an anti-thesis to the concepts developed in this paper, I cite a recent book by Alexander Bird which has the title of this section [32]. Bird defines the only fundamental natural properties as 'potencies' which, linguistically at least, are akin to potentialities. This dispositional monism gives him the foundation for the—necessary—laws of nature. As I stated in [9], the contradictorial relation between actuality and potentiality in LIR thus provides arguments against attacks on the reality of 'potencies', defined as dispositional properties that include potential manifestations. My demonstration that what is potential as well as what is actual is real answers the critique that only the actual is real. The modal argument (*possibilia* are not things that exist in other worlds but not in this one) against the objection that potencies involve unrealized manifestations of possibilities that, accordingly, violate naturalism is supported by a view of unrealized possibilities as real potentialities, but ones whose reality does not depend on their manifestation if this is prevented by an actuality.

Bird sees the elimination of invariance as a desirable feature, part of a general strategy of eliminativism: symmetry principles and conservation laws may be eliminated as being "features of our form of representation rather than features of our world requiring to be accommodated within our metaphysics". I do not contest—here—Bird's argument. I consider it an example of the Lupascian standpoint possible, namely, that a total separation of the world and our representations of it is neither necessary nor desirable. However, I would exclude his overall thesis from the domain of Natural Philosophy.

With this scientific–philosophical background, let us now look at one of the areas of major interest to contemporary philosophy, that of process.

### *4.3. The Philosophy of Process*

An area to which it is natural to apply the logical system outlined above is that of process. To the extent that it refers to real, physical and mental phenomena, placing the philosophy of process in the domain of Natural Philosophy should be self-evident. That it is not entirely so is a measure of the problem which this paper addresses. I analyze here the work of two contemporary philosophers.

#### 4.3.1. A. N. Whitehead: Consistency, Coherence, and Concrescence

Curiously, the criteria proposed in this paper place Whitehead's concepts of consistency and coherence both outside and inside the domain of Natural Philosophy. As summarized by Soelch [33], Whitehead supplements James's notion of an empirical, rational but subjective domain by a logic, but this logic is based on not more than standard rules of inference and the law of non-contradiction. I consider that this doctrine remains here at the level of epistemology, that "the fundamental ideas in terms of which a scheme is developed presuppose each other, so that in isolation they are meaningless". I note a reference to propositional truth. However, Whitehead's focus, anticipating phenomenology, is on the "texture of human experience". Coherence is also defined as the body (*sic*) of our theoretical knowledge, but at the same time it is "a basic inventory of concepts", an inert Peircean classification.

Much closer to NP in my view, which I discussed in [10], is Whitehead's concept of 'concrescence', extended in his *Process and Reality* [4] toward real systems: "The coherence, which the system (organism) seeks to preserve, is the discovery that the process, or concrescence, of any one actual entity involves the other actual entities among its components. In this way the obvious solidarity of the world receives its explanation."

4.3.2. Nicolas Rescher

The foundational work of Rescher on process metaphysics and process semantics is well known [5], and I have summarized my views of it elsewhere [9]. Rescher's mission for process philosophy is "enabling us to characterize, describe, clarify and explain the most general features of the real." Further, he relates his view of the processual structure of reality to energy, the entities of quantum mechanics entering into more and more complex arrangements.

In an Appendix to his [5], Rescher proposes a Process Semantics as an alternative to standard predicate logic as the conceptually most versatile and philosophically most fundamental tool for reasoning and understanding reality. His semantical (*sic*) strategy dispenses with object/subject terms and replaces them with verbs and adverbs indicative of processes. According to Rescher, these are capable of accomplishing what a semantics of individuals can do with properties and relations. His process semantics is thus at the basis of his ideas of process philosophy and process metaphysics. What he called the mainstream logical theory of the West, which takes an approach to truth that is committed to its static fixity, was and is unable to meet this challenge.

I can agree here with Gare's suggestion [34] that the resulting process doctrine looks like a logic whose terms are those of processes, including living processes. From an LIR standpoint, the notion of logic can be extended to include Gare's construction, which goes beyond Rescher's. The latter states that "dispositional processes accomplish exactly the needed job of rendering predicational terms of the form G[the-x(Fx)] contingently true or false". We are thus clearly in a truth-functional, linguistic domain. Logic in Reality of course is about nothing but properties and relations and their dynamics, but it is in a non-truth-functional, non-linguistic domain. Rescher does call attention to the lack of fixity of his conception of truth and the fluidity and analogue character of natural processes. On the other hand, he suggests their "kinship" to the continuities captured by differential equations, which is not adequate, as no reference is made to the continuity-discontinuity dualism.

Going now from Process Semantics to his major theme of Process Metaphysics, Rescher correctly states that matters of cognition and communication cannot be substance-like 'things', but are processual phenomena. These are described, we would now say, by the science and philosophy of information (see for example one of my papers with Wu Kun [35] and the discussion below). His processual view of scientific inquiry is equally important for the break it makes with the standard philosophy of science. As a process metaphysics which includes all these ideas, Rescher's philosophical 'system' does provide a distinctive and illuminating window on the world. He himself seems to have had an intuition of the transitional character of his doctrine and this is where I would position him, somewhere 'between' philosophy and natural philosophy. LIR describes change in terms of dynamic opposition and captures some of the features of process described by Rescher. In the absence of any other formal logical system that does so, LIR can be seen as the preferred logic of, in and for process. With this addition, we may consider the philosophy of process as being in the domain of Natural Philosophy.

4.3.3. Johanna Seibt

Among contemporary philosophers, Johanna Seibt, a student of Rescher, has extended the work of Whitehead and provides a basis for its potential naturalization into Natural Philosophy. I say 'potential' because I do not believe Seibt has fully achieved a naturalization in the terms of this paper. Her standard categorial entities in this formal ontology are theoretical entities with only axiomatic characterization. The only things to which she says we are ontologically committed by the use of abstract singular terms are linguistic entities, without explanatory force. In Lupasco, the term 'explanatory force' of non-linguistic entities (items) is not only a metaphor.

In correcting the 'The Myth of the Given', Sellars says [36] that non-propositional items cannot serve as what is given, but inferential relations are always between items with propositional form.

However, even Sellars, I would like to believe against his will, is forced into making 'distinguos'—yes or no positions due to the absence of a principled manner in which they can be seen as operating jointly, synchronically, or diachronically as the case may be.

I have suggested that the exclusion of contradiction from logic has overly constrained its applicability. Similarly, Seibt has shown how characteristic Aristotelian presuppositions have constrained ontology to a substance paradigm. From her standpoint, Seibt sees a trend in ontological theories that leads from traditional substance-ontological schemes operating with concrete, particular, static, and 'causally separate' entities (including abstract and general entities) to schemes whose basic entities are concrete but non-particular, dynamic, and 'causally interlaced' or 'overlapping'. LIR implies a dynamics for moving from the first group of entities to the second and a physical meaning to 'interlaced or overlapping'. This founds a metaphysical to and accordingly to a further new ontology, one of which the physical dynamics are an explicit part. Only such an ontology would meet my criteria for a role in Natural Philosophy.

### *4.4. Information Ethics and Digital Ontology*

Rafael Capurro has made pioneering contributions to the fields of the science, philosophy, and ethics of information based on his unique philosophical perspective of the position of humankind in the world. For Capurro, the field of information ethics defines the essentially social nature of meaningful information. In his formulation of a digital ontology [37], Capurro emphasizes that our ways of understanding ourselves and the world cannot be separated from the effects of the world on us but are radically grounded in them. He is in effect saying "ontology is not a discipline distinct from ethics; it is ethics in its original sense". In today's world, ethics and information ethics cannot be considered independently of one another.

From my dynamic logical perspective, Capurro's critical Heideggerian concepts of human existence have been naturalized, brought into a non-reductionist relation to science, and can be considered part of Natural Philosophy. They can be seen as part of a convergence of science and philosophy directed toward a revitalization of the concepts of the commons and of the common good.

### *4.5. Philosophy in the Flesh*

In their major 1999 study [2], George Lakoff and Mark Johnson make a devastating indictment of standard philosophy and—analytical and formalist philosophy in general, and they give full ontological value to the constructs of cognitive science. "The results of second-generation cognitive science stand squarely opposed to the analytic and formalist philosophical traditions ... on (1) the embodiment of concepts and of mind in general; (2) the cognitive unconscious; (3) metaphorical thought; and (4) the dependence of philosophy on the empirical study of mind and language." Their position on the relationship between science and philosophy is similar to the one taken in this paper: empirical scientific results, especially through an informational perspective, take precedence over *a priori* philosophical theories.

In their conclusion, the authors make a trenchant case for the importance of metaphor in philosophy, to ensure that "philosophical theories work". Metaphorical metaphysics "is not some quaint product of antiquated and naïve philosophical views. Rather, it is a characteristic of all philosophies, because it is a characteristic of all human thought." "Metaphors are the very means by which we can understand abstract domains and extend our knowledge into new areas."

I can agree with basically all of the critique of Lakoff and Johnson—their embodied realism—as an absolutely necessary part of a philosophy that is, as they say, creative and synthetic. I have some questions about the role assigned to metaphor. By saying that the logical structure of Aristotle's reasoning is metaphorical, and that his ontological commitments come out of the metaphors, our authors seem to have inversed ontological priority. They make metaphors—metaphorically—do more philosophical work to bind thought, knowledge, and imagination into an organic whole than I think they are capable of. I will refer again to their work in the Section 5 on Naturalization and Merleau-Ponty.

### 4.6. *Dé-Coïncidence (Decoincidence)*

The French philosopher and sinologist François Jullien has recently coined the term '*dé-coïncidence*' (decoherence/incoherence) to describe the dynamics of the evolution of cognitive and social processes [38]. Currently discredited theories of mind postulated quantum phenomena occurring in microtubules in the brain as the physical basis of thought. In fact, these would be 'washed out' by thermal noise, that is, they would no longer be coherent.

Jullien associates, very much in the spirit of Lupasco, decoincidence with temporality, emergence, symmetry breaking, and the foundations of ethics in opposition to the coherent inhuman world of quantum phenomena, timeless, changeless, and ethically neutral. One must follow the advice of von Bertalanffy and avoid pushing analogies to far, but in the context of Jullien's deep knowledge of Chinese philosophy and logic, the coincidences (*sic*) between the principles of LIR and his concept are striking.

## 5. Phenomenology and the Naturalization of Phenomenology

The reworking of some additional subjects within Philosophy seems necessary to eliminate what amount to category errors, ascribing to natural phenomena logical properties which are essentially fictions. These subjects are thus the main targets for the naturalization proposed in this paper. I will now discuss how this grid might apply to them, in other words, 'move' them to Natural Philosophy where possible. The precursor to naturalization as a process [39] was 'scientization', defined as the incursion of empirical science into areas of knowing previously the purview of theology and philosophy. An example of this is the attempted naturalization of intentionality [40], which has been only partially successful. If one looks explicitly for precedents to naturalization in philosophy, one finds that the term is generally used to describe a kind of grafting of philosophy onto science studies. This conceptual dead end suggests that the entire domain requires reconceptualization.

### 5.1. *Husserl and the Naturalization of Phenomenology*

In contemporary philosophy, phenomenology occupies a strange position: on the one hand, it seems to place major ontological value on appearance while at the same time denying access to it by science. Perhaps it is best seen from an historical standpoint as a reaction, perfectly understandable in the 20th Century, to the hegemony of reductionist scientific views of a universe in which a transcendental deity no longer had a place.

The 'naturalization of phenomenology' might however be considered an oxymoron to the extent that phenomenology was designed by Husserl to exclude physical reality. My view of physical reality is simply the world independent of our thought processes which are nevertheless part of it and without which it would not have meaning), as in the weak objectivity of D'Espagnat. Hussserl's approach of focusing on the unique lived character of experience available to individuals has led to the familiar definition of phenomenology. Familiar, also, is Husserl's later bracketing of the question of the existence of the natural world and its relation to experience vs. a realist ontology. As discussed below, the informational approach leads to alternate, and from an LIR standpoint preferable, descriptions of the co-existence of meaning and non-meaning in the world.

In the *Naturalizing Phenomenology* compendium of 1999, Roy [43] confirms that Husserl's phenomenological theory of intentionality is based entirely on the assumption that "truly adequate characterization of intentional phenomena can only be achieved by renouncing all forms of naturalism, both ontological and epistemological." I obviously agree with Roy that this is too high a philosophical price to pay. Although in Husserl every intentional state is conceived as one entity mediated by another, his relation of interpretation resembles that of Peirce with an ontological 'cut' between the interpretation and its intentional correlate. There is 'identity within difference', but not semantic, in my terms real, interaction between them.

### *5.2. Semiotics: Peirce and Brier*

The semiotician Sören Brier has claimed that the semiotics of Charles S. Peirce can deliver the missing philosophical framework for phenomenology through his semiotic conception of a fundamental triadic structure of the universe. Semiotics is a transdisciplinary doctrine that studies how signs in general—including codes, media, and language, plus the sign systems used in parallel with language—work to produce interpretation and meaning in human and nonhuman living systems such as prelinguistic communication systems. For Peirce, a sign is anything that stands for something or somebody in some respect or context.

Sören Brier has pointed out the weaknesses in much of standard philosophical and sociological thought in general and phenomenology in particular. He thus writes [44] that Husserl, Heidegger, Merleau-Ponty, and Luhmann were unsuccessful in developing a proper philosophical framework for phenomenology. They did not offer any adequately deep picture of things in themselves in relation to appearance. Thus both Wu Kun (see below, Section 8) and Brier state that Husserl's transcendental idealism makes no contact with the world or the natural sciences. In particular, Wu has provided a unique analysis of Husserl from an informational standpoint [45]. I will simply reiterate here his key conclusion, namely, the complexity of human individual and social existence and experience cannot be captured by reference to a "life-world" and "intersubjectivity" that exclude the detailed functional role of information, information processing and the operation of the physiological and psychological structures necessary for that processing.

Peirce's introspectional method leads him to ascribe a foundational role to chance and spontaneity as causal factors. The subsequent classification of reality into "Firstness, Secondness and Thirdness" follows. I have argued that Peirce's system remains one of classification of phenomena in terms of representation by signs and symbols. It adds nothing that helps us understand the ontological basis of the way the world evolves. Signs obviously refer to existing therefore natural objects, but they are abstractions from them, and the corresponding relationship is not natural-philosophical as no dynamic, ontological relations obtain between the entities involved.

The above considerations are the basis of Brier's thesis outlined in his major book *Cybersemiotics* [44] whose sub-title is "*Why Information is not Enough?*". My reply is that semiotics is not enough since it does not incorporate in its 'flesh', to use the Merleau-Ponty and Lakoff concept, the dynamic, energetic changes from actual to potential, present, and absent that the term 'information' refers to.

### *5.3. The 'Flesh': Merleau-Ponty and Lakoff and Johnson*

The contribution of Merleau-Ponty and his existentialist followers can be seen as a necessary reaction to the transcendentalism of Husserl. In his *Phenomenology of Perception*, Merleau-Ponty emphasized the role of the body in human experience. In the terms of Logic in Reality, his body-image is a kind of "included middle" between the mental and mechanical-physical domains. The human subject is inseparable from both his body and the world. Arran Gare has provided recent [47] authoritative discussion of Merleau-Ponty's trajectory which led him ultimately to embrace natural philosophy as the framework for his thought.

Unfortunately, by focusing on the human body (the 'flesh') as the primary philosophical entity, Merleau-Ponty effectively eliminated any foundational role for the properties of the underlying physical components of the 'flesh'. In my view, these properties that are not only consistent with consciousness and life but underlie their emergence as real and not epiphenomenal.

It is perhaps more than anecdotal to note that in a competition for a key position in the *Collège de France* in the 1950s, Merleau-Ponty was chosen over his contemporary rival—Lupasco. The marginalization of Lupasco can be dated to this event. As I have suggested in a paper in French [48], it is high time for this 'noble' marginalization to end. Finally, as I have discussed in another reference to Capurro's work [49], phenomenology should never, *pace* Husserl, have been conceived of as being a science in the first place.

### 5.4. *Speculative Realism: 'Ends'*

The basic concept of this paper is that the natural philosophical stance is augmented by inclusion of the logic of Lupasco outlined above. One of the consequences of my interpretation it that it becomes otiose to talk about the 'end' of phenomenology, like Sparrow, as in Sparrow's Speculative Realism [50] or even of the end of philosophy, as Heidegger famously did. If there is an 'end' to something, it is the splendid isolation of philosophy from science that amounts to a simplistic idealistic position. Philosophy, as opposed to phenomenology retains some transcendental aspects as essential to its existence as a domain of knowledge, even if concessions to satisfactory aspects of the scientific paradigm may have to be made. Philosophy and Natural Philosophy retain their specificities as disciplines within a transdisciplinary framework of which science and LIR are a part. The LIR categorical feature of non-separability denies the traditional philosophical division between theory and practice and looks for ways in which they overlap and inform one another. This process, and the mental movements it entails, are those which take place when a logic—LIR—is and should be considered as part of knowledge as a whole, including science, in what I have called the 'logical rejunction' of logic with knowledge initiated by Lupasco [51].

Let us now see, therefore, what a Philosophy of Information in relation to phenomenology and Natural Philosophy might bring to the table.

## 6. Luciano Floridi: Information Philosophy and Informational Structural Realism (ISR)

The concept of a specific Philosophy of Information was introduced by Luciano Floridi in Europe in order to bring some order into the many theories of and approaches to information. The debate went back to Wiener's "proto-physical" view of the nature of information—information is information, not matter or energy. LIR approaches the realist/anti-realist debate from a logical and scientific standpoint in which information as data or propositions are not primitive. From my perspective, Wiener's statement can no longer be accepted without some additional qualification. If the important properties of non-digital information are processual, causal, and value-bearing, in the LIR ontology, it is also energetic in nature.

I have discussed Floridi's Informational Structural Realism (ISR) [52], which I consider is supported by LIR at several points, in detail in my book, *Logic in Reality* [9] and in [53] and I will not repeat them here. I believe ISR is a useful tool to block radical anti-realist and anti-scientific scepticism. ISR, however, lacks the ontological dimension of LIR and cannot be included in the domain of Natural Philosophy. This position is supported by Beni in [54].

In the next section, I will show why I believe the Philosophy and Metaphilosophy of Information developed by Wu Kun in China can so be included.

## 7. Wu Kun and the Philosophy of Information

Working for over thirty-five years on a Philosophy of Information (PI) that includes an informational theory for all major fields of knowledge [7], Wu recovers dialectics as an appropriate strategy for philosophy and science, including social and political science. The basic insight of his Philosophy of Information is that the concept of objective reality = objective existence is too poor to describe the informational world. A proper new ontology and worldview is needed to describe the phenomenological characteristics of that existence. The development of Wu's thought, in and of itself, is equivalent to an 'emergence' from the ideological dialectical materialism of standard Marxism-Leninism. A more appropriate designation for Wu's doctrine is 'dialectical realism', a concept associated with the work of Theodor Adorno.

Wu's new informational view of the need for unification of critical disciplines and their formulation as a metaphilosophy constitute a major contribution, as yet little recognized outside China, to any general theory of information [55,56]. His theories constitute part of a new transdisciplinary paradigm, in which information has a central role in the transformation of the society and its approach to knowledge and the classical separation of the academic disciplines. In fact, Wu's approach constitutes and new, original and in my view necessary critique of the bases of modern philosophy as a whole.

In [57], Wu repeats his conviction that an informational ontological doctrine would provide the foundation for change in all other areas of philosophy, including epistemology. This statement of a new "open problem" has been addressed by Wu and the writer in a compendium relating information and the 'quest' for transdisciplinarity [58]. Our paper suggests convergence of science and philosophy in the area of information, and we propose reasons why this could be a phenomenon defining the contours of the Philosophy of Science and Philosophy in general.

Wu's picture confers an ontological dimension to the categorial discussions of information theory that have been largely epistemological, for example, the Philosophy of Information of Luciano Floridi (see above). In the perspective of this paper, the complex physical and non-physical real properties of information place the philosophy applicable to them within a generalized Natural Philosophy. This approach is consistent with my view of 'information-as-process' set out in my 2014 paper [10].

### *7.1. Information as Process*

In the LIR view, real informational entities are processes, binary and non-binary, that are not independent of and cannot be discussed without reference to the *a priori* non-binary transfers of energy that are their source, in some real situation, at all levels of reality. The LIR approach thus incorporates and provides for a relation between information as well-formed, meaningful and truthful data (Floridi) and information as real energetic processes. Information-as-processes can function as higher-level operators, capable of causing change on information-as-data and higher level entities.

The approach of the sociologist and systems theorist Wolfgang Hofkirchner approach to a Unified Theory of Information (UTI) [59] is to eliminate the absolute and in my view artificial separation between critical concepts of information in favor of a dialectical relationship similar to the ancient intuition of 'unity-in-diversity'. Specifically, his "UTI seeks a concrete-universal concept of information rather than an abstract one". Hofkirchner considers information as a "superconcept", which includes a group of overlapping concepts—such as message, signal, etc.—as they apply to communication, cognition and cooperation between human and non-human organisms. Hofkirchner asks how matter and idea, mind, information, etc. can be grasped as complements and with them information as a thing (a structure, a flow) or as a human construction. Hofkirchner gives a dialectical answer to the implied division between subject and object, suggesting that mind, and with it information, is of a different 'materiality' than 'non-emergent' states of matter.

From the LIR standpoint, mind and information can be seen as "complements" if one sees them as processes. Structure, flow and "human processing activity" all follow the same real, physical dialectics. If matter and information are differentiated in a "common genus", for LIR, that genus is simply energy, and within it both follow its logical patterns of evolution, avoiding the problems of the term "different materiality". Logic in Reality is, also, a logic of emergence or "emergent materialism". In this view, information is, *pace* Wiener, an energetic phenomenon that instantiates real contradictions.

My conception of information as process should not be taken to exclude other perspectives. Marcin Schroeder seeks [60] the structural characteristics of information—syllogisms—using a combination of philosophical and mathematical perspectives (one/many; Boolean algebra; lattices of closed sub-sets). Such structures can be carriers of some new qualitative properties of information, for example the level of information integration which reflects the mutual interdependence of the elements of a variety. Schroeder has called the lattices involved the logic of the information system, by loose analogy to quantum logic.

However, the basic logic of this approach is in my opinion still a logic of propositions or their mathematical equivalents. The qualitative properties of information which are described are formal; these structural characteristics have no meaningful implications for real phenomena beyond their (clear) formulation. Accordingly, they are not within Natural Philosophy in the sense of this paper.

It is, rather, non-Boolean algebras together with non-Kolmogorovian probabilities that are appropriate systems for analysis.

*7.2. Wu Contra Husserl*

Wu expressed his views of the critical role of information in 2011 [61]. As noted above, in the light of information theory, the weaknesses of modern philosophy, from Kant through Husserl become apparent. It is the existence of information, even more than, but in concordance with, the logic of and in reality (LIR), that breaks the traditional absolute separation of subject and object. As noted above, although Husserl found a way of beginning to describe the reality of consciousness, his one-dimensional phenomenological reduction maintains, in another form, the disastrous (for human society) polarization of standard bivalent logics. As a hermeneutic process, Husserl's bracketing is thus fundamentally flawed. My conclusion from this discussion of phenomenology is that in the informational terms of Wu Kun, it can be included in Natural Philosophy. In its initial formulation by Husserl it cannot.

In the work of both philosophers and neuroscientists such as Searle and Deacon as well as Wu Kun, the basic worldview of natural science, namely, that consciousness is part of nature is upheld. As is discussed below, the advantage of an informational standpoint, or 'stance', is that information serves as the unifying concept between the fields of physics, biology, neuroscience and mind. In this sense, the philosophy of information is a more scientific and reasonable explanation of the mechanism of human understanding than in phenomenology.

Following Wu, I propose an informational ontology in which we as humans have (self-evidently) access to "things-in-themselves" as a 'natural phenomenology' that is objective or better objective and subjective in its interpretation of the structure of the world. We live, also as indicated in the dialectics of Lupasco, by adhering to route on which "the natural noumenon's own movement explains the world".

Thus, functional and operational definitions of information have their role to play in practical applications. However, they fail to capture both the intrinsic dynamics of complex processes and the nature of information itself which is instantiated in them. For the understanding of knowledge and knowledge propagation, drastic modifications of points in standard epistemology, also foreseen in LIR, have to be made.

*7.3. The Science-Philosophy of Information*

The insights gained in the study of the unique scientific and philosophical characteristics of information are summarized in [58]. Wu's original idea is that what is taking place in philosophy is a 'scientification' of philosophy and a 'philosophization' of science, his terms for the convergence of the disciplines under the influence of the unique properties of information processes. The term Unified Science of Information has been applied to characterize the convergence, but this is not strictly accurate, as the convergent theory includes the Philosophy of Information as a proper part, without conflation. We therefore proposed the term Unified Science-Philosophy of Information (USPI) as the best possible description of this field.

The philosophical stance of USPI may be usefully compared to Hofkirchner's proposal [15] of a praxio-onto-epistemology (POE) as "a response to the current developmental requirements of humanity". According to Hofkirchner, (I invert his order of points) we need to (1) reflect the unity of the physical world by the unity of the world of knowledge; (2) the unity of the social world presupposes the unity of the physical world; (3) the survival of civilization itself depends on establishing a new world order, a unity of the social world. Traditional approaches are apparently stuck in the three disciplines of epistemology, ontology, and praxiology as alternatives. POE offers a transdisciplinary response for going beyond them. It is a synthesis, and a concept for inclusion in a new Synthetic Philosophy that resembles that of LIR and the USPI in this respect.

Wu and I concluded that what has been defined is both new content of the philosophy of science and new dynamics of the relations between a science and its philosophy. The dynamics of the processes can be captured in the concept of a trend toward an Informational Metaphilosophy of Science as the most appropriate model of knowing and reasoning. This Philosophy-Science justifies a new non-reductionist view of the world in which it is ethically impossible to maintain any scientific basis for economic, social or ethical exclusion. The use of this doctrine to promote the development of an information commons and the common good is thus a moral as well as a methodological imperative.

From the point of view of this paper, everything that could be considered part of such a Unified Science-Philosophy of Information, or which could be described as a science-philosophy in general would be part of Natural Philosophy. The Philosophy of Science itself could thus also be segmented based on the same criterion.

### *7.4. The Philosophy of Natural Computation*

Computational approaches are currently at the center of developments in the theory and philosophy of information; what form of computationalism is most adequate is a metaphilosophical issue. The theory comes in two major forms, (1) pan-computationalism or strong computationalism, which includes statements that the universe operates like a computer; and (2) a weaker form, developed by Gordana Dodig-Crnkovic [27], informational or info-computationalism (ICON) which reflects Floridi's view of the universe as an informational structure (see above), in which natural computation governs the dynamics of information.

Natural computation represents implementation of physical laws on an informational structure within a living system. Her work thus presents a synthesis of two paradigms within contemporary philosophy—computationalism and informationalism - into a new dual-aspect info-computationalist framework. The dualism itself does not mean that the phenomena are separated, and exclude each other. On the contrary, they are mutually determining, constraining, and completely indissoluble. Structures and the processes are inseparably interwoven by physical laws, as described by Dodig-Crnkovic, and LIR gives logical underpinning to the dynamics of "interwoven". ICON, as a naturalized epistemological approach, it conceptualizes information as both here (intelligence), there (world) and on the interface, as information constitutes the basic 'stuff' of existence. It grasps many features of natural processes.

In the context of this study, computationalism as natural computation thus appears as an acceptable, natural philosophical component of a Metaphilosophy of Information as I have defined Natural Philosophy.

### *7.5. The Logic of the Third*

In his approach to a Unified Theory of Information (UTI), Hofkirchner does not refer to the fields of philosophy or the philosophy of information as such. However, many of his concepts and formulations illuminate core philosophical, logical and ethical problems, in the context of the 'informational turn' and with a clearly stated objective of furthering a Global Sustainable Information Society (GSIS).

As Hofkirchner writes [15], a UTI should be a logical as well as an historical thesis, explaining not only the historical appearance (emergence) of new information processes and structures but how these processes and structures are logically linked. Hofkirchner explicitly excludes standard deduction as incapable of accomplishing this task, but LIR would appear to be an acceptable candidate for doing so.

His combination of critical thinking and systems thinking—of Critical Theory and Systems Theory—includes what he calls the Logic of the Third [63]. The (informal) Logic of the Third is the foundation of a critical social systems theory, in which "criticism is a method oriented toward recognising and sublating contradictions". Hofkirchner is an adept of Hegel; I will only remind readers here that real contradictions have a positive valence in Lupasco and LIR. 'Management' rather than elimination of them is my preferred strategy.

Hofkirchner states that given a society characterized by agonisms, legitimate agonistic differences can and do degenerate into antagonistic denials of the 'other' when social actors try to impose their own interests exclusively. This phenomenon can be considered as one principle of this Logic of the Third:

only the social relations that reinforce one's own position enter into consideration as a 'mechanism' that operates for the transformation of agonisms into antagonisms. The most important question is if and how a needed 'mechanism' of turning antagonisms into agonisms can work, how it can take the edge off them, how it can sustainably de-escalate them—a question to be answered according to the same Logic of the Third. A conjunction between Hofkirchner's approach and Logic in Reality is easily found: Lupasco's central 1951 book is entitled, in English, "The Principle of Antagonism and the Logic of Energy" [16]. LIR is, also, a logic of an emergent 'third' element in real processes and included without difficulty the real antagonism between human beings as logical in this sense.

Another classical philosophical problem, with which both LIR and Hofkirchner are concerned, is the relation between the 'one' and the 'many'; identity and diversity; and identity and difference. This is a key concept in Lupasco's dynamic logic of/in reality in which movement from primarily diversity or heterogeneity to unity or homogeneity was as fundamental as that between actuality and potentiality in the basic structure of the universe.

Hofkirchner proposes the relation between identity and difference as describing four ways of thinking: reductionism, projectivism, disjunctivism, and integrativism. The first two yield unity without diversity, the third diversity without unity. The fourth, as also expressed by the contemporary philosophers Edgar Morin, yields the necessary unity-in-diversity and diversity-in-unity. Hofkirchner applies these concepts to information in a doctrine of emergent materialism (EM) that goes beyond materialistic and idealistic monism and (even) interactive dualism. The dialectics of EM recognizes, like the theory of Wu Kun, the identity and difference of matter and information. EM is a philosophy of mind, "overarching all manifestations of information and not only mind."

Logic in Reality is compatible with part but not all of this approach. LIR provides a realistic interpretation of the physical, dialectical relation, a grounded 'interactive dualism' between identity and diversity, a unity-in-diversity and a diversity-in-unity as well as between the terms of other critical physical and philosophical dualities. As stated above LIR, in contrast to standard bivalent or multivalent propositional logics, it provides the basis for an ethics as the finality for the intellectual process, a principle which also pervades the work of Hofkirchner. It thus satisfies both my formal and moral criteria for a Natural Philosophy.

### 7.6. *The 'Incomplete Nature' of Terrence Deacon*

The currently prevailing assumptions about the nature of information are still based largely on computational extensions of Shannon's original ideas, sufficient to explicate its minimal physical characteristics but insufficient to define its representational character or its functional, qualitative, and normative value. The biologist Terrence Deacon has proposed a new approach to information as a process instantiating a complex dynamics that starts with thermodynamics and continues throughout higher ontological levels of form (morphodynamics) and intentionality (teleodynamics). In his *Incomplete Nature* [14], Deacon extends a thermodynamic concept of energy derived from statistical mechanics to yield a complete and cohesive description of complex processes, in which absence, the fact of being not or not completely present, plays a critical role in the emergence of living systems, mind, and information.

Deacon shows the central role of negative relationships defined with respect to absence. The concepts of information, function, purpose, meaning, intention, significance, consciousness, change and human value are intrinsically defined by their fundamental incompleteness.

This is similar to the LIR picture of energy as an energy-matter duality, with a critical role of potential as well as actual properties of processes. My own presentation of a concept of information focused on its dynamic characteristics—information as a process constituted by energy but carrying meaning [65]. Deacon shows how the operation of both Shannon entropy and Boltzmann entropy must be taken into account in information, and Logic in Reality (LIR) further suggests that information involves non-Markovian processes.

In my 2012 paper [28], I demonstrated the complementarity of the LIR and Deacon approaches to what is not, or not fully, present—not "there"—in gaining an understanding of the dynamics of complex phenomena, especially, of intentionality, information and ethics. My own presentation of a concept of information focused on its dynamic characteristics—information as a process constituted by energy but carrying meaning.

Deacon showed that the key feature of information is its absent content, a resultant function of the necessary physicality of information processes. LIR shows that presence (actuality) and absence (potentiality) in such processes must be related dynamically. While the importance of a concept of absence for information was indicated by Marijuan 10 years ago, it is Deacon's detailed current development that now calls for our attention.

LIR provides a necessary further *validation* of the role of absence as defined by Deacon, in relation to presence, and prepares its *valuation*. Valuation of absence and negation in general is logically equivalent to the valuation of the other, immanently. Thus in addition to explicating the evolution of complex processes, Logic in Reality, unlike all standard logics, founds an ethics and this implies, today, an ethics of information.

The work of Deacon and Logic in Reality share the ontological feature of being firmly grounded in physical processual reality. The latter enables a critique of the former such that principles of the combined theories offer a new platform for progress in the science and philosophy of life. Meaning, morality, emergence have their own logic and real dynamics and do not need to import natural philosophical principles from outside of physics. In more recent work [66], Deacon and Cashman explored further the philosophical implications of absence as incompleteness, emphasizing that it is a necessary component for the description of a real world that includes meaning and human values. I thus see his work as a major contribution to a new Natural Philosophy.

## 8. Conclusions

The theory outlined in this paper starts from a logic grounded in science and applied to philosophy. This non-standard logic of processes in/of reality, LIR, is a rigorous alternative to bivalent or multivalent propositional logic as a requirement for a valid system.

LIR can be a method of distinguishing between Natural Philosophy and philosophy *tout court*. It is based on the assumption that energy deploys itself in all existence, in particular in human existence and complex cognitive and social processes, in a movement from actuality to potentiality and vice versa, alternately and reciprocally, without either totally disappearing, except in trivial static cases. This logic, which I call Logic in Reality, supports and is supported by parts of doctrines from many different and disparate sources, including some of the informal perspectives of Eastern, in particular Chinese world-views. This logical approach establishes non-separability as a basic ontological principle and, among other things, supports the role of 'the other' in society, an argument in favor of social-economic justice and the common good.

The domain of philosophy-as-such, 'just' philosophy, as a separate discipline is best directed toward the study of general principles, such as the unity of knowledge and speculative, 'fundamental' questions such as "why is there something rather than nothing?" A characteristic feature of such questions is that they do not change, although an individual's interpretation of them will obviously be a function of his or her context. In this domain I include apparently dynamic theories such as category theory, semiotics and quantum-type logics applicable to macroscopic phenomena which in fact retain the principles of standard propositional and mathematical logics. Their capability of describing the 'interesting', that is, interactive, changing and moral aspects of phenomena is accordingly limited.

The phenomenon of human and animal consciousness is placed squarely in the domain of Natural Philosophy. Representations and beliefs are natural *qua* the mental processes from which they develop; they are only pure philosophy with regard to content, even if they refer to real objects and can be verified *a posteriori*. As in the case of organism evolution, it is only by examining the dynamics of lower-level emergent processes that we will be able to adequately explain the sentience, representation, perspective, and agency that are the hallmarks of mental experience as a dynamic proces. Rather than being the ultimate "hard problem" of philosophy and neuroscience, the subjective features of neural dynamics are the expected consequences of its emergent hierarchy, as discussed by Deacon [66]. The so-called mystery of consciousness may be a false dilemma, created by our failure to understand the causal efficacy of emergent constraints.

I have addressed two major errors that have been made in the discussion of lived experience: one is to 'bracket' it, following Husserl; the other is to deny that it has a scientific or at least regular, partly reproducible properties, structure and dynamics. The anti-scientific approach had perhaps the laudable intention of avoiding reductionism, but it lacks the necessary coherence to function as a guide to ethical behavior. Transcendental intuition is not a concept within Natural Philosophy as discussed in this paper.

The formulation of LIR does not preclude and welcomes the development of alternative, opposing logical systems, in which some logic is explicit or implied. I have suggested elsewhere the work of Derrida [67] on "grammatology as a positive science" and the process philosophy of Seibt as examples. However, I cannot accept as candidates for any such newer, expanded theory those which aim at some absolute truth or certainty. My 'philosopher's stone' tests for the absence of pure concepts, conceptions of pure 'things'—identities, static concepts, and unstructured diversities without a minimum of self- and hetero-organization. LIR seeks the presence of physical processes-in-progress, all of which are meaningful and capable of being re-cognized as such.

If one accepts that Natural Philosophy should be a coherent but dynamic doctrine with the above properties, capable of integrating science without falling into 'scientism', Logic in Reality is a tool for achieving this 'naturalization'. Accordingly, I look forward with great interest to reading the other papers in this special issue and the revisions and additions to Logic in Reality, as well as other ideas that they may suggest.

**Funding:** This research received no external funding.

**Acknowledgments:** I would like to acknowledge my particular gratitude to Rafael Capurro and Arran Gare for their pertinent comments and encouragement. There are two other authors in particular whose work should be considered as contemporary Natural Philosophy and would therefore be relevant to the objective of the special issue: Robert Ulanowicz, whose paper on ecology appears in it, and Marc-Williams Debono, who has developed a concept of 'plasticity' in thought and other natural phenomena. However, the number of topics in this paper is already large. They also have encouraged me in it, and I hope to do justice to their work in forthcoming papers.

**Conflicts of Interest:** The author declares no conflict of interest.

## References

1. Ayer, A. *Language, Truth and Logic*, 2nd ed.; Dover Publications, Inc.: New York, NY, USA, 1946.
2. Lakoff, G.; Johnson, M. Philosophy in the Flesh. In *The Embodied Mind and its Challenge to Western Thought*; Basic Books: New York, NY, USA, 1999.
3. Bennett, M.R.; Hacker, P.M.S. *Philosophical Foundations of Neuroscience*; Blackwell Publishing: Malden, MA, USA, 2003.
4. Whitehead, A. *Process and Reality. Corrected Edition*; The Free Press: New York, NY, USA, 1998.
5. Rescher, N. *Process Metaphysics*; State University of New York Press: Albany, NY, USA, 1996.
6. Seibt, J. Free Process Theory: Towards a Typology of Occurrings. In *Process Theories: Cross-Disciplinary Studies in Dynamic Categories*; Seibt, J., Ed.; Kluwer Academic Publishers: Dordrecht, The Netherlands, 2003.
7. Wu, K. The Basic Theory of the Philosophy of Information. In Proceedings of the 4th International Conference on the Foundations of Information Science, Beijing, China, 21–24 August 2010.
8. Floridi, L. *The Philosophy of Information*; Oxford University Press: Oxford, UK, 2010.
9. Brenner, J. *Logic in Reality*; Springer: Dordrecht, The Netherlands, 2008.
10. Brenner, J. Process in Reality: A Logical Offering. *Log. Log. Philos.* **2005**, *14*, 165–202. [CrossRef]
11. Deleuze, G.; Guattari, F. *Qu'est-ce que la Philosophie?* Les Éditions de Minuit: Paris, France, 1991.
12. Capurro, R. Capurro provides his conceptions, in the text E-mail, of the difference between philosophy and Natural Philosophy. Private E-mail to the author. 28 July 2018.

13. Priest, G. Inconsistency in the Empirical Sciences. In *Inconsistency in Science*; Meheus, J., Ed.; Kluwer Academic: Dordrecht, The Netherlands, 2002.
14. Deacon, T. *Incomplete Nature. How Mind Evolved from Matter*; W.W. Norton & Co.: New York, NY, USA, 2011.
15. Hofkirchner, W. Emergent Information. In *A Unified Theory of Information Framework*; World Scientific: Singapore, 2013.
16. Lupasco, S. *Le Principe D'antagonisme et la Logique de l'énergie*; Éditions du Rocher: Paris, France, 1987; (Originally Published in Éditions Hermann: Paris, France, 1951.).
17. Nicolescu, B. *Nous, la Particule et le Monde*; Éditions du Rocher: Paris, France, 2002; (Originally published in Éditions Le Mail: Paris, France, 1985.).
18. Brenner, J. Information in Reality: Logic and Metaphysics. *Triple-C* **2011**, *9*, 332–341. [CrossRef]
19. Brenner, J. Consciousness as Process: A New Logical Perspective. *APA Newsletter/Philosophy and Computers* **2018**, *18*, 9–23.
20. Lupasco, S. *Qu'est-ce qu'une structure?* Christian Bourgois: Paris, France, 1967.
21. Ladyman, J.; Ross, D. *Every Thing Must Go. Metaphysics Naturalized*; Oxford University Press: Oxford, UK, 2007.
22. Cao, T. *Conceptual Developments of 20th Century Field Theories*; Cambridge University Press: Cambridge, UK, 1997.
23. Schroeder, M. The Philosophy of *Philosophies*. Synthesis through Diversity. *Philosophies* **2016**, *1*, 68–72. [CrossRef]
24. Gare, A. Natural Philosophy and the Sciences: Challenging Science's Tunnel Vision. *Philosophies* **2018**, *3*, 33. [CrossRef]
25. Fichte, J. *Science of Knowledge*; Cambridge University Press: Cambridge, UK, 1982.
26. Kedrov, B. *Dialectique, Logique, Gnoséologie: Leur Unité*; Éditions du Progrès: Moscow, Russia, 1970.
27. Dodig-Crnkovic, G. Nature as a network of morphological infocomputational processes for cognitive agents. *Eur. Phys. J. Spec. Top.* **2017**, *226*, 181–195. [CrossRef]
28. Brenner, J. The Logical Dynamics of Information; Deacon's "Incomplete Nature". *Information* **2012**, *3*, 676–714. [CrossRef]
29. Sklar, L. *Philosophy of Physics*; Westview Press: Boulder, CO, USA; San Francisco, CA, USA, 1992.
30. Bishop, R.; Brenner, J. Potentiality, Actuality and Non-Separability in Quantum and Classical Physics: Heisenberg's *Res Potentiae* in the Macroscopic World. *arXiv*, 2018; arXiv:1801.01471.
31. Kuhlmann, M.; Pietsch, W. What Is and Why Do We Need Philosophy of Physics? *J. Gen. Philos. Sci.* **2012**, *43*, 209–214. [CrossRef]
32. Bird, A. *Nature's Metaphysics. Laws and Properties*; Oxford University Press: Oxford, UK, 2007.
33. Soelch, D. From Consistency to Coherence. Whitehead's Transformation of James's Epistemic Conservatism. *Eur. J. Pragmatism Am. Philos.* **2011**, *III*. [CrossRef]
34. Gare, A. Private E-mail to the author. 20 September 2018.
35. Philosophy of Information: Revolution in Philosophy. Towards an Informational Metaphilosophy of Science. *Philosophies* **2017**, *2*, 22. [CrossRef]
36. Rosenberg, J. Wilfrid Sellars. *The Stanford Encyclopedia of Philosophy (Summer 2006 Edition)*. Zalta, E.N., Ed.; Available online: http://plato.stanfordedu/archives/sum2006/entries/sellars/ (accessed on 29 April 2012).
37. Capurro, R. Towards an ontological foundation of information ethics. *Eth. Inf. Technol.* **2006**, *8*, 175–186. [CrossRef]
38. Jullien, F. *Dé-Coïncidence*; Grasset: Paris, France, 2017.
39. Feldman, R. Naturalized Epistemology. In *The Stanford Encyclopedia of Philosophy Summer 2012 Edition*; Zalta, E.N., Ed.; The Metaphysics Research Lab Center for the Study of Language and Information, Cordura Hall Stanford University: Stanford, CA, USA, 2012; Available online: http://plato.stanford.edu/archives/sum2012/entries/epistemology-naturalized/ (accessed on 12 August 2013).
40. Jacob, P. *Intentionality, The Stanford Encyclopedia of Philosophy (Winter 2014 Edition)*. Zalta, E.N., Ed.; Available online: http://plato.stanford.edu/archives/win2014/entries/intentionality/ (accessed on 23 February 2015).
41. Petitot-Cocorda, J. *Physique du Sens*; CNRS Éditions: Paris, France, 1999.

42. Smith, D. Intentionality Naturalized? In *Naturalizing Phenomenology. Issues in Contemporary Phenomenology and Cognitive Science*; Petitot, J., Varela, F.J., Pachoud, B., Roy, J.-M., Eds.; Stanford University Press: Stanford, CA, USA, 2011; pp. 83–110.
43. Roy, J. Saving Intentional Phenomena: Intentionality, Representation and Symbol. In *Naturalizing Phenomenology*; Petitot, J., Varela, F., Pachoud, B., Roy, J.-M., Eds.; Stanford University Press: Stanford, CA, USA, 1999.
44. Brier, S. *Cybersemiotics. Why Information is not Enough*; University of Toronto Press: Toronto, ON, Canada, 2008.
45. Wu, K. The Complex Characteristics of Multidimensional Emergence: Critique of Husserl's Phenomenological Reduction. In Proceedings of the International Symposium on Cutting-edge Issues of the Contemporary Philosophy of Science and Mind, Guangzhou/Macau, China, 13–17 December 2010.
46. Brenner, J. The Philosophical Logic of Stéphane Lupasco. *Log. Log. Philos.* **2010**, *19*, 243–285.
47. Kauffman, S.; Gare, A. Beyond Descartes and Newton: Recoverinng life and humanity. *Prog. Biophys. Mol. Biol.* **2015**, *119*, 219–244. [CrossRef] [PubMed]
48. Brenner, J. Stéphane Lupasco: Vers la fin d'une noble marginalité. *Sociétés* **2013**, *1*, 71–78. [CrossRef]
49. Brenner, J. The 'Naturalization' of the Philosophy of Rafael Capurro. In *A Festschrift in Honor of Rafael Capurro*; Kelly, M., Bielby, J., Eds.; Springer Fachmedien: Wiesbaden, Germany, 2016; pp. 45–64.
50. Sparrow, T. The End of Phenomenology. In *Metaphysics and the New Realism*; Edinburgh University Press: Edinburgh, UK, 2014.
51. Brenner, J. Stéphane Lupasco et la rejonction métalogique. In *A la Confluence de Deux Cultures—Lupasco Aujourd'hui*; Editions Oxus: Paris, France, 24 March 2010.
52. Floridi, L. A Defence of Informational Structural Realism. *Synthese* **2008**, *161*, 2008. [CrossRef]
53. Brenner, J. Information: A Personal Synthesis. *Information* **2014**, *5*, 134–170. [CrossRef]
54. Beni, M. Epistemic Informational Structural Realism. *Minds Mach.* **2016**, *26*, 223–239. [CrossRef]
55. Wu, K. The Essence, Classification and Quality of the Different Grades of Information. *Information* **2012**, *3*, 403–419. [CrossRef]
56. Wu, K.; Brenner, J. Informational Thinking and Systems Thinking: A Comparison. In Proceedings of the Foundations of Information Conference, Moscow, Russia, 13 June 2013.
57. Wu, K. The Development of Philosophy and Its Fundamental Turn. In Proceedings of the 1st International Conference on the Philosophy of Information, Xi'An, China, 18 October 2013.
58. Wu, K.; Brenner, J. A Unified Science-Philosophy of Information. In *Information Studies and the Quest for Transdisciplinarity*; World Scientific: Singapore, 2017.
59. Hofkirchner, W. How to achieve a unified theory of Information. *Triple-C* **2009**, *7*, 357–358. [CrossRef]
60. Schroeder, M. Dualism of Selective and Structural Manifestations of Information in Modelling of Information Dynamics. In *Computing Nature. Turing Centenary Perspective*; Dodig Crnkovic, G., Giovagnioli, R., Eds.; Springer: Berlin, Germany, 2013; pp. 125–137.
61. Wu, K. The Fundamental Turn of Philosophy and Basic Philosophical Issues. *Hebei Acad. J.* **2011**, *4*, 11–21. (In Chinese)
62. Depraz, N. When Transcendental Genesis Encounters the Naturalization Project. In *Naturalizing Phenomenology. Issues in Contemporary Phenomenology and Cognitive Science*; Stanford University Press: Stanford, CA, USA, 1999; pp. 464–489.
63. Hofkirchner, W. On the Validity of Describing 'Morphogenic Society' as a System and Justifiability of Thinking about it as a Social System. In *Late Modernity. Trajectories toward Morphogenic Society*; Archer, M., Ed.; Springer: Cham, Switzerland, 2014; pp. 119–141.
64. Batterman, R. *The Devil in the Details. Asymptotic Reasoning in Explanation, Reduction and Emergence*; Oxford University Press: Oxford, UK, 2002.
65. Brenner, J. The Logic of the Physics of Information. *Information* **2014**, *5*, 389–403. [CrossRef]
66. Deacon, T.; Cashman, T. Steps to a Metaphysics of Incompleteness. *Theol. Sci.* **2016**, *14*, 401–429. [CrossRef]
67. Derrida, J. *Of Grammatology*, Corrected ed.; The Johns Hopkins University Press: Baltimore, MA, USA; London, UK, 1997.

# 10

# Philosophy of Information and Revolution in Philosophy: Towards an Informational Metaphilosophy of Science

**Kun Wu** [1] **and Joseph Brenner** [1,2,*]

1 International Center for the Philosophy of Information, Xi'an Jiaotong University, Xi'an 710048, China; wukun@mail.xjtu.edu.cn
2 International Center for Transdisciplinary Research, Paris c/o Chemin du Collège 1, Les Diablerets 1865, Switzerland
* Correspondence: joe.brenner@bluewin.ch

**Abstract:** In the most general if unconventional terms, science is the study of how man is part of the universe. Philosophy is the study of man's ideas of the universe and how man differs from the rest of the universe. It has of course been recognized that philosophy and science are not totally disjointed. Science is in any case not a monolithic entity but refers to knowledge as the results of reasoning and both invasive and non-invasive experiment. We argue that the philosophy of science, in studying the foundations, methods and implications of science and the link between philosophy and science, must now take into account the impact of the rapidly developing science and philosophy of information. We suggest that the philosophy of information is in fact a metaphilosophy, since informational processes operate in all the sciences and their philosophies. The simplest definition of (a) metaphilosophy is that of a set of statements about (a) philosophy, and any definition of a metaphilosophy thus requires one of philosophy and of the task of philosophy as well. According to Sellars, "the aim of philosophy is to understand how things in the broadest possible sense of the term hang together in the broadest possible sense of the term". In this paper, we focus on the recursive thought underlying those statements as real processes, occurring both in and between the fundamental and the meta-level. We propose a non-standard logic, Logic in Reality, as the logic of those processes. The metaphilosophy of information is thus a framework for talking about the scientific aspects of philosophy and the philosophical aspects of science. Both Logic in Reality and the metaphilosophy of information provide a basis for understanding the physical and epistemological dynamics of existence, that is, from where the properties of things come that enable both them and the concepts of them to contrast, conflict and ultimately "hang together". We conclude that the current convergence of science and philosophy under the influence of information science constitutes a revolution in philosophy, that is, in how science and philosophy are done. Many of the issues discussed in the metaphilosophy of information may thus be viewed as part of an emerging informational metaphilosophy of science.

**Keywords:** convergence; science; society; logic; metaphilosophy; philosophy; non-separability; information; revolution

---

## 1. Introduction

### 1.1. *Philosophy, Science and Information*

Human beings seem driven to gain knowledge (The concept (or belief) that knowledge is justified true belief and therefore that belief is primitive will not be discussed here.) about themselves and the world beyond that required for immediate survival. Science and philosophy are the two major modes of thought to satisfy this drive, and knowledge is gained in the former by some combination of observation, of trial and error, and ultimately of experiment. The knowledge gained in philosophy is the result of recursive introspection and speculation about man's place in the universe—at the same time an integral part of it and different by virtue specifically of the capacity for recursive thought. Thus, in the most general terms, philosophy is primarily the study of ideas of the universe and how man differs from the rest of the universe. Science is the study of how man is part of the universe. This unconventional definition of science is an attempt to recognize and incorporate the concept that thought must in some way reflect the physical processes that constitute thinkers. The philosophy of science, in studying the foundations, methods and implications of science, not only functions as a link between philosophy and science but also has the as yet not fully recognized or accepted consequence of demonstrating their non-separability. This paper will discuss (1) the current trend toward a convergence of science and philosophy under the influence of the rapidly developing science and philosophy of information and (2) whether this trend constitutes or should be considered a revolution in philosophy. We conclude that we are witnessing the emergence of an informational metaphilosophy of science.

At the start of the 20th century, the advent of quantum mechanics radically changed the foundations of science and our philosophical conceptions of the ground of existence. In the last 25 years, a comparable rapid development in the field of information has taken place whose implications are just beginning to be understood. The development has moved from the technology and science of information, including quantum information, to the emergence, most recently, of philosophies of information. Floridi in the West [1] and independently Wu in China [2] proposed philosophies of information (PI) in response to a perceived need to place the field of information and its technology on a sound intellectual basis. The objective was to bring order into the large number of different understandings of the nature and function of information. Further, in China, Wu proposed the consideration of his philosophy of information as a metaphilosophy, incorporating all the sciences of information and that the resulting convergence of the science and philosophy of information constitutes a revolution in philosophy itself [3].

### *1.2. Naturalistic Realism*

As an early precursor to this research in the West, we cite the 1975 article by C. A. Hooker [4] which defined the concept of Naturalistic Realism (NR) and explored the relationship between a science, its philosophy and an applicable metaphilosophy. Hooker's approach was congenial to us in its rejection of the distinctions of standard binary logic and an acceptance of a dialectical interaction between the physical and cognitive domains. Wu's concepts of the complex structural role of information in the extant domain, in which the purely physical-energetic and cognitive-energetic components are not totally separated or separable, is an informational version of NR.

Hooker defined a Philosophy of Science as follows: "The content of a philosophy of science comprises a theory. The theory is of the same kind as those of science in every philosophically relevant respect except logical role, insofar as the subject matter of the philosophy is science (or a science) itself". A scientific aspect of Hooker's work is its essential humanism, including (1) the idea that the goal of rational thought, the rational acceptance of beliefs and means in both science and life in general, is the maximization of human potential as well as of the depth and scope of understanding and (2) the rehabilitation of intuition as part of rational function and hence of science and (3) maintaining awareness that philosophical work does not take place in a social and ideological vacuum. These ideas, in particular that intuition and knowledge are dialectically interacting cognitive processes, are central to the non-standard logic and epistemology of Stéphane Lupasco, outlined below in Section 5.5 and discussed in detail in by Brenner in [5].

Further in this spirit, the Philosophy of Information Science is to be distinguished from Information Science by its focus on issues similar to those that serve to distinguish the philosophy of physics from physics, as discussed in a recent compendium [6]. These include questions on the one hand of the interpretation of physical theories as such and how these inform philosophical discussions, and on the other underlying "substrate" of the theories expressed as statements about reality, probability, space-time and so on. In the case of information, the Philosophy of Information provides a framework for inclusion of the simplest as well as the most complex "philosophical" features of Information Science, especially, meaning and value. In both cases, we feel that the emphasis should be placed on the absence of absolute separation between a science and its philosophy. This should be, in our view, a key doctrine of the Philosophy of Science. Not only are they not separated but their non-separability is their most essential categorial feature, as it is in the Logic of Reality which the cognitive dynamics of the relationship follow (Section 4.4). As we will see, our approach cuts through the debate as to whether a Philosophy of Science follows the rules and logic of philosophy, science or both.

### *1.3. Outline of Paper*

It is the new functional role that we attribute to information that is central to this paper, and we therefore begin in Section 2 with an outline of the recent evolution and current status of the field of information, of which the study of information is a part. Section 3 summarizes the basic concepts of the structure and role of Wu's Philosophy and Metaphilosophy of Information, based on his segmentation of the existential field and the concept of grades of information. Section 4 consists of a summary of the key aspects of Brenner's Logic in Reality—LIR [5] necessary to show the basis for its application to the science and philosophy of information. This section includes our concept of non-separability as a categorial feature that is central to our ontological approach. As a general logic of *change*, LIR applies to the major changes that constitute revolution. For the subsequent discussion, as we were dissatisfied with aspects of standard approaches to science for this discussion, we suggested an additional perspective in Section 5.

We then summarize, in Section 6, the concept, extensively discussed since the work of Thomas Kuhn, of revolution in science and contrast it with the limited literature on revolution in philosophy. Section 7 returns to the theory of the philosophy of information as a metaphilosophy of Wu and on the impact of information on philosophy. This is the background for our discussion of the paradigmatic status of what we describe as an informational turn. It is an introduction to Section 8, which looks more deeply into the impact of information on philosophy and Section 9, which presents evidence for the current interaction and convergence of the science and philosophy of information. Section 10 discusses whether or not unity and unification, including a potential Unified Science-Philosophy of Information (USPI), are appropriate goals of theory.

In Section 11, we argue that the current developments in Information Science and Philosophy leading to a USPI, that is, a convergence of science and philosophy, under the influence of information, defines a discontinuity in thought that justifies calling this informational turn a revolution in philosophy itself. We therefore suggest that any proper new philosophy of science is an informational metaphilosophy, in that (the science of) information defines both new content of the philosophy of science and new dynamics of the relations between a science and its philosophy. We conclude that all of the issues and attitudes discussed in this Special Issue may be viewed as part of an emerging informational metaphilosophy of science.

## 2. Information and Information Science

### *2.1. From Communication and Information Theory to Information Science*

As analyzed by Wu [7], from an historical standpoint, the universal character of the concepts of information and information systems had as a consequence that the scientific study of information problems went rapidly beyond the field of communication science. After the birth of information theory, there was a rapid and general expansion of the fields of its application. Not only were formed the three major branches of information theory—technology information theory; semantic information theory and information utility theory, but also informational concepts, processes and methods were found and applied in almost all fields of natural and social science and thought. There has never been any single subject that has had such a wide range of adaptability and comprehensive application to human knowledge as information in the fields of organization, linguistics, neurology, physiology and psychology to mention only a few.

With development of information theory and related subjects in science including electronics, automation, computer science, and other technical and theoretical subjects, communication theory evolved into the new discipline of Information Science (IS). IS included and integrated systems and methods especially from computer science and Artificial Intelligence as well aspects of the operation of these methods in all standard sciences from physics to the cognitive and life sciences and cosmology.

The establishment and development of Information Science as a separate discipline is thus a new development in science itself. Information Science is not a single or cross-disciplinary subject, but an inter- or transdisciplinary subject system consisting of many levels and disciplines. We see the practice of Information Science, involving the attention paid to the complex interactions between fields, as taking on a wider causal role in the transformation of the essential forms and functions of the sciences in general. This transformation can be considered as part of a new scientific or knowledge paradigm in which information theory and science are the dominant modes of knowledge acquisition.

One of the consequences of the rapidity of these changes is that there is no language to describe adequately the profound informational transformation of the form and function of science. That language has itself to be "informational", and it is this idea that suggested the term "informational scientification" to represent the recursive coupling of the interdependent components of science and information science [2].

An earlier version of this paper included a hierarchical ordering of the fields and sub-fields of the complex system of disciplines of Information Science as follows: a General Theory of Information (1), a Philosophy of Information (2), a Unified Theory of Information (3), Information Science (4), different kinds of Informatics (5) and an Informational Knowledge Paradigm (6). In the interim, this classification has become less significant than the changes that we have identified in Information Science and the Philosophy of Information in the direction of their convergence. Questions of unity and unification in science and philosophy remain of central interest and are discussed in Section 9.

## Informatics

This paper would not be complete without some additional comments on the characteristics of Informatics, considered by some of its practitioners as a full-fledged, integrated science in its own right, with its own laws and methods [8]. The evolution of Informatics roughly tracks that of Information Science and has been studied in China by Xueshan Yan, Huacan He and others. In 2008, Zong-Rong Li and his colleagues suggested a new framework for Information Science in terms of six categories—"1 + 4 + 3"—in which 1 refers to Theoretical Informatics; 4 to the underlying theories and technologies, communication theory, cybernetics, computer science and robotics; and 3 to three levels of application in engineering, social science and humanities. The work of the Authors of this paper can be considered within the scope of Theoretical Informatics [9]. In Li's view, it embodies the philosophy of information, an informational worldview, the relation of matter-energy and information and so on, in other words the issues touched on in this paper.

Any debate about whether Information Science, Informatics, or a Philosophy or Metaphilosophy of Information or Informatics is more adequate as a framework for discussion will not be entered into here. As noted above, the work of Wu in China and the publications of A. D. Ursul in Russia since the 1970s are classical works in the area [10]. To the extent that the theories of Ursul, K. K. Kolin [8] and Li illuminate the nature of information there is no necessary disjunction with ours, but it would be outside the scope of this paper to make a further comparative analysis of them. In the view of Xueshan Yan, despite some prior questioning, the term Informatics remains necessary to delineate at least two applied aspects of information theory: research in information technology and research about information. The term Theoretical Informatics is close to that of "Foundations of Information Science" of Marijuan and of "Metaphilosophy of Information" of Wu. A complete picture of the implications of the various usages has been presented by Yan [11] in his recent book in Chinese.

### *2.2. Further Definitions and Functions of Information Science*

Typical academic definitions of Information Science are (1) the foundation of various disciplines which take information as the main object of study; (2) a discipline that studies the laws and movement of information; and (3) a comprehensive interdisciplinary subject that uses information theory to describe, simulate and control the flow of information in real systems. It can be called one of the three leading-edge disciplines together with the life sciences and materials science.

However, just as information and information systems have the most general and universal character and the broadest meaning and scope, in comparison with matter and material systems, Information Science has the broadest scope of any science including as its subjects of study the analysis, collection, classification, manipulation, storage, retrieval, laws of movement and dissemination of information, divided into appropriate levels and categories. The subjects are highly interdependent and cannot be completely separated. The material (energetic) and non-material aspects of information and its laws of evolution transmission, reception are always inherently unified as discussed by Wu [12]. As noted above, Information Science cannot be regarded as a single simple discipline, and it cannot be explained comprehensively just by the terms of cross-, inter- or transdisciplinarity and comprehensiveness, although all of these terms can be useful.

The position and role of Information Science can also not be simply compared with the life sciences and material sciences since it is more universal than them. They must now incorporate relevant theories and methods provided by Information Science. The life sciences study the general laws and methods of the occurrence, development, movement, transformation, change and recombination of essential biological and genetic information, and the material sciences study the general mechanism and methods of the functioning, processing, compounding and construction of the essential informational structure of material objects. From this point of view, the essential informational content of research in these disciplines is contained within Information Science.

Information Science (IS) has developed concomitantly with related approaches to modern science, including systems theory and science. In fact, IS cannot be totally separated from subjects also studied in Systems Science. However, as shown in a recent paper [13], Information Science and what Wu has called Informational Thinking (IT) go beyond Systems Science and Systems Thinking (ST) with respect to many if not all major areas of current research.

A key link between the science and philosophy of information has been made by Marcin Schroeder [14] who writes, speaking of the concept of information: "Also, it is important to develop some standards of inquiry, which would make information scientific studies accessible to philosophical analysis and reflection. In turn, contributions of information science to the resolution of problems identified within philosophy will give the best measure of maturity for information science as a discipline." Let us now turn directly to the Philosophy of Information.

## 3. The Philosophy and Metaphilosophy of Information of Wu

### *3.1. The Information Age*

It has become commonplace to say that we live in an Information Age and/or that we belong to an Information Society, but there is still little agreement on what information is. In our opinion, part of the difficulty in achieving a workable consensus about information is its multi-faceted nature, in which technological, scientific-theoretic and philosophical components are present. In this regard, work in the relatively new domain of the Philosophy of Information, in Russia, China and in the West as noted above, has resulted in some new epistemological and ontological concepts of information independently of its origins in communication theory and its embodiment and functioning in computational technology and Information Science.

It has also become common to deplore the multiplication of disciplines and the consequent fragmentation of knowledge, in part facilitated by the availability of the Information and Communication Technologies (ICTs). In this paper, we offer a more optimistic view, suggesting the possibility of a partial defragmentation of knowledge by the identification and application of some general informational principles within science, philosophy and logic, which have gone unnoticed to date. The operation of these principles is particularly visible not only in establishing the nature and properties of information and information processes, but also in analyzing their impacts on science and philosophy themselves.

### *3.2. The Emergence of a Philosophy of Information*

The first work on the Philosophy of Information on which this paper is based was carried out by Wu [2] starting in the 1980s. A. D. Ursul in (now) Russia should receive historical credit for the earliest publication in this field [9], work like that of Wu hidden behind the language barrier. A small part of Wu's work became available in English [15,16] after the 4th International Conference on the Foundations of Information Science in Beijing in 2010. In particular, the comprehensive, recursive informational process of development was named by Wu "The Informational Scientification of Science" [15] (Wu prefers the neologism of "scientification" to the more familiar one of naturalization since, as should be obvious, the latter only applies to domains of knowledge that are normally considered outside science.). Following this Conference the authors found that this theory is supported by the extension of logic to real phenomena by Brenner—Logic in Reality; LIR [5], grounded in the dualistic quantum-mechanical properties of energy. In our joint theory, there is an informational and logical continuum from the Philosophy of Information to that of the sciences of perception, cognition and social evolution and their respective philosophies as well as to the other sciences formalized as their informational counterparts.

The Italian philosopher Luciano Floridi, now at the University of Oxford in U.K., is the pioneer of the field of the Philosophy of Information in the West as Wu is in China [1]. In the definition of Floridi, the Philosophy of Information (PI) "is the philosophical field concerned with (a) the critical investigation of the conceptual nature and basic principles of information, including its dynamics, utilization and sciences; and (b) the elaboration and application of information-theoretic and computational methodologies to philosophical problems. The dynamics of information is further defined (in part) as "the constitution and modeling of information environments, including their systemic properties, forms of interaction, internal developments, etc." We will return to his work later in connection with the metaphilosophy of Wu.

The first consequence is that to approach correctly today the concept of science, that is, within the context of a Philosophy of Science, we must see what the effect of the incorporation of a science of information might be. The impact of the informationalization of science is thus taking place on two levels: on science (1) as an experimental, intrusive practice and (2) as a cognitive discipline in which the major object is as elusive as change itself. We submit that these notions lead, *ipso facto*, to a new picture of the Philosophy of Science as a complex together with the Philosophy of Information. Some consensus is developing that information is a new kind of object of scientific study, instantiating a fundamental dualism. Based on this dualism, Wu has presented a new interpretation of critical philosophical concepts, especially, the segmentation of the existential field, leading to a formulation of a Metaphilosophy of Information having a central role in the acquisition of knowledge [17]. Let us now look at Wu's approach in detail.

### *3.3. The Segmentation of the Existential Field*

Information is somehow associated with or constitutive of existence, but it has proven notoriously difficult to define and characterize, due to its multiple duality: it has both physical and apparently non-physical components. Information is both meaningful and a carrier of meaning. Information can be viewed as well-defined data [1], processes [18], referring to what is not or not yet "there" [19] and in many other ways. As Wu has stated elsewhere, to approach correctly a concept considered part of standard science—information—we must reexamine the entire philosophical structure of transmitted human knowledge!

Thus, for us the most important innovation has been Wu's Basic Theory of the Philosophy of Information (BTPI) [2] that states that a new segmentation of the field of existence (the extant domain) is required to properly define information. In order to explore the essence of information, it is necessary to first examine the scope of the field of existence itself—the existential field. In this approach, all the "existence" in the whole universe (the world, nature) can be put into the categories of objective reality, objective unreality and subjective unreality as its three major divisions. The scope of objective existence is thus broader than objective reality (matter). The material category does not include the entire mental "world". There is a field of "objective unreality" between the material and mental to which traditional science and philosophy have not paid adequate attention, even when it is given a physicalist interpretation.

Wu thus defines information from a philosophical perspective as a category that indicates the presence of indirect existence, which is a self-display by material entities (with direct existence) of the status and trajectory of that existence. In Wu [20] in English, based in part on articles published only in Chinese over the last 30 years, information is shown to include three basic forms: in-itself, for-itself and regenerated information, which is constituted by the first two. Information in these three basic forms establishes the essence of information, which is further developed in a fourth form—social information.

Information is further characterized by the qualities of its three different grades, corresponding to these forms: The quality of first-grade information demonstrates direct objective existence and indirect objective existence; the quality of second-grade information demonstrates multiple levels of direct objective and indirect objective existence; the quality of third-grade information is that of the subjective relationships in human understanding that are encoded as information.

The grounding of information in the ontological structure of the world gives it a central role in the approach to knowledge, constituting a new and necessary critique of the classical separation of the academic disciplines and the bases of modern philosophy. This leads to a new worldview, a new existential picture of world in informational terms. In particular, we will see that our approach confers an ontological dimension to the categorial discussions of information theory that have been largely epistemological. We will return to this conception of information after we look at problem of a logic for information in relation to the Philosophy of Information and Information Science.

## 4. Logic and the Nature of Information

### *4.1.The Problem of Logic*

In his discussion of the computational philosophy of science [21], Thagard noted that processes going beyond standard deductive logic were required in scientific discovery, but did not propose anything more radical that the adjunction of induction and abduction. In fact, few discussions of logic are to be found to date in discussions of complex phenomena such as change, intentionality, intelligence and information for the good, if unfortunate, reason that standard propositional, truth-functional logics, even in their modern modal and epistemic forms, are incapable of handling the recursive and topic non-neutral features of complex processes and, indeed, of information other than at the lowest computationally defined level. Binary truth-functional propositional logics, even in their modern modal, doxastic and deontic forms, serve as the underpinnings of a current scientific paradigm from which the validity of certain $1^{st}$-person experience and questions of human values are almost totally absent. If such issues are discussed in terms of logic at all, it is essentially metaphorically, as a more or less classically structured system of beliefs and practices. Standard logics, and the entirely equivalent disciplines of set and category theory, are not designed for the analysis of either fundamental ontological questions or complex psychological and socio-economic phenomena, such as that of art.

The exclusion of critical domains of thought involving questions of change, consciousness and the self and ethics from logic and, therefore, from science in its original conception of knowledge of all nature, seems unsatisfactory. Change is ubiquitous in existence and experience. Theories of change, however, have focused on making it mathematically, computationally and logically tractable, within the framework of standard logic. In fact, change is contradictory: it is regular and irregular; consistent and inconsistent; continuous and discontinuous. Since the only logics available are incapable of accepting real contradictions, they have been incapable of describing change.

All approaches to such phenomena thus suffer from more or less explicit dependence on underlying logics, bivalent or multivalent, that are semantic and truth-functional, including their most recent modal, epistemic, doxastic and paracomplete (intuitionist) versions. These logics require, among other things, absolute separation of continuity and discontinuity, space-time and matter, chance and necessity, etc., and lead to the paradoxes with which we are all familiar. Even paraconsistent logics, which accept contradiction, capture only the linguistic, as opposed to the physical, aspects of processes, although some real inconsistencies in simple change (Sorites problems) are accepted. Logics of epistemic change [22] are based on linguistic abstractions from which physical processes have been largely eliminated.

### *4.1. Logic in Reality (LIR)*

The new logical approach, which we will argue is applicable to complex cognitive and informational processes, is an extension and updating of original work by the Franco-Romanian thinker Stéphane Lupasco (Bucharest, 1900—Paris, 1988). This new perspective, which Brenner has designated as Logic in Reality (LIR) [5] focuses on the connections, rather than the distinctions, between phenomena and provides a new basis for the discussion of moral issues in a more principled, scientific manner. LIR is thus an entirely new kind of non-propositional logic grounded in the fundamental self-dualities and dualities in the nature of energy or its effective quantum field equivalent. These antagonistic dualities can be formalized as a structural, logical and metaphysical principle of opposition or contradiction instantiated in complex higher-level phenomena. The fundamental postulate of LIR is that for all energetic phenomena (all phenomena) alternate between degrees of actualization and of potentialization of themselves and their opposites or "contradictions" but without either going to the absolute limits of 0 or 100%.

The LIR logical system has a formal part—axioms, semantics and calculus; an interpreted part consisting of a metaphysics and a categorial ontology; and a two-level framework for analysis relating levels of explanation. LIR is neither a physics nor a cosmology but a logic that enables stable patterns of inference to be made, albeit with reference to probability-like metavariables. In LIR, processes are constituted by series of series, etc., of reciprocally determined actualizations and potentializations of entities and their opposites, and emergent states, driven by the overall energy gradient of the universe. Causality, determinism and indeterminism, time and space, parts and wholes, etc. receive non-standard interpretations in this theory.

LIR captures the dynamic structure of the non-separable and inconsistent aspects of complex entities, processes and events at biological, cognitive and social levels of reality. Real entities can be described as encoding significant energy in potential form, as capacity for interaction. Both the actual and potential states of particles at lower levels—atoms, molecules, biopolymers, cells, etc.—are functional. The residual potentialities of entities at any level are the carriers of the information necessary for upward causation and emergence at the next higher level. This grounds, in basic physics, the concepts of "auto"-catalysis and "self"-organization in evolution and morphogenesis.

### *4.2. Information in LIR*

Given its contradictorial approach to all complex real phenomena, LIR can be seen as a logical methodology that would encourage the retention and use of partially conflicting notions and theories of information, among others. LIR thus can provide bridging concepts or "glue" between the concept of semantic information at the lowest data level and broader applications. LIR places this concept, and thus Hofkirchner's "superconcept" [23] of information, in a naturalized physical, metaphysical and logical context. Information is both a means to model the world and part of the world that is modeled, and LIR describes the dialectic relation between them. An anonymous reviewer has referred—negatively—to our references to dialectics as "Leninist" logic. Hegel distinguished between dialectics and formal logic—which was for him the Aristotelian logic of his day. The law of non-contradiction holds in formal logic, but it is applicable without modification only in the limited domain of the static and changeless. In what is generally understood as dialectical logic, which Logic in Reality superficially resembles, the law of non-contradiction fails. The subsequent developments of formal logic, starting with Frege and Russell, have forced Hegel's conception of contradiction to be rejected or interpreted non-literally. Lenin is a neo-Hegelian some of whose ideas are close to LIR: "Logical concepts have an abstract form but at the same time express things in themselves". One must focus on the dynamic interaction between subject and object, identity and difference. Consequently, readers should not think that any use of the term "dialectics" implies the untenable political positions of Marxism-Leninism. Some of its philosophical insights are valid and do not need or deserve to be discarded a priori.

Floridi found the concept that semantic information is true if it points to the actual state of the world somewhat equivocal, but I believe its fits the LIR processual logic, in that logical (in the LIR sense) information, as a set of informational processes, is the actual state of the world.

To repeat, Logic in Reality does not pretend to offer or to constitute an independent theory of information that would supersede any or all existing approaches. LIR provides a new interpretation of the concept of qualitative information or information-as-process as contrasted with quantitative information. We distinguish between information-as-process (information-in-itself) and information processing. The latter is usually thought of as computation, but our approach includes non-computational operations of thought. What LIR does offer is a way of explicating aspects of the dualistic nature of information, (properties that one could say LIR is "designed" to handle) as they appear, for example, in the theory of Wu.

We do not claim to be the first to emphasize the need for scientific disciplines to accept the qualitative properties of physical phenomena as logical elements of them. Colin McGinn recognized this in his Basic Structures of Reality [24] referring to the intuition of Bertrand Russell that percepts cannot be reduced to the structural-mathematical abstractions of physics. Physics gives only the causal skeleton of physical reality, but percepts are "thick" realities that cannot be reduced to what is ontologically "thin". The (relative) thinness of physics needs to be supplemented by the thickness supplied by percepts, but our informational-logical approach provides the basis for going beyond McGinn's "mysterian" concept. Cognition and perception are informational processes that follow the dynamic logic of interaction [25], while avoiding slippage in the direction of a pan-psychism that is as false as standard physicalism.

### *4.3. Further Implications for Philosophy*

Symons [26] has given several arguments explaining why logic has had a minimal role in the mainstream Philosophy of Science, but he himself has applied epistemic logic directly to the neuroscientific study of perception and identification and showed that epistemic logic can model the natural phenomenon of knowledge seeking. LIR supports this applied approach. To use Quine's phrase, as "a compendium of the broadest traits of reality" [17] rather than a linguistic system, LIR offers a principled way of establishing a link between empirical science and logic, with empirical evidence logically able to support a unified system of knowledge, better, a Unified Science of Information, which in the view of Wu includes related fields of knowledge such as design and engineering (see his discussion of the Philosophy of Information below).

Derrida [27] questioned the structure of standard binary oppositions, and said that "différance" "invites us to undo the need for balanced equations, to see if each term in an opposition is not after all an accomplice of the other." LIR takes this intuition and provides a new "structure" of oppositions and reading of "being an accomplice". The "difference" in the famous statement of Bateson, that information is a difference that makes a difference, can be seen as a différance.

In LIR, the structure of reality does not depend on any transcendental notion of human experience as proposed by Heidegger and in the neo-Kantian phenomenology of Petitot. The dynamics of physical processes may be described without reduction. This logic is not that of logical positivism or of Hempel. It is part, rather, of a new ontological turn in philosophy (see below, Section 8.1 on the informational turn).

### 4.4. *Non-Separability*

In discussing the philosophy of a science, one begins by assuming that that the science has subject matter, goals or objectives and a methodology for attempting to reach those goals. If we also require of a philosophy that it tell us something about reality, both as described by that field and others, it should be obvious, as it was to Hooker that there is no total separation between the science and its philosophy. Even if the latter is best described by the term "reflections on", this term conveys the idea of a higher level, reflexive or recursive cognitive process. This description, we believe, applies in general to the Philosophy of Science.

The problem is that non-separability as a logical as well as scientific principle is not widely accepted as such for the common but bad reason that it conflicts with standard propositional and Boolean logics, as well as standard set and category theory. These doctrines are (still) at the basis of much reasoning about topics in both science and philosophy. However, they fail to provide access to much of reality that cannot be modeled mathematically, that is, for which no algorithm can be written. Inconsistent or paraconsistent logics only go part of the way toward reality, as they retain the linguistic, truth-functional criteria of standard logics [28]. In this section, we discuss several concepts central to our approach to which the principle of non-separability as defined ontologically in LIR is essential.

#### 4.4.1. Dogmatism and Scientism

We are not so naïve as to believe that there are no countervailing trends in philosophy as LIR would predict. Wu has discussed the need to "fight" against the unconditional separation between science and philosophy. In a compendium on the "Future of Philosophy", philosophy is defined as "the transdiscipline that questions the assumptions and interrogates the values and claims to knowledge of all other disciplines recognizing their significant value in relation to each other and asking new questions and opening new paths of inquiry". Philosophy opposes science only as scientism, viewing science and its standard methods as exclusive, which "far from advancing science, has only advanced technoscience". Genuine science is the systematic effort, inseparable from philosophy (emphasis ours), to comprehend the world in all its diversity [29].

Despite the absence of references to information, we can agree with this statement, but not with the superannuated doctrine in a compendium in the same series entitled "Foundations of Mind: Cognition and Consciousness" [30]. Here we read that science is to be characterized in terms of nihilism, not in what science implies, but as the very essence of science as such, a perpetual disavowal of subjectivity due to the repressed Cartesian split at its core. This is one expression of the gap we hope that LIR and the science and philosophy of information may help to bridge.

#### 4.4.2. Complementarity

Bohr's principle of complementarity as a fundamental aspect of quantum objects is one of the major advances in thought of the 20th century. Bohr asked physicists, essentially, to accept A and non-A, wave and particle characteristics of a quantum particle, and its space-time description (kinematic) and causal (dynamic) descriptions at the same time. More accurately, the explanandum was that A or non-A was observed depending on what theoretical or experimental questions were being asked.

However, what could this mean? In the absence of a firm definition by Bohr, the complementarity principle came to be discussed as something like a simple juxtaposition.

The LIR view of complementarity is in total disagreement with that presented by the physicist and philosopher of science John A. Wheeler. Wheeler wrote [31] that complementarity ... represents in one sense the most revolutionary (emphasis ours) conception of our day; the title of the sub-section was "Complementarity: Powerful Guard against Contradictions". He also wrote, "free will and determinism are complementary concepts, not contradictory; the two can never come into use at the same time". Brenner has amply documented the need to rehabilitate contradiction in logic and philosophy.

Bohr was apparently suspicious of the ability of various modifications of classical logic, as it was understood in the mid-20th century, to assist in the definition of quantum physics, although the failure of non-commutativity and non-distributivity of quantum variables, which suggest non-Boolean algebra and logics, were well known. It was only in the 1980s, with the advent of paraconsistent logics, that a new approach to the formal explanation of the principle of complementarity became possible. However, the paraconsistent logician Béziau states that "there is no principle of complementarity, and complementarity is just a word for some philosophical ideas, for an insight that Bohr was never able to formulate in a clear way." It is correct to say that the common understanding of complementarity is too vague to be of metaphysical value. However, I also feel that Bohr, toward the end of his life, seems to have moved toward a more ontological interpretation: phenomena or information were mentioned as being complementary, rather than descriptions. "The phenomenon by which in the atomic domain objects exhibit the properties of both particles and waves that in classical, macroscopic physics are mutually exclusive categories." This is a coherent philosophy in that it accepts a concept, which is the fundamental concept of LIR, of the complementarity of opposites in both an epistemological and ontological sense.

If, as suggested by Lupasco [5], dynamic opposition is a fundamental principle of existence, a real contradictorial relation in quantum phenomena is neither physically nor logically unacceptable, and it can have both epistemological and ontological aspects. It is not physically unacceptable because wave and particle properties are not fully instantiated at the same time, until the measurement of one potentializes the other. It is not logically unacceptable for exactly the same reason. Two answers can be given to the objection that this formulation simply restates the result of experiment: (1) if the particle aspects are actualized, the wave aspects must be present as potential, and vice versa, otherwise it is difficult to explain how they could reappear; (2) it is not in the LIR view that there is any problem with the observed duality of quantum entities in the first place.

### 4.4.3. The Metalogical Rejunction

There is a further reason for including the Lupasco discussion of the relation of science and logic in this paper on the relation of science and philosophy. The original work of Lupasco can also be seen as a bridge or intermediate explanatory structure between the disciplines and the realities they discuss. Brenner feels that Lupasco effected a return of logic to its original sense of a global science of nature, which one might call a metalogical "rejunction" [32]. No diminishing of the value of standard logic in its appropriate domain of evaluation of statements about reality is intended or implied. However, Lupasco's logical theory [33] and LIR are at the same time scientific theories and, to the extent that their physical postulates or underpinnings could be disproved, they could meet Popper's criterion of falsifiability. In another sense, they are metatheories that propose analyzing the extent to which other theories adequately represent the non-separable properties of real phenomena. Thus, there is in Lupasco and LIR a possible new criterion of falsifiability as partial falsehood. However, it is clear that their more general acceptance and application require a shift from focus on the axioms and formalism of classical and neo-classical propositional or mathematical logic as the criteria of a valid logical system. One corollary of LIR is the necessary logical existence hence the scientific nature of irrational, non- or anti-scientific positions. Such positions are supported by a great deal of energy and obviously correspond to certain fundamental human structures and needs. They can, however, be easily assimilated into the Philosophy of Science in our informational framework and the motivations and reasons for their existence understood.

The Philosophy of Information of Wu [2] that now accompanies the expansion of the fields of Information Science and Technology deserves our attention because it illustrates the principle of the Lupasco logic indicated above. To summarize this section, we may say that it is the inherent inability of standard logics to handle change that disqualifies them as a basis for understanding the world. LIR attempts to take the world as it is, in all its complexities and contradictions or better countervalences as the basis for understanding it. It provides a counterexample to the view, in a standard late 20th century text by Hesse, that the logic of science is "circular" because theory and data constrain one another [34].

The characteristics of information, as they are codified in the Philosophy of Information as a Metaphilosophy, have impacts on science and philosophy that in fact indicate the reduction of the separation between them. It is this relation that we will explore as the major new contribution of Wu for which the LIR of Brenner provides some of the tools. Since, however, we were not satisfied with the monolithic use of the term "science", we suggest some necessary distinctions.

## 5. What Is "Science"?

### *5.1. A Segmentation of Science*

As we pursued this research, we found it important to emphasize that "science" should not be viewed and referred to as an identity, but as composed of many different types of system for gaining of knowledge of the world. We therefore prefer to refer to two aspects of science: (1) its rough segmentation along the lines of "hard" and "soft", experimental and conceptual; and (2) the traditional relative independence of different scientific disciplines of both types. In fact, in much of the literature on the content of the term "science", the most that one can say of the many attempts to define its domains is that they are not very scientific. Designations like the natural sciences and humanities or social sciences, exact or hard and soft, allow a primitive classification, but do not show what such activities have in common or what the critical differences between them may be. To say that the scientific method is used in chemistry and anthropology adds little to the knowledge of how these sciences are carried out. Given the enormous variety of the targets or substrates of scientific effort, it appears to us more logical to define different domains of science according to the up-stream processes that occur and operate on the different substrates. We therefore refer to two domains of science, Science I and Science II, designated as Conceptual-Creative and Pragmatic-Invasive respectively.

In this picture, the creative cognitive processes of Science I, intuitive or reasoned, are in this picture essentially the same for all sciences, including mathematics and, as Lupasco suggested, also for art [33]. From a systems perspective they apply primarily to open systems, living and non-living, accessible and inaccessible. The processes of Science II apply to closed, prepared and primarily non-living systems to which changes can be made without ethical concerns, a chemical reactor, or more broadly computational science systems. Environmental science is clearly in the group of Science I, since the environment is not a closed system. Medicine is also, as the invasive changes it makes are in living beings, primarily human, involve ethical concerns and are far from being exact or independent of the critical patient-physician interaction. However, that they are limited in scope and the existence of some overlap between the two groups is not fatal to the discussion. In fact, as Hesse suggested in Hesse [34], continuum rather than dichotomy is the more appropriate model for the relation of the natural and human sciences.

### *5.2. Science as Separation?*

In a standard account of the development of science, or scientific knowledge, two interacting processes occur: scientists start by making experimental observations and use these to generate laws and theories but also start with the latter to make predictions that are checked experimentally against them. In both cases, however, the target or object of the investigation will have been relatively narrowly defined. The derivation of the term from the Latin to cut or separate is well known. Objects and processes are separated from others to facilitate their analysis according to specific methodologies.

As a particular science becomes more complex, its development and understanding is facilitated by the use of knowledge and methods of other disciplines, which may be other sciences, mathematics, logic and so on. As a reviewer suggested, the German word *Wissenschaft*, which conveys the concept of the production of knowledge is in some ways more appropriate than science. We may call this contemporary stage that of multi-, inter- and transdisciplinarity of which one major acceptation is that of Nicolescu [35]. This process is being accelerated by the increasing computational power of the Informational and Communications Technologies (ICTs). A concomitant development is that of Systems Science, in which systems are described, not just as originally by von Bertalanffy as "complexes of elements standing in interaction" [36] but also ones from which physical parts cannot be removed without irreversibly damaging or destroying their ability to function.

### 5.3. Methodology

Although the concept of scientific method is too complex for further analysis here, there are other concepts of methodology, meaningful in the contemporary practice of science that we wish to keep at the center of our attention. The first group of these is, obviously, computational methods. They can be and are applied routinely in all the sciences. In addition, they have acquired associated disciplines such as the by now well-known computational philosophy of science [21], the philosophy of computation and other sub-disciplines. I suggest the work of Gordana Dodig Crnkovic as a primary reference in this area [37].

The second kind of method, which seems strictly limited to the human domain, is the application of an operative or organizational principle to an individual or social cognitive process to determine its dynamics, what "forces are at work". The target can be either the nominal subject of the science or the way in which the science can be structured. In the more formal logic of Lupasco [38], this would mean to seek, for each phenomenon, what phenomenon is primarily opposing it and to what extent the first is repressing or being repressed by the second. We will return to this methodology following the presentation below of this extension of logic to real phenomena made by Lupasco and developed further by Nicolescu and Brenner that is applicable to the discussion in this paper. For us, a critical word is "design"; the design of all scientific experiments, regardless of field, is a thought process that is itself a Science I.

The impact on science of the different properties and processes subsumed under the concept of information will depend on what kind of science is under discussion. As we will see, the non-standard, non-propositional logic proposed by Lupasco is for us is a key tool in understanding the dualistic nature of information, its philosophy and its science, and what we will show is a "revolution" in their currently evolving relation.

## 6. Revolution in Philosophy

### 6.1. The Kuhnian Model

The canonical model for this research on the revolutionary aspects of information is the now classical 1962 study by Thomas Kuhn: The Structure of Scientific Revolutions. It is immediately clear from subsequent work by Kuhn and others, both his followers and detractors, that there is no consensus either on what criteria define a revolution in science or whether the changes in progress in science and society constitute one or more revolutions. In this paper, well address two separate but obviously related questions: (1) is it correct to say that science and philosophy are converging in some manner and (2) is it important and useful to call attention to this development? Judging from the enormous amount of discussion of Kuhn's work that has taken and is still taking place, it would seem that whether or not a set of concepts constitute a revolution or not is a subject of great academic interest, if nothing else. Nickles has reviewed the literature on scientific revolutions in an authoritative article [39] from which we will take just one of the many questions asked: do all revolutions have the same structure and function, or are there diverse forms of rupture, discontinuity, or rapid change in science? Our answer is clearly yes.

This study has, however, identified an essential way in which a revolution in philosophy differs conceptually from a revolution in science: the latter refers to the dynamic form of changes in scientific theory; the former points to discontinuities in world-views. It should be clear that revolution does not automatically imply ethical progress but may only involve a change of authority. The National-Socialist (Nazi) seizure of power in 1933 that ended the democratic Weimar Republic was as much a revolution as the one that brought it into being by ending the Hapsburg monarchy in 1918. Regressions of this kind, albeit on a smaller scale, have been part of political history since at least the Peloponnesian Wars in Greece in the 5th century BCE. The further application of a term from political and social science to science in general has led to controversies which are by now familiar. The simplest and most informative way of deciding whether a development in knowledge or "thinking" has the character of a revolution is to define the latter as a major qualitative discontinuity, while recognizing that for any complex natural process, no discontinuity is absolute but always involves a degree of continuity.

Even in the case of science, we feel that there is a 4th logical and ontological dimension of incommensurability as a marker for revolution in addition to the epistemological dimensions identified by Kuhn. It is this logical dimension that is most relevant for a concept of revolutions in philosophy that it would now seem desirable to explore. The essence of standard notions of incommensurability is that scientific revolutions alter the very definition of science itself. They change the structural relations between pre-existing kind terms, breaking the non-overlap principle and resulting in a new ontology. The problem we have with this standard form of analysis is that it is essentially epistemological, without reference to real processes of knowledge acquisition which instantiate a dynamic ontology themselves.

We may thus ask first if an informational revolution in philosophy alters the very definition of philosophy itself. The answer is "yes". We can also ask if it results in a change in ontology. Our answer is "yes" but not in the "hard" incommensurable sense [40]: changes whether rapid or "revolutionary" cannot not embody, especially in the informational sense we discuss here, elements of prior knowledge and method. In our definition, all change is ontological.

### 6.2. Current Concepts of a Revolution in Information

As noted above, the concept of one or several revolutions in science has been accepted as a valid topic of research for some time. However, if one looks today at current volume of a major Western philosophical journal such as SYNTHESE, it is difficult to find references to any specific role of information, let alone a revolutionary one, even in articles dealing with foundational issues of ontology and quantum mechanics. The exception, of course, is the work of Luciano Floridi [41] and his identification of a "Fourth Revolution".

It thus has been a major objective of this article and of our joint work is to begin to redress this situation by documenting the way in which information can have a major impact on philosophy, on science and hence on the philosophy of science itself. As noted at the start of this paper, the concept of one or several revolutions in science has been accepted as a valid topic of research for some time. One notes of course the work of Thomas Kuhn and his commentators. The concept of a revolution in philosophy has also previously been formalized by Marx and in the 1950 by Ayer [42] and others, but it is certainly not the subject of extensive current debate. However, from the point of view of Wu, a new "quiet" revolution in philosophy has been taking place in China since the early 1980s, with the recognition of the major impact on philosophy of the philosophy of information, considered as a metaphilosophy. This revolution is expressed in radical changes to the way fundamental philosophical problems can be conceived of and discussed. Wu has stated that in fact a revolution is occurring from the standpoint of the Philosophy of Information although the number of individuals involved, judged from a rough survey of publications, is probably still very limited.

The hermeneutic link that we establish is the following: information requires the re-introduction into science as well as philosophy of the neglected (because poorly grounded) dialectics of subject and object. To the extent that some non-Chinese thinkers embody and support a subject-object dialectics in their work, they participate ipso facto in the revolution in philosophy. The underlying humor in this situation is not a basis for not giving it the serious attention it deserves. The establishment and development of information science and technology occupy a unique and critical position in the 20th century science, constituting in the views of some workers a scientific and technological revolution. In 1999, Fang listed no less than six types of revolution in this field [43]. In the concept of Floridi [41], information is the 4th major revolution in the series communication (Gutenberg)—industrial—scientific. We are witnessing the establishment of an economy of knowledge and information and the emergence of a knowledge-based [44] information society.

This paper focuses on some of the theoretical aspects of the current revolution in philosophy, which we have identified. As Wu points out, the application of the Philosophy of Information involves a fundamental theoretical transformation operating the level of the highest paradigm of philosophy, that which discusses the structure of existence. It is this fundamental theoretical transformation that constitutes the revolution of philosophy. Its consequences can be expected to be further changes in all basic and non-basic problems and fields of philosophy.

### *6.3. The Logic of Change and Revolution*

Change is ubiquitous in nature, and change in living systems, especially human thought and behavior is the most complex form of which we know. For human beings, two terms characterize change as rate, slow evolution and rapid revolution. The first applies to the biological or cognitive realm, the second only to cognitive disciplines and social structures. These processes can be further characterized by (1) their relation, that is, whether there is a continuous spectrum of change between them, or whether revolution implies a discontinuity; and (2) generality, the number of individuals involved and their degree of consciousness of being involved in drastic change. We claim that a change in the domain of philosophy has occurred and is occurring that, although neither instantaneous nor widespread, is sufficiently drastic to be called a revolution. Logic in Reality is a logic of change par excellence, and it would seem to provide both a framework and a language for the discussion of the revolutionary changes in philosophy.

### *6.4. In Relation to Information Science*

As noted above, Wu has characterized his Philosophy of Information as a Metaphilosophy since it discusses ways in which all theories are constituted and operate in the evolving informational world. Following his outline for information, one may construct an "informational" model of knowledge that includes as its proper parts Information Science and its data. In the framework of Logic in Reality, the essential point is to recognize what brings together, rather than what differentiates or separates, the epistemological and ontological elements of information. In my LIR view, these are part of the content of Information Science.

There is an additional consequence of the proposed convergence occurring in thought. It is that if the philosophical implications of a scientific discovery are equally fundamental and revolutionary. In this case, it becomes more and more difficult to give priority to science as opposed to its philosophy, although they remain distinct. In the Copernican revolution, man was forced to see himself as being no longer at the center of a solar universe. Later, our importance was reduced further by the understanding that our solar system is a tiny spot at the edge of average galaxy, of which there are billions. Today, we must absorb and integrate into our thinking and being that the form of "ordinary" matter-energy of which we are composed is again only a small fraction of the total of which the universe is composed and evolves. A "logic of duality" enables one to be more comfortable about living with the ignorance that accompanies, dialectically, such increases in knowledge. They must be accompanied by increases in humility, or one becomes lost in Promethean technological fantasies.

### *6.5. In Relation to Science in General*

Nothing in our discussion so far requires that any revolutionary movement be absolute, and one therefore must be able to distinguish degrees of revolutionarity. The criticism to be made here is that there will be two sets of observers whose positions must be taken into account: those who consider that a theory is moderately revolutionary, despite the absence of major discontinuity. Such a position cannot be distinguished from some forms of evolution. In fact, the absence of total separation between revolution and evolution is a second-order dialectical opposition to which the principles of LIR apply. Another process, to which attention is being paid in the field of biology, is devolution, a movement backwards toward prior states, and either more or less complex. Revolution and devolution thus constitute another duality in the same sense, often referred to today as evodevo (We note that evodevo has been taken by the editors of this Special Issue as a topic for discussion in the framework of a metaphilosophy of science).

It is important to note that there are other fields, such as biology, in which a convergence of science and philosophy has taken place without their necessarily being considered revolutionary. Neuroscience, on the other hand is being considered as undergoing a cognitive revolution. This consists in rejecting standard two-level views in favor of a fully integrated science of cognition. Boone and Piccinini [45], much in the spirit of this study, urge that the philosophical implications of this revolutionary shift in understanding be taken into account.

We now return to the theory of the philosophy of information as a metaphilosophy of Wu and on the impact of information on philosophy.

## 7. The Metaphilosophy of Information

### *7.1. Philosophy and Metaphilosophy*

A standard definition of the term metaphilosophy, one that is apparently simple and non-controversial, is a statement or set of statements about philosophy. The Journal of Metaphilosophy lists the following definitions in its Aims and Scope: the foundation, scope, function and direction of philosophy, the following; the interrelations among schools or fields of philosophy; aspects of philosophical systems; the relation of philosophy to other disciplines and the justification (presumably by some form of truth-preservation) of philosophical methods and arguments. The concept that is lacking in this otherwise most desirable set of objectives, and also in the literature in general, is that of structure or functioning, in other words, the "how" rather than the "what" of philosophical argument.

We first note that a discussion of metaphilosophy requires a definition of both philosophy and the task of philosophy as well. In that of Sellars [46] "the aim of philosophy is to understand how things in the broadest possible sense of the term hang together in the broadest possible sense of the term". Sellars contrasted the understanding of the world that is possible for perceiving human beings, considered as free, rational agents, capable of self-perception ("manifest images") and the entities present in the macro- and micro-physical world that is understood through science ("scientific images"). His intent was ultimately the merging of these two conceptions, one self-referential and one not, in a synoptic vision or synthesis of "persons-in-the-world". Both Logic in Reality and Wu's Basic Theory of the Philosophy of Information provide a basis for understanding both the physical and epistemological dynamics of existence, that is, from where the properties of things come from that enable both them and the concepts of them to contrast, conflict and ultimately "hang together".

The recursive relation between philosophy and metaphilosophy instantiates this principle: (1) no aspect of one is totally devoid of aspects of the other, and any absolute division into first- and second-order problems is arbitrary; (2) the question of an infinite regress of "philosophies" does not arise. In the epistemology of LIR, iteration, in this case of real relations, stops after two or three stages because no new information is added by subsequent stages. The elements of knowledge and the knowledge of that knowledge are in a contradictorial relationship that exhausts the available mental configuration space. One can imagine an infinite regress as a process that does not stop, but in reality one stops it, or it stops itself [5], a reality noted by Aristotle himself.

A theory of metaphilosophy that talks only in terms of categorial separation or distinction between elements, disciplines or methodologies in philosophy is that of Toulmin [47]. In our view, any such theory has a certain limited domain of validity, in which it is more or less adequate or appropriate to the philosophy in question. The broader role of a Metaphilosophy of Information and by implication for all other disciplines has been given by Wu: "Now, my research is still basically limited to elucidate the general basic theory of philosophy of information from the angle of a metaphilosophy. At such a level, there is a lot of work we should do to define the philosophical essence of information, the philosophical shape and form of information; the nature of the different levels of information; a philosophical measure of information; the relationship between information and various prior definitions of its scope; information ontology, information epistemology, information methodology; the evolution of the informational world; information in material and social evolution; informational sociology and psychology; informational esthetics: an informational theory of value; there are still have very abundant and a large number of branch issues in the each area field of that listed above [48]." In our view, this conception of "meta-" does not conflict with that above of a recursive conceptual analysis. Philosophy and metaphilosophy are not totally disjunct in the process of philosophical ascent.

The article by Sebastian Sequoiah-Grayson, a collaborator of Floridi, entitled "The Metaphilosophy of Information [49] is one of the few on this subject. It supports Floridi's concept of strongly semantic information, but in fact indicates only two items of content of a "metaphilosophy of information": (1) that it should include "Shannon's Premonition" that there will always be a multiplicity of theories of information and (2) explications of the pre-theoretical notion of information are to be judged by their usefulness. These ideas are more or less acceptable in the context of this paper, but they do not say very much. We have found no other serious references to a Metaphilosophy of Information. Wu, through the substantial exposition and explicit references in [2] should be considered the pioneer in this field.

Our view thus offers a novel dialectic perspective on philosophy, metaphilosophy and their recursive relation. It naturalizes this relation, eliminating any implied circularity, since it does not require the total independence of premises and conclusion of standard logics. Starting from the fundamental properties of matter-energy, my theory permits a new approach to critical issues in both philosophy and science that is both logical and metaphilosophical. Wu's metaphilosophical view of information is not directed toward the codification of a Metaphilosophy of Information as yet another static discipline or body of knowledge. It is rather an attitude toward the position of an adequate Philosophy of Information as encompassing a critical component of all disciplines, beyond the scientific content specific to them. Metaphilosophy is not something "more abstract" than philosophy and it must be able to deal with the essential aspects of all disciplines and their theories.

### *7.2. Informational Thinking and the Metaphilosophy of Information*

The Metaphilosophy of Information requires attention to the informational aspects of complex processes as a methodological necessity, in a process that Wu calls Informational Thinking. Informational Thinking (IT), as conceived of by Wu, refers to a way of grasping and describing the essential characteristics and attributes of things by reference to the structure and dynamics of the information involved in their evolution, from their historical origins to future possibilities and probabilities. This strategy involves something like a Husserlian bracketing of the details of any complex process to consider the ways in which information functions in its dynamics, as well as the dialectical relations between its logical elements as proposed by LIR. However, the difference between Wu's theory and that of Husserl is obvious: the purpose of Wu's original Philosophy of Information is to clarify the nature of the dual existence and dual evolution of material and information in the objective world, starting from the logic of the existence and dynamics of the natural human self. The phenomenology of Wu, unlike that of Husserl, does not have to be "naturalized", that is, brought into the domain of natural science. It is already there. The naturalization of Husserlian phenomenology was the subject of a major 1999 study [50]. Wu's approach eliminates the arduous task of finding natural equivalents for Husserl's transcendental intuitions. Wu then discloses directly the mechanisms of the processes involved in an individual's understanding at the level of the integrated object and subject, with internal and external interactions providing the necessary multi-level objective and subjective mediation.

### *7.3. The Question of Phenomenology*

In this sense, all of the cognitive issues addressed by Wu, especially informational values, valence and social evolution, have implied the use of Informational Thinking for their analysis. IT requires the abandonment of thinking in absolute material terms while retaining their commonsense foundations. IT is basically a methodological concept that, via the definitions of carriers and codes of information, enables inferences to be made about the historical and potential or probable future states of an information system. IT dialectically unifies energy factors and informational factors, determinism and indeterminism, internal and external feedback processes, independence (autonomy) and interdependence. LIR provides the additional logical structure for the dialectic interpretation of such a unified approach, based as we repeat on the impossibility of any total logical or physical separation between these dualities. In fact, Informational Thinking is the Metaphilosophy of Information in other terms. To the extent that Informational Thinking requires the consideration of all the philosophical and scientific facets of information, we believe that we are close to a new scientific (and logical) paradigm, a Unified Science of Information in which Informational Thinking, as opposed to thinking in terms of entities, results in new interpretations of, among other things, traditional disciplines and their theories. Above all, we see the (meta-) philosophy and (meta-) logic of information outlined here as a contribution to the naturalization of a process view of information as a whole. In other words, by seeing the relations between the changes in values that take place in human informational activities and the forms of society, a more profound understanding of information is possible that could be a contribution to overall progress and sustainable development of human civilization. Information Science, Metaphilosophy, Metalogic and Thinking may thus facilitate what Wu calls for, namely, a change in the commitment to and the interpretation of the dynamic oppositions in all complex natural processes in informational terms. Through the study of information as one of the most basic features of existence, and the formalization of informational activities, the Metaphilosophy of Information of Wu can and should change the way basic philosophical—metaphysical, epistemological and ontological—issues are discussed.

## 8. The Impact of the Philosophy of Information on Philosophy

### *8.1. The Naïve Concept of the Opposition between Science and Philosophy*

The reality of the separation between science and philosophy refers to the opposing views of scientists and philosophers, in the absence of a satisfactory critique of science by philosophers and vice versa. As Wu discussed in detail in Wu and Li [51], it is an artifact of the conventional segmentation of existence in philosophy into matter-energy and mind. The Information Science and the Philosophy of Information have shown, as discussed in Section 4.2 above that there is (a) an in-itself world of information not identical to matter-energy and (b) the modality of mind is an informational activity constituted by for-itself and regenerated information. The mode of existence of the informational world is indirect, and information is a philosophical category indicating that indirect existence, which displays the state of the direct existing mode of the material world.

Based on this, we can say that the world is the co-existence of matter-energy and information (direct and indirect existence). However, then the basic question of philosophy must be changed to correspond with it to include the relationship not only between matter and mind but also matter and information and information and mind [7] (Wu often uses the term "spirit" in the Western sense of mind, pointing that the same word is used for both in Chinese).

### *8.2. The Co-Evolution of Matter and Information*

A first consequence of the dual existence of matter and information is that both evolve in a synchronized way. "Things" (processes) being a composite of direct and indirect existence, they are both material and informational entities. This leads to an interior unification of time and space that complements the exterior unification of general relativity. In our theory, the information about the direct existence of past time is stored in patterns of space indirectly and the information about past time indicates changes in space, because the information about past time directly indicates the current structure or pattern of space.

This concept of the effective operation of the spatialization and the temporization of space as a logical interpretation of the Einstein theory was proposed by Lupasco in 1951 [38]. The interactions of "things" are, then, the processes of assimilation of the information in/of "things". The indirect existence of history constructs direct existence in its evolution and "passes it down" so to speak. This replacement of things by informationally functional processes is close to the recent naturalization of metaphysics by Ladyman and his associates in their provocatively entitled 2007 book Every Thing Must Go [52].

### *8.3. Towards a New Theory of Knowledge, Man and Society*

We can only give some brief indications in this section of the major implications for philosophy of the above informational approach. We can now see that the maintenance of the relation between subject and object, but at the same time their recasting (See the work of Rafael Capurro [53] for further development of this important philosophical concept.) in informational terms makes possible an new understanding of the emergence of cognitive ability. The (human) subject's distinguishing of the object's information uses the subject's own characteristics to make clear the necessary relation of difference that defines cognitive content, which is knowledge.

The philosophical distinctions between nature and society, the essences of biology and psychology and so on can be eliminated in our new informational discourse. The origins and evolution of both humans and human society are cooperative processes of biologically inherited information patterns, psychological patterns of informational activity and informationally defined patterns of behavior. As Wu puts it, "A man is a multidimensional unification of natural and social existence, psychology, biology and behavior." The open-ended character of this multi-dimensional existence implies for human existence that, as postulated in Logic in Reality, it instantiates both determinism and indeterminism.

Finally, here, the understanding of the role of the informational world makes possible a new discussion of the value of information, and consequently of a new philosophy of value. The theory of the dual existence and dual evolution of matter-energy and information has the effect that their value is formed in their synchronous and diachronous interaction. As is discussed among other places in the field of Relational Quantum Mechanics [54], it is the interactions that are the primary existential mode, and "things" (see above), without their various interior and exterior interactions, do not exist. It is the universality of these interactions that confirm the fact and existence of value. Mental or cognitive value is the highest modality of informational value, but it is always, in the social field integrated with material value and in-itself information value. We believe our approach "naturalizes" a Durkheimian legitimation of metaphysics and the place of science in society, although we prefer a language of social processes to one of social facts.

### 8.4. Information Science, Again

The existence of the subjects of a new field of existence—the informational world distinguished from the world of matter-energy which grounds it—within information science results in a new set of principles for scientific interpretations, especially one of holism rather than the reductionism prevalent in traditional philosophy. (This reductionism is unfortunately also present in many concepts of Information Science, which "stop" at the initial ones of Shannon derived from communications theory.) Our theory goes beyond their unity as expressed in the 1980s by Hofstadter [55] and also of their interaction, the fact that they do not totally conflict and contradict. Material entities and informational entities are always unified innately and concretely. Compared to the standard research principles of, say, systems science, self-organization, etc., the research principle of Information Science is more fundamental, more integrated and more representative of the complex processes of real existence. It refers to the modalities of systems, beyond their matter-energy, as types of relation, patterns, ways of organization and series of structures, and there relationships, patterns, ways of organization and series of structures can only be explained by the concept of information activity, where, again, matter—energy is only the carrier.

## 9. The Informational Turn and the Convergence of Science and Philosophy

### 9.1. A Series of Turns. The Informational Turn

We may summarize the view of the Philosophy of Information as a Metaphilosophy outlined in Section 6 above by stating that it provides a new bridge between science and philosophy which points toward their convergence. Information science and philosophy not only are not separated but also dynamically interact in the direction of a scientification of philosophy and a philosophization of science. The impact of the rapidly developing science of information on science, on philosophy and on the philosophy of science is thus an extremely complex recursive process, of which only a part has received detailed study. The changes in both the philosophy and science of information are reflected in what could be described from a philosophical standpoint as a foundational informational turn.

The evolution of philosophy starting in the last century can be summarized as a series of turns: the first is a linguistic turn, away from ontology toward epistemology. Its logic is standard linguistic logic. Next occur phenomenological and existential turns, whose logic is pure formal, linguistic logic. This is followed by the 1st ontological turn, due to the failure of descriptions of reality based on analytical, semantic criteria of truth toward what is. Its logic is paraconsistent, but still linguistic.

This 1st ontological turn implied a radical shift in science that should favor really scientific that is, non-absolute knowledge. However, the logical and philosophical tools were lacking for this purpose. The consequence has been the on-going narrowness and specialization of contemporary philosophy and an increasing separation of philosophy and science. As discussed by Wu [7], these so-called turns were not fundamental since they did not change the traditional ontological paradigm of classical Western philosophy, namely, the dualistic formula that existence = matter + mind. Such a philosophy has "lost its capacity to explain and transform the world as a general view of it". Many aspects of the standard Philosophy of Science remain limited by their reliance on more or less classical concepts of models, semantics, and logic.

This has led to what we call a 2nd ontological turn, becoming the informational turn, taking on in the process its "revolutionary" character [53,56]. The logic of this turn is the Logic in Reality of Brenner indicated above.

### 9.2. The Convergence

As a consequence of the development of science, the universal, dualistic character of information has emerged clearly. In this view, in which science and philosophy are both present in a dialectical relationship, the world is constituted by matter-energy and information as its fundamental elements as discussed in Section 4. In the remainder of this section, we will discuss further implications of the informational turn for philosophy and the convergence of science and philosophy.

Evidence for the convergent trend we have identified, outside that of Information Science and Philosophy itself, comes from a number of different sources, both in China and the West. Examples are:

- Systems Science
- Intelligence Science
- Cybersemiotics
- Cognitive Semiotics
- Transdisciplinarity
- Angeletics (Messaging Theory)
- Information Ecology
- New (natural) Computational Theory

These disciplines share, in part, the cognitive dynamics of Information Science and the Philosophy of Information. The emphasis is on what unifies complex phenomena rather than on what appears to separate them, and on the joint applicability, at least in part, of conflicting theories. As Brenner has noted in Brenner [57], the intentionality of natural computation, presented in detail by Gordana Dodig Crnkovic [37], overlaps that of LIR as a description of reality.

9.2.1. The Question of Computationalism vs. Natural Computation

It is by now well established that computational approaches are at the center of developments in the theory and philosophy of information. It is clear that what form of computationalism is most adequate is a metaphilosophical issue. The theory comes in two major forms, (1) pan-computationalism or strong computationalism, which includes statements that the universe operates like a computer; and (2) a weaker form, developed by Gordana Dodig Crnkovic, informational- or info-computationalism which reflects Floridi's view of the universe as an informational structure, in which natural computation governs the dynamics of information.

Gordana Dodig Crnkovic has defined an Informational-Computational approach as follows: "Info-computationalism (ICON) relates to Floridi's program for the Philosophy of Information by contrasting it with a pan-computational stance, that of Zuse, Lloyd and others, which takes the universe to be a computer. With the universe represented as a network of computing processes at different scales or levels of granularity, ICON sees information as a result of (natural) computation. Adopting Floridi's Informational Structural Realism (see Section 9.3), which argues for the entire existing physical universe being an informational structure, natural computation can be seen as a process governing the dynamics of information.

It is thus necessary to distinguish carefully such approaches from that of a computational universe which assert that the universe is actually a digital, Turing-like computer that in fact computes using some digital code. While remaining agnostic about the question of fundamentality, Gordana Dodig Crnkovic replaces the emphasis where it belongs, namely on understanding that part of natural phenomena which may be subsumed under the concept of computation. It is to these ideas that the term natural computation, that is, information processing by natural systems, can be usefully applied. As Gordana Dodig Crnkovic points out, computationalism is not the world; it is a modeling framework that is acceptable within certain domains and does not exhaust our possibilities to relate to the world.

Within ICON, information and matter/energy are represented by information and computation. Computation presents implementation of physical laws on an informational structure. Instead of describing the world in terms of matter/energy (where energy stands for equivalent of matter) and information, as does Wu, the info-computationalist approach makes the distinction between structure (information) and a process (computation). The mind/body problem is solved in a simple way. In this framework, there is no Cartesian divide between body and mind. Mind is a process, information processing, and body is a structure (proto-information). Thus, mind is a process of natural computation that results from dynamical reconfiguration/re-structuring of the information in the brain, in tune with the rest of the body, which connects it with the physical world.

Freed from the burden of the dogma of the computational universe, computationalism as natural computation appears as an acceptable component of a Metaphilosophy of Information. It grasps (a term often used by Wu many features of natural processes. This naturalized epistemology approach, conceptualizes information as both here (intelligence), there (world) and on the interface, as information constitutes the basic "stuff" of existence. Its structural changes are the results of computational processes. Within this framework of dual-aspect informationalism/computationalism (info-computationalism), matter may be viewed as a structure (information), in a permanent process of flow—natural computation. This subject has been discussed in detail by Gordana Dodig Crnkovic in a recent compendium [58].

This work thus presents a synthesis of two paradigms within contemporary philosophy—computationalism and informationalism into a new dual-aspect info-computationalist framework. The dualism itself does not mean that the phenomena are separated, and exclude each other. On the contrary, they are mutually determining, constraining and completely indissoluble. The structures and the processes are inseparably interwoven by physical laws, and LIR gives logical underpinning to the dynamics of "interwoven".

The key further moments of Wu's latest views of the origin and characteristics of convergence of science and philosophy are as follows.

9.2.2. Rationality

If science reflects the rational thinking of human beings, the thinking that corresponds to the reception of sensorial evidence, from experiment, cannot be separated from a more universal form of rational thought, which Wu calls rationality or universal rationality. Science incorporates or involves, from the beginning, concepts that are primarily philosophical or we might say metascientific—a worldview, an epistemology, a methodology but it ends in universal rationality. For a more standard but still useful view of rationality we refer to the 2001 book of the philosopher J. D. Searle, Rationality in Action [59] in which a distinction, but not an absolute classical separation between internal and external reasons for action is established.

We thus see, for the description of the cognitive evolution of phenomena, that its science and philosophy are reciprocally related, as conjugate variables, with sensitivity maximized in science and rationality maximized in philosophy. Another way of expressing this idea is by using the Lupasco logic: one can say, for phenomena at the lowest physical level that their science is actualized and their philosophy is potentialized and for highest level phenomena that their philosophy is actualized and their science is potentialized (that is, not absent or eliminated but not focused on). This reciprocity applies also to the views of science by philosophy and vice versa: each considers the other field more limited, and this should be an indication that both are true and not true at the same time, which is a logical statement within Logic in Reality. Both science and philosophy instantiate their inherent relations of unity and complexity.

The norm for us is that the universal scientific rationality is saturated with philosophical concepts. The unity of philosophy and science cannot be seen as just an external convergence, but as an inherent amalgamation in which, however, the disciplines do not totally lose their identity and specificity.

Despite the criticism by some authors of the concept of cognitive levels, in the case of both universal rationality and science, we consider that it applies naturally. It is not that the highest level is philosophy and the lowest science, but there is no philosophy that is not partly science and no philosophy that is not partly science. We may state the same thing for the science and philosophy that Brenner stated for science and logic: at the beginning they were integrated; then were separated and today, under the influence of information in the broadest sense, they can be viewed as undergoing a metaphilosophical (or metascientific) rejunction. It should be obvious that this process does not take place equally or at the same rate for all the sciences, but we are looking here at a general trend.

The strongest force for change in philosophy (or human thought in general) is thus science, in particular information science, and this state of affairs must influence the foundations of the Philosophy of Science per se. This does not mean that philosophy has only a passive role in this process. On the contrary, if there are no philosophical initiatives, the Philosophy of Science could not evolve on its own. We thus need to add to the basic concept of the non-separability of philosophy and science the further layer of critique of the Philosophy of Science. Note also the comment above regarding the relevance of the German term *Wissenschaft*—knowledge-production—to the discussion. We point towards such a new critique in our concluding Section 11.2.

### *9.3. The Self-Critique of Philosophy and the Philosophy of Information: Wu and Floridi*

In the view of Wu, the natural self-transformation of philosophy is achieved by the transition between levels of scientific rationality, with the assimilation of new, external information. This, however, must accept the regulation of philosophy itself, that is, to be exposed to choice and critique. There is a double effect in this process of assimilation: on the one hand, external information is criticized by philosophy; on the other hand, because that critique changes the original structure of philosophy, this ipso facto constitutes as critique of philosophy.

It is the contemporary Philosophy of Information, especially in Wu's acceptation of it, which shows the development of philosophy through this form of dual criticism. It enables the debate about information to proceed on a new basis, avoiding the analogies used to match information with conceptions of the outmoded paradigm of traditional philosophy (information is a property of matter; information is meaning; information is a mental entity, etc.).

In summary, this Philosophy of Information that shows the general character of information transcends the basic beliefs and theories of traditional philosophy. The new PI is based on the concept that philosophy impacts science at the same time that philosophy acts on itself. We conclude that the birth of the modern Philosophy of Information leads to the first fundamental turn of philosophy itself.

We are now in a position to analyze the similarities and differences between the approaches of Wu and Floridi to the Philosophy of Information. It is clear that these are different, partially complementary views in which all the major issues of the foundations of information are addressed. Brenner has outlined these views in the readily accessible [57], and we provide a summary here. As we have seen in this paper, the work of Wu is better described as a Metaphilosophy of Information, since it includes a vision of the operation of the Philosophy of Information as drastically changing the content of philosophy itself.

In 2004, Floridi listed some eighteen open problems in the philosophy of information [60]. One of the most important was whether meaning can at least partly be grounded in an objective, mind-, and language-independent notion of information (naturalization of intentionality). Is it possible to analyze both information and meaning not truth-functionally but as having the potential or being a mechanism to change the informational context? (Our answer is of course yes.)

Floridi provided a detailed theory (action-based semantics) of how data acquire meaning as the indispensable foundational picture of semantic information and information processing upon which the informational aspects of theories of meaning and of society can be soundly based. The question that Floridi did not ask, however, is whether some form of ontological commitment is necessary for a complete theory of information. We obviously think that one is and that this is a crucial aspect of the Philosophy of Information of Wu.

Floridi does argue, for example, in his Philosophy of Information [1] that digital ontology, according to which the ultimate nature of reality is digital or computational, should be carefully distinguished from informational ontology, according to which the ultimate nature of reality is structural. Floridi avoids the Boolean digital vs. analogue dichotomy in favor of an Informational Structural Realism (ISR), according to which knowledge of the world is knowledge of its structures.

The most reasonable ontological commitment favors an interpretation of reality as the totality of its structures, energetic entities, dynamically interacting with one another. His Informational Structural Realism (ISR) thus appears to provide an ontology applicable to both sub-observable and to observable structural objects by translating them into informational objects, defined as cohering clusters of data, not in the alphanumeric sense of the word, but in an equally common sense of differences de re, i.e., mind-independent, concrete points of lack of uniformity.

These cohering clusters of data as relational entities are the elementary relata required in Floridi's ISR. The structuralism in question here is based on relational entities (understood structurally) that are particular, not on patterns that are abstract and universal (We recall the key feature of non-separability of the LIR ontology. LIR simply extends it as an accurate general ontological picture of the dynamic processes of change. A complex process and its opposite or contradiction "come together" or do not exist).

Floridi's position is that the ultimate nature of reality is informational, and it makes sense to adopt a view of reality as mind-independent and constituted by structural objects that are neither substantial nor material (they might well be, but we have no need to suppose them to be so) but informational. Logic in Reality, however, offers a principled basis for saying that they are and suggests the logical rules they follow. As Brenner has also shown [61], the Floridi ontology fails to capture the evolution of real informational processes. The critical aspect of information, to which Hofkirchner and others are now turning, is its dualistic relation to the energy of which it is constituted. In our view, it is this duality or dualism that is the actual "driver" of informational processes.

## 10. Unity; Towards a Unified Science of Information

### *10.1. The Question of Unity*

As one philosophical consequence of our theory of the omnipresence of information in science and knowledge, we ask ourselves if it is relevant to the question of the Unity of Science. We note first that when almost any subject is presented as a unity, it is always with a positive valence. A unity is something desirable and desired in whatever forms the unity presents itself: a unified theory, a search for invariants and so on. In a perhaps too rapid analysis, Lupasco associated our search for invariants, e.g., in 20th century physics and other unities as a psychological expression of the logical antagonism of ourselves as living beings, that is, instantiations of diversity, growth and death.

Without going more deeply into this question, if one looks at the authoritative article by Cat in the Stanford Encyclopedia of Philosophy [62], one is struck by the diversity of senses that can be given to the definition of unity! These range from the possible single nature of the underlying "stuff" of the universe, to the unification of the disciplines within science and with regard to these whether on is dealing with concepts or terms or the higher-level entity of theory and whether the relations are ones of reduction, explanation or logical inference.

Cat suggests that the concept of unity can have value at the practical level in science, to justify approaches and goals, and in philosophy to help choose what philosophical questions to pursue and what target areas to explore. The Unity of Science could suggest what science is to be referenced by philosophy as authoritative. He touches upon our point in the first paragraph by suggesting "unities and unifications help us meet cognitive and practical demands upon our life ... , contribute to our self-image and be seen as a source of aesthetic value, providing a grip on our intellectual imagination".

Our approach extends this view: this picture of the value of the Unity of Science, self-referentially, is itself a unity of a sort that neglects, intentionally or not, the value of diversity, or, as we believe is equivalent, believes that it is necessary to do so explicitly. Informational processes however, as we have seen throughout this paper, are a composite of unities and diversities, in the complex dynamic structures of the LIR perspective. Our dualism has been well captured by Marcin Schroeder in his contribution to the concept of natural computation [63]. "The naturalistic perspective on computing is based on the observation that every computation is inherently analogue, and the distinction between analogue and digital is only a matter of its meaning". In the LIR picture of the evolution of real processes, of course, the (logical) elements involved are all "analogue".

Let us discuss two of the components of our proposed Unified Science of Information.

### *10.2. A General or Unified Theory of Information*

The objective of finding a unifying information theory that would synthesize all existing approaches in an amalgamated structure of ideas, constructions, methods and applications has been perhaps best approached by Mark Burgin in his General Information Theory [64]. We first note that a General Theory of Information (GTI) is not a Unified Science or Theory of Information. The former involves only practical information science at the basic theoretical level, while the latter is part of a broader informational paradigm, as we will see.

In his book, Burgin integrated perspectives on information from logic, epistemology and systems theory in a rigorous, parametric mathematical framework. In the case of the GTI, the parameter is very general. This parametric approach provides a tool for building the GTI as a synthesis, which organizes and encompasses all main directions in information theory. Abstract categories allow one to develop flexible models for information and its flow, as well as for computers, networks and computation. Another type of model establishes functional representation of infological systems representing information as an operator in functional spaces.

Burgin considers his GTI has provided solutions to various problems via the unifying concept of an infological system, concepts of different types of information and types of different concepts of information. At the highest cognitive level, the qualitative dimension of information, in particular, meaning and its evolution are clearly listed by Burgin among the critical areas for further work, "to form a unified system of information quality characteristics and measures and study their properties in the context of a GTI". Although Burgin favors mathematical modeling of intelligence, mind and instinct also in the context of a GTI, he nowhere excludes non-mathematical approaches.

From our perspective, there are cognitive and other informational processes which are non-computable, that is, algorithms cannot be written for them. Although the mathematical approach has and will retain an essential relation to these also, any explanation of these must therefore ultimately be based on principles that go beyond those parts of those processes that can be modeled mathematically.

In a recent article, Brenner has summarized a number of other currently debated theories of information of interest by Luhn, Markov and Marijuan but none of these are as exhaustive as that of Burgin and they will not be discussed further here. We now turn to the next level, that of a Unified Theory of Information.

We note first that the scheme of principled distinctions proposed by Wu has a relationship to and a place in the conceptual approaches that Hofkirchner has recently listed for a Unified Theory of Information (UTI). Hofkirchner [23] among others has argued for the desirability of a UTI that would encompass the different manifestations of information processes. Such a UTI should be capable of balancing the apparently contradictory properties of information—physical and non-physical, universal and particular—without reduction. Its underlying principle should be "as abstract as necessary but as concrete as possible at the same time".

Hofkirchner considers information as a "superconcept", which includes a group of overlapping concepts such as message, signal, etc. as they apply to communication, cognition and cooperation between human and non-human organisms. Hofkirchner asks how matter and idea, mind, information, etc. can be grasped as complements and with them information as a thing (a structure, a flow) or as a human construction. Hofkirchner gives a dialectical answer to the implied division between subject and object, suggesting that mind, and with it information, is of a different "materiality" than "non-emergent" states of matter. His own approach to a Unified Theory of Information (UTI) is to eliminate the absolute and in my view artificial separation between critical concepts of information in favor of a dialectical relationship similar to the ancient intuition of "unity-in-diversity". Specifically, his "UTI seeks a concrete-universal concept of information rather than an abstract one". Hofkirchner wishes to avoid reliance on a "formal-logical figure of necessary and sufficient conditions" and use a way of thinking that integrates as well as differentiates the particular and universal", with is consistent with Logic in Reality.

### *10.3. Toward a Unified Science-Philosophy of Information*

In contrast to the above designations, a Unified Science of Information (USI) would include them, as major levels, together with a Philosophy of Information, a General Theory of Information and various forms of Informatics covering the technological aspects of information. However, a USI would not be limited to these fields. It would be both the effect of the convergence of science and philosophy, including those of information, and the cause of further integration of science and philosophy in which the philosophical sense of the science of information and the scientific character of the philosophy of information would be completely present in a new integrated pattern of human knowledge.

As a result of its continuity across all levels of human knowledge from philosophy to science to technology, a USI would be a disciplinary system that can be described in Chinese by the metaphor of "standing upright between heaven and earth". This metaphor captures the role of information in providing a link between phenomena at the lowest physical level and at the highest human cognitive level.

The further development of a Unified Science of Information (USI) should lead, in this view, to further integration of science and philosophy in which the philosophical character of Information Science and the scientific character of the Philosophy of Information (PI) become readily apparent. The Philosophy of Information (PI) could be viewed as a part of a USI, and the USI would achieve its real ground as a general provision of philosophy as a whole. In other words, the USI is the scientific basis of the PI, and the PI is the general philosophical precondition of a USI. The convergence of the two represents an integrated pattern of development of contemporary human knowledge.

As we have seen, there is a set of new and unique relationships that are developing between the classical disciplines of science and philosophy as a consequence of new understandings of the science and philosophy of information. The overall movement is that of a philosophization of science and a scientification of philosophy leading to their convergence. However, in this paper and elsewhere, we have used the term Unified Science of Information. This is not strictly accurate, as our convergent theory includes the Philosophy of Information as a proper part, without conflation. We therefore propose, despite its awkwardness, the term Unified Science-Philosophy of Information (USPI) as the best possible description of our field of endeavor.

The philosophical stance of USPI may be usefully compared to Hofkirchner's proposal [65] of a Praxio-Onto-Epistemology (POE) as "a response to the current developmental requirements of humanity". While traditional approaches are apparently stuck in the three disciplines as alternatives, POE offers a transdisciplinary response for going beyond them, resembling LIR in this respect.

### *10.4. Towards an Informational Metaphilosophy of Science*

We can conclude from the above that a proper new philosophy of science is an informational metaphilosophy, in that (the science of) information defines both new content of the philosophy of science and new dynamics of the relations between a science and its philosophy. A question of interest to readers will be that of the consequences of this convergence for the Philosophy of Science itself. In the spirit of this paper, we suggest that as the special sciences become more and more informational, their respective philosophies can be included as part of the philosophical aspects of the Unified Science-Philosophy of Information (UPSI). At the same time, logically, the informational-philosophic aspects of the USPI can become part of the general Philosophy of Science. All of these considerations, however, are clearly metaphilosophical, since they touch on the content of the respective philosophies (of information and science). We therefore tentatively conclude that the dynamics of the processes can be captured in the concept of a trend toward an Informational Metaphilosophy of Science as the most appropriate model of knowledge. This Philosophy-Science justifies a new non-reductionist view of the world in which it is ethically impossible to maintain any scientific basis for economic, social or ethical exclusion. The use of this doctrine to promote the development of an information commons and the common good is thus a moral as well as a methodological imperative. We consider this, therefore, a necessary area for further research.

## 11. Conclusions. A Revolutionary Attitude

### *11.1. Summary*

In this paper, we have first presented the concept of a process by which the properties of information, collated in Information Science and Philosophy, enable it to function as an operator [66] to change the nature of science and philosophy themselves, with a functional role in the emerging information society, including how science and philosophy are done. We see the Informational Stance of the practitioners of Informational Science as a guarantee of avoiding limited, reductionist positions and applications of our informational approach in the areas of perception and cognitive science, consciousness and the understanding of personal identity. As this approach affects disciplines, in view of the prestige that information has even at the lowest intellectual levels, it may become a basis for application to the social and political structures of society.

We have shown, in our discussion, the central role of Logic in Reality (LIR) a non-standard, non-propositional logic that can handle the contradictions and inconsistencies of the real, informational world. LIR provides a logical framework for the most important interactive relations discovered by Wu in the relation between the informational world and the world of matter-energy on which it is based. Although we do not deny that in principle another such non-propositional logic system might accomplish the same task, neither we nor anyone who has ever commented on our logic has ever been able to identify one.

### *11.2. The Question of "Turn' vs. "Revolution". The Revolutionary Attitude*

We conclude that the current informational revolution defines a discontinuity in thought that justifies calling it a revolution in philosophy itself, but we specify that it be as a change in attitude that the revolution could become concretized. Wu has defined the Informational Attitude or Stance (IS) as a philosophical position most appropriate for, and not separated nor isolated from, the emerging science and philosophy of information itself. IS requires attention to the informational aspects of complex processes as a methodological necessity.

Application of an Informational Stance would involve defining, for each concept in information research, in all of science and in fact of all knowledge not only its scientific and philosophical aspects but also their interaction and co-modification. The major consideration of such a stance associated with a Unified Science-Philosophy of Information is thus that of giving proper value to its qualitative, non-measurable and non-computable components. It should never be said that qualitative relations and inequalities that follow the rules of Logic in Reality are more important or necessary than the quantitative equalities, only that they are no less fundamental.

We consider that a Revolutionary Attitude is now a necessary part of the intellectual world, embodying several functions. It would be revolutionary for people to change the dynamics of their acceptance of the published literature, exercising the principle of tolerance but also rigor that Nicolescu has insisted are the main attributes of the Transdisciplinary Attitude. Other multi- and interdisciplinary movements, such as that of Translational Medicine, emphasize the need for a radical break with accepted ways of realizing the medical benefits to the patient of fundamental research in biology. The consequences of such a Revolutionary Attitude remain to be defined, but they hopefully would accompany a corresponding positive change in the economic and social structure of society as a whole.

**Author Contributions:** Both authors contributed to this paper.

**Conflicts of Interest:** The authors declare no conflict of interest.

## References

1. Floridi, L. *The Philosophy of Information*; Oxford University Press: Oxford, UK, 2010.
2. Wu, K. The Basic Theory of the Philosophy of Information. In Proceedings of the 4th International Conference on the Foundations of Information Science, Beijing, China, 21–24 August 2010.
3. Wu, K. The Interaction and Convergence of the Science and Philosophy of Information. *Philosophies* **2016**, *1*, 228. [CrossRef]
4. Hooker, C.A. Philosophy and Meta-Philosophy of Science: Empiricism, Popperianism and Realism. *Synthese* **1975**, *32*, 177–231. [CrossRef]
5. Brenner, J. *Logic in Reality*; Springer: Dordrecht, The Netherlands, 2008.
6. Kuhlmann, M.; Pietsch, W. What Is and Why Do We Need Philosophy of Physics? *J. Gen. Philos. Sci.* **2013**, *43*, 209–214. [CrossRef]
7. Wu, K. The Development of Philosophy and Its Fundamental Informational Turn. *Information* **2015**, *6*, 693–703. [CrossRef]
8. Kolin, K.K. The Globalization of Social Information and Humanistic Revolution. In Proceedings of the Chinese-Russian Conference on Information Science, Wuhan, China, 20 September 2013.
9. Li, Z. The Worldview and Methodology of Information Science. In Proceedings of the International Conference on Philosophy of Information, Xi'an, China, 18–21 October 2013.
10. Ursul, A. On the Nature of Information. *Probl. Philos.* **1965**, *3*. (In Russian) [CrossRef]
11. Yan, X. *Information Science: Concept, System and Perspective*; Beijing Press: Beijing, China, 2016. (In Chinese)
12. Wu, K. The Partition of the Existent Field and the "Whole New" Sense of the Philosophy of Information. *Humanities. J.* **2013**, *5*, 1–6. (In Chinese)
13. Wu, K.; Brenner, J. Informational Thinking and Systems Thinking: A Comparison. In Proceedings of the Foundations of Information Conference, Moscow, Russia, 13 June 2013.
14. Schroeder, M.J. Foundations for Science of Information: Reflection on the Method of Inquiry. *Triple-C* **2011**, *9*, 377–384.
15. Wu, K. The Informational Scientification of Science. *Qinghai Soc. Sci.* **1997**, *2*, 53–59. (In Chinese)
16. Brenner, J. Wu Kun and the Metaphilosophy of Information. *Int. J. Inf. Theor. Appl.* **2011**, *18*, 103–128.
17. Wu, K.; Brenner, J. The Informational Stance: Philosophy and Logic. Part I: The Basic Theories. *Log. Log. Philos.* **2013**, *22*, 453–493.
18. Brenner, J. Information in Reality: Logic and Metaphysics. *Triple-C* **2011**, *9*, 332–341.
19. Deacon, T.W. *Incomplete Nature. How Mind Evolved from Matter*; W.W. Norton & Co: New York, NY, USA, 2011.
20. Wu, K. The Essence, Classification and Quality of the Different Grades of Information. *Information* **2012**, *3*, 403–419. [CrossRef]
21. Thagard, P. *Computational Philosophy of Science*; The MIT Press: Cambridge, MA, USA, 1993.
22. Brenner, J. A Logic of Ethical Information. *Knowl. Technol. Policy* **2010**, *23*, 109–133. [CrossRef]
23. Hofkirchner, W. How to achieve a unified theory of Information. *Triple-C* **2009**, *7*, 357–358.
24. McGinn, C. *Basic Structures of Reality. Essays in Meta-Physics*; Oxford University Press: Oxford, UK, 2011; p. 160.
25. Wu, K.; Brenner, J. An informational ontology and epistemology of cognition. *Found. Sci.* **2014**, *20*, 249–279. [CrossRef]
26. Symons, J. Applying Logic; Some remarks on the reciprocal influence of experimental and formal investigations of identification. In *Open Problems in Epistemology*; Hintikka, J., Ed.; Philosophical Society of Finland: Helsinki, Finland; Available online: http://www.johnsymons.net/wp-content/uploads/2012/04/Apply-Logic.pdf (accessed on 8 August 2017).
27. Derrida, J. *Of Grammatology*; Johns Hopkins University Press: Baltimore, MD, USA; London, UK, 1974.
28. Priest, G. Paraconsistent Logic. In *Handbook of Philosophical Logic*; Gabbay, D., Guenthner, F., Eds.; Kluwer Academic: Dordrecht, The Netherlands, 2000.
29. Gare, A. Introduction: The Future of Philosophy. *Cosm. Hist. J. Nat. Soc. Philos.* **2012**, *8*, 1–17.
30. Cifone, M. Nothingness and Science (A Propadeutic). *Cosm. Hist. J. Nat. Soc. Philos.* **2014**, *10*, 251–274.

31. Wheeler, J. *At Home in the Universe*; American Institute of Physics Press: Woodbury, NY, USA, 1994.
32. Brenner, J. Stéphane Lupasco et la Rejonction Métalogique. In *À la confluence de deux cultures. Lupasco aujourd'hui. Actes du colloque international UNESCO*; Éditions Oxus: Paris, France, 2010; pp. 251–286.
33. Lupasco, S. *Logique et Contradiction*; Presses Universitaires de France: Paris, France, 1947.
34. Hesse, M. *Revolutions and Reconstructions in the Philosophy of Science*; Indiana University Press: London, UK, 1980.
35. Nicolescu, B. *Manifesto of Transdisciplinarity*; State University of New York Press: Albany, NY, USA, 2002.
36. Von Bertalanffy, L. *General System Theory*; George Braziller: New York, NY, USA, 1969.
37. Dodig Crnkovic, G. Nature as a network of morphological infocomputational processes for cognitive agents. *Eur. Phys. J. Special Topics.* **2017**, *226*, 181–195. [CrossRef]
38. Lupasco, S. *Le Principe D'antagonisme et la Logique de L'énergie*; Éditions du Rocher: Paris, France, 1987; Originally published in Paris: Éditions Hermann, 1951.
39. Nickles, T. Scientific Revolutions. In *The Stanford Encyclopedia of Philosophy (Winter 2016 Edition)*; Zalta, E.N., Ed.; Stanford University: Stanford, CA, USA, 2014; Available online: http://plato.stanford.edu/archives/win2016/entries/scientific-revolutions/ (accessed on 17 March 2017).
40. Oberheim, E.; Hoyningen-Huene, P. The Incommensurability of Scientific Theories. In *The Stanford Encyclopedia of Philosophy (Winter 2016 Edition)*; Zalta, E.N., Ed.; Stanford University: Stanford, CA, USA, 2014; Available online: http://plato.stanford.edu/archives/win2016/entries/incomensurability/ (accessed on 7 January 2016).
41. Floridi, L. *The Fourth Revolution. How the Infosphere is Reshaping Human Reality*; Oxford University Press: Oxford, UK, 2014.
42. Ayer, A.; Kneale, W.; Paul, G.; Pears, D.; Strawson, P.; Warnock, G.; Wollheim, R. *The Revolution in Philosophy*; Macmillan: London, UK, 1950.
43. Fang, I. *A History of Mass Communication. Six Information Revolutions*; Focal Press: Waltham, MA, USA, 1997.
44. Leydesdorff, L. *The Knowledge-Based Economy*; Universal Publishers: Boca Raton, FL, USA, 2006.
45. Boone, W.; Piccinini, G. The Cognitive Neuroscience Revolution. *Synthese* **2016**, *193*, 1509–1534. [CrossRef]
46. De Vries, W. Wilfrid Sellars. In *The Stanford Encyclopedia of Philosophy (Winter 2016 Edition)*; Zalta, E.N., Ed.; Stanford University: Stanford, CA, USA, 2014; Available online: http://plato.stanford.edu/archives/win2016/sellars/ (accessed on 8 August 2017).
47. Toulmin, S. *Knowing and Acting. An Invitation to Philosophy*; Macmillan: New York, NY, USA; London, UK, 1976.
48. Wu, K. *Philosophy of Information—A New Spirit of the Time*; Shaanxi Normal University Press: Xi'an, China, 1989. (In Chinese)
49. Sequoiah-Grayson, S. The Metaphilosophy of Information. *Minds Mach.* **2007**, *17*, 331–334. [CrossRef]
50. Petitot, J.; Varela, F.; Pachoud, B.; Roy, J.-M. (Eds.) *Naturalizing Phenomenology Issues in Contemporary Phenomenology and Cognitive Science*; Stanford University Press: Stanford, CA, USA, 1999.
51. Wu, K.; Li, P. Scientific Evolution: The transformation of the scientific worldview and way of thinking. *J. Chin. Renmin Univ.* **2008**, *3*, 41–46. (In Chinese)
52. Ladyman, J.; Ross, D. *Every Thing Must Go. Metaphysics Naturalized*; Oxford University Press: Oxford, UK, 2007.
53. Brenner, J. The 'Naturalization' of the Philosophy of Rafael Capurro. In *A Festschrift in Honor of Rafael Capurro*; Kelly, M., Bielby, J., Eds.; Springer Fachmedien: Wiesbaden, Germany, 2016; pp. 45–64.
54. Laudisa, F.; Rovelli, C. Relational Quantum Mechanics. In *The Stanford Encyclopedia of Philosophy (Spring 2002 Edition)*; Zalta, E.N., Ed.; Stanford University: Stanford, CA, USA, 2002; Available online: http://plato.stanford.edu/archives/spr2002/entries/qm-relational/ (accessed on 13 November 2007).
55. Hofstadter, D.; Dennett, D. *The Mind's I*; Basic Books: New York, NY, USA, 1981.
56. Wu, K. The Interaction and Convergence of the Philosophy and Science of Information. In Proceedings of the 2nd International Conference on the Philosophy of Information, Vienna, Austria, 6 June 2015.
57. Brenner, J. Information: A Personal Synthesis. *Information* **2014**, *5*, 134–170. [CrossRef]
58. Dodig Crnkovic, G.; Giovagnioli, R. (Eds.) *Computing Nature. Turing Centenary Perspective*; Springer: Berlin, Germany, 2013.
59. Searle, J. *Rationality in Action*; MIT Press: Cambridge, MA, USA, 2001.
60. Floridi, L. Open Problems in the Philosophy of Information. *Metaphilosophy* **2004**, *35*, 554–582. [CrossRef]

61. Brenner, J. Levels of Abstraction; Levels of Reality. In *Luciano Floridi's Philosophy of Technology*; Demir, H., Ed.; Springer: Dordrecht, The Netherlands, 2012.
62. Cat, J. The Unity of Science. In *The Stanford Encyclopedia of Philosophy (Winter 2014 Edition)*; Zalta, E.N., Ed.; Stanford University: Stanford, CA, USA; Available online: http://plato.stanford.edu/archives/win2014/entries/scientific-unity/ (accessed on 28 February 2017).
63. Schroeder, M. Dualism of Selective and Structural Manifestations of Information in Modelling of Information Dynamics. In *Computing Nature. Turing Centenary Perspective*; Dodig Crnkovic, G., Giovagnioli, R., Eds.; Springer: Berlin, Germany, 2013; pp. 125–137.
64. Burgin, M. *Theory of Information. Fundamentality, Diversity and Unification*; World Scientific: Singapore, 2010.
65. Hofkirchner, W. *Emergent Information. A Unified Theory of Information Framework*; World Scientific: Singapore, 2013.
66. Burgin, M.; Brenner, J. Operators in Nature, Science, Technology and Society: Mathematics, Logic and Philosophy. *Philosophies* **2017**, *2*, 21. Available online: http://www.mdpi.com/2409-9287/2/3/21 (accessed on 17 September 2017). [CrossRef]

# 11

# The Interaction and Convergence of the Philosophy and Science of Information

**Kun Wu**

International Center for the Philosophy of Information, Xi'an JiaoTong University, Xi'an 710048, China; WuKun@mail.xjtu.edu.cn

Academic Editor: Marcin J. Schroeder

**Abstract:** Under the impact of information technology and the information sciences, major changes are occurring in both science and philosophy that constitute an informational turn. The recently developed Philosophy of Information has integrated the unique dualistic ontological properties of information, and scientific rationality can now be seen to include an interactive relationship between science and philosophy. Information, in particular Information Science is thus part of the structure, and not just of the content, of philosophy. In this mode of knowledge development, science transforms philosophy and philosophy can critique both science and itself. I see a process of convergence taking place that is leading to a Unified Science-Philosophy of Information, a system of disciplines of which the Philosophy of Information is a part, and Information Science achieves an additional dimension based on this fundamental philosophical stance. I argue further that a proper new Philosophy of Science would be an informational metaphilosophy in that a Unified Science-Philosophy of Information includes both a new content of Science and new dynamics of the relations between a science and its philosophy.

**Keywords:** convergence; informational turn; interaction; philosophy of information; philosophy of science; Unified Science of Information; universal rationality

---

## 1. Introduction

The rapid expansion of the information sciences after emerging from the domain of communication has raised many philosophical questions about the nature of information and its mode of existence. Although involving the transfer of energy in some way, information is a unique complex of energy and meaning. A philosophy of information thus requires inclusion of or reference to the energetic, accordingly scientific aspects of information generation, transfer and reception. The approach I have taken is to start from the assumptions of philosophy as they were understood in the last quarter of the 20th Century and see what the implications are of the properties of information for a proper discussion of information science, philosophy and their relation.

One objective of this paper is to find an appropriate framework and language in which philosophy and the sciences, including standard Information Science can be discussed together. As we will see, information needs to be part of the structure, not just content, of philosophy itself. Concepts of information as a complex process rather than data can be applied to philosophy and assist in the understanding of it. The major problem addressed is to properly characterize the changes that are taking place in knowledge as a whole. These movements, I suggest, can be described as a convergence leading to a Unified Science-Philosophy of Information, a system of disciplines of which the Philosophy of Information is a part, and Information Science achieves an additional dimension based on this fundamental philosophical stance. I argue further that a proper new Philosophy of Science would be an informational metaphilosophy in that a Unified Science-Philosophy of Information includes both a new content of Science and new dynamics of the relations between a science and its philosophy.

To anchor my theory in philosophy, I will start with one of the basic topics in philosophy, the question of existence.

### 1.1. *The Question of Existence*

In a most general sense, at the heart of knowledge is a philosophy of Being, a metatheory of philosophy, of which a theory of existential domains is the central part. This philosophical metatheory is the highest paradigm of philosophy, where paradigm is understood as a pattern in the Kuhnian sense. Whether or not a philosophical theory can stand on its own in a "high-level philosophical forest" can be decided by whether a unique ontology for it has been established.

In traditional Western philosophy, existence is partitioned into three basic existential domains:

> God as objective idea; matter; and personal individual spirit or soul. The theory of these basic existential domains refers to these domains and their interrelations. As science developed, revealing the materiality of ostensibly divine nature, the concept of God gradually disappeared from the forefront of science and philosophy. Therefore, it is now more reasonable to define a corresponding ontological paradigm of Western philosophy as "existence = matter + spirit", (excluding some doctrines in specifically religious studies), where "spirit" has the non-transcendental meaning discussed below.

In my research [1], I have shown that the recently developed Philosophy of Information partitions the existential domain again and suggests a new ontological paradigm: "existence = matter + information", where information consists of objective and subjective informational domains. In the scientific worldview corresponding to this paradigm, the world is constituted by matter-energy and information as its fundamental elements. Compared to the ontological paradigm of traditional philosophy, the new one reveals a new existential domain—the objective informational world—and redefines the nature of spirit in the sense of complex levels of informational activities [2].

### 1.2. *The Question of "Spirit"*

An introductory comment is necessary for the comprehension of this article pertaining to the term "spirit". There are two major meanings of the term "spirit": that of (1) an "objective" existing spirit which refers to God or an Absolute idea; and (2) a personal spirit of human beings, corresponding to the terms "mind" or "consciousness" in Western thought. In modern Chinese philosophical terminology, the term "spirit" can be used in both cases.

Both Chinese and Western materialists, of whom I am one, do not accept the existence of an objective spirit as usually defined. The so-called objective spirit, which does not exist in the real objective world, is only a creation of personal spirit. It is unnecessary to distinguish the two concepts of spirit in Chinese, but my use of the terms spirit and spiritual in this paper is exclusively in the personal, that is, immanent sense.

### 1.3. *A Philosophical Definition of Information: Direct and Indirect Being; Subjective and Objective*

In my philosophy of information, I give the following definition of information: "Information is a philosophical category indicating indirect being. It is the self-manifestation of the existing mode and status of matter (direct being)" [3]. Information can be distinguished into two fields: objective indirect being (objective information) and subjective indirect being (spirit, or subjective information). Thus, the formula mentioned above "existence = matter + information" can also be rewritten as "existence = matter + objective information + subjective information (spirit) = direct being + objective indirect being + subjective indirect being". Such a world view is a reflection of a fundamental change in the traditional world view of matter and spirit dualism, as it can describe the relation between matter and spirit as a process of mutual transition and transformation through the medium of information. The philosophy of information thus effectively dissolves the simple dichotomy of matter and spirit.

If we investigate further the relationship between direct being and indirect being, we will see that the world of indirect being is derived from the interaction of the world of direct being, which is the world of the manifestation, presentation, mapping, representation or subjective reflection and subjective reform of the concept of nature, the world of the mode and status of direct being. A simple example can be given which illustrates the forms of beings and the correspondence relations between them. We can propose three kinds of modes of existence of the moon (or of any other real but not directly accessible object): the moon in the sky, the moon in the water (the moon in a reflecting surface) and the pattern of the moon in our brain. Those three kinds of moon respectively correspond to the direct being moon, objective indirect being moon and subjective indirect being moon. In fact, what the world of objective indirect being reveals is the relational aspect of the universal connection of objective things.

In my classification of the morphology of information, the information does not equal subjective "meaningfulness" or "significance". Beyond the subjective world there is also, following Sartre, an objective "in-itself information" world, but the subjective spirit is the "for-itself" form of information. Here, for-itself information refers to the information which is grasped by cognitive agents. A further form of information is "regenerated" information—new information that is processed and created by the thoughts of cognitive agents. The next level is that of social information, that involved in the interactions of cognitive agents. The essential points of my work on the philosophical nature and classification of information and the fundamental theory of information philosophy, published in Chinese, have recently become available in English [4–6].

### *1.4. Outline of Paper*

In the next Section 2, I will discuss the informational turn taking place in science and philosophy. In Section 3, the convergence of science and philosophy under the impact of this turn will be discussed from the viewpoint of knowledge and universal reason. Section 4 goes more deeply into this convergence and the relation between science, philosophy and universal scientific rationality. Section 5 introduces the concept of a Unified Science-Philosophy of Information (USPI) and its incorporation of philosophy. In my final Section 6, the work of Y. X. Zhong in Information Science and mine in the Philosophy of Information are contrasted as exemplifying trends in current thought in China that are relevant to a potential USPI. Section 7 summarizes briefly the results of this study.

## 2. The Informational Turn of Contemporary Science and Philosophy

As I have discussed recently, at the Vienna Information 2015 Summit Conference, there are several theories of philosophical turns proposed by Western philosophers including the phenomenological turn, existential turn, axiological turn, praxiological turn and so on. The two most important are the turns from ontology to epistemology, and the consequent linguistic turn. However, these turns are concerned only with a shift of philosophical horizons, rather than any transformation at the highest level of metaphilosophical paradigm, and are not fundamental.

On the other hand, because of its universal character, information has a fundamental significance for the transformation of both philosophy and science, given its transdisciplinary properties and multiple levels and dimensions. It is the Philosophy of Information considered as metaphilosophy [7] that exemplifies the first fundamental turns in philosophy and science [8,9]. These "informational" turns are in fact not separate processes, but two sides of a single unified course of development of contemporary knowledge.

### *2.1. Information Science*

For the nature of the subject in information science and other traditional disciplines, people usually only use labels like interdisciplinary subject, transdisciplinary subject, or comprehensive discipline to explain them. Even though these labels cannot be seen as inappropriate, yet just staying at the level of these labels is far from enough to reveal the significance and value of overall and radical reform that Information Science brings to traditional science. In essence, Information Science requires a transformation of the scientific paradigm, which will result in a brand-new scientific system which uses information theory as the predominant approach to cognition, forcing general information theory to be seen as interacting with traditional scientific systems. In this case, Information Science itself is a modern scientific system rather than a single field or discipline.

### 2.2. *Philosophy of Information as a Metaphilosophy*

My formulation of the concept of information as a basic category of philosophy defines the central role of information and information science in all relevant disciplines such as ontology and epistemology as well as in science. This is a metaphilosophical principle, since it has to do with the content of philosophy itself. Justification for my calling my Philosophy of Information a Metaphilosophy, "a highest philosophy", to be distinguished from all others, is its unique and universal character, its new worldview, as an informational conception of history, society, values, knowledge, science and technology.

A standard definition of the term metaphilosophy is a statement or set of statements about philosophy. I first note that a discussion of metaphilosophy requires a definition of both philosophy and the task of philosophy as well. As Brenner has pointed out, in that of Sellars, "the aim of philosophy is to understand how things in the broadest possible sense of the term hang together in the broadest possible sense of the term". My Basic Theory of the Philosophy of Information provides one basis for understanding both the metaphysical and epistemological dynamics of existence, that is, from where the properties of things come from that enable both them and the concepts of them to contrast, to conflict and ultimately to "hang together".

A theory of metaphilosophy that talks only in terms of categorial separation or distinction between elements, disciplines or methodologies in philosophy is that of Toulmin [10]. In my view, any such theory has a certain limited domain of validity, in which it is more or less adequate or appropriate to the philosophy in question. In an article in Chinese [11], I have given a broader role of metaphilosophy for information studies (and by implication for other disciplines): "Now, my research is still basically limited to elucidate the general basic theory of philosophy of information from the angle of a metaphilosophy. At such a level, there is a lot of work we should do to define the philosophical essence of information, the philosophical shape and form of information; the nature of the different levels of information; a philosophical measure of information; the relationship between information and various prior definitions of its scope; information ontology, information epistemology, information methodology; the evolution of the informational world; information in material and social evolution; informational sociology and psychology; informational esthetics: an informational theory of value; there are still have very abundant and a large number of branch issues in the each area field of that listed above". My view thus offers a novel dialectic perspective on philosophy, metaphilosophy and their recursive relation. It naturalizes this relation, eliminating any implied circularity, since it does not require the total independence of premises and conclusion of standard logics.

As indicated in the Introduction, my metaphilosophical view of information is not directed toward the codification of a Metaphilosophy of Information as yet another static discipline or body of knowledge. It is rather an attitude toward the positioning of an adequate Philosophy of Information as encompassing a critical component of all disciplines, beyond the scientific content specific to them. In this approach, metaphilosophy is not something "more abstract" than philosophy and it must be able to deal with the essential aspects of all disciplines and their theories. A metaphilosophical approach is essential to avoid unnecessary and misleading distinctions between disciplines and their informational aspects. One of the consequences is that the comprehensive nature of such a metaphilosophy, within a transdisciplinary paradigm, establishes the role of those involved as a socio-political role, involving them in the social and ethical aspects of the informational components of reality.

The Metaphilosophy of Information as such requires further attention to the informational aspects of complex processes as a methodological necessity, in a process that I have called Informational Thinking. Informational Thinking (*IT*) refers to a way of grasping and describing the essential characteristics and attributes of things by reference to the structure and dynamics of the information involved in their evolution, from their historical origins to future possibilities and probabilities. This strategy involves something like a Husserlian bracketing of the details of any complex process to consider the ways in which information functions in its dynamics, as well as the dialectical relations between its logical elements. However, the difference between my theory and that of Husserl is obvious: the purpose of the original Philosophy of Information is to clarify the nature of the dual existence and dual evolution of material and information in the objective world, starting from the logic of the existence and dynamics of the natural human self. This phenomenology, unlike that of Husserl, does not have to be "naturalized", that is, brought into the domain of natural science (The naturalization of Husserlian phenomenology was the subject of a major 1999 study: *Naturalizing Phenomenology. Issues in Contemporary Phenomenology and Cognitive Science.* Eds. Jean Petitot et al. Stanford University Press, Stanford. My approach eliminates the arduous task of finding natural equivalents for Husserl's transcendental intuitions). It is already there, in the real processes involved in an individual's understanding at the level of the integrated object and subject, with internal and external interactions providing the necessary multi-level objective and subjective mediation. In this sense, all cognitive issues, especially informational values, valence and social evolution, have implied the use of Informational Thinking for their analysis. *IT* requires the abandonment of thinking in absolute material terms in traditional material while retaining its commonsense foundations. *IT* is basically a methodological concept that, via the definitions of carriers and codes of information, enables *inferences* to be made about the historical and potential or probable future states of an information system. *IT* dialectically unifies energy factors and informational factors, determinism and indeterminism, internal and external feedback processes, independence (autonomy) and interdependence. In fact, Informational Thinking is the Metaphilosophy of Information in other terms.

## 3. The Intrinsic Unifying Convergence of Science and Philosophy

### 3.1. *Knowledge and Universal Reason: The Basis of the Convergence of Science and Philosophy*

In the most general sense, we can view philosophy as an activity of seeking universal reason, while scientific observation and experiment have the characteristics of concrete perceptual activity. (For more details about this paragraph and the next see [12]). On the basis of this, philosophy and science have generally been considered as separate disciplines.

In fact, general reasoning and concrete perception should not be separated completely in any form of human cognitive activity. Human beings inevitably evaluate all kinds of sense data in the framework of reasoning. It is one of the obvious differences between human consciousness and the animal mind, as well as the ultimate ground of philosophy and science as an intrinsically unified knowledge system.

Science is essentially constituted by principles of universal rationality. For a discussion of scientific rationality in English, the reader is directed to the recent article in the *Stanford Encyclopedia of Philosophy* [13]). Those principles are not equal to direct narratives about facts of observation and experiment. They depend on certain concepts, rules and methods of abstract philosophical thinking to ascend from narrations of facts to principles of universal rationality. We can thus begin to see how philosophy is in science, and how science is in the rules of philosophical paradigms. There is an intrinsic, implied philosophical concept in any scientific universal rationality, which therefore can be viewed as the "offspring" of certain philosophical concepts and concrete narratives combining with one another. The unity of philosophy and science cannot be considered exclusively as an external join, but as an inner convergence as well.

Most scientists believe that scientific theories are established on the basis of observed, experimental data and facts, the concrete perceptual characteristics of which define the concrete perceptual characteristics of science itself. Only if those data and facts are accurate will the scientific conclusions obtained from them be precise. However, have scientists considered seriously by what concrete means those data and facts are obtained and explained?

### 3.2. Information and Cognition

Human beings do not cognize the objective world directly. There are many complex kinds of intermediate relationships between cognition and the objects of cognition, as discussed in a paper in English [6]. In related research on the Philosophy of Information, I proposed a complex emergent theory which explains the occurrence of cognition in terms of five intermediate aspects: (1) an objective informational field; (2) a subjective physical structure; (3) a subjective knowledge structure; (4) subjective material instruments; (5) a subjective genetic-historical dimension.

In view of these five intermediate aspects, the phenomena seen directly in observation and experiment are not the "objective facts" themselves, but the macroscopic informational signs of "objective facts" remaining after transfer through intermediate structures. Accordingly, to draw valid scientific conclusions is possible only by explaining those signs. The corresponding explanations depend not only on the analysis of the experimental results of observation, with or without instruments, but also on the scientific theoretical paradigms applied to recognize those structures.

Thus, no kind of science can be determined solely by so-called concrete sense data. Scientific knowledge is the combined product of sense data and general reasoning. In this approach, philosophy can no longer be considered something transcendental, irrelevant to and outside science. I do not wish to conflate, that is, eliminate all distinctions between philosophy and science. Both have targets and methodologies that are unique to them, but mutual influence and interaction seems the correct term for the relation between them.

### 3.3. The Content of Scientific Experiment

During the process of scientific observation and experiment, the content observed by scientists through complicated instruments of observation is not the original status of any actual objects. In the macroscopic observation area which can be realized by human senses or simple instruments, the effect of information conversion and transformation happening via medium are still inconspicuous. However, such effects cannot be ignored in modern science; because of the observation of the universe which is beyond the macroscopic world and microscopic world we have to use very complicated scientific instruments which magnify such effects to a significant extent. In fact, the things which can be directly observed in scientific survey and experiments by scientists are some macroscopic marks: the trajectory and structure of point, ray, curve, colored tape or picture, left by the relevant information of "object fact" after transformed by intermediary apparatus, rather than the so called "object fact" itself. We have to give relevant explanations to the marks of these trajectories and structures, so that we can obtain a valid scientific judgment from them. These relevant explanations, however, not only rely on the analysis of the performance of observation instruments and apparatuses used by scientists, but also depend on the related scientific paradigm existing in the scientists' cognitive structure. Thus, between the "objective facts" (the observed objects) and the "scientific facts" (marks left by information transformation by instruments), between the "scientific fact" and the "scientific judgment" and between the "scientific judgment" and "scientific theory", there exist complicated intermediate relationships. Thus, in fact no kind of science can be determined by sensibility alone; science is by its nature a product of combining concrete sensibility and universal rationality. Better, sensibility and rationality are present in thought as conjugate variables of a kind, varying in reciprocal proportions between the limits of 0 and 1: philosophy is at one limit and science at the other.

In this way, philosophy is no longer transcendental, having nothing to do with science or being beyond science. Philosophy is something that is integrated into the science, working as a part of its organic composition, acting as its "soul in a metaphorical sense" and playing a core role in a scientific paradigm. By "soul in a metaphorical sense" I mean high-level cognitive approaches to acquiring, explaining and handling observational experimental materials, methods of normalizing them and the capacity for constructing scientific theories. Beyond perception, the worldview, epistemology, and methodological considerations on how to undertake scientific research, how to process experimental data are important concepts that are an intrinsic part of scientific activity. Additionally, the fact that science draws on hypotheses and abductions shows the most crucial and important effects, significance and values of philosophical (and logical) considerations and gives a creative intellectual pattern to its development.

Some may argue that mathematics is pure logic and does not need to include any observational end experimental materials to be valid. Actually, however, due to the fact that mathematics is a kind of theory studying the quantitative relation and spatial, structural relation between things, it never can avoid interpreting the relevant relationships in the real world, involving not only elementary and advanced mathematics, but also Euclidean and non-Euclidian geometry, fractal theory and chaos theory). Mathematics also refers to various logics and language systems for computer programming. The point worthy to notice is no more than the difference of idealization of exceeding actual quantity and space relationship obtained by diverse mathematical forms. Theoretical physics also cannot be constituted only by pure logic and idealistic speculation. Even diverse idealized experiments regarding quantum theory, relativity and cosmology in general also need to find their explanation and proof in the relevant real world [14].

### *3.4. The Level of Universal Rationality: The Relative Mutual Definition of the Partition of Science and Philosophy*

Because all scientific disciplines are systematically constituted by universal principles, what establishes the differences between them is their degree of universal rationality, not the presence or absence of such rationality. In other words, science at whatever level of depth has a philosophical sense from which we can determine the approximate boundary between philosophy and science. The inner differences of levels or degrees of universal rationality define the hierarchy of philosophy and science.

There exist complex interactions of mutual effect and definition between the levels of universal rationality, which can be considered a bi-univocal relationship between them. In one respect, the lower universal rationality is the foundation on which the higher universal rationality is established, the latter being derived by abstracting, generalizing and summarizing the former; in the other respect, the lower universal rationality is the instantiation of a higher universal rationality in a concrete area, the consequence and the product of the higher universal rationality determining it.

The problem of the existence and nature of levels in philosophy has been the subject of much debate, to which Floridi has contributed, among others, with the concept of Levels of Abstraction [15]. He is reluctant to accept any theory that postulates ontological levels of organization existing independently of the level of abstraction at which they are conceptualized. In my view, however, levels of rationality correspond to real mental structures (processes) which are not static within a level and are subject to change via recursivity. If we take engineering as a "concrete" area, it is always subject to reflection about its existential and moral implications, which, hopefully, are taken into account in practice.

The dual characteristics of the lower and higher rationalities inevitably induce them to converge, again without conflation, that is, while maintaining essential differences in targets and methodologies as indicated below.

In this process, the higher universal rationality illuminates, constrains and controls the lower universal rationality, while the lower universal rationality not only embodies certain normative principles belonging to higher universal rationality at its own level, but also provides valid basic foundations for higher universal rationality from its own material contents and activities.

The interactions between levels of rationalities will necessarily result in a holographic unified relationship of internal convergence, on which different degrees and levels of rationality are based. Holographic means here that they are mutually embodied, constrained and reciprocally defined.

Ordinarily, the higher-level system of universal rationality is called philosophy, and what underlies this system is called science. However, such a distinction of the disciplines of science and philosophy is not fully correct, because it implies that philosophy and science are disjunct. In fact, the absolute partition between science and philosophy is only present in a historical phase when neither of them has been adequately developed. Philosophy must not be detached from and override science; rather it should be considered a (natural) *kind* of science, since science is in complete accord with the outputs of correct rational thinking, and science should be a *kind* of philosophy.

Any subject of human knowledge is constituted by a certain proportion of concrete sensibility, that is, of science and of universal rationality, philosophy. The ratio of these two ingredients varies reciprocally from 0% to 100% [16].

## 4. The Transformation of Science into Philosophy. The Critiques of Science by Philosophy. The Self-Critique of Philosophy

### *4.1. The Transition between Levels of Universal Rationality*

A true Philosophy of Science, which should obviously be grounded in science, thus cannot be separate from and supervene on science. The current dependence of philosophical development on scientific development indicates that science is the strongest and most basic driving force for the transformation of philosophy.

In general, new scientific concepts and principles that can reveal the nature of things and phenomena are always rationalities that are first proposed in certain narrow scientific domains and therefore have narrow functional areas of application. There exist, however, concepts and principles of a more universal character which can break through the initial narrow disciplinary limitations.

Such concepts or principles can transition to a higher level of universal rationality, and illustrate its most general aspects.

If the new concept and principle is not completely contrary to the old one, or there is just a small partial contradiction between them, then the old rational system will not change substantially or only be modified in small details. However, sometimes there is a situation where the new universal rationality conflicts with the fundamental universal rationality at the higher level, forcing the higher-level system to take one of the following two attitudes: (1) repel the new system to protect itself; (2) use the new one to change or replace the old contrary one to renew the entire general system of rationality. The former attitude is usually the one accepted by conservative theory, while the latter attitude might initiate a revolution at that level.

In the history of philosophy and science, the transforming effect of science on philosophy is obvious. Consider ontology: in ancient Greek philosophy, there was a theory of atomism, a world constructed by indivisible material particles. Later, from the point of view of classical mechanics, the world is constructed integrally by particles whose basic properties result from the interactions of forces. "Quality" was considered by modern materialists and physicists as the symbol of the existence of matter, and the "weight" of quality as the standard magnitude of measuring matter. In other words, materialist philosophers all conflated matter with "quality" in science and viewed it as the origin of the world. Next, matter-energy was shown to be a more basic form of reality than quality by electromagnetic field theory, relativity and quantum mechanics. This new development in science made traditional materialism lose its *raison d'être*, which led to corresponding transformations in philosophy, the emergence of modern energetics, a new realism and a new materialist philosophy.

Now, it is seen to be necessary to investigate the world and the things in it from an informational viewpoint, beyond that of matter/energy alone. The contemporary scientific worldview turns out to be an integral, complex informational theory and the scientific thinking turns out accordingly to be an informational thinking as well [1].

Following the middle of the last century, following the emergence and development of a basic Science of Information, the significance and value of an informational world at different levels of existence has appeared in stages. New developments in science challenged requirements for a dichotomy between the matter and spirit and subject and object of traditional philosophy, and resulted in the emergence of the contemporary Philosophy of Information. Based on the new "fruits" from the development of the Science of Information, the Philosophy of Information establishes new philosophical and scientific paradigms based on the dual existence and dual evolution of matter and information, which as noted not only brings about the first fundamental turn in philosophy, but also establishes the precondition for a Unified Science of Information.

Recent developments relevant to the problematic of unity have been well summarized by Jordi Cat in his article on the Unity of Science [17]. These can be read as avoiding any principle of "unity for the sake of unity". Cat notes several positive, anti-reductionist trends in the philosophy of science, for example in moving from dependence on concepts primarily from physics. Cat suggests that the concept of unity can have value at the practical level in science, to justify approaches and goals, and in philosophy to help choose what philosophical questions to pursue and what target areas to explore. Reference to the Unity of Science could be made to describe what science is to be considered by philosophy as authoritative.

### *4.2. Exclusion of the Limit of Lower Universal rationality. The Critique of Science by Philosophy*

The transformation of philosophy is achieved by the transition from levels of scientific universal rationality, but this does not imply that philosophy is a passive participant in this process. In contrast, without the initiative in philosophy, the transformation of science to philosophy could not be achieved. Here, it is useful to emphasize another aspect of the relationship between philosophy and science: the critique of Science by Philosophy.

The universal rationality of science is of much greater universality and can surpass the narrow limits of the disciplines from which it was originally generated toward higher form of universal rationality. Hierarchical transition is a process of the self-sublimation of universal rationality, and the reconsideration or re-evaluation of the concept of a universal rationality itself. This higher universal rationality defines and processes the original lower general rationalities by taking them as objects of investigation. In other words, the higher universal rationality imposes its methodology on lower rationalities while generalizing, summarizing and assimilating the lower general rationalities, implementing a kind of philosophical critique in the process.

The fact that philosophy must enrich and develop itself through science, however, does not mean that philosophy is just a "vassal" of science. Philosophy has a critical role at its own level. In the development of the concepts of the unity of science and philosophy, it is inevitable to have to take into account aspects of the transformations effected on philosophy by science and critiques made of science by philosophy. In the process of the development of science and philosophy, the (partial) transformation of science to philosophy and the critiques by philosophy of science are clearly manifested.

In the second phase of the scientific revolution, after the acceptance of the achievements of electromagnetic field theory, relativity field theory and quantum mechanics revealed the more basic nature of energy as compared to matter in the real world, the idea of fighting against materialism with energetics occurred to some scientists and philosophers. They preferred to call themselves realists rather than materialists. In this situation, the transformation of science seriously challenged the older materialism explained by material substance, which indicates how the development of science can require that philosophy transform and develop itself. However, where the emergence of energetics induced philosophy to change depended on the critical function of philosophy itself. At that time, there were two different philosophical critiques: one was to consider the relationship of quality and energy in a mechanistic and replace materialism by energetics. Another critique was is to consider that relationship in a dialectical way, view them as different forms of objective reality, and accordingly reveal the material nature of objective reality by critical analysis in order to establish a new kind of materialism that could include both matter and energy. The explanatory principle of objective reality not only sublimates the concept of energy in science to the level of general philosophy, but it also makes possible a materialist explanation of energy and energetics by a philosophical critique in which the transformation of science to philosophy could be seen, and the general characteristics of the achievements of science could be sublimated into philosophical conceptions and theories as well [18]. The process by which the contemporary Philosophy of Information was established thus illustrates its dual effect: the transformation of science to philosophy and the critique of science by philosophy.

### 4.3. The Problem of the Nature of Information

As we know, the communicational theory of information of Shannon and the informational cybernetics of Wiener in 1948 both belong to the field of technological informational science. Wiener's suggestion [19] of an ontological meaning of information as different from matter and energy has led to many discussions and investigations of the philosophical problems of a Science of Information. These have taken the form of a search, by Eastern and Western scholars, for an interactive, realist theory of a Unified Science of Information (USI), based on the development of both the Science and Philosophy of Information (see Section 5 below). Recognizing the limitations of his initial theory, Wiener did try to emphasize the general philosophical character of information, discussing the nature of information from a philosophical view while considering information as negative entropy from a view of pragmatic informational theory. He had two famous ideas: one was that "information is information, neither matter nor energy". The other one was that "information is a name for the content of what is exchanged with the outer world as we adjust to it, and make our adjustment felt upon it" [20]. Although Wiener did not define what exactly information is directly, he thus emphasized the independent value and meaning of information compared to matter and energy., while seeing the necessity of considering information from "the exchanged content" point of view as well.

However, these explanations of information remained at the functional level of technological pragmatism. Until now, their definitions of information are still the basic doctrines in scientific circles: information is indetermination that has been removed (Shannon); information is negative entropy (Wiener).

Obviously, both of these are just relative and quantitative definitions of information made from a consideration of the sender's unidirectional relation to the receiver. Although they have pragmatic value in the fields of communication and cybernetics, they do not reveal the general nature of information.

Scientists and philosophers, who missed the critical aspects of these definitions, adopted the method of simple analogies of the theoretical conceptions and the disciplinary characteristics related to pragmatic informational science and technology and traditional philosophy for the explanation of information. Several research approaches to studies of information problems can be listed: the computational, the information ethical, the communication informational, the information cognitional, the sign informational, the information phenomenological, and so on. However, because these approaches are dependent on a given concrete philosophy or science, they are consciously or unconsciously constrained by the narrow and limiting characteristics of their original theories and disciplines. Accordingly, these theories do not reveal the truly unique and revolutionary significance of informational considerations. A Unified Information Theory founded on them cannot be considered as a higher Science of Information, let alone a general Philosophy of Information, a Unified Science of Information, or, in the formulation I now prefer, a Unified Science-Philosophy of Information.

The transformation of philosophy by science thus cannot be achieved automatically by counting on scientific successes in themselves, but depends on relevant critiques of science by philosophy. This is a two-sided interactive process, to which both science and philosophy contribute. Thus, in his pioneering work on the Philosophy of Information in the West, Luciano Floridi has called the impact of information science and technology an informational revolution [21]. His proposal of an "informational ontology" correctly critiques the limited, computational concept of a digital ontology.

However, as the I have pointed out, Floridi has not addressed the core problem of the nature of information and the impact of the philosophy of information on philosophy in general.

One important contribution to the field that Floridi has made is his concept of Informational Structural Realism (ISR). Thus, Floridi argues, for example, in [15] that *digital ontology*, according to which the ultimate nature of reality is digital or computational, should be carefully distinguished from *informational ontology*, according to which the ultimate nature of reality is structural [22]. Floridi avoids the Boolean digital vs. analogue dichotomy in favor of ISR, according to which knowledge of the world is knowledge of its structures. The most reasonable ontological commitment favors an interpretation of reality as the totality of its structures, energetic entities, dynamically interacting with one another. In my view however, the Floridi limited ontology fails to capture the evolution of real informational processes.

Floridi's position is that the ultimate nature of reality is informational, mind-independent and constituted by structural objects that are neither substantial nor material (they might well be, but we have no need to suppose them to be so). The Logic in Reality of Brenner [23] offers a principled basis for saying that they are and suggests the logical rules they follow. In the mutual transformation process of matter (mass-energy) interaction in the nature itself, the information exhibiting the corresponding process and quality is intertwined in the interactive matter by the way of spatio-temporal conversion and mutual mapping and transformation among matter. Consequently, the information world reveals the matter world that has been created, and this information world is specifically embedded in the relevant structure of matter world. Logic in Reality describes the movements in nature such that the whole world and everything in the world are dualities of matter and information. According to this idea, we can say that Logic in Reality [7] may become one of the theoretical foundations of for unifying information science and information philosophy. I had completely independently written a book discussing logics of nature which presents an intensive investigation of the relevant questions [24].

The critical aspect of information, to which Hofkirchner and others are now turning, is its dualistic relation to the energy of which it is constituted. In the view of Brenner as well as me, it is this duality or dualism that is the actual "driver" of informational processes.

### *4.4. Meaning from an Informational Standpoint*

A key issue in philosophy is the emergence of meaning in human activities, which I propose can be looked at from an informational standpoint. First, two kinds of epistemological theories of meaning can be identified: (1) a semantic theory which assigns semantic contents to expressions of a language; and (2) a foundational theory of meaning which states the facts in virtue of which expressions have the semantic contents that they have. My conception of meaning is ontological and foundational. According to Aristotle, philosophy is a doctrine about "existent being", so the primary problem faced by philosophy is "What does exist?", the domains of being, and the relation between them. It is how this question is answered that defines the fundamental nature of philosophy, as well as stipulates the basic approaches and methods of dealing with the problems in other fields. Therefore, the ontological doctrine of a specific philosophical system becomes the criterion for judging the nature of that system and deciding whether it is able to stand firmly at the level of meta-philosophy.

Human cognitive activities are involved in processes of the mutual selection and matching, reorganization and reconstruction, creation, according to a non-deterministic model, of new subjective information processes. I designate as teleological (in the Deacon sense) or purposeful information that created by human beings to achieve or insure the success of practical activities. Thus, human activities of material production, from my informational standpoint, imply the process of planning to implement purposeful, structural information to create material objects, effect actions, etc. I am particularly concerned about the way in which new information is created in the recombination of available modes of communication between human beings. In the process of transmission of information from sender (subject) to receiver (object), the teleonomy of the subject implies that its information will be realized in the object. Meaning emerges in this process that I propose follows both the dialectic principles of Logic in Reality [23] and the Teleodynamics of Deacon [25]. The true definition of meaning is then new content in the information. Once high-level information activity patterns are created, they acquire the properties of meaning and value for a person by a process of self-reference, which adds a new element to the person's entire information activity system. Of course, meaningless information involved in the relations between objective things, their mappings and their presentations is widespread in nature. This part of information I call "in-itself" information, for which there is no cognitive interpreter.

### *4.5. The Constructive Transformation of Advanced Universal Rationality. The Self-Critique of Philosophy*

The critique of philosophy has a dual significance: the critique not only aims at specific boundary of science, but also points at philosophy itself. The purpose of a critique to science from philosophy is to eliminate a certain parochialism and the limitations of some category theories. The criticism to itself from philosophy is to break down a facet which is ossified, dogmatic, outdated and conservative. Philosophy has always had a two-sidedness: conservativeness and criticalness, sluggishness and activeness, backwardness and vision. Nevertheless, philosophy also is the spirit of the era and cannot lag behind it in the long term. The development of science and society demands that philosophy exhibit sufficiently its positive characteristics, while recognizing that, as for all real systems, contradictions and regressions will never be totally absent. In other words, philosophy, that is, philosophers, have to have the ability for self-criticism to develop and transform themselves.

The transition of a lower universal rationality to a higher level referred to above and the critiques of philosophy by science proved that philosophy is an open system, which needs "information" from outside. However, this information from outside must accept the methodological primitives of philosophy itself, namely choice and critique. Only when it (information) is integrated critically into the *structure* of philosophy can information be assimilated to the *content* of philosophy. As a result of this assimilation and regulative self-critique, philosophy can transform itself naturally by itself. In this process of assimilation, the following dual effects are achieved: on the one hand, external information is critiqued by philosophy; on the other, because that kind of critique changes the original construction of philosophy-in-itself, philosophy as a whole is critiqued as well. If the change of construction is comprehensive and if that critique acts on the most basic concepts and principles that represent the highest paradigm of philosophy, a fundamental transformation is possible.

The contemporary Philosophy of Information reveals the problems that affected the development of philosophy in regard to the above critical issues. In fact, for a long time, to explain the nature of information, there had been a tendency to use not only the simple analogies discussed above, but also analogies from related theories and traditional conceptions of philosophy.

For example: "information is a property of matter"; "information is a way of existence of matter"; "information is an existing state of matter"; "information is a character of spiritual entity"; "information is the externalization of movement"; "information is an interactive concept of matter"; "information is reflection"; "information is meaning", and so on. These all tried to match information to simple traditional philosophical concepts. Far from revealing the new, unique and universal character of information, they castrated it, eliminated its comprehensive and fundamental significance for transformation and value, leaving it in the decayed cage of the old paradigm of traditional philosophy. It is impossible to establish a Philosophy of Information in accordance with and reflecting the spirit of the time and its innovative significance by way of analogies. As von Bertalanffy pointed out in relation to systems, "analogies are scientifically worthless" [26]. This is why the work of only a few philosophers has been relevant to the establishment of either a systematic Philosophy of Information or a Unified Science-Philosophy of Information.

As long as the constraints of the traditional philosophical paradigm continue to be used, complete with their traditional philosophical concepts, theories and methods, the emergence of any kind of truly new philosophy will be difficult and very long in coming.

The general characteristics of information transcend the basic premises and theoretical structure of traditional philosophy. A Philosophy of Information that truly shows these general characteristics establishes the critiques that philosophy makes of science, and the critiques that philosophy makes of itself as well. To repeat, the new ontology of the Philosophy of Information changes the basic doctrine of traditional philosophy: "existence = matter + spirit" into "existence = matter + information (spirit being only a complex form of information)". Thus, the subjective-objective relationship of traditional philosophy is transformed into a more complex interactive relationship that includes the multiple informational intermediary activities of the spiritual (cognitive) subject and object. This transformation realizes the fundamental innovation of philosophical ontology and epistemology, philosophical evolution theory, philosophical value theory and philosophical methodology as well. Due to the dual-critical process of the philosophical critique of science and philosophy itself, the Philosophy of Information achieves a comprehensive transformation of traditional philosophy, which results in the first fundamental turn in history of philosophy, as discussed in Section 2 [27].

## 5. A Unified Science of Information "Upright between Heaven and Earth"

As a result of establishing the fundamental role of information in the existential domain, the Philosophy of Information provides a kind of dual-existential and dual-evolutionary theory of matter and information which describes information as a general phenomenon existing in everything in the cosmos. That leads to the acknowledgement of the dual dimension of matter and information in all forms of research. Because the lack of an informational dimension in traditional philosophy and science, it is necessary to transform them completely to take into account the new scientific paradigm provided by the current Science and Philosophy of Information. By means of that transformation, all scientific and philosophical domains become involved in an integrating, developing trend of paradigm transformation, which I have called the "informational scientification of science" [28].

The current interaction and convergence of the Science and Philosophy of Information represents a fundamental and basic path for the development of scientific and philosophical knowledge. This "philosophization of science" and "scientification of philosophy", anticipated in the progression from ancient philosophy to modern science and philosophy, now represents a completely new way of thinking that is that distinct from that of the contemporary Western philosophy of consciousness. It resists an absolute separation between science and philosophy and establishes interactive, mutually defining feedback loops between science and philosophy which emphasizes their interrelation.

With the emergence of this completely new trend, philosophy and science are now facing a new situation, which might be considered as a rationale for establishing a general Unified Science of Information, better, a Unified Science-Philosophy of Information that would include all the domains of philosophy, science, technology and mechanics. The idea of establishing first a Unified Science of Information was initiated by a group of European scholars in the 1990s. Since then, from different levels and disciplinary viewpoints, many scientists and philosophers from all over the world have made efforts in that direction including A. D. Ursul and Konstantin Kolin from Russia; Pedro Marijuán, Wolfgang Hofkirchner, Søren Brier, Rafael Capurro and Joseph E. Brenner from Europe; Yi Xin Zhong, Ming Li, Changlin Liu, Litian Shen, Xianhan Luo, Dongsheng Miao, Kang Ouyang, Xueshan Yan and I from China; and Luciano Floridi, John Collier and Albert Borgmann from other countries.

This research suggests the independence and universality of the informational world. It anticipates and is the precondition for the establishment and development of a needed new modern paradigm for science and philosophy, a new worldview in which Unified Science-Philosophy of Information would have a central role.

The informational world, of course, is not independent of the material world. It is the complexity of its dual aspects of information-as-energy and information-as-meaning that is the source of the difficulties in its comprehension. However, they have different modes of existence, and information flows in its own, unique mode according to its own rules. In this sense, information is *relatively* independent of the material world, while not being separate from it. Logic in Reality provides the framework for the interactive dialectic relation between them.

*The Disciplines of Information Science*

Elsewhere, I have proposed a model of a potential Unified Science of Information classified according to six major levels: the Philosophy of Information; a General Theory of Information (GTI); Regional Informatics, in which the basic principles of the GTI are collated in three major disciplinary sub-groups: natural informatics, social informatics, cognitive informatics); Category Informatics; Branch informatics (several branches); and Engineering Technological Informatics [29]. In the meantime, this classification has become somewhat less relevant and useful at a practical level.

In the West, the concept of a GTI was first stated explicitly by Mark Burgin [30], later expanded and developed in a major book [31]. The concept of a Unified *Theory* of Information has been developed most completely by Wolfgang Hofkirchner [32,33].

In contrast, a Unified Science of Information (USI), to use a Chinese metaphor, would be a disciplinary system "upright between heaven and earth" that is, including all human knowledge levels from philosophy to science to engineering technology. Such a Unified Science of Information would favor further convergent integration of science and philosophy, toward a Unified Science-Philosophy of Information. In this integration, the philosophical sense of the Science of Information and the scientific character of the Philosophy of Information would be fully present. Thus, the Philosophy of Information could be viewed as a part of a general Science of Information, and the Science of Information as achieving its real unity by its foundation in the general principles of philosophy. In this vision, the Unified Science-Philosophy of Information is the scientific basis of a general Philosophy of Information, and the Philosophy of Information is the general theoretical precondition of a unified and unifying Science of Information.

In my opinion, the establishment of a Unified Science-Philosophy of Information and the mature development of a Philosophy of Information should be a process of convergence, two sides of a new and integral developing pattern of contemporary human knowledge.

## 6. Information Science and Philosophy in China: A Comparison of Wu Kun and Yi Xing Zhong

In China, there is a kind of natural understanding and interactive relationship has emerged in joint discussions of the Science of Information proposed by Yi Xing Zhong and the Philosophy of Information proposed by myself. The disciplines are different in approach but equally satisfactory in their conclusions.

In October 2014, the tenth forum of the Journal *Philosophical Analysis*: entitled "A National Conference on the Philosophical Spirit of the Informational Era" was held in Xi'an by the editorial department of *Philosophical Analysis*, the International Center for the Philosophy of Information in Xi'an Jiaotong University and the Research Society of Natural Dialectics in Shaanxi province. Zhong discussed five aspects of his understanding of that relationship in his conference paper entitled "The Consideration of the Philosophy of Information from a viewpoint of the Science of Information" [34]. The detailed comparison of our views is outlined below.

### 6.1. Characteristics: Harmonious But Different

My Philosophy of Information is broad and general, while Zhong's Science of Information is deep and systematic. They both capture key problems in their respective ways and answer the basic questions such as "what is information?" and "what is the rule of movement of information". Their conclusions have their own focal points and respective characteristics, but they prove each other as well.

### 6.2. The Partition of Existence: Philosophy Opens the Way

As we have seen, traditional philosophy states: existence = matter + spirit. My Philosophy of Information keeps the term "spirit" but gives it a new reading in terms of information. Zhong's Science of Information maintains that "information is a kind of universal existence in the fields of nature, human society and spirit". This supports the preferred interpretation of "existence = matter + information" in my Philosophy of Information.

### 6.3. A Basic Concept: Different Melodies Played with Equal Skill

My basic definition of information is that "information demonstrates by itself the existential mode and state of matter". Zhong's Science of Information establishes a hierarchy of definitions of information. Ontological information as an ultimate source of all levels of information is defined as: "the apparent way in which things change", where "things" are material or spiritual.

Zhong's and my theory possess their own philosophical and scientific characteristics with different words and phrases, but their connotations are consistent: "appear" has the same meaning as "show"; "a state of movement and mode of change" is virtually equivalent to "the existential mode and state of matter".

### 6.4. Informational Epistemology: Enhancing Each Other's "Beauty"

My Informational Epistemology proposes five levels of informational activities involved in the process of human cognition: in-itself activities of information, perceptual intuition and cognition of information, memory and storage of information, subjective creation of information, social realization of information. He discussed the holographic top-down controlling and the progressively increasing bottom-up relations from between those five levels, as well as an integrative participating and mutually transforming relation. Obviously, this is a comprehensive discussion of principle, a complete analysis from informational ontology to informational epistemology. Zhong's Science of Information [35] defines information as "form (grammatical information), meaning (semantic information), effect (pragmatic information) of states of movement state and mode of change effected by cognitive subjects". He calls this trinity "complete information". Based on this, an "informational transforming rule" reveals the mechanism for going from objective "ontological information" to subjective "intelligent strategy and action". It is interesting that the "informational transforming rule" in the Philosophy of Information and the "informational analysis of levels" in Zhong's work enhance each other's meaning "beauty". They are "beautiful" theories. The Philosophy of Information illustrates the broad principles of Informational Epistemology, while the Science of Information explains the deep mechanism of informational transformations; Zhong and I thus hold the same view.

### 6.5. The Concept of "Informational Intermediaries": Respective Discoveries

As mentioned above [6], my informational epistemology views the human cognitive process as virtual informational activities carried out via multiple intermediaries, which eliminates any mystery about the interactive process occurring between subject and object.

Zhong considers that informational effects provide an intelligent strategy to recognizing and transforming the world for human subjects through a series of "informational transitions" from ontological information to epistemological information, then to knowledge, to basic consciousness, to emotion, to reason, to intelligent strategy, finally to intelligent action. The objective is to realize the benefit of both the subjective and objective worlds and improve the existing and developing environment. Therefore, an "informational transforming rule" and an "informational virtual intermediary construction" reveal the informational mechanism of subjective and objective interaction on the levels of science and philosophy respectively. They both make discoveries and prove and supplement one another.

Zhong said in the last part of his paper: "It stretches the imagination that the Science and Philosophy of Information are so harmonious with one another while their investigators carry out each other's researches independently". In my opinion, in Chinese research, it is not a coincidence that the studies on the Science and Philosophy of Information are naturally concordant, interactive, illuminating and different in approach but give equally satisfactory results. Firstly, it is the reflection of the universal character of information; secondly, it is the reflection of the unity of philosophy and science; thirdly, it is the reflection of the communication between and convergence of research in philosophy and science, on which a Unified Science-Philosophy of Information should be based; fourthly, it is the reflection of Chinese scholars' persistence in a new use of dialectical thinking.

For a long time, the dogmatic aspects of the textbook system of Chinese dialectic materialistic philosophy were serious, but if one does not stick to its dogma, and adds explanations from complexity thinking, one can then see the true sense of dialectics as a methodology. Ways of convergence of informational thinking, systematical thinking and complexity thinking are then possible, endowing science with the characteristics of what I prefer to call dialectical realism and philosophy with characteristics of complexity. By doing this, the definition and impact of philosophy on science, the transformation and reconstruction of science into philosophy, and the critical development of philosophy itself can be demonstrated.

To summarize, this dialectical and integrative process in science and philosophy is in my view the general mode of Chinese development of the Science and Philosophy of Information: the informational philosophization of informational science and the informational scientification of informational philosophy. Here, it is not only a transformation and sublimation of science, but also a transformation and sublimation of philosophy.

## 7. Conclusions

In this paper, I have shown how the incorporation of the existential properties of information in philosophy leads to the convergence of science and philosophy in general and to an emerging Unified Science-Philosophy of Information (USPI). The USPI is thus a highly complex metaphilosophical system for organizing and discussing knowledge at the interface between science and philosophy. I believe we are witnessing the emergence of a new system of science, a metascience in a complex, dynamic reciprocity with philosophy that amounts to a paradigmatic revolution in thought. However, much work remains to be done to make the tools offered by a Unified Science-Philosophy of Information capable of being used constructively and routinely.

The achievements of science and philosophy in China [12] as well as the rest of the world have brought new hope for establishing such a Unified Science-Philosophy of Information. In view of the potential benefits to society, the establishment and healthy development of such a new philosophical conception of knowledge seems desirable. This paper is my proposed contribution to such a development.

**Acknowledgments:** I thank Joseph E. Brenner, Vice-President—Inter- and Transdisciplinarity of the International Society for Information Studies (IS4SI), Vienna and Associate Director of my Center for the Philosophy of Information in Xi'an for his comments and suggestions regarding this manuscript.

**Conflicts of Interest:** The author declares no conflict of interest.

## References

1. Wu, K.; Li, P. Scientific Evolution: The transformation of the scientific worldview and way of thinking. *J. Chin. Renmin Univ.* **2008**, *3*, 41–46. (In Chinese)
2. Wu, K. The Partition of the Existent Field. *Sci. Dialect. Mod.* **1986**, *2*, 32–33. (In Chinese)
3. Wu, K. The philosophy of information classification. *Potential Sci. J.* **1984**, *3*, 33–35. (In Chinese)
4. Wu, K. The Essence, Classification and Quality of the Different Grades of Information. *Information* **2012**, *3*, 403–419. [CrossRef]
5. Wu, K. The Development of Philosophy and Its Fundamental Informational Turn. *Information* **2015**, *6*, 693–703. [CrossRef]
6. Wu, K.; Brenner, J.E. An Informational Ontology and Epistemology of Cognition. *Found. Sci.* **2015**, *20*, 249–279. [CrossRef]
7. Brenner, J.E. Wu Kun and the Metaphilosophy of Information. *Int. J. Inf. Theor. Appl.* **2011**, *18*, 103–128.

8. Wu, K. The Partition of the Existent Field and the "Whole New" Sense of the Philosophy of Information. *Hum. J.* **2013**, *5*, 1–6. (In Chinese)
9. Wu, K. The Interaction and Convergence of the Philosophy and Science of Information. In Proceedings of the 2nd International Conference on the Philosophy of Information, Vienna, Austria, 6 June 2015.
10. Toulmin, S.E. *Knowing and Acting: An Invitation to Philosophy*; Macmillan: New York, NY, USA; London, UK, 1976.
11. Wu, K. On the Relation of Science and Philosophy. *Sci. Technol. Dialect.* **2004**, *1*, 1–3. (In Chinese)
12. Wu, K. *Philosophy of Information—A New Spirit of the Time*; Shaanxi Normal University Press: Xi'an, China, 1989. (In Chinese)
13. Matheson, C.; Dallmann, J. Historicist Theories of Scientific Rationality. In *The Stanford Encyclopedia of Philosophy (Summer 2015 Edition)*; Edward, N.Z., Ed.; Stanford University: Stanford, CA, USA, 2014. Available online: http://plato.stanford.edu/archives/sum2015/entries/rationality-historicist/ (accessed on 29 August 2015).
14. Wu, K. The crisis of philosophy and the informational turn of philosophy. *J. Xi'an Jiaotong Univ.* **2014**, *1*, 2–4. (In Chinese)
15. Floridi, L. *The Philosophy of Information*; Oxford University Press: Oxford, UK, 2011.
16. Wu, K. *The Philosophy of Information: Theory, System and Method*; The Commercial Press: Beijing, China, 2005; Volume 266, pp. 27–29. (In Chinese)
17. Cat, J. The Unity of Science. In *The Stanford Encyclopedia of Philosophy (Winter 2014 Edition)*; Edward, N.Z., Ed.; Stanford University: Stanford, CA, USA, 2014. Available online: http://plato.stanford.edu/archives/win2014/entries/scientific-unity/ (accessed on 13 April 2015).
18. Wu, K. The development of philosophy and its fundamental turn from the viewpoint of an informational world. *J. Chin. Renmin Univ.* **2014**, *3*, 72–78. (In Chinese)
19. Wiener, N. *Cybernetics*; Hao, J., Translator; Science Press: Beijing, China, 1963; p. 133. (In Chinese)
20. Wu, K. *Philosophy and Turns of Philosophy: Review of the Uniformity of Internal Integration between Science and Philosophy*; People's Publishing House: Beijing, China, 2014; Volume 3.
21. Floridi, L. *The Fourth Revolution: How the Infosphere is Reshaping Human Reality*; Oxford University Press: Oxford, UK, 2014.
22. Floridi, L. Against Digital Ontology. *Synthese* **2009**, *168*, 151–178. [CrossRef]
23. Brenner, J.E. *Logic in Reality*; Springer: Dordrecht, The Netherlands, 2008.
24. Wu, K. *The Logics of Nature*; Northwest University Publishing House: Kirkland, WA, USA, 1990.
25. Deacon, T.W. *Incomplete Nature: How Mind Evolved from Matter*; W.W. Norton & Company: New York, NY, USA, 2012.
26. Von Bertalanffy, L. *General System Theory*; George Braziller: New York, NY, USA, 1969.
27. Wu, K. Objective Reality, Substantial Materialism, Energetics and the Non-Substantial Trend of Materialism. *J. Xi'an Jiaotong Univ.* **2004**, *2*, 69–75. (In Chinese)
28. Wu, K. The basic problem of philosophy and its fundamental turn. *J. Hebei* **2011**, *4*, 11–21. (In Chinese)
29. Wu, K. The Informational Scientification of Science. *Qinghai Soc. Sci.* **1997**, *2*, 53–59. (In Chinese)
30. Burgin, M. Information theory: A multifaceted model of information. *Entropy* **2003**, *5*, 146–160. [CrossRef]
31. Burgin, M. *Theory of Information*; World Scientific: Singapore, 2010.
32. Hofkirchner, W. How to achieve a unified theory of Information. *Triple C* **2009**, *7*, 357–358.
33. Hofkirchner, W. *Emergent Information: A Unified Theory of Information Framework*; World Scientific: Singapore, 2013.
34. Zhong, Y.X. Information Science and Its View of Information Philosophy. *Philos. Anal.* **2015**, *1*, 17–31. (In Chinese)
35. Zhong, Y.X. Unity-Based Diversity: System Approach to Defining Information. *Information* **2011**, *2*, 406–416. [CrossRef]

# 12

# The Career of the Lógos: A Brief Biography

**D. H. Williams**

Department of Religion, Baylor University, Waco, TX 76798-7284, USA; DH_Williams@Baylor.edu

Academic Editor: Marcin J. Schroeder

**Abstract:** This paper is a review of the influence that lógos has had on ancient Greek, Jewish, and Christian writings. During the philosophical era known as Middle Platonism, the concept/ontology of the lógos played a unique role in enabling Pagan, Jewish, and Christian intellectuals to communicate on a small space of common ground.

**Keywords:** lógos; episteme; Middle Platonism; Sophia; memra; lógos spermatikos; lógos prophorikos

---

## 1. Introduction

Ancient Greek philosophy bequeathed to subsequent cultures its unique methods of investigating the being of the universe through reason. Two of the most important problems generally addressed are well known. The first has to do with proposing realities of stability and permanence in an ever changing world; the second is the problem of the "One and the Many", that is, how to relate the diversity and plurality of visible things to an orderly and unified cosmos. In their search for such principles, the Greeks argued that the cosmos—from stars to souls—was perfectly arranged, possessed coherence, and could therefore be explained. However, implicit to these problems was the most important question of all: how did the divine, or utterly transcendent, invisible, and immutable interface or intersect with the material, temporal, and mutable world. This was the great philosophical quest—within all the Greek schools and for most religions as well. Related to this, for those schools of thought that posited the necessity of an intersection, there was a problem about how this occurred and how far it occurred. This problem was only further compounded by the supposition that the material and mutable had its origin from the unseen and immutable, as one finds in Platonism and Judaism. The "problem", as I'm calling it—something common to Pagan, Jewish, and, later, Christian believers—was the ontological tension that the unseen, immutable, or divine (as in the case of Heraclitus) must act in forming the mutable, temporal world, without violating the nature or properties of its divine essence or power. As we will see, this all has bearing on the role of the "lógos" (λόγοσ) in its Greek development, whether this be Pagan, Jewish, or Christian.

The concept of the lógos (λόγοσ) came to serve as a cohesive principle or universal reason, though it did not begin this way. Its origins were more chaotic. Debate about the lógos was exceedingly common among different schools of philosophy, though most agreed in principle that the concept of lógos was polysemic in that it conveyed several meanings at the same time. During the fourth through fifth centuries B.C., the greatest evolution occurred in the use of lógos in a rational sense, which determined the relation of unseen realities from the mere appearance of things (the seen). Etymologically speaking, the Greek noun lógos is derived from the verb légein, "say"; this linguistic origin was permanently etched into its meaning, as we will see. Greek philosophers certainly made extensive use of it in a wide range of meanings—word, assertion, definition, interpretation, explanation, reason, criterion, proportion, relation, argument, and rational discourse—but also used *lógos* with the general and indeterminate meaning of "report", "presentation", and "narrative of or about something."

The multivalent interpretation of lógos is perhaps best demonstrated by attempts to translate it into another language. In Latin texts, lógos is translated as *sermo* or *verbum* [1], both of which had more to do with a mode of speech (i.e., proverb, discourse) or with the manner of speaking (such as conversation), but it might occasionally be transliterated "lógos" in order to preserve the breadth of its meaning. In English, lógos is most often translated as "word", adhering to the Latin limitation, though it is just as accurate to use the nouns: reason, mind, intellect, and other synonyms.

Among its many transformations and applications, the lógos supremely became the ultimate communicative act of God toward animate and inanimate creation. Given the centrality of the essence of lógos within varied philosophical systems (which include Judaism and Christianity), I wish to show more precisely its importance as a comprehensive designation in the ancient Mediterranean world. Most everyone imparted to the lógos a necessary operation of the Divine in the world that made possible knowledge and ethics. Strangely, scholarly work on understanding the lógos through the ages is lacking attention, though much has been written about lógos in ipsum. Most who write about the lógos do so on the way to some larger topic. In a short paper, I cannot do justice to the subject, so I wish to offer several examples of how the concept was first utilized in several contexts and draw some implications.

One must confront the fact that there has been no uniform understanding about the lógos in the sense that there has been no unifying doctrine. Even within the same philosophical "school", there may be several definitions. Nevertheless, there is a platform of common features that the varied fragments and statements demonstrated about the identity of lógos. By the early Hellenistic period, it was used to express the rationality in man as well as the divine. In the course of its evolution, the lógos also functions as the divine law or will of God as expressed in the natural universe or by special revelation. However it was applied, the lógos was first and foremost a philosophical utterance that offered metaphysical transcendence as much as immanence. In other words, the lógos could serve as an ontological bridge connecting the seen and unseen realms.

## 2. Pre-Socratics

Attempts to trace the use of the word in detail have proved to be unsuccessful. It is, however, evident that lógos was already being used by the Pre-Socratics, chiefly in Heraclitus of Ephesus (sixth century B.C.). We find the term lógos for the first time in the fragments of Heraclitus, not only as a designation for his own understanding and interpretation of things, but also as the only unifying formula for the arrangement of things in the world. Heraclitus of Ephesus, who lived in the sixth century, B.C., was the first philosopher we know of to give lógos a philosophical or theological interpretation. Heraclitus might in fact be called the first Western philosopher, since his writings were perhaps the first to set forth a coherent system of thought akin to what we now term philosophy. Although his writings are preserved in approximately 130 fragments, we know that he described an elaborate system touching on the ubiquity of change, the dynamic interplay of opposites, and a profound unity of things [2]. The lógos seemed to figure heavily in his thought, making him the first philosopher we know of to give lógos a philosophical or theological interpretation. He described it as a universal, underlying principle through which all things come to pass and in which all things share.

Fragments 1 and 2 remain critical to formulating a basis for understanding [3].

1. "Although this *lógos* always exists, men are ignorant [of it] both before they hear and after they have once heard. For even though all things happen in accordance with this *lógos,* they are like men of no experience when they experience words and deeds such as these..."
2. "... it is necessary to follow the common. However, although the *lógos* is common, the many live as if they had a private understanding."

Lógos as a cause and universal (common) also has a regulating function in that everything is governed and ordered by it. Human ignorance is not an obstacle to the efficacy of the lógos. Its activity may catch certain people by surprise since they live according to their limited dictates of conscience or knowledge. Nonetheless, the lógos should be regarded as "common" or, presumably, a universal endemic to reality.

Here, lógos was an immanent principle that was omnipresent in things. Heraclitus' lógos also appeared to have a material embodiment, as if it were a physical force, related in a sense to the primordial element fire. The human lógos was in a position to comprehend that lógos, since human reason (lógos) in particular, existed as part of the universal lógos; as per Fragment 115: "The soul has a *lógos* which increases itself [within the soul]. A very similar conception is shared by Isocrates (from the fourth to the fifth century B.C.), which is that the lógos has a regulating function in that everything is governed and ordered by it. Stoicism will find this line of thought central to its own purposes.

### 2.1. Plato

It has been noted in the past that Plato omits a surprising amount of pre-Socratic thought [4]. Moreover, it seems likely that Plato and Aristotle were simply ignorant of many important pre-Socratic ideas. However, this picture does not tally with the lógos appearing as the faculty of reason both in Plato (*Laws* 689D; *Tim.* 89D) and Aristotle (*Eth. Nic.* 102b 26); Aristotle employs lógos to mean the definition or essence of a thing (*Meta.* 993a 17) and the principles that exists in law (*Pol.* 1286a 17), whereas Plato speaks of lógos as that which is added to true opinion to make it knowledge (*Theat.* 201C). Plato's use of lógos in the *Theaetetus* has been a matter of ongoing debate. The question at the center of this dialogue is about the problem of knowledge, "How do I know that my judgement (my opinion) is true?" That is, what is the criterion for distinguishing true from false judgement? A lógos is an account (or explanation) that records a distinguishing mark or nature of an object [5,6]. The *Theaetetus* seems to end on a negative note as if to say we will fail to come to an understanding of the nature of knowledge based only on our sensations and our opinions. Yet Theaetetus reports a definition of *epistêmê* as "true belief with logos" (Theaet 201c–d.), and Socrates seems to agree.

> Clearly, lógos is an essential ingredient for possessing a true knowledge of anything. However, there is also in Plato the lógos that makes virtue possible.
>
> one sees and contemplates things that are set in a regular arrangement and are always in the same condition—things that neither do injustice to one another nor suffer it at one another's hands, but remain all in order according to reason (lógos)... (*Rep.* 500c).

The lógos makes possible the harmonious arrangement of the eternal and unchanging order which is the foundation for our imitation and growth in virtue.

While there seems to be two applications of the lógos, it has been argued that Plato presents broadly similar interpretations of lógos, namely, that which transforms Platonic quasi-virtue into full virtue, and that which transforms lesser states of knowing (one's experience or opinion) into a certain *epistêmê*, or other forms of wisdom [7]. Exactly how one goes about achieving an appropriation of the lógos seems to be another aspect of the allusiveness often encountered in the Platonic dialogues.

### 2.2. Stoics

Lógos doctrine is a capital element in the system of the Stoics and may be said to have contributed the most to the lógos' application toward arriving at meaning and morality [8]. Very much has been written on this subject that I cannot treat here (The major discussions are found in [9–12]). Broadly stated, the Stoic perspective regards physics and theology as correlatives. The material universe pulsates with living being, the lógos or rational principle that resides in everything, including the human soul. This intrinsic reality is in fact God or the governing principle of all things, meaning that everything operates according to providential ordering imbued with the lógos.

For the Stoics, the lógos within everything can be accurately described as pantheism, about which the North African writer Tertullian remarks how Zeno of Citium (the reputed founder of Stoicism) taught that the lógos pervaded throughout the material world as honey runs through the honeycomb (Tertullian, Ad nat. II. 4). The point here is that the lógos functions as an active principle imbuing and determining the course of the cosmos. Unlike early Platonic thought, Zeno is said to have considered "the lógos is the creator and adjuster of everything in nature." As a spiritual power, "the lógos authored the world and pervaded every part of it." (Tertullian, Apol. 21). For this reason, the lógos was known in Greek as the "lógos spermatikos" (seeding of rationality). At the same time, Stoicism also embraced a kind of panentheism (Cicero, De Nat. Deo. I. 40–41; Athenagoras, Plea, 6.4; 22.5); that is, the divine does not merely produce all, but the divine soul is within all. Because the Divine Reason inhabited everything, a moral order existed in the creation as well as within the human soul. It is no wonder that the Stoics defined philosophy as "striving after wisdom."

As far as Hierocles the Stoic was concerned, the gods are immutable and fixed in their judgments, never wavering from what they originally decreed [13]. However, it was no less true, Hierocles acknowledged, that "epic poetry", that is, the creative expression of realities, gives credence to how pliable and mutable the gods are in their actions toward human affairs, since they are manifestations of a unitary divine power. Early twentieth-century scholars [14] criticized Stoicism for misconstruing the earlier understanding of lógos, but this seems unnecessary. Even if we grant that the Stoic lógos was a more metaphysically extended concept than Heraclitus would have entertained, it does not follow that the Stoics totally misrepresented Heraclitus in this regard. It is not possible to pass off so simply that the cosmic-metaphysical interpretation of Heraclitus' lógos was a completely Stoic invention (Miller, 165).

Some explanation was necessary if the world (*kósmos*) were orderly and the lógos were the general plan according to which everything happened—or the model for the harmony and balance between the diverse opposing forces in the universe. The unity of the Heraclitean fragments—the comprehension, continuity, and progression of ideas—is such that the lógos idea, if not the word itself, pervades the whole.

### *2.3. Philo Ioudaios (Judaeus)*

We now turn to Philo, a Jewish *literati* who lived in Alexandria during the same years that Christ lived. A prolific writer with some forty-eight separate treatises to his credit, Philo was ironically used widely by Christians though not by Jews. With the exception of Josephus (another Hellenist Jew from the first century), neither Talmud nor the Midrash ever mention him [15].

Most of what we know about Hellenistic Judaism is drawn from Philo (some from Josephus), his writings supplying valuable data for the philosophical eclecticism of Platonist, Stoic, and Pythagorean elements known as Middle Platonism, which was considerably influential upon the later Christian Platonists in Alexandria. It is not difficult to find on nearly every page of Philo's writings an intimate knowledge of Greek literature; Homer, poets such as Euripides and Demosthenes, and especially Plato (his favorites being the *Timaeus* and the *Phaedrus*). It was said of Philo that not only did he talk like a Greek, but he also had the soul of a Greek. As noted earlier, Philo read and studied the Bible, not in Hebrew but in Greek. There was nothing contradictory in his mind between Scripture and philosophy, the latter being the means by which one obtained wisdom. "For philosophy is the practice and study of wisdom, and wisdom is the knowledge of things divine and human and their causes" (On Consorting with the Preliminary Studies XIV. 79).

The Pentateuch, the first five books of the Hebrew Bible, was the unquestioned authority in all matters of belief and practice: indeed, a great many of Philo's treatises are commentaries on the Bible. Greek culture and philosophy is the unmentioned but omnipresent backdrop by which the principles about God and ethics could be understood or be realized. In particular, Philo selected the Platonic paradigm of being and becoming, immutability and change, and knowledge and ignorance as the system of thought most suitable for the task of expounding and interpreting the truth revealed to Moses. Plato is often admired by Philo as the Pagan thinker closest to the truth of biblical revelation [16]. At the same time, the greater revelation for Philo was how the apparently primitive Jewish collection of texts—Genesis, Exodus, Leviticus, Numbers, and Deuteronomy—when read with a properly trained eye through allegorical and metaphorical reasoning, contained the highest and most profound philosophy [17].

Even greater than Plato, Moses was himself the greatest of philosophers, whose teaching laid the groundwork for Greek thinking on all matters of ethics and metaphysics. However suspect modern historians may find his historical framework, Philo was drawing on an already common argument in antiquity. Another Egyptian Jew named Aristobulus asserted two centuries earlier that the ideas of the best Greek poets and philosophers were anticipated by Moses in the Torah (Cited in Eusebius of Caesarea, Prep. Evang. IX. 27). These same themes resurface in Josephus, who re-asserted the antiquity of Jewish legislation and custom (Which he had already done in his twenty books entitled, Antiquity of the Jews.), declaring that Moses was the father of Greek philosophy (Contra Apion II. 168). In the Jewish mind, Mosaic chronological priority helped to explain why there existed so many ostensible parallels between Greek and Hebrew scriptural ideas [18].

It was likewise Philo who widely integrated the multivariate notion of the lógos, using it more than 1300 times in references to the lógos as the Divine Reason, by participation in which humans are rational; the model of the universe; the superintendent or governor of the universe; and the first-born son of God. Characteristic of Middle Platonism, Philo joined Platonic and Stoic streams of identifying the Divine lógos as the Supreme Principle, distinguishing the lógos as a second subordinate divine principle, and combined them to form an intelligible pattern that strongly impinged on Christian thought. On the one hand, the Supreme Deity is the God of the Old Testament, the God of Abraham, Isaac, and Jacob. This God is the same as the Platonist Highest Good or Supreme God, whose being possesses many of the philosophical hallmarks as utter transcendence and the Absolutely One and Simple (Philo, Allegorical Laws II. 21, 86; On the Migration of Abraham 125; Alleg. I. 51; II.2, 3).

On the other hand, the wholly transcendent God was made known to humanity in time and creation through the agency of the lógos, whom Philo describes variously as a Divine mediator between God and the world. The lógos, in this latter instance, exists as a subordinate, intermediate being, although it is not always clear what Philo has in mind, nor does he ever render for the reader a concrete definition (At other times in his writings, the lógos seems to be a representative force or special presence of God.).

Philo shares with his philosophical era the portrayal of the Divine lógos usually as a personification of the Platonic Ideas, in a manner similar to the way a builder is said to have implanted in his mind a plan for constructing a city (On Fashioning the World 4.17). Thus, too, the lógos functioned as God's noetic tool for creating the world. Along lines similar to Platonism, the lógos functions as the demiurge of the *Timaeus*, completely subordinated to the Supreme God (*Republic*). It is God who creates the world via the lógos. Without trying to be too confusing, Philo seems to have subjoined the transcendent God of Platonism with the immanent lógos of the Stoics, though in his own configuration [19]. This was an essential insight that Christians would later adopt. Knowing of the close nexus of Greek thought and Judaism in the centuries before the time of Jesus, it is not surprising that Christianity assumed a proportionally greater degree of the Greek philosophical tradition through the Philonian matrix.

At the same time, Philo does not avoid the language of the personal God found in the Old Testament. In those places where we find immanent moments of God interacting with creation (Gen 1–3) or human beings (Abraham, Gen 12; Moses, Ex 19–20), we are reminded that this is accomplished through the agency of the lógos as the mediator between the utterly transcendent God and the material world.

### *2.4. The Lógos of John and Greeks*

The Gospel of John begins with a prologue that is quite unlike the other gospels and is itself a most remarkable statement: "In the beginning was the lógos and the lógos was with God and the lógos was God." Like the surrounding intellectual culture, the term lógos here contains an elasticity of meaning that qualified the unique self-expression of God that always existed, always acted as the Divine reason or intellect, and had been the agent whereby God creates the visible world. Some New

Testament scholars have argued that the occurrence of this term as a divine name cannot be due to the influence of Greek philosophy [20], but this is disputable. While we will never know the exact original intention of the author of the prologue, philosophers—both Christian and Pagan—came to regard the statement as the epitome of a philosophical ontology. Indeed, Christian intellectuals in the second and third centuries often presented Christianity not merely as a philosophy, but as the sole and eternal philosophy [21]. The conceptuality of the lógos played a central role in making this happen.

Among the countless models invoked as an ideological prototype for John's pre-existent lógos, Werner Kelber has contended that Jewish Wisdom is the best candidate. Coming forth from the mouth of the Most High, Wisdom existed at the beginning before the world was created (Wis 9:1–2; Prov 8:22–23). Subsequent to her participation in the work of divine creation (Prov 8:27–31), she was sent down from the heavenly abode to make a dwelling place on earth (Wis 9:1–2; Sir 24:8ff). Whoever finds her will find life (Prov 8:35), for she is like a tree spreading forth its branches of glory and grace (Sir 24:16). However, she cannot herself find a resting place on earth, because all foolish men reject her (En 42:2). This Wisdom presentation in the canonical and apocryphal books of the Hebrew Bible offers "good parallels for almost every detail of the prologue's description of the Word." It clearly provides us with a key to the principal operations of the lógos [22].

If Kelber is right, then why does the prologue introduce the Son as lógos and not as wisdom? Use of lógos is clearly deliberate and presents a philosophical context by which this gospel begins. In response to Kelber, surely Hellenistic Judaism has just as much a role to play in interpreting the prologue. It was common by the first century to use wisdom and lógos as synonyms. That is, in Hellenic Judaism, there was an interchangeability of *sophia* with lógos as exemplified by Philo's transference of *sophia* attributes upon the lógos. To this one should also add the role of the meaning of the Hebrew "memra" (dibbur). It is difficult to say how far the rabbinical concept of the memra ("dibbur"), which was used in parallel to the divine Wisdom, had come under the influence of the Greek term lógos. However, Philo must have been aware of the memra as a cosmic power that extended from God to affect His will [23].

Considering John's prologue more carefully, the lógos is said to be with God, which suggests a distinction between God and his Word. However, the lógos is also named as God of God, as if it were an aspect (*species*) of divinity [24]. Pierre Hadot has contended that Christian philosophy was made possible by the ambiguity (or polysemy) of the Greek lógos. As "Word", "rational force", "discourse", or "explanation", the lógos was easily fused with other personifications. John's prologue does not at first fully identify the lógos, but by John 1:14 it is announced that the lógos is the Son of the Father. Such language had already been used by Philo, just as we saw Philo's reference to lógos as "first-born son." However, it should be said that we cannot be certain that Philo is the source—certainly not the sole source—for the prologue author's portrayal of the lógos.

An equally likely place to find precedents is the "Wisdom literature" of the Hebrew Scriptures (Ps, Prov, Job, and others). Given the strengths of these precedents, one scholar has argued that we should ignore Philo and look solely at the Scriptural evidence [25]. In several instances, we find the term "word" used (either as lógos or rhēma), usually being linked with God's majesty or action. Ps 106:20 states that the word is *sent by God to heal:* "He sent His *word (lógos)*, and healed them," and Ps 147:15 reads, "God Who sends forth his speech throughout the earth: His *word (lógos) runs swiftly*." We might also look at the Apocryphal OT: "By *his word* (lógos) all things are regulated" (*Ecclus* 43: 28). It all sounds much like Jn 1:3 and 9: He is the one through whom God "made all things" and is "the true light that enlightens every man."

Of course we are drawn to Prov 8, where we do find Wisdom (*Sophia*) in a personified form.

> 22 The Lord created me at the beginning of his work,
> the first of his acts of old.
> 23 Ages ago I was set up,
> at the first, before the beginning of the earth...
> 30 then I was beside him, like a master workman;

and I was daily his delight, rejoicing before him always,
31 rejoicing in his inhabited world
and delighting in the sons of men. [26]

For theological and apologetic reasons, a hypostasized "wisdom" (vv. 22–28) will often be found in Christian writers from the second to the fourth centuries as a description of the lógos and of Christ, as the Word or Wisdom of God.

Still, the Scripture-only argument seems both unnecessary and is probably too wary of the influence of non-Christian sources on Christian texts. However, such influences are undeniable. By the mid-second century, Christian thinkers were presenting the lógos in terms that were familiar to Platonists and Stoics. From evidence we have about secular Hellenist opinion, the Prologue was construed as a philosophical text. The Neo-Platonist Amelius, who was no friend to the Christians, calls John "a barbarian," yet affirms the remarks in the prologue:

> This then was the lógos, on whose eternal being depended the existence of things that were made, as Heracleitus also would maintain... the Barbarian maintains that He *was with God and was God: through whom* absolutely *all things were made (Eusebius, Prep. Evang. XI. 19).*

It seems that Amelius understood a close connection between the Gospel's vocabulary and what is proper to philosophical inquiry (Hadot, 239). This was not an isolated case. Later, we see a marked resemblance in *Confessions* (Conf. VII. ix,13), where Augustine states quite clearly that he had recently read "some books of the Platonists." It was within these books, though not in the exact words but "with the same sense," that he first encountered the meaning expressed in the prologue of John 1, which he quotes: "What was made was life in him [the lógos], and that life was the light of men. The light shined in the darkness, and the darkness did not comprehend it." The Platonists could not have said it better. As a former materialist and skeptic, Augustine turned from the restless and temporary world to the Divine lógos whom Christians and philosophers identified as God. There is no hint of surprise in Augustine's description that the biblical lógos stood in close proximity to the ontological ordering of the (neo-)Platonists.

It should be noted that rhēma (ῥῆμὰ) and lógos (the two terms are used interchangeably by John) employed in the Fourth Gospel are already used in a theologically and christologically suggestive manner—specifically in Jn 12:48 ("He who rejects me and does not receive my sayings has a judge; the word that I have spoken will be his judge on the last day") and 17:8a,14 ("...the words [rhēmata] which you gave me I have given to them...I have given to them your word"). Both lógos and rhēma abound in the Fourth Gospel, occurring fifty-one times (lógos 39; rhēma[ta], 12). Even Miller admits that the reason why lógos (not rhēma) was chosen in the prologue had to do with its rich character and varied usages that suggest a fuller expression. From whence did this "rich character and varied usages" come?

*2.5. The Christian Philosopher Justin*

In a defense of Christianity written in the mid-second century in order to gain rational credibility among the Romans, Justin shows varied intersecting links between Christian and Greek philosophies. Here again we see effects of Middle Platonism though it should be noted that Justin harnesses philosophical vocabulary for actuating Biblical teaching. His chief interests is in the ways in certain philosophical wisdom is a partial reflection of scriptural principles. At one point, he makes a startling comment: "when we say also that the lógos, who is the first-birth of God, was produced without physical union, and that He, Jesus Christ, our Teacher, was crucified and died, and rose again, and ascended into heaven [...] By this we propound nothing different from what you believe about those whom you esteem sons of Jupiter" (Justin, Apol. 21). Justin is interested in the principle of similarity, which is not to say that he believes Divine generation is found equally between the Christian Gospel and Pagan religion. In fact, Justin is very careful to signal the distinction between classical philosophy and Pagan religion.

In another text of Justin, he uses the lógos *spermatikos* principle, but with limitations. He does not hesitate to say that "the seed of God, the lógos is found throughout the world. We have declared above that He is the Word of whom every race of men were partakers" (Apol. 46). This means that all humanity participates in the rationality of the lógos. Justin shows just how Stoicized he is. Plato and Socrates are included since the inner lógos enabled them to come as close to the truth without the benefit of Scriptural revelation. As a result, Justin claims, the teaching of Plato and Pythagoras "have been as a wall and fortress of philosophy to us" (Dial. 5). Elsewhere it is stated: "For whatever lawgivers or philosophers have at any time uttered well or was achieved with hardship according to finding and contemplating the Logos" (II Apol. 10.2). Anyone who led a life directed by reason (lógos) is de facto a Christian, even if he or she knew nothing of Christ. The same governing principle of the lógos is applied to the work of any Pagan philosopher. It is worth quoting Justin here at length.

> What each of them proclaimed was good when he saw from a part of the divine spermatic lógos what is connatural to it. But when they contradict themselves in their principal teachings they are shown not to have a secure understanding and infallible knowledge. Therefore whatever things were rightly said by anyone belongs to us Christians because after God, we worship and love the Logos who is from the unbegotten and ineffable God (II Apol. 13.3).

For Justin, all human wisdom as displayed in ethics and pursuing the truth is a result of the lógos implanted in human nature. "We know that the followers of Stoic opinions were decent at any rate with regard to their ethical doctrine, as were also the poets in some respects... for the seed of the lógos had been implanted in the whole human race" (II Apol. 7.1. The phrase "lógos spermatikos" only appears in this apology.). On account of the shared lógos, the great philosophers of history offered good guidance, even if this was partial and incomplete. Since the lógos was finally revealed as the Christ of the Christians, the Jews and ultimately the Christians best understood God's purposes as revealed in the lógos.

While a great many Christian thinkers wrote subsequently on the lógos, Justin's constructions remain mostly intact. There was after Justin, however, a shift away from an emphasis on the lógos *spermatikos* to the lógos *prophorikos*. This latter is initially articulated by Theophilus of Antioch (Ad Autol. 2. 22). This wholly intrinsic and substantially unified relation within the Godhead might have endured forever had it not been for the act of creation. At this juncture, the lógos "within" (*endiathetos*) comes forth or, as God's Word, is "spoken" (*prophorikos*). Here, the translation of lógos as "Word" serves as a metaphor of God's utterance. In that act (not "moment") of God's "speaking", the Word comes forth as a distinctive reality: the lógos who is God is also with God and is now reckoned to be God's agent of creation and inspiration. Origen's commentary on Matthew provides a case study.

> [T]he disciples say: "We have no more than five loaves and two fish (Mt 14:17). In this way they hint that the five loaves are the perceptible words of the Scriptures, and for this reason equal in number to the five senses. Surely the two fishes suggest the Word made manifest and the Word hidden, as these happen to be a taste of those perceptible things in the Scriptures" (Origen, In Matt 11. 1–2).

For the Christians, however, the lógos *prophorikos* was not a simple *demiurgos*. Tertullian is insistent that this reifying act of the lógos does not mean that God created a second god to do his bidding. Any notion of a God begetting a second god seemed too close to the sort of Pagan polytheism that Tertullian radically opposed. Instead, the lógos is said to have been issued from the very substance of the eternal Being and emerged (not divided from) hypostatically for the purpose of revealing God through the creation. Nor is the substance separated—it is only extended in the divine generation of the lógos; He is a spirit of a spirit, God of God (Tertullian, Apol. 21.13).

Somewhere between Justin and Tertullian, Tatian, from Syria, knew and embraced lógos theology as a suitable means of explaining Christian teaching about the Father and Son. Closer to Tertullian's account, Tatian lays stress on the way the lógos became known as the utterance of the Father. In this moment of utterance when the lógos is externalized, he is not distinguished from God as if a part of God had been cut off. Using metaphors of speech and fire (Tatian, Orat. 5.2), Tatian holds that the utterance of the Word from the Speaker (God) underscores the distinction between the Speaker and self-existing Word, whereas in the other metaphor it is the same fire that passes from torch constituting no loss or change in the transfer in either flame. More impressive, if lesser known, is the Christian philosopher Athenagoras, who takes us to the very threshold of Origin's "eternal generation" by declaring that God's lógos or Nous is called "firstborn" "not because he came into existence", since he was "eternally rational (logikòs)" within the eternal mind of God. Our familiar passage of Prov 8:22 is quoted in confirmation: "For the Lord, it says, made me the beginning (cf. Jn 1:1) of his ways for his works."

Whereas Athenagoras is not intent, as Justin was, to show the divine revelation of the lógos toward all creation, he wishes to demonstrate that the lógos, as the mind (nous) and reason (lógos) of the Father, does not fall ontologically into the category of created things. In a way that anticipates Origin, Athenagoras makes a sharp division between divine or eternal being and created being. The Son can only be a partaker of eternal being. Philo's legacy begins to slip to the side.

### *2.6. Shared Metaphysical and Ethical Ground*

One thinks immediately of divine immutability, a concept that remained permanently etched in Christian theology for defending the inviolability of the divine nature. Others included immortality of the soul, understanding God by way of negation, and the necessity of divine providence in the world. Most of all—and often underestimated—is Christianity's assumption of philosophy as a way of life. In various ways, Greek philosophy served as a model for the rise of Christian philosophy. We have already seen that Christian intellectuals explained Christianity as a philosophy, even as *the* philosophy. Christians were not prepared to follow the religious elements woven into Greek and Roman philosophical analyses, but it is arguable that Christianity adopted the philosophical cultural structure, which was "a style of life and a mode of being" (Hadot, 240–41). Throughout antiquity, *philosophia* designated not so much a theory or method of epistemology as it signified a lived wisdom and a way of acting in accordance with reason. Christian philosophy, thus, consisted in living in accordance with the lógos. Since Christianity was certainly connected with a way of life, it was not difficult to present Christianity with a philosophical outlook.

## 3. To Conclude

One cannot fail to notice how much overlap existed between the philosophical theologies of the ancient Mediterranean world, especially between Jewish, Greek, and Christian theologies, whose apprehension of the universe was both rational (or explanatory) and good.

A second characteristic of Greek philosophical systems is their naturalism. This means that the foundations for human behavior are inherent within the design of the cosmos. Stoics, Platonists, and Pythagoreans operate with the task of knowing and responding to the character of the world. The lógos is both the designer and the design within all reality. However, there is also a significant difference on this point. Christianity makes a sharp divide between creator and creation. Augustine maintained what had become the standard Christian understanding by his time: that Greek philosophy brought good guidance to the searching mind, but only imperfectly. There was no question in Augustine's mind how much Platonist metaphysics had shaped his own thinking [27]. Meanwhile, Plato raised the right questions but could never fully answer them. Only the Wisdom of God, the lógos, was capable of healing the heart and the affections. In the Christian way, this lógos was not a mere principle but, as Clement of Alexandria stated it, "the heavenly Word, the true champion, who is being crowned upon the stage of the whole world" (Protreptikos 1 (Loeb 92.7)).

In sum, we should not fail to recognize an obvious feature about the above narrative. The lógos, through its various overlapping stages, came to function as a kind of glue or adhesive that enabled comparable systems to intersect. While this was not an inevitable state of affairs, the pliability of the lógos nonetheless made it an ideal philosophical and theological construct that offered solutions to fundamental problems that had to do with connecting transcendence and imminence. Despite the Greek amalgamation of the poetic and the rational, or Judaism and Christianity's "parting of the ways", the lógos nevertheless became and remained an indelible element of diverse religious systems.

**Conflicts of Interest:** The author declares no conflict of interest.

### References and Notes

1. The flexibility with the use of verbum came the closest to lógos. Lactantius, a Latin writer (late third century) explains how the Greek lógos is much more expressive of the creator of the world than Latin terms. *Div. Inst.* IV. 9: "But the Greeks speak of Him as the *lógos*, more befittingly than we do as the word (verbum), or speech: for *lógos* signifies both speech and reason, inasmuch as He is both the voice and the wisdom of God."
2. The "lógos-fragments" make one group distinguished from others.
3. Of course our construction of Heraclitus' views is just that: a construction of fragments that lack context and relation to each other. This leads to a greater danger of misrepresentation that we wish to avoid. Fortunately there are a great deal of testimonia concerning Heraclitus that makes it possible to have enough confidence in the few conclusions we draw from the evidence.
4. It is well known to pre-Socratic scholars that Plato and Aristotle at many points misunderstood and misrepresented their predecessors.
5. Shields, C. The lógos of 'lógos': Theaetetus 206c–210b. *Apeiron* **1999**, *32*, 107–124.
6. Cross, R.C. lógos and Forms in Plato. *Mind* **1954**, *63*, 433–450. [CrossRef]
7. Moss, J. Right Reason in Plato and Aristotle: On the Meaning of Logos. *Phronesis* **2014**, *59*, 181–230, Both Plato and Aristotle, moreover, broadly agree on what is needed to transform proto-virtue into genuine virtue: some intellectual quality. Sometimes they put this point by saying that the proto-virtuous lack *phronêsis* (*Phaed.* 69b, *EN* 1144b17, *Pol.* 1277b25) or *nous* (*Men.* 100a; *Phaed.* 82b, *EN* 1144b12). At other points, however, they put the point in an apparently quite different way: one must have or grasp a *lógos*, or more specifically the correct or right (*orthos*) *logos*. [CrossRef]
8. Gericke, J. Dimensions of the logos: From lógos-Philosophy to logos-Theology. *Acta Patrist. Byzantina* **2000**, *11*, 93–116, at 95.
9. Colish, M. *The Stoic Tradition from Antiquity to the Early Middle Ages*; Brill: Leiden, The Netherlands, 1985.
10. Rist, J.M. *Stoic Philosophy*; Cambridge: Cambridge, UK, 1969.
11. Long, A. *Stoic Studies*; University of California Press: Oakland, CA, USA, 2001; (originally published 1996).
12. Inwood, B. (Ed.) *The Cambridge Companion to the Stoics*; Cambridge University Press: Cambridge, UK, 2006.
13. How Should One Behave toward the Gods? 1.3, 53. In *On Appropriate Acts. Hierocles the Stoic: 'Elements of Ethics', Fragments and Excerpts*; Ramelli, I.; Konstan, D. (Eds.) SBL: Atlanta, GA, USA, 2009; p. 65.
14. Notably is Glasson, T.F. A British scholar, Glasson argued that the only lógos in Heraclitus was Heraclitus' own discourse; that is, that there was no cosmic metaphysical principle called the lógos. Glasson, T.F. Heraclitus' Alleged lógos Doctrine. *J. Theol. Stud.* **1952**, *3*, 231–238. [CrossRef]
15. "It is plain therefore that pre-Christian Judaism cannot be judged as a whole. After the Dispersion had begun, the Jewish people ceased to be a homogeneous body: its fortunes varied with its geographical distribution, and with its fortunes its attitude towards Hellenism." Gregg, J.A.F. Judaism and Hellenism in the Second Century before Christ. *Ir. Church Q.* **1908**, *4*, 291–308, Judaism in Egypt shows the greatest influence of the Greek spirit, but there is no question that Palestine became thoroughly Hellenized (with the exception of Judaea proper) until the time of the Maccabean revolt. [CrossRef]
16. Runia, D.T. How to Read Philo. In *Exegesis and Philosophy: Studies on Philo of Alexandria*; Variorum: Aldershot, UK, 1990; p. 186, Philo's use of Greek philosophical literature and, in particular, his exploitation of Plato's famous cosmological dialogue, the *Timaeus*, is extensive.
17. Dillon, J. *The Middle Platonists 80 BC to AD 220*; Cornell University Press: Ithaca, NY, USA, 1977; p. 141.

18. Philo, however, was not only influential among Christian authors, since it is highly probable that it is also under his influence that a second-century pagan philosopher, Numenius says: "What More is Plato than a Moses Writing Good Greek?" Van Der Horst, P.W. Plato's Fear as a Topic in Early Christian Apologetics. *J. Early Christ. Stud.* **1998**, *6*, 1–14. [CrossRef]
19. The rationality of the lógos is detected in the universe, but being Jewish, he could not subscribe to Stoic pantheism. Both Jews and Christians will draw hard and fast lines between the creator and creation.
20. Ed. Miller wants to claim there is no need to look beyond the gospel of John itself. Miller, E.L. The Johannine Origins of the Johannine Logos. *J. Biblic. Lit.* **1993**, *112*, 445–457. [CrossRef]
21. Hadot, P. *What is Ancient Philosophy?* Harvard University Press: Cambridge, MA, USA, 2002; orig. ed., 1995; p. 237.
22. Kelber, W.H. The Birth of a Beginning: John 1:1–18. *Semeia* **1990**, *52*, 121–144.
23. E.g., Ps 32:6 (LXX 33) "By the word of the Lord (τῷ λόγῳ τοῦ Κυρίου) the heavens were established;" Ps 119:89; LXX 120:89), "For ever, O Lord, thy word (ὁ λόγος) is settled in heaven." Lógos may not always be the equivalent in the LXX. Gen 15:1: "the word (ῥῆμα) of the Lord came to Abram"; Is 55:11, "so shall my word (ῥῆμά) be, whatever shall proceed out of my mouth, it shall by no means turn back." The two Greek words have different etymologies but together they combine the conceptualizing of an inner idea/though (lógos) and the rhēma as God's utterance or communication.
24. Tertullian, *Adv. Prax.* 2 explicitly mentions that the members of the Trinity are the same substance "in aspect." [T]res autem non statu, sed gradu, nec substantia sed forma, nec potestate sed specie, unius autem substantiae et unius status et unius potestatis, quia unus deus ex quo et gradus isti et formae et species in nomine...
25. May, E. The Logos in the Old Testament. *Cathol. Biblic. Q.* **1946**, *8*, 438–447, This view assumes Philo would have been largely unaware of or uninterested in the Scriptural evidence which seems unlikely.
26. Also in *Ecclus* 24, Wisdom is introduced as celebrating her heavenly origin and rule over the created order. Cf. Ecclus 1:1–2: "I came, out of the mouth of the most High..." From this first of the two verses we gather that Wisdom's origin is from God, but as an expression of revelation of God, and Wisdom 9:1: "God of my fathers, and Lord of mercy, who has *made all things with your word (lógos).*"
27. *De vera rel.* iii.3: You have persuaded me that truth is not seen with the bodily eyes but by the pure mind ...[That] mind has to be healed so that it may view the immutable form of things which remains ever the same, preserving its beauty unchanged and unchangeable, knowing no spatial distance or temporal variation, abiding absolutely one and the same.

# 13

# Exploring the Computational Explanatory Gap

**James A. Reggia [1,*], Di-Wei Huang [2] and Garrett Katz [2]**

[1] Department of Computer Science and Institute for Advanced Computer Studies, University of Maryland, College Park, MD 20742, USA

[2] Department of Computer Science, University of Maryland, College Park, MD 20742, USA; dwh@cs.umd.edu (D.-W.H.); garrett.katz@gmail.com (G.K.)

* Correspondence: reggia@cs.umd.edu

Academic Editor: Jordi Vallverdú

**Abstract:** While substantial progress has been made in the field known as artificial consciousness, at the present time there is no generally accepted phenomenally conscious machine, nor even a clear route to how one might be produced should we decide to try. Here, we take the position that, from our computer science perspective, a major reason for this is a computational explanatory gap: our inability to understand/explain the implementation of high-level cognitive algorithms in terms of neurocomputational processing. We explain how addressing the computational explanatory gap can identify computational correlates of consciousness. We suggest that bridging this gap is not only critical to further progress in the area of machine consciousness, but would also inform the search for neurobiological correlates of consciousness and would, with high probability, contribute to demystifying the "hard problem" of understanding the mind–brain relationship. We compile a listing of previously proposed computational correlates of consciousness and, based on the results of recent computational modeling, suggest that the gating mechanisms associated with top-down cognitive control of working memory should be added to this list. We conclude that developing neurocognitive architectures that contribute to bridging the computational explanatory gap provides a credible and achievable roadmap to understanding the ultimate prospects for a conscious machine, and to a better understanding of the mind–brain problem in general.

**Keywords:** machine consciousness; artificial consciousness; cyberphenomenology; computational explanatory gap; cognitive phenomenology; phenomenal consciousness; executive functions; gated neural networks

---

## 1. Introduction

Can computational studies contribute to our understanding of phenomenal consciousness? By "phenomenal consciousness" we mean the subjective qualities (qualia) of sensory phenomena, emotions and mental imagery, such as the redness of an object or the pain from a skinned knee, that we experience when awake [1]. Consciousness[1] is very poorly understood at present, and many people have argued that computational studies do not have a significant role to play in understanding it, or that there is no possibility of an artificial consciousness. For example, some philosophers have argued that phenomenal machine consciousness will never be possible for a variety of reasons: the non-organic nature of machines [2], it would imply panpsychism [3], the absence of a formal definition of consciousness [4], or the general insufficiency of computation to underpin consciousness [5,6]. More generally, it has been argued that the objective methods of science cannot

---

[1] Here and below, we use the term "consciousness" to mean "phenomenal consciousness" unless specifically indicated otherwise.

shed light on phenomenal consciousness due to its subjective nature [7], making computational investigations irrelevant.

These arguments and similar ones are bolstered by the fact that no existing computational approach to artificial consciousness has yet presented a compelling demonstration or design of instantiated consciousness in a machine, or even clear evidence that machine consciousness will eventually be possible [8]. Yet at the same time, from our perspective in computer science, we believe that none of these arguments provide a compelling refutation of the possibility of a conscious machine, nor are they sufficient to account for the lack of progress that has occurred in this area. For example, concerning the absence of a good definition of consciousness, progress has been made in artificial intelligence and artificial life without having generally accepted definitions of either intelligence or life. The observation that only brains are known to be conscious does not appear to entail that artifacts never will be, any more than noting that only birds could fly in 1900 entailed that human-made heavier-than-air machines would never fly. The other minds problem, which is quite real [9,10], has not prevented studies of phenomenal consciousness and self-awareness in infants and animals, or routine decisions by doctors about the state/level of consciousness of apparently unresponsive patients, so why should it prevent studying consciousness in machines?

What then, from a purely computational viewpoint, is the main practical barrier at present to creating machine consciousness? In the following, we begin to answer this question by arguing that a critical barrier to advancement in this area is a *computational explanatory gap*, our current lack of understanding of how high-level cognitive computations can be captured in low-level neural computations [11]. If one accepts the existence of cognitive phenomenology, in other words, that our subjective experiences are not restricted to just traditional qualia but also encompass deliberative thought processes and high-level cognition [12], then developing neurocomputational architectures that bridge this gap may lead to a better understanding of consciousness. In particular, we propose a route to achieving this better understanding based on identifying possible *computational correlates of consciousness*, computational processes that are exclusively associated with phenomenally conscious information processing [13]. Here, our focus will be solely on *neuro*computational correlates of high-level cognition that can be related to the computational explanatory gap. Identifying these correlates depends on neurocomputational implementation of high-level cognitive functions that are associated with subjective mental states. As a step in this direction, we provide a brief summary of potential computational correlates of consciousness that have been suggested/recognized during the last several years based on past work on neurocomputational architectures. We then propose, based on the results of recent computational modeling, that the *gating mechanisms* associated with top-down cognitive control of working memory should be added to this list, and we discuss this particular computational correlate in more detail. We conclude that developing neurocognitive architectures that contribute to bridging the computational explanatory gap provides a credible roadmap to better understanding the ultimate prospects for a conscious machine, and to a better understanding of phenomenal consciousness in general.

## 2. The Computational Explanatory Gap

There is a critically important barrier to understanding the prospects for machine consciousness that is not widely recognized. This barrier is the *computational explanatory gap*. We define the computational explanatory gap to be a lack of understanding of how high-level cognitive information processing can be mapped onto low-level neural computations [11]. By "high-level cognitive information processing" we mean aspects of cognition such as goal-directed problem solving, reasoning, executive decision making, cognitive control, planning, language understanding, and metacognition—cognitive processes that are widely accepted to at least in part be consciously accessible. By "low-level neural computations" we mean the kinds of computations that can be achieved by networks of artificial neurons such as those that are widely studied in contemporary computer science, engineering, psychology, and neuroscience.

The computational explanatory gap can be contrasted with the well-known *philosophical explanatory gap* between a successful functional/computational account of consciousness and accounting for the subjective experiences that accompany it [14]. While we argue that the computational explanatory gap is ultimately relevant to the philosophical explanatory gap, the former is *not* a mind–brain issue per se. Rather, it is a gap in our general understanding of how computations (algorithms and dynamical processes) supporting goal-directed reasoning and problem solving at a high level of cognitive information processing can be mapped into the kinds of computations/algorithms/states that can be supported at the low level of neural networks. In other words, as illustrated in Figure 1, it is a purely computational issue, and thus may initially appear to be unrelated to understanding consciousness.

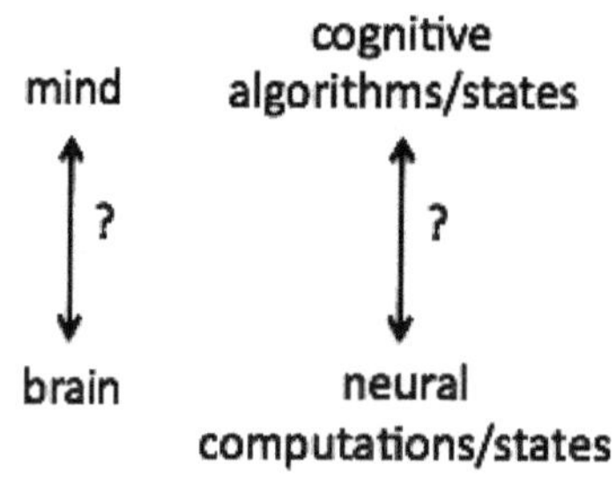


**Figure 1.** The well-known philosophical explanatory gap (on the **left**) and less recognized computational explanatory gap (on the **right**). The arguments presented here are that the latter can also be viewed as a fundamental problem, and that focusing on solving it may be central to advancing future work on phenomenal machine consciousness.

The computational explanatory gap is also not an issue specific to computers or even computer science. It is a generic issue concerning how one type of computations at a high level (serial goal-directed deliberative reasoning algorithms associated with conscious aspects of cognition) can be mapped into a fundamentally different type of computations at a low level (parallel distributed neural computations and representational states). It is an *abstraction* independent of the hardware involved, be it the electronic circuits of a computer or the neural circuits of the brain.

Further comparison of the computational explanatory gap and the philosophical explanatory gap is informative (see Figure 2). In philosophy, the computational explanatory gap relates to the long-standing discussion concerning the "easy problem" of accounting for cognitive information processing versus the "hard problem" of explaining subjective experience, the latter being associated with the philosophical explanatory gap [15]. This characterization of the easy problem is sometimes qualified by comments that the easy problem is not really viewed as being truly easy to solve, but that it is easy to imagine that a solution can be obtained via functional/computational approaches, while this is not the case for the hard problem (e.g., [1]). Nonetheless, the easy/hard contemporary philosophical distinction tends to largely dismiss solving the computational explanatory gap, as it is just part of the easy problem. Such a dismissal fails to explain why the computational explanatory gap has proven to be largely intractable during more than half a century of efforts (since McCulloch and Pitts [16] first captured propositional-level logical inferences using neural networks). This intractability is somewhat mysterious to us as computer scientists, given that the brain somehow readily bridges this gap. While the brain's structure is of course quite complex, it appears unlikely that this complexity alone could be the whole explanation, given that mainstream top-down artificial intelligence (AI) systems (which are much simpler than brain structure/function) have been qualitatively more successful in modeling high-level cognition when compared to neurocomputational methods. We believe that something more fundamental is being missed here. From our perspective, the computational explanatory gap is actually a fundamental, difficult-to-resolve issue that is more relevant to the hard problem than is generally recognized, and that once the computational explanatory gap is bridged, the philosophical explanatory gap may prove to be much more tractable than it currently appears.

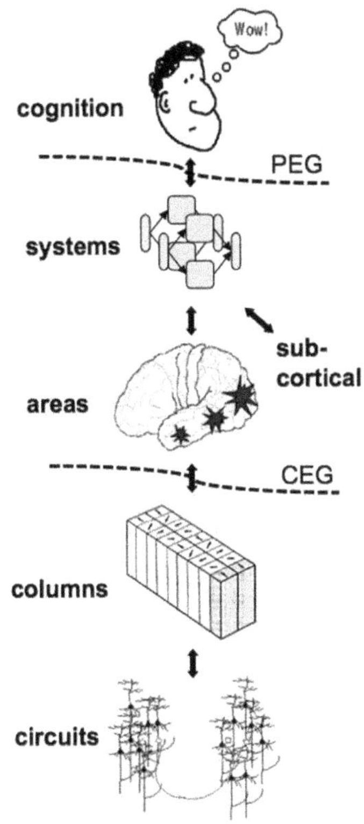


**Figure 2.** The philosophical and computational explanatory gaps address different problems. The philosophical explanatory gap (top dashed line labeled PEG) refers to our inability to understand how subjective mental experiences can arise mechanistically from a material/physical substrate, the brain. In contrast, the computational explanatory gap (bottom dashed line labeled CEG) refers to our inability to understand how high-level cognitive algorithms and any macroscopic correspondences that they may have in the brain can be accounted for by the low-level computational mechanisms supported by the microscopic neurocomputational processes and algorithms of neural circuitry, artificial or otherwise.

Comparing the philosophical and computational explanatory gaps as above is closely related to what has been referred to as the "mind–mind problem" [17]. This framework takes the viewpoint that there are two senses of the word "mind": the phenomenological mind involving conscious awareness and subjective experience, and the computational mind involving information processing. From this perspective, there are two mind–brain problems, and also a *mind–mind problem* that is concerned with how the phenomenological and computational minds relate to one another. Jackendoff suggests, inter alia, the theory that "The elements of conscious awareness are caused by/supported by/projected from information and processes of the computational mind that (1) are active and (2) have other (as yet unspecified) privileged properties." The computational explanatory gap directly relates to this theoretical formulation of the mind–mind problem. In particular, the notion of "privileged properties" referenced here can be viewed as related to what we will call computational correlates of consciousness in the following. However, as we explain later, our perspective differs somewhat from that of Jackendoff: We are concerned more with cognitive phenomenology than with traditional sensory qualia, and our emphasis is on correlations between phenomenological and computational states rather than on causal relations.

The computational explanatory gap is also clarified by the efforts of cognitive psychologists to characterize the properties that distinguish human conscious versus unconscious cognitive information processing. Human conscious information processing has been characterized as being serial, relatively slow, and largely restricted to one task at a time [18–20]. In contrast, unconscious information processing is parallel, relatively fast, and can readily involve more than one task simultaneously with limited interference between the tasks. Conscious information processing appears to involve widespread "global" brain activity, while unconscious information processing appears to involve more localized activation of brain regions. Conscious information processing is often associated with inner speech and is operationally taken to be cognition that is reportable,[2] while unconscious information processing has neither of these properties. The key point here is that psychologists explicitly trying to characterize the differences between conscious and unconscious information processing have implicitly, and perhaps unintentionally, identified the computational explanatory gap. The properties they have identified as characterizing unconscious information processing—parallel processing, efficient, modular, non-reportable—often match reasonably well with those of neural computation. For example, being "non-reportable" matches up well with the nature of neurocomputational models where, even once a neural network has learned to perform a task very successfully, what that network has learned remains largely opaque to outside observers and often requires a major effort to determine or express symbolically [21]. In contrast, the properties associated with conscious information processing—serial processing, relatively slow, holistic, reportable—are a much better match to symbolic top-down AI algorithms, and a poor match to the characteristics of neural computations. In this context, the unexplained gap between conscious cognition and the underlying neural computations that support it is strikingly evident.

Resolving the computational explanatory gap is complementary to substantial efforts in neuroscience that have focused on identifying *neural correlates of consciousness* [22]. Roughly, a neural correlate of consciousness is some minimal neurobiological state whose presence is sufficient for the occurrence of a corresponding state of consciousness [23]. Neurobiologists have identified several candidate neurobiological correlates, such as specific patterns in the brain's electrical activity (e.g., synchronized cortical oscillations), activation of specific neuroanatomical structures (e.g., thalamic intra-laminar nuclei), widespread brain activation, etc. [24]. However, in spite of an enormous neuroscientific endeavor in general over more than a century, there remains a large difference between our understanding of unconscious versus conscious information processing in the brain, particularly in our limited understanding of the neural basis of the high-level cognitive functions. For example, a great deal is currently known at the macroscopic level about associating high-level cognitive functions with brain regions (pre-frontal cortex "executive" regions, language cortex areas, etc.), and a lot is known about the microscopic functionality of neural circuitry in these regions, all the way down to the molecular/genetic level. What remains largely unclear is how to put those two types of information processing together, or in other words, how the brain maps high-level cognitive functions into computations over the low-level neural circuits that are present, i.e., the computational explanatory gap (bottom dashed line CEG in Figure 2). It remains unclear why this mapping from cognitive computations to neural computations is so opaque today given the enormous resources that have been poured into understanding these issues. The key point here is that this large gap in our neuroscientific knowledge about how to relate the macroscopic and microscopic levels of information processing in the brain to one another is, at least in part, also a manifestation of the abstract underlying computational explanatory gap.

### 3. The Relevance to Consciousness

Why is bridging the computational explanatory gap of critical importance in developing a deeper understanding of phenomenal consciousness, and in addressing the possibility of phenomenal machine consciousness? The reason is that bridging this gap would allow us to do something that is currently beyond our reach: It would allow us to directly and cleanly compare (i) neurocomputational mechanisms associated with conscious high-level cognitive activities; and (ii) neurocomputational

---

2 Although such a criterion has substantial limitations, being verbally reportable has long been widely used in experimental psychology as a major objective criterion for accepting that a person is conscious of (subjectively aware of) an event [18,20].

mechanisms associated with unconscious information processing. To understand this assertion, we need to first consider the issue of cognitive phenomenology.

The central assertion of *cognitive phenomenology* is that our subjective, first-person experience is not restricted to just traditional qualia involving sensory perception, emotions and visual imagery, but also encompasses deliberative thought and high-level cognition. Such an assertion might seem straightforward to the non-philosopher, but it has proven to be controversial in philosophy. Introductory overviews that explain this controversy in a historical context can be found in [25,26], and a balanced collection of essays arguing for and against the basic ideas of cognitive phenomenology is given in [12]. A recent detailed philosophical analysis of cognitive phenomenology is also available [27].

Most of this past discussion in the philosophy literature has focused on reasons for accepting or rejecting cognitive phenomenology. Philosophers generally appear to accept that some aspects of cognition are accessible to consciousness, so the arguments in the literature have focused on the specific issue of whether there are phenomenal aspects of cognition that cannot be accounted for by traditional sensory qualia and mental imagery. For example, an advocate of cognitive phenomenology might argue that there are different non-sensory subjective qualities associated with hearing the sentence "I'm tired" spoken in a foreign language if one understands that language than if one does not, given that the sensory experience is the same in both cases.

While there are those who do not agree with the idea of cognitive phenomenology, there appears to be increasing acceptance of the concept [28]. For our purposes, here, we will simply assume that cognitive phenomenology holds and ask what that might imply. In other words, we start by *assuming* that there exist distinct non-sensory subjective mental experiences associated with at least some aspects of cognition. What would follow from this assumption? One answer to this question is that cognitive phenomenology makes the computational explanatory gap, an apparently purely computational issue, of relevance to understanding consciousness. Since the computational explanatory gap focuses on mechanistically accounting for high-level cognitive information processing, and since at least some aspects of cognitive information processing are conscious, it means that computational efforts to mechanistically bridge the computational explanatory gap have direct relevance to the study of consciousness. In particular, we hypothesize that such neurocomputational studies provide a route to both a deeper understanding of human consciousness and also to a phenomenally conscious machine. This hypothesis makes a large body of research in cognitive science that is focused on developing neurocomputational implementations of high-level cognition pertinent to the issue of phenomenal consciousness. This work, while recognized as being relevant to intentional aspects of consciousness, has not generally been considered of direct relevance to phenomenology. This implication is an aspect of cognitive phenomenology that has apparently not been recognized previously.

## 4. A Roadmap to a Better Understanding of Consciousness

From a computational point of view, the recognition that high-level cognitive processes may have distinct subjective qualities associated with them has striking implications for computational research related to consciousness. Cognitive phenomenology implies that, in addition to past work explicitly studying "artificial consciousness", other ongoing research focused on developing computational models of higher cognitive functions is directly relevant to understanding the nature of consciousness. Much of this work on neurocognitive architectures attempts to map higher cognitive functions into neurocomputational mechanisms independently of any explicit relationship between these functions and consciousness. Such work may, intentionally or inadvertently, identify neurocomputational mechanisms associated with phenomenally conscious information processing that are not observed with unconscious information processing. This would potentially provide examples of computational correlates of consciousness, and thus ideally would provide a deeper understanding of the nature of consciousness in general, just as molecular biology contributed to demystifying the nature of life and deprecating the theory of vitalism. In effect, this work may allow us to determine whether or not there are computational correlates of consciousness in the same sense that there are neurobiological correlates of consciousness.

A computational correlate of consciousness can, in general, be defined to be any principle of information processing that characterizes the differences between conscious and unconscious information processing [13]. Such a definition is quite broad: It could include, for example, symbolic AI logical reasoning and natural language processing algorithms. Consistent with this possibility, there have been past suggestions that intelligent information processing can be divided into symbolic processes that represent conscious aspects of the mind, and neurocomputational processes that represent unconscious aspects of cognition [29–32]. However, while such models/theories implicitly recognize the computational explanatory gap as we explained it above, they do not attempt to provide a solution to it, and they do not address serious objections to symbolic models of cognition in general [33]. The critical issue that we are concerned with here with respect to the computational explanatory gap is how to *replace* the high-level symbolic modules of such models with neurocomputational implementations. How such replacement is to be done remains stubbornly mysterious today.

Accordingly, in the following, we use the term "computational correlate of consciousness" to mean minimal neurocomputational processing mechanisms that are specifically associated with conscious aspects of cognition but *not* with unconscious aspects. In other words, in the context of the computational explanatory gap, we are specifically interested in *neuro*computational correlates of consciousness, i.e., computational correlates related to the representation, storage, processing, and modification of information that occurs in neural networks. Computational correlates of consciousness are a priori distinct from neural correlates [13]. As noted above, proposed neural correlates have in practice included, for example, electrical/metabolic activity patterns, neuroanatomical regions of the brain, and biochemical phenomena [23]—correlates within the realm of biology that are not computational. Computational correlates are abstractions that may well find implementation in the brain, but as abstractions they are intended to be independent of the physical substrate that implements them (brain, silicon, etc.).

Our suggestion here is that, as computational correlates of consciousness as defined above become discovered, they will provide a direct route to investigating the possibility of phenomenal machine consciousness, to identifying candidate properties that could serve as objective criteria for the presence of phenomenal consciousness in machines, animals and people (the problem of other minds), and to a better understanding of the fundamental nature of consciousness. In other words, what we are suggesting is that a complete characterization of high-level cognition in neurocomputational terms may, along the way, show us how subjective experience arises mechanistically, based on the concepts of cognitive phenomenology discussed above.

## 5. Past Suggestions for Computational Correlates of Consciousness

If one allows the possibility that the computational explanatory gap is a substantial barrier both to a deeper understanding of phenomenal consciousness and to developing machine consciousness, then the immediate research program becomes determining how one can bridge this gap and identify computational correlates of consciousness. Encouragingly, cognitive phenomenology suggests that the substantial efforts by researchers working in artificial consciousness and by others developing neurocognitive architectures involving high-level cognitive functionality are beginning to provide a variety of potential computational correlates. Much of this past work can be interpreted as being founded upon specific candidates for computational correlates of consciousness, and this observation suggests that such models are directly related to addressing the computational explanatory gap. In the following, we give a description of past computational correlates that are identifiable from the existing literature, dividing them into five classes or categories:

- representation properties
- system-level properties
- self-modeling

- relational properties
- cognitive control

All of these correlates are based on neurocomputational systems. We give just a brief summary below, using only a single example of each class, to convey the general idea. Further, we will consider these potential correlates uncritically here, deferring the issue of whether they correlate *exclusively* with consciousness until the Discussion section. A more detailed technical characterization and many further examples in each class can be found in [34].

One class of computational correlates of consciousness is based on *representation properties*, i.e., on how information is encoded. This refers to the intrinsic properties of the neural representation of information used in cognitive states/processes. For example, a number of theoretical arguments and several early recurrent neural network models of consciousness were based on hypothesizing that neural activity *attractor states* are associated with or characterize consciousness [13,35–39]. At any point in time, a recurrent neural network has an activity state, a pattern of active and inactive neurons that represents/encodes the contents of the network's current state (Figure 3). Over time, this pattern of activity typically changes from moment to moment as the activities of each neuron influence those of the other neurons. However, in networks that serve as models of short-term working memory, this evolution of the activity pattern stops and settles into a fixed, persistent activity state (Figure 3, right). This persisting activity state is referred to as an "attractor" of the network because other activity states of the network are "attracted" to be in this fixed state. It is these attractor states that have been proposed to enter conscious awareness and in this sense to be a computational correlate of consciousness. This claim appears to be consistent with at least some neurophysiological findings [40]. Of course, there are other types of attractor states in recurrent neural networks besides fixed activity patterns, such as periodically recurring activity patterns (limit cycles) [41], and they could also be potential computational correlates. In particular, it has been proposed that instantaneous activity states of a network are inadequate for realizing conscious experience—that qualia are correlated instead with a system's *activity space trajectory* [35]. The term "trajectory" as used here refers to a temporal sequence of a neural system's activity states, much as is pictured in Figure 3, rather than to a single instantaneous activity state. Viewing a temporal sequence of activity patterns as a correlate of subjective experience overcomes several objections that exist for single activity states as correlates [35].

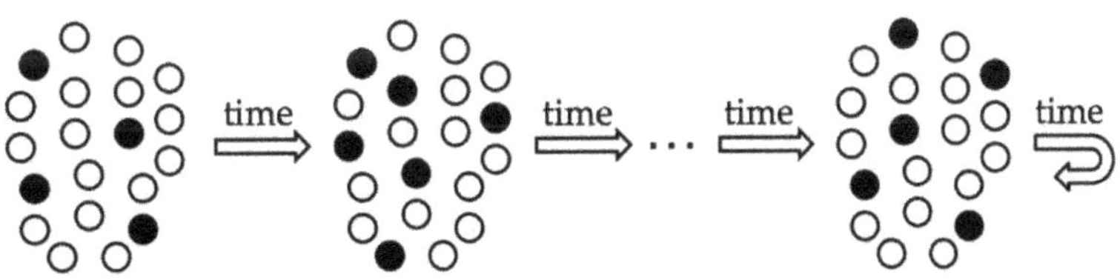


**Figure 3.** On the left is a set of artificial neurons that are widely connected to one another (the connections are not shown to keep the diagram simple). An arbitrary initial activity state has been assigned to the network. This is shown schematically by indicating those neurons that are active (on, firing, excited, etc.) by filled circles and those neurons that are inactive (off, silent, inhibited, etc.) by unfilled circles. As time passes, the activity state typically changes repeatedly (middle), but under appropriate conditions, eventually reaches a state that no longer changes with time (rightmost). The network's activity state is then said to have reached a fixed point, and this latter activity pattern is said to be an *attractor state* of the network because other transient states of the network are "attracted" to become this persistent state. Attractor states in neural networks of this sort often represent stored information in working memory or the solutions to problems.

A second class of computational correlates of consciousness is based on *system-level properties* of a neurocomputational system. This term is used here to mean those computational properties that characterize a neurocomputational system as a whole rather than, as with representational properties, depend on the specific nature of neural activity patterns that represent/encode cognitive states and processes. We use *global information processing* as an example here. The terms local and global, when applied to neurocognitive architectures, generally refer to the spatial extent of information processing. A number of empirical studies have suggested that information processing during conscious mental activities is widely distributed ("global") across cerebral cortex regions and also associated with increased inter-regional communication [42–44]. Inspired by this, a number of neural network models have been studied in which conscious/effortful information processing is associated with computational processes involving the recruitment of hidden layers and hence widespread network activation of a "global workspace" [45,46]. An example neural architecture of this type is illustrated schematically in Figure 4. This specific example concerns a Stroop task where one must either read aloud each seen word ("green", "blue", etc.) or name the color of the ink used in the word, the latter being more difficult and effortful with incongruous words. Significant widespread activation of the "global workspace" occurs when the model is dealing with a difficult naming task that requires conscious effort by humans, and not with the easier, more automatic word reading task, making global activation a potential computational correlate of consciousness. It has been suggested elsewhere that global information processing provides a plausible neurocomputational basis for both phenomenal and access consciousness [47].

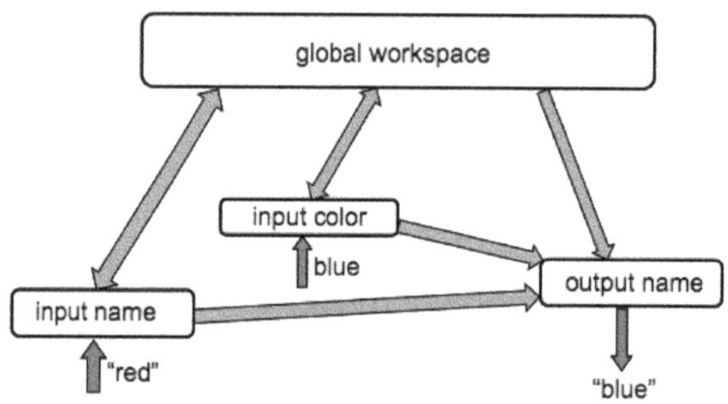


**Figure 4.** A schematic representation of the architecture of a neural global workspace model for a word-color Stroop task [46]. Each box represents a set/layer of neurons. Local processing occurs in the input and output layers, while with global processing, substantial activation also occurs throughout the workspace layer.

A third class of computational correlates of consciousness involves *self-modeling*, that is, maintaining an internal model of self. Self-awareness has long been viewed as a central aspect of a conscious mind [48,49]. For example, analysis of the first-person perspective suggests that our mind includes a *self-model* (virtual model, body image) that is supported by neural activation patterns in the brain. The argument is that the subjective, conscious experience of a "self" arises because this model is always there due to the proprioceptive, somatic and other sensory input that the brain constantly receives, and because our cognitive processes do not recognize that the body image is a virtual representation of the physical body [50]. Accordingly, AI and cognitive science researchers have made a number of proposals for how subjective conscious experience could emerge in embodied agents from such self-models. An example of this type of work has studied "conscious robots" that are controlled by recurrent neural networks [51]. A central focus of this work is handling temporal sequences of stimuli, predicting the event that will occur at the next time step from past and current events. The predicted next state and the actual next state of the world are compared at each time step, and when these two states are the same a robot is declared to be conscious ("consistency of cognition and behavior generates consciousness"). In support of this concept of consciousness, these expectation-driven robots have been shown to be capable of self-recognition in a mirror [52], effectively passing the "mirror test" of self-awareness used with animals [53] and allowing the investigators to claim that it represents self-recognition. The predictive value of a self-model such as that used here has previously been argued by others to be associated with consciousness [54].

A fourth class of potential computational correlates of consciousness is based on *relational properties*: relationships between cognitive entities. *Higher-order thought theory* (HOT theory) of consciousness [55] provides a good example of a potential computational correlate of consciousness involving relational properties. HOT theory is relational: It postulates that a mental state *S* is conscious to the extent that there is some other mental state (a "higher-order thought") that directly refers to *S* or is about *S*. In other words, consciousness occurs when there is a specific relationship such as this between two mental states. It has been suggested that artificial systems with higher-order representations consistent with HOT theory could be viewed as conscious, even to the extent of having qualia, if they use grounded symbols [56]. Further, HOT theory has served as a framework for developing *metacognitive networks* in which some components of a neurocomputational architecture, referred to as higher-order networks, are able to represent and access information about other lower-order networks [57], as illustrated in Figure 5. It is the second-order network's learned reference to the first-order network's internal representations that makes the latter at least functionally conscious, according to HOT theory. The claim is that "conscious experience occurs if and only if an information processing system has learned about its own representation of the world" [57], and that the higher-order representations formed in metacognitive models capture the core mechanisms of HOT theories of consciousness [58].

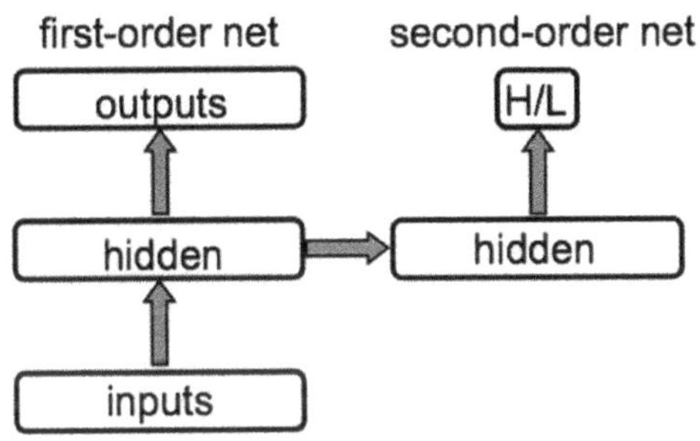


**Figure 5.** A caricature of a typical metacognitive neural architecture. Boxes indicate network layers, and gray arrows indicate all-to-all adaptive connections between layers. The first-order network on the left is used to learn pattern classification tasks. The second-order network on the right monitors the first-order network's hidden layer representation and outputs an estimate as to the correctness of the first-order network's output for each input pattern. The correctness of this output over time reflects the extent to which the second-order network has learned a meta-representation of the first-order network's representation.

A fifth class of computational correlates of consciousness is based on *cognitive control*, the executive processes that manage other cognitive processes [59]. Examples of cognitive control include directing attention, maintaining working memory, goal setting, and inhibiting irrelevant signals. Most past neurocomputational modeling work of relevance here has focused on attention mechanisms. While attention and conscious awareness are not equivalent processes, normally they are closely linked and highly correlated [60–62]. It is therefore not surprising that some computational studies have viewed attention mechanisms as computational correlates of consciousness. For example, Haikonen [63] has proposed a conscious machine based on a number of properties, including inner speech and the machine's ability to report its inner states, in which consciousness is correlated with *collective processing of a single topic*. This machine is composed of a collection of inter-communicating modules. The distinction between a topic being conscious or not is based on whether the machine as a whole attends to that topic. At each moment of time, each specialized module of the machine broadcasts information about the topic it is addressing to the other modules. Each broadcasting module competes to recruit other modules to attend to the same topic that it is processing. The subject of this unified collective focus of attention is claimed to enter consciousness. In other words, it is the collective, cooperative attending to a single topic that represents a computational correlate of consciousness. Recently implemented in a robot [64], this idea suggests that a machine can only be conscious of one topic at a time, and like global workspace theory (from which it differs significantly), this hypothesis is consistent with empirical evidence that conscious brain states are associated with widespread communication between cerebral cortex regions.

## 6. Top-Down Gating of Working Memory

We have now seen that past research relevant to the computational explanatory gap has suggested or implied a variety of potential computational correlates of consciousness. It is highly likely that additional candidates will become evident in the future based on theoretical considerations, experimental evidence from cognitive science, the discovery of new neural correlates of consciousness, and so forth. In this section, we will consider a recently-introduced type of neural models focused on cognitive control of working memory. These models incorporate two potential computational correlates of consciousness: temporal sequences of attractor states, something that has been proposed previously as a computational correlate, and the top-down gating of working memory, something that we will propose below should also be considered as a computational correlate within the category of cognitive control. To understand this latter hypothesis, we need to first clarify the nature of working memory and characterize how it is controlled by cognitive processes.

### *6.1. Cognitive Control of Working Memory*

The term *working memory* refers to the human memory system that temporarily retains and manipulates information over a short time period [65]. In contrast to the relatively limitless capacity of more permanent long-term memory, working memory has substantial capacity limitations. Evidence suggests that human working memory capacity is on the order of roughly four "chunks" of information under laboratory conditions [66]. For example, if you are playing the card game bridge, your working memory might contain information about some recent cards that have been played by your partner or by other players during the last few moves. Similarly, if you are asked to subtract 79 from 111 "in your head" without writing anything down, your working memory would contain these two numbers and often intermediate steps (borrowing, etc.) during your mental calculations. Items stored in working memory may interfere with each other, and they are eventually lost, or said to decay over time, reflecting the limited storage capacity. For example, if you do ten consecutive mental arithmetic problems, and then you are subsequently asked "What were the two numbers you subtracted in the third problem?", odds are high that you would no longer be able to recall this information.

The operation of working memory is largely managed via cognitive control systems that, like working memory itself, are most clearly associated with prefrontal cortex regions. It is these top-down "executive processes" that are at issue here. Developing neural architectures capable of modeling cognitive control processes has proven to be surprisingly challenging, both for working memory and in general. What computational mechanisms might implement the control of working memory functionality?

One answer to this question is that top-down gating provides the mechanisms by which high-level cognitive processes control the operation of working memory, determining what is stored, retained and recalled. In general, the term "gating" in the context of neural information processing refers to any situation where one neurocomputational component controls the functionality of another. However, neural network practitioners use this term to refer to such control occurring at different levels in neurocomputational systems. At the "microscopic" level, gating can refer to local interactions between individual artificial neurons where, for example, one neuron controls whether or not another neuron retains or loses its current activity state, as in long short-term memory models [67]. While simulated evolution has shown that localized gating of individual neurons can sometimes contribute to the reproductive fitness of a neural system [68], we do not consider this type of localized gating further.

Instead, in the following, we are concerned solely with gating at a much more "macroscopic" level where one or more modules/networks as a whole controls the functionality of other modules/networks as a whole. Such large-scale gating apparently occurs widely in the brain. For example, if a person hears the word "elephant", that person's brain might turn on speech output modules such as Broca's area (they repeat what they heard), or alternatively such output modules may be kept inactive (the person is just listening silently). In such situations, the modules not only exchange information via neural pathways, but they may also control the actions of one another. A module may, via gating, turn on/off the activity or connections of other modules as a whole, and may determine when other modules retain/discard their network activity state, when they learn/unlearn information, and when they generate output.

*6.2. Modeling Top-Down Gating*

To illustrate these ideas, we consider here a recently-developed neurocomputational model that addresses high-level cognitive functions and the computational explanatory gap. This model incorporates a control system that gates the actions of other modules and itself at a "macroscopic" level [69,70]. In this model, the control module learns to turn on/off (i.e., to gate) the actions of other modules, thereby determining when input patterns are saved or discarded, when to learn/unlearn information in working memory, when to generate outputs, and even when to update its own states.

As a specific example, consider the situation depicted in Figure 6, which schematically illustrates a neural architecture described in [70]. On the left is an arrangement of 16 cards that each display a pattern on one face, where all but two of the cards shown are face down on a table top. On the right is pictured a neurocomputational agent that can see the card configuration and that has the ability to select specific cards on the table by pointing to them. The goal is for the neurocognitive agent to remove all of the cards from the table in as few steps as possible. On each step, the agent can select two cards to turn over and thereby reveal the identity of those two cards. If the two cards match, then they are removed from the table and progress is made towards the goal. If the selected cards reveal different patterns, as is the case illustrated in Figure 6, then they are turned back over and remain on the table. While it may appear that no progress has been made in this latter case, the agent's neural networks include a working memory in which the patterns that have been seen and their locations are recorded and retained. Accordingly, if on the next step the agent first turns over the upper left card and discovers that it has horizontal stripes on its face, then rather than selecting the second card randomly, the agent would select the (currently face down) rightmost card in the second row to achieve a matching pair that can be removed.

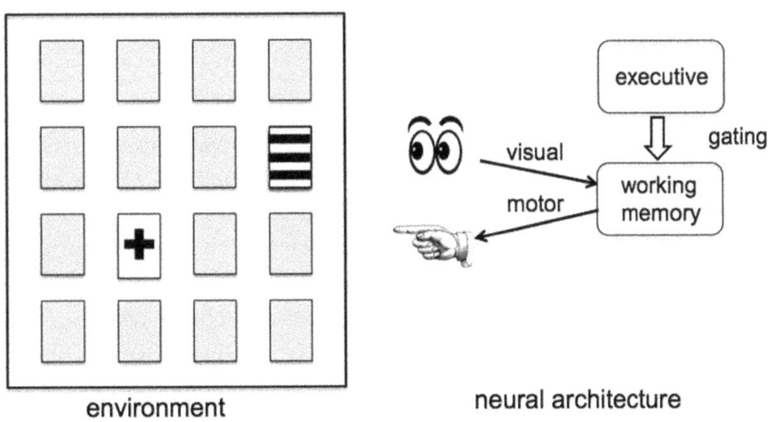


**Figure 6.** On the left, a set of 16 cards is spread out on a table, with all but two of the cards face down. On the right, the top-level structure of a neurocomputational agent is shown schematically, where the agent can see the current card configuration and can act by pointing at face-down cards to indicate that they should be turned over. The agent has a working memory that allows it to retain in memory the identities and locations of a few recent cards that it has seen (subject to decay), and an executive control system that directs the agent's working memory and output motor actions.

The most interesting aspect of our architecture's underlying neurocomputational system is the executive module (upper right of Figure 6) that directs and controls the actions of the rest of the system. The executive module is initially trained to carry out the card removal task and acts via top-down gating mechanisms to control the sequence of operations that are performed by the agent. The agent's neural architecture pictured on the right side of Figure 6 is expanded into a more detailed form in Figure 7, indicating the neurocomputational model's actual components and connectivity. The visual input arrow of Figure 6 is implemented at the top left of Figure 7 by components modeling the human "what" (object) and "where" (location) visual pathways, while the motor output arrow of Figure 6 is implemented as a motor system at the bottom of Figure 7. The agent's working memory in Figure 6 is seen on the left in Figure 7 to consist of multiple components, while the executive system is implemented as a multi-component control module on the right in Figure 7. The top-down gating arrow between executive and working memory systems in Figure 6 is implemented as nine gating outputs exiting the control module at the bottom right of Figure 7 and from there traveling to a variety of locations throughout the rest of the architecture.

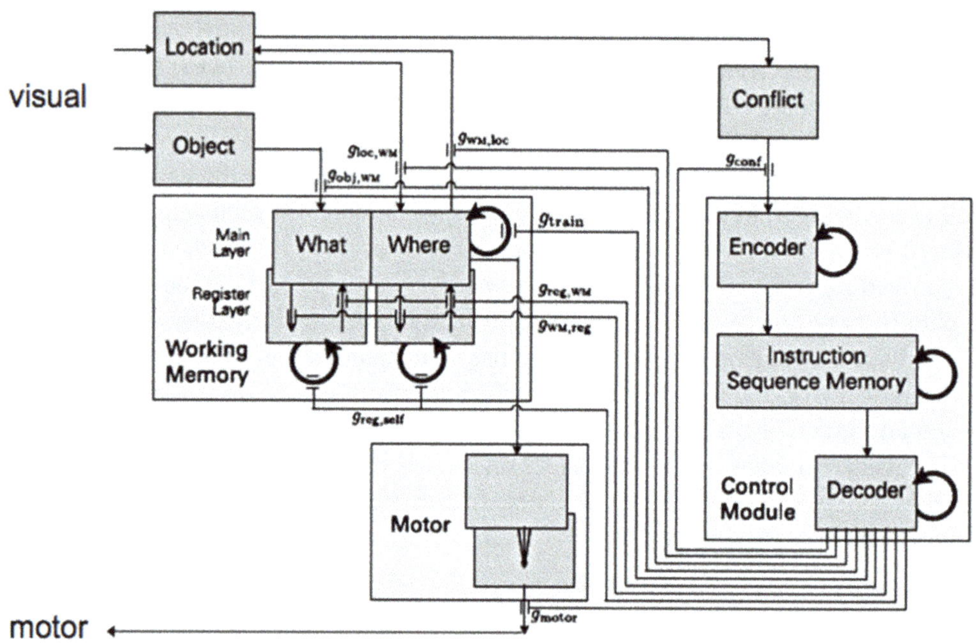


**Figure 7.** A more detailed depiction of the neurocomputational mechanisms controlling the card matching task agent illustrated in Figure 6. Each gray-shaded box represents a neural network module, while the arrows represent connection pathways between these modules. On the left, an operational system consists of visual pathways feeding into the working memory, the latter driving the agent's motor actions. Many of these modules are recurrently connected (broad circular arrows). The control module, or executive system, is pictured on the right. Its gating outputs, originating at the bottom right of the picture, control the operational system's actions as described in the text.

In the neurocomputational architecture shown in Figure 7, incoming visual information passes through the visual pathways to the working memory, and can trigger motor actions (pointing at a specific card to turn over); these neural components form an "operational system" pictured on the left. The working memory stores information about which cards have been observed previously by learning, at appropriate times, the outputs of the location and object visual pathways. This allows the system subsequently to choose pairs of cards intelligently based on its past experience rather than blindly guessing the locations of potential matches, much as a person does. Working memory is implemented as an auto-associative neural network that uses Hebbian learning. It stores object-location pairs as attractor states. This allows the system to retrieve complete pairs when given just the object information alone or just the location information alone as needed during problem solving. This associating of objects and locations in memory can be viewed as addressing the binding problem [71].

The control module shown on the right in Figure 7 directs the actions of the operational system via a set of gating outputs. The core of the control module is an associative neural network called the instruction sequence memory. The purpose of this procedural memory module is to store simultaneously multiple instruction sequences that are to be used during problem solving, in this case simple instruction sequences for performing card matching tasks. Each instruction indicates to the control module which output gates should be opened at that point in time during problem solving. Informally, the instruction sequence memory allows the system to learn simple "programs" for what actions to take when zero, one, or two cards are face up on the table. The instruction sequence memory is trained via a special form of Hebbian learning to both store individual instructions as attractor states of the network, and to transition between these attractors/instructions during problem solving—it essentially learns to perform, autonomously, the card matching task.

The control module's gating connections direct the flow of activity throughout the neural architecture, determine when output occurs, and decide when and where learning occurs. For example, the rightmost gating output labeled $g_{motor}$ (bottom center in Figure 7) opens/closes the output from the motor module, thus determining when and where the agent points at a card to indicate that it should be turned over. Two of the other gating outputs, labeled $g_{obj,WM}$ and $g_{loc,WM}$, determine when visually-observed information about a card's identity and/or location, respectively, are stored in working memory. Other gates determine when learning occurs in working memory ($g_{train}$), when comparison/manipulation of information stored in working memory occurs ($g_{reg,WM}$, $g_{WM,reg}$, $g_{reg,self}$), when the top-down focus of visual attention shifts to a new location ($g_{WM,loc}$), and when the executive control module switches to a new sequence of instructions ($g_{conf}$).

The control module's gating operations are implemented in the underlying neural networks of the architecture via what is sometimes referred to as multiplicative modulation [72]. At any point in time, each of the nine gating connections signals a value $g_x$, where $x$ is "*motor*" or "*loc,WM*" or other indices as pictured in Figure 7. These $g_x$ values multiplicatively enter into the equations governing the behaviors of the neural networks throughout the overall architecture. For example, if the output of a neuron $j$ in the motor module has value $o_j$ at some point in time, then the actual gated output seen by the external environment at that time is the product $g_{motor} \times o_j$. If $g_{motor} = 0$ at that time, then no actual output is transmitted to the external environment; if on the other hand $g_{motor} = 1$, then $o_j$ is transmitted unchanged to the outside world. The detailed equations implementing activity and weight change dynamics and how they are influenced by these gating control signals for the card matching task can be found in [70].

When an appropriate rate of decay is used to determine how quickly items are lost from working memory, this specific architecture for solving card matching task produced accuracy and timing results reminiscent of those seen in humans performing similar tasks [70]. Specifically, this system successfully solved every one of hundreds of randomly-generated card matching tasks on which it was tested. We measured the number of rounds that the system needed to complete the task when 8, 12 or 16 cards were present, averaged over 200 runs. The result was 8.7, 13.0, and 21.2, respectively, increasing as the number of cards increased as would be expected. Interestingly, when we had 34 human subjects carry out the same task, the number of rounds measured was 7.9, 13.5, and 18.9 on average, respectively. While the agent's performance was not an exact match to that of humans, it is qualitatively similar and exhibits the same trends, suggesting that this neural architecture may be capturing at least some important aspects of human cognitive control of working memory.

### 6.3. *Top-Down Gating as a Computational Correlate of Consciousness*

There are actually two innovative aspects of this agent's neurocontroller that are potential computational correlates of consciousness, one a representational property proposed previously, the other a mechanism that relates to cognitive control. The first of these involves the instruction sequence memory that forms the heart of the control module (see Figure 7). Prior to problem solving, sequences of operations to carry out in various situations are stored in this memory, much as one stores a program in a computer's memory [70]. Each operation/instruction is stored as an attractor state of this memory module, and during operation the instruction sequence memory cycles through these instructions/attractors consecutively to carry out the card matching or another task. In other words, the instruction sequence memory transitions through a sequence of attractor states in carrying out a task. As we discussed in Section 5, it has previously been hypothesized that an activity-space trajectory such as this is a computational correlate of consciousness [35]. Since the execution of stored instructions here is precisely a trajectory in the instruction sequence memory's neural network activity-space, that aspect of the card-removal task agent's functionality can be accepted as a potential computational correlate of consciousness based on the activity-space trajectory hypothesis.

However, our primary innovative suggestion here is that there is a second mechanism in this neurocontroller that can be viewed as a potential computational correlate of consciousness: the use of *top-down gating of working memory* that controls what is stored and manipulated in working memory. Arguably these gating operations, driven by sequences of attractor states in the executive control module, correspond to consciously reportable cognitive activities involving working memory, and thus they are a potential computational correlate of consciousness. To understand this suggestion, we need to clarify the relationship of working memory to consciousness. Working memory has long been considered to involve primarily *conscious* aspects of cognitive information processing. Specifically, psychologists widely believe that the working memory operations of input, rehearsal, manipulation, and recall are conscious and reportable [65,73–75]. Thus, on this basis alone any mechanisms involved in implementing or controlling these working memory operations merit inspection as potential correlates of consciousness.

In addition, cognitive phenomenology appears to be particularly supportive of our suggestion. Recall that cognitive phenomenology holds that our subjective first-person experience includes deliberative thought and high-level cognition. Our viewpoint here is that high-level cognitive processes become intimately associated with working memory via these top-down gating mechanisms. In particular, it seems intuitively reasonable that the controlling of cognitive activities involving working memory via top-down gating mechanisms might convey a conscious sense of ownership/self-control/agency to a system. Top-down gating of working memory may also relate to the concept of mental causation sometimes discussed in the philosophy of mind literature (especially the literature concerned with issues surrounding free will). The recent demonstration in neurocomputational models that goal-directed top-down gating of working memory can not only work effectively in problem-solving tasks such as the card matching application, but also that such models exhibit behaviors that match up with those observed in humans performing these tasks, supports the idea that something important about cognition (and hence consciousness, as per cognitive phenomenology) is being captured by such models.

Top-down gating of working memory is clearly a distinct potential correlate of consciousness that differs from those described previously (summarized in Section 5). It is obviously not a representational property, although gating can be used in conjunction with networks that employ attractor states as we described above. It is not a system property, like a global workspace or information integration, nor does it explicitly act via self-modeling. It is perhaps somewhat closer to relational properties in that gating can be viewed as relating high-level cognitive processes for problem-solving to working memory processes. However, top-down gating is quite different than relational models that have been previously proposed as computational correlates of consciousness. For example, unlike with past neurocomputational models based on HOT theory that are concerned with metacognitive networks/states that *monitor* one another, gating architectures are concerned with modules that *control* one another's actions. Our view is that top-down gating fits best in the class of computational correlates of consciousness involving cognitive control. This latter class has previously focused primarily on aspects of attention mechanisms, such as the collective simultaneous attending of multiple modules to a single topic [63,64] or the generation of an "efference copy" of attention control signals [76]. Our proposed correlate of top-down gating of working memory differs from these, but appears to us to be complementary to these attention mechanisms rather than an alternative.

**7. Discussion**

Past progress in the field known as artificial consciousness has made significant strides over the last few decades, but has mainly involved computationally simulating various neural, behavioral, and cognitive aspects of consciousness, much as is done in using computers to simulate other natural processes [8]. There is nothing particularly mysterious about such work: Just as one does not claim that a computer used to simulate a nuclear reactor would actually become radioactive, there is no claim being made in such work that a computer used to model some aspect of conscious information processing would actually become phenomenally conscious. As noted earlier, there is currently no existing computational approach to artificial consciousness that has yet presented a compelling demonstration or design of phenomenal consciousness in a machine.

At the present time, our understanding of phenomenal consciousness in general remains incredibly limited. This is true not only for human consciousness but also for considerations about the possibility of animal and machine consciousness. Our central argument here is that this apparent lack of progress towards a deeper understanding of phenomenal consciousness is in part due to the computational explanatory gap: our current lack of understanding of how higher-level cognitive algorithms can be mapped onto neurocomputational algorithms/states. While those versed in mind–brain philosophy may generally be inclined to dismiss this gap as just part of the "easy problem", such a view is at best misleading. This computational gap has proven surprisingly intractable to over half a century of research on neurocomputational methods, and existing philosophical works have provided no deep insight into *why* such an "easy problem" has proven to be so intractable. The view offered here is that the computational explanatory gap is a fundamental issue that needs a much larger collective effort to clarify and resolve. Doing so should go a long way in helping us pin down the computational correlates of consciousness.

Accordingly, we presented several examples of candidates for computational correlates of consciousness in this paper that have emerged from past work on artificial consciousness and neurocognitive architectures. Further, we suggested and described an additional possible correlate, top-down gating of working memory, based on our own recent neurocomputational studies of cognitive control [69,70]. It is interesting in this context to ask how such gating may be occurring in the brain. How one cortical region may directly/indirectly gate the activity of other cortical regions is currently only partially understood. This is an issue of much recent and ongoing interest in the cognitive neurosciences. Gating interactions might be brought about in part by direct connections between regions, such as the poorly understood "backwards" inter-regional connections that are well documented to exist in primate cortical networks [77]. Further, there is substantial evidence that gating may occur in part indirectly via a complex network of subcortical nuclei, including those in the basal ganglia and thalamus [78]. Another possibility is that gating may arise via functional mechanisms such as oscillatory activity synchronization [72,79]. In our related modeling work, the details of implementing gating actions have largely been suppressed, and a more detailed examination comparing alternative possible mechanisms could be an important direction for future research.

The examples that we presented above, and those suggested by other related studies, are very encouraging in suggesting that there now exist several *potential* computational correlates of consciousness. However, an important difficulty remains: Many hypothesized computational mechanisms identified so far as correlates of consciousness are either known to also occur in neurocomputational systems supporting non-conscious activities, or their occurrence has not yet been definitively excluded in such settings. In other words, the main difficulty in identifying computational correlates of consciousness at present is in establishing that proposed correlates are *not* also present with unconscious aspects of cognitive information processing. For example, viewing neural network activity attractor states as computational correlates of consciousness is problematic in that there are many physical systems with attractor states that are generally not viewed as conscious, leading to past suggestions that representing conscious aspects of cognition in such a fashion is not helpful: An attractor state may relate to the contents of consciousness, but it is arguably not a useful explanation of phenomenology because there is simply no reason to believe that it involves "internal experience" [80] or because it implies panpsychism [13]. Similarly, the metacognitive neural networks that HOT theory has inspired suggest that information processing in such neural architectures can be taken to be a computational correlate, but there are possibly analogous types of information processing in biological neural circuits at the level of the human brainstem and spinal cord that are associated with apparently unconscious processing. Thus, "second-order" information processing in neural architectures *alone* apparently would not fully satisfy our criteria for being a computational correlate of consciousness. Similarly, global/widespread neural activity per se does not appear to fully satisfy our criteria because such processing also occurs in apparently unconscious neural systems (e.g., interacting central pattern generators in isolated lamprey eel spinal cord preparations produce coordinated movements involving widespread distributed neural interactions [81], but it is improbable that an isolated eel spinal cord should be viewed as being conscious). Very similar points can be made about HOT theories, gating mechanisms, integrated information processing, and self-modeling.

For this reason, it remains unclear at present which, if any, of the currently hypothesized candidates for neurocomputational correlates of consciousness will ultimately prove to be satisfactory without further qualifications/refinements. This is not because they fail to capture important aspects of conscious information processing, but primarily because similar computational mechanisms have not yet been *proven* to be absent in unconscious information processing situations. These computational mechanisms are thus not yet *specifically* identifiable only with conscious cognitive activities. Future work is needed to resolve such issues, to pin down more clearly which aspects of cognition enter conscious awareness and which do not, and to further consider other types of potential computational correlates (quantum computing, massively parallel symbol processing, etc.).

**Acknowledgments:** This work was supported in part by ONR award N000141310597.

**Author Contributions:** The authors contributed jointly to all aspects of this work.

**Conflicts of Interest:** The authors declare no conflict of interest. The funding sponsors had no role in the design of the study; in the collection, analyses, or interpretation of data; in the writing of the manuscript, and in the decision to publish the results.

## References

1. Block, N. On a Confusion about a Function of Consciousness. *Behav. Brain Sci.* **1995**, *18*, 227–247. [CrossRef]
2. Schlagel, R. Why not Artificial Consciousness or Thought? *Minds Mach.* **1999**, *9*, 3–28. [CrossRef]
3. Bishop, M. Why Computers Can't Feel Pain. *Minds Mach.* **2009**, *19*, 507–516. [CrossRef]
4. Bringsjord, S. Offer: One Billion Dollars for a Conscious Robot; If You're Honest, You Must Decline. *J. Conscious. Stud.* **2007**, *14*, 28–43.
5. Manzotti, R. The Computational Stance is Unfit for Consciousness. *Int. J. Mach. Conscious.* **2012**, *4*, 401–420. [CrossRef]
6. Piper, M. You Can't Eat Causal Cake with an Abstract Fork. *J. Conscious. Stud.* **2012**, *19*, 154–180.
7. McGinn, C. *Consciousness and Its Origins*; Oxford University Press: Oxford, UK, 2004.
8. Reggia, J. The Rise of Machine Consciousness. *Neural Netw.* **2013**, *44*, 112–131. [CrossRef] [PubMed]
9. Harnad, S. Animal Sentience: The Other-Minds Problem. *Anim. Sentience* **2016**, *1*, 1–11.
10. Reggia, J.; Huang, D.; Katz, G. Beliefs Concerning the Nature of Consciousness. *J. Conscious. Stud.* **2015**, *22*, 146–171.
11. Reggia, J.; Monner, D.; Sylvester, J. The Computational Explanatory Gap. *J. Conscious. Stud.* **2014**, *21*, 153–178.
12. Bayne, T.; Montague, M. (Eds.) *Cognitive Phenomenology*; Oxford University Press: Oxford, UK, 2011.
13. Cleeremans, A. Computational Correlates of Consciousness. *Prog. Brain Res.* **2005**, *150*, 81–98. [PubMed]
14. Levine, J. Materialism and Qualia: The Explanatory Gap. *Pac. Philos. Q.* **1983**, *64*, 354–361.

15. Chalmers, D. *The Conscious Mind*; Oxford University Press: Oxford, UK, 1996.
16. McCulloch, W.; Pitts, W. A Logical Calculus of the Ideas Immanent in Nervous Activity. *Bull. Math. Biophys.* **1943**, *5*, 115–133. [CrossRef]
17. Jackendoff, R. *Consciousness and the Computational Mind*; MIT Press: Cambridge, MA, USA, 1987.
18. Baars, B. *A Cognitive Theory of Consciousness*; Cambridge University Press: Cambridge, UK, 1988.
19. Baars, B. The Conscious Access Hypothesis. *Trends Cognit. Sci.* **2002**, *6*, 47–52. [CrossRef]
20. Dehaene, S.; Naccache, L. Towards a Cognitive Neuroscience of Consciousness. *Cognition* **2001**, *79*, 1–37. [CrossRef]
21. Huynh, T.; Reggia, J. Symbolic Representation of Recurrent Neural Network Dynamics. *IEEE Trans. Neural Netw. Learn. Syst.* **2012**, *23*, 1649–1658. [CrossRef] [PubMed]
22. Crick, F.; Koch, C. Towards a Neurobiological Theory of Consciousness. *Semin. Neurosci.* **1990**, *2*, 263–275.
23. Chalmers, D. What is a Neural Correlate of Consciousness? In *Neural Correlates of Consciousness*; Metzinger, T., Ed.; MIT Press: Cambridge, MA, USA, 2000; pp. 17–39.
24. Metzinger, T. *Neural Correlates of Consciousness*; MIT Press: Cambridge, MA, USA, 2000.
25. Bayne, T.; Montague, M. Cognitive Phenomenology: An Introduction. In *Cognitive Phenomenology*; Bayne, T., Montague, M., Eds.; Oxford University Press: Oxford, UK, 2011; pp. 1–34.
26. Siewert, C. Phenomenal Thought. In *Cognitive Phenomenology*; Bayne, T., Montague, M., Eds.; Oxford University Press: Oxford, UK, 2011; pp. 236–267.
27. Chudnoff, E. *Cognitive Phenomenology*; Routledge Press: Abingdon-on-Thames UK, 2015.
28. Jorba, M.; Vincente, A. Cognitive Phenomenology, Access to Contents, and Inner Speech. *J. Conscious. Stud.* **2014**, *21*, 74–99.
29. Chella, A. Towards Robot Conscious Perception. In *Artificial Consciousness*; Chella, A., Manzotti, R., Eds.; Imprint Academic: Charlottesville VA, 2007; pp. 124–140.
30. Kitamura, T.; Tahara, T.; Asami, K. How Can a Robot Have Consciousness? *Adv. Robot.* **2000**, *14*, 263–275. [CrossRef]
31. Sun, R. Accounting for the Computational Basis of Consciousness. *Conscious. Cognit.* **1999**, *8*, 529–565. [CrossRef] [PubMed]
32. Sun, R. *Duality of the Mind*; Erlbaum: Hillsdale, NJ, USA, 2002.
33. Dodig-Crakovic, G. The Architecture of Mind as a Network of Networks of Natural Computational Processes. *Philosophies* **2016**, *1*, 111–125. [CrossRef]
34. Reggia, J.; Katz, G.; Huang, D. What are the Computational Correlates of Consciousness? *Biolog. Inspir. Cognit. Archit.* **2016**, in press. [CrossRef]
35. Fekete, T.; Edelman, S. Towards a Computational Theory of Experience. *Conscious. Cognit.* **2011**, *20*, 807–827. [CrossRef] [PubMed]
36. Grossberg, S. The Link between Brain Learning, Attention, and Consciousness. *Conscious. Cognit.* **1999**, *8*, 1–44. [CrossRef] [PubMed]
37. Mathis, D.; Mozer, M. On the Computational Utility of Consciousness. In *Advances in Neural Information Processing Systems*; Tesauro, G., Touretzky, D., Leen, T., Eds.; MIT Press: Cambridge, MA, USA, 1995; Volume 7, pp. 10–18.
38. O'Brien, G.; Opie, J. A Connectionist Theory of Phenomenal Experience. *Behav. Brain Sci.* **1999**, *22*, 127–196. [CrossRef] [PubMed]
39. Taylor, J. Neural Networks for Consciousness. *Neural Netw.* **1997**, *10*, 1207–1225. [CrossRef]
40. Libet, B. The Neural Time Factor in Conscious and Unconscious Events. In *Experimental and Theoretical Studies of Consciousness*; Wiley: New York, NY, USA, 1993; pp. 123–137.
41. Huang, D.; Gentili, R.; Reggia, J. Self-Organizing Maps Based on Limit Cycle Attractors. *Neural Netw.* **2015**, *63*, 208–222. [CrossRef] [PubMed]
42. Baars, B.; Ramsey, T.; Laureys, S. Brain, Conscious Experience, and the Observing Self. *Trends Neurosci.* **2003**, *26*, 671–675. [CrossRef] [PubMed]
43. Massimini, M.; Ferrarelli, F.; Huber, R.; Esser, S.K.; Singh, H.; Tononi, G. Breakdown of Cortical Effective Connectivity during Sleep. *Science* **2005**, *309*, 2228–2232. [CrossRef] [PubMed]
44. Tagliazucchi, E.; Chialvo, D.; Siniatchkin, M.; Amico, E.; Brichant, J.F.; Bonhomme, V.; Noirhomme, Q.; Laufs, H.; Laureys, S. Large-Scale Signatures of Unconsciousness are Consistent with a Departure from Critical Dynamics. *J. R. Soc. Interface* **2016**, *13*. [CrossRef] [PubMed]

45. Connor, D.; Shanahan, M. A Computational Model of a Global Neuronal Workspace with Stochastic Connections. *Neural Netw.* **2010**, *23*, 1139–1154. [CrossRef] [PubMed]
46. Dehaene, S.; Kerszberg, M.; Changeux, J. A Neuronal Model of a Global Workspace in Effortful Cognitive Tasks. *Proc. Natl. Acad. Sci. USA* **1998**, *95*, 14529–14534. [CrossRef] [PubMed]
47. Raffone, A.; Pantani, M. A Global Workspace Model for Phenomenal and Access Consciousness. *Conscious. Cognit.* **2010**, *19*, 580–596. [CrossRef] [PubMed]
48. Samsonovich, A.; Nadel, L. Fundamental Principles and Mechanisms of the Conscious Self. *Cortex* **2005**, *41*, 669–689. [CrossRef]
49. Searle, J. *Mind*; Oxford University Press: Oxford, UK, 2004.
50. Metzinger, T. The Subjectivity of Subjective Experience. In *Neural Correlates of Consciousness*; Metzinger, T., Ed.; MIT Press: Cambridge, MA, USA, 2000; pp. 285–306.
51. Takeno, J. *Creation of a Conscious Robot*; Pan Stanford: Singapore, 2013.
52. Takeno, J. A Robot Succeeds in 100% Mirror Image Cognition. *Int. J. Smart Sens. Intell. Syst.* **2008**, *1*, 891–911.
53. Gallup, G. Chimpanzees: Self-Recognition. *Science* **1970**, *167*, 86–87. [CrossRef]
54. Ascoli, G. Brain and Mind at the Crossroads of Time. *Cortex.* **2005**, *41*, 619–620. [CrossRef]
55. Rosenthal, D. A Theory of Consciousness. In *The Nature of Consciousness*; Block, N., Flanagan, O., Guzeldere, G., Eds.; MIT Press: Cambridge, MA, USA, 1996; pp. 729–753.
56. Rolls, E. A Computational Neuroscience Approach to Consciousness. *Neural Netw.* **2007**, *20*, 962–982. [CrossRef] [PubMed]
57. Cleeremans, A.; Timmermans, B.; Pasquali, A. Consciousness and Metarepresentation: A Computational Sketch. *Neural Netw.* **2007**, *20*, 1032–1039. [CrossRef] [PubMed]
58. Pasquali, A.; Timmermans, B.; Cleeremans, A. Know Thyself: Metacognitive Networks and Measures of Consciousness. *Cognition* **2010**, *117*, 182–190. [CrossRef] [PubMed]
59. Schneider, W.; Chein, J.M. Controlled and Automatic Processing: Behavior, Theory, and Biological Mechanisms. *Cognit. Sci.* **2003**, *27*, 525–559. [CrossRef]
60. Graziano, M.; Webb, T. A Mechanistic Theory of Consciousness. *Int. J. Mach. Conscious.* **2014**, *6*, 163–175. [CrossRef]
61. Koch, C.; Tsuchiya, N. Attention and Consciousness: Two Distinct Brain Processes. *Trends Cognit. Sci.* **2006**, *11*, 16–22. [CrossRef] [PubMed]
62. Lamme, V. Why Visual Attention and Awareness are Different. *Trends Cognit. Sci.* **2003**, *7*, 12–18. [CrossRef]
63. Haikonen, P. Essential Issues of Conscious Machines. *J. Conscious. Stud.* **2007**, *14*, 72–84.
64. Haikonen, P. *Consciousness and Robot Sentience*; World Scientific: Singapore, 2012.
65. Baddeley, A. Working Memory and Conscious Awareness. In *Theories of Memory*; Collins, A., Conway, M., and Morris, P., Eds.; Erlbaum: Hillsdale, NJ, USA, 1993.
66. Cowan, N.; Elliott, E.; Scott Saults, J.; Morey, C.; Mattox, S.; Hismjatullina, A.; Conway, A. On the Capacity of Attention: Its Estimation and Its Role in Working Memory and Cognitive Aptitudes. *Cognit. Psychol.* **2005**, *51*, 42–100. [CrossRef] [PubMed]
67. Monner, D.; Reggia, J. Emergent Latent Symbol Systems in Recurrent Neural Networks. *Connect. Sci.* **2012**, *24*, 193–225. [CrossRef]
68. Chabuk, T.; Reggia, J. The Added Value of Gating in Evolved Neurocontrollers. In Proceedings of the International Joint Conference on Neural Networks, Dallas, TX, USA, 4–9 August 2013; pp. 1335–1342.
69. Sylvester, J.; Reggia, J.; Weems, S.; Bunting, M. Controlling Working Memory with Learned Instructions. *Neural Netw.* **2013**, *41*, 23–38. [CrossRef] [PubMed]
70. Sylvester, J.; Reggia, J. Engineering Neural Systems for High-Level Problem Solving. *Neural Netw.* **2016**, *79*, 37–52. [CrossRef] [PubMed]
71. Feldman, J. The Neural Binding Problem. *Cognit. Neurodyn.* **2013**, *7*, 1–11. [CrossRef] [PubMed]
72. Akam, T.; Kullmann, D. Oscillatory Multiplexing of Population Codes for Selective Communication in the Mammalian Brain. *Nat. Rev. Neurosci.* **2014**, *15*, 111–122. [CrossRef] [PubMed]
73. Baddeley, A. Working Memory: Theories, Models and Controversies. *Annu. Rev. Psychol.* **2012**, *63*, 1–29. [CrossRef] [PubMed]
74. Baars, B.; Franklin, S. How Conscious Experience and Working Memory Interact. *Trends Cognit. Sci.* **2003**, *7*, 166–172. [CrossRef]

75. Block, N. Perceptual Consciousness Overflows Cognitive Access. *Trends Cognit. Sci.* **2011**, *15*, 567–575. [CrossRef] [PubMed]
76. Taylor, J. CODAM: A Neural Network Model of Consciousness. *Neural Netw.* **2007**, *20*, 983–992. [CrossRef] [PubMed]
77. Van Essen, D. Corticocortical and Thalamocortical Information Flow in the Primate Visual System. *Prog. Brain Res.* **2005**, *149*, 173–185. [PubMed]
78. Sherman, S.; Guillery, R. *Exploring the Thalamus and its Role in Cortical Function*; MIT Press: Cambridge, MA, USA, 2006.
79. Singer, W. Dynamic Formation of Functional Networks by Synchronization. *Neuron* **2011**, *69*, 191–193. [CrossRef] [PubMed]
80. Taylor, J. Neural Models of Consciousness. In *Handbook of Brain Theory and Neural Networks*; Arbib, M., Ed.; MIT Press: Cambridge, MA, USA, 2003; pp. 263–267.
81. Ijspeert, A. Central Pattern Generators for Locomotion Control in Animals and Robots. *Neural Netw.* **2008**, *21*, 642–653. [CrossRef] [PubMed]

# Permissions

All chapters in this book were first published in PHILOSOPHIES, by MDPI; hereby published with permission under the Creative Commons Attribution License or equivalent. Every chapter published in this book has been scrutinized by our experts. Their significance has been extensively debated. The topics covered herein carry significant findings which will fuel the growth of the discipline. They may even be implemented as practical applications or may be referred to as a beginning point for another development.

The contributors of this book come from diverse backgrounds, making this book a truly international effort. This book will bring forth new frontiers with its revolutionizing research information and detailed analysis of the nascent developments around the world.

We would like to thank all the contributing authors for lending their expertise to make the book truly unique. They have played a crucial role in the development of this book. Without their invaluable contributions this book wouldn't have been possible. They have made vital efforts to compile up to date information on the varied aspects of this subject to make this book a valuable addition to the collection of many professionals and students.

This book was conceptualized with the vision of imparting up-to-date information and advanced data in this field. To ensure the same, a matchless editorial board was set up. Every individual on the board went through rigorous rounds of assessment to prove their worth. After which they invested a large part of their time researching and compiling the most relevant data for our readers.

The editorial board has been involved in producing this book since its inception. They have spent rigorous hours researching and exploring the diverse topics which have resulted in the successful publishing of this book. They have passed on their knowledge of decades through this book. To expedite this challenging task, the publisher supported the team at every step. A small team of assistant editors was also appointed to further simplify the editing procedure and attain best results for the readers.

Apart from the editorial board, the designing team has also invested a significant amount of their time in understanding the subject and creating the most relevant covers. They scrutinized every image to scout for the most suitable representation of the subject and create an appropriate cover for the book.

The publishing team has been an ardent support to the editorial, designing and production team. Their endless efforts to recruit the best for this project, has resulted in the accomplishment of this book. They are a veteran in the field of academics and their pool of knowledge is as vast as their experience in printing. Their expertise and guidance has proved useful at every step. Their uncompromising quality standards have made this book an exceptional effort. Their encouragement from time to time has been an inspiration for everyone.

The publisher and the editorial board hope that this book will prove to be a valuable piece of knowledge for researchers, students, practitioners and scholars across the globe.

# List of Contributors

**Corey Anton**
School of Communications, Grand Valley State University, 210 LSH, 1 Campus Drive, Allendale, MI 49401-9403, USA

**Patricia C. Brunsteins**
Escuela de Filosofía, Facultad de Filosofía y Humanidades, Universidad Nacional de Córdoba, Pabellón Francia, Ciudad Universitaria, Córdoba, C.P. 5000, Argentina

**Sabrina Haimovici**
Facultad de Filosofía y Letras, Instituto de Filosofía "Dr. Alejandro Korn", Consejo Nacional de Investigaciones Científicas y Técnicas (CONICET), Universidad de Buenos Aires, Buenos Aires, C.P. 1406, Argentina

**Laura Danón**
Centro de Investigaciones de la Facultad de Filosofía y Humanidades, Facultad de Filosofía y Humanidades, Universidad Nacional de Córdoba (National University of Córdoba), Pabellón Agustín Tosco 1 Piso, Ciudad Universitaria, Córdoba 5000, Argentina

**Marlie Tandoc**
Book and Media Studies, University of St. Michael's College, University of Toronto, 60 St. George, Toronto, ON M5S 1A7, Canada

**Robert K. Logan**
Department of Physics, University of Toronto, 60 St. George, Toronto, ON M5S 1A7, Canada

**Matthew McManus**
Department of Political Science and International Relations, Tec de Monterrey, C.P 52926 Atizapan, Mexico

**Robert Prentner**
Department of Cognitive Sciences, University of California, Irvine, CA 92627-5100, USA
Department of Humanities, Social and Political Science, ETH Zürich, 8091 Zürich, Switzerland

**Gennady Shkliarevsky**
Historical Studies Program, Bard College, Annandale-on-Hudson, NY 12504, USA

**Joseph E. Brenner**
International Center for the Philosophy of Information, Xi'an Jiaotong University, Xi'An 710049, China

**Kun Wu**
International Center for the Philosophy of Information, Xi'an Jiaotong University, Xi'an 710048, China

**Joseph Brenner**
International Center for the Philosophy of Information, Xi'an Jiaotong University, Xi'an 710048, China
International Center for Transdisciplinary Research, Paris c/o Chemin du Collège 1, Les Diablerets 1865, Switzerland

**D. H. Williams**
Department of Religion, Baylor University, Waco, TX 76798-7284, USA

**James A. Reggia**
Department of Computer Science and Institute for Advanced Computer Studies, University of Maryland, College Park, MD 20742, USA

**Di-Wei Huang and Garrett Katz**
Department of Computer Science, University of Maryland, College Park, MD 20742, USA

# Index

CPSIA information can be obtained
at www.ICGtesting.com
Printed in the USA
LVHW060849030122
707669LV00002B/45

9 781647 261559